Advance Praise for *Evolve!*

"*Evolve!* presents fascinating evidence and makes a powerful case for both the promise and the perils of ever-expanding Internet use. Kanter's entertaining stories show that the new requirements for success touch all of us, whether in our professional roles or in daily life. This appealing book is not just for the wealthy or the wired—it is a must-read for all who care about the future."

—Alan Dershowitz
    Professor, Harvard Law School, and Author, *Genesis of Justice*

"*Evolve!* offers so much wisdom at such a fast pace! While investors will appreciate Kanter's practical insights about success or failure in the Internet age, entrepreneurs will seize her advice about crafting a collaborative culture. Everyone else will simply enjoy a great book about the world ahead of us."

—Bill Hambrecht
    Founder, Chairman, and CEO, WR Hambrecht + Co., and
    Co-founder, Hambrecht & Quist

"If you're an e-entrepreneur or a business executive, or you just want to puzzle out where the world of business is heading, strap yourself in and ride along with Rosabeth Moss Kanter as she expertly guides you through cyberspace and recounts the many dumb mistakes and shrewd moves others have taken. You will come back from a thrilling ride into the future armed with her wisdom."

—Ken Auletta
    Writer, *The New Yorker* "Annals of Communication," and
    Author, *World War 3.0: Microsoft and Its Enemies*

"Rosabeth Moss Kanter brings to light the profound change that is taking place in the American workplace and what will be required to lead it. She backs up her theory—that the Internet has changed the very nature of corporate culture—with a concrete selection of best practices and models to emulate. Executives of new and traditional companies will want to discuss *Evolve!* widely."

—Geraldine Laybourne
    President and CEO, Oxygen Media

Evolve!

Other Works by Rosabeth Moss Kanter

Rosabeth Moss Kanter on the Frontiers of Management

Innovation: Breakthrough Strategies at 3M, DuPont, General Electric, Pfizer, and Rubbermaid (co-edited)

World Class: Thriving Locally in the Global Economy

The Challenge of Organizational Change (co-edited)

When Giants Learn to Dance: Mastering the Challenges of Strategy, Management, and Careers in the 1990s

Creating the Future (co-authored)

The Change Masters: Innovation and Entrepreneurship in the American Corporation

A Tale of "O": On Being Different in an Organization

Life in Organizations: Workplaces as People Experience Them (co-edited)

Men and Women of the Corporation

Work and Family in the United States

Another Voice (co-edited)

Creating and Managing the Collective Life (edited)

Commitment and Community

Evolve!

Succeeding in the
Digital Culture of Tomorrow

ROSABETH
MOSS
KANTER

HARVARD BUSINESS SCHOOL PRESS
BOSTON, MASSACHUSETTS

Library of Congress Cataloging-in-Publication Data

Kanter, Rosabeth Moss.
Evolve! : succeeding in the digital culture of tomorrow /
Rosabeth Moss Kanter.
p. cm.
Includes index.
ISBN 1-57851-439-8 (alk. paper)
1. Information technology. 2. Internet—Economic aspects.
3. Organizational change. 4. Success in business.
HC79.I55 K358 2001
658.4'062--dc21
00-047241

To Barry, Matt, and Browser—
always young, always exploring, always together in spirit

EVOLVE!—THE SONG
Lyrics by Rosabeth Moss Kanter

[chorus]

Get ready for the next step,
Select the best step.
It's a leap in evolution
From the Internet revolution.
Just pick a direction
In this world of connection.
So many problems to solve—
You've got to evolve.

I

When outcomes are uncertain, answers hard to devise,
That's time to form a team, tap dreams, and improvise.
Listen to your audience, build a scene on every hope,
Shake up thinking, see new patterns in the kaleidoscope.
You don't have to play alone, so start placing your bet
On links to lots of partners, near and far across the Net.
Join hands beyond tall silos, step out of the lonely cells,
Seek a common state, collaborate, for community wealth.

[chorus]

II

Putting lipstick on a bulldog won't transform enough,
Makeup can't hide everything; change takes deeper stuff.

Shift the mood, adjust your attitude, before you go online;
Find new habits of mind, don't just dwell on what's behind.
Don't be trapped by old divisions, on a patch of tiny turf,
That means settling for less—there's more you could be worth.
Think big! Think bold! Think of new things to create.
First-rate prizes go to leaders who can innovate.

[chorus]

III

Why are you so silent, has the mouse got your tongue?
Tech talk is what the older folks can learn from the young.
But the Net generation must absorb from the past,
Enduring values of service, how to build things that last.
So rally people power, make the world a better place,
Because we live on the ground, not in cyberspace.
The computer can help us but it's only just a tool;
It's humanity's goals that should make all the rules.

Get ready for the next step,
Select the best step.
It's a leap in evolution
From the Internet revolution.
Just pick a direction
In this world of connection.
So many problems to solve—
You've got to evolve.

CONTENTS

Evolve!

INTRODUCTION
The New Economy Lobotomy

We want to learn from the past. But we want our dreams to wipe away our memories.

—Christopher Galvin, CEO of Motorola

LIFE IS NOW DEFINED BY where we stand with respect to the Internet. Real mail (the kind that comes in envelopes and doesn't require downloading) is called "snail mail" because e-mail has become the standard. At meetings, people cut off discussion by saying "Let's continue that conversation offline," even though they are meeting face to face, not online; "offline" is a new synonym for "in private," as though everything public were now on the Internet. We have switched from understanding screen-life by using real-life analogies—desktops, trash barrels, real estate, stores, and malls—to defining all of life in terms of the World Wide Web. A *New Yorker* cartoon shows St. Peter requesting user name and password before admitting a man to heaven. Another one features "The Off-Line Store"— "All items are actual size! Take it home as soon as you pay for it! Merchandise may be handled prior to purchase!"[1]

You don't have to be in business to see the cultural changes wrought by

1

the Internet, but business is a good starting point. Soon there could be only three main types of companies in the world: dotcoms, dotcom-enablers, and wannadots.

Dotcoms are the pure Internet companies, operating online businesses. Their activities tend to exist primarily in cyberspace. Many were formed in the heady last half of the 1990s, and most died fast. But successful pioneers such as eBay, Amazon.com, and Yahoo! have already transformed industry dynamics, opened new career aspirations, and become emblematic of a new workplace style. Others threaten to revolutionize industries, from Napster's attack on the recorded music business to the rapidly multiplying e-learning companies challenging colleges and universities. Already the purely digital are swallowing real-world companies, from AOL acquiring TimeWarner to Amazon acquiring warehouses.

Dotcom-enablers are the technology and service providers who spread the Internet gospel. Sun Microsystems's mission, its leaders say, is to "dotcom" the world, to be the "lumberyard for the Internet." IBM is now an e-evangelist for e-business and the world's largest e-business itself. Cisco Systems uses its own lean e-business model to convince others to buy its routers and communications products. Lucent Technologies, once the research and manufacturing arm of Ma Bell, aspires to be a venture capitalist, business incubator, and fast-moving provider of Internet infrastructure. For a time, the growth companies among consulting firms and advertising agencies were a raft of new Web strategy firms, such as Razorfish, iXL, Digitas, Mainspring, and Brand Farm. Operating in Internet time themselves, the Web technology and service companies are change agents that can succeed only if they turn everyone else into Net-based companies. Their rhetoric makes it sound like we are witnessing the Second Dot-Coming.

Wannadots are everyone else—existing businesses, schools, hospitals, and other established organizations. Corporate giants that were once the industry standard are now defined as "not-Internet"—referred to as offline, land based, or bricks and mortar (BAMs). Or they are known by how much they have embraced the Web—for example, multichannel "clicks and mortar" or "bricks and clicks" companies. They follow a variety of paths to cyberspace (and we will trace their journeys, later in this book). Cookware catalog and retailer Williams-Sonoma took several years to become convinced of the importance of e-commerce despite its direct marketing know-how. After a modest experiment during the 1998 holiday season, it launched a wedding gift registry in the spring of 1999 and a full e-commerce department six months later—but still has to work out the relationship between stores, catalogs, and e-commerce. NBC had several early starts before relaunching CNBC.com as a financial services website and now talks about how closely the website should be aligned with the television channel—where they should be tightly coupled and where they should diverge. Arrow Electronics, a leading semiconductor distributor, knew it could be driven out of business by online procurement. So Arrow approached its own online marketplace; if its business was going to be cannibalized, at least Arrow stockholders would be the ones enjoying the meal. General Electric CEO Jack Welch points to "a number of our units you could call DestroyYourBusiness.Com aimed at attacking our existing businesses."

The three types aren't pure types, of course. Dotcoms are developing land links, wannadots are morphing into multichannel hybrids, and a range of dot-orgs and dot-nets are increasingly hard to classify. The largest e-commerce companies in the world are not dotcoms, they are IBM and Cisco. In Taiwan, hardware manufacturer Acer founded more than forty software or dotcom subsidiaries between 1997 and early 2000, investing in Internet-related businesses in Greater China and Asia Pacific and forming alliances with—who else?—IBM and Cisco. In the United Kingdom, two of the largest portals through which users get their e-mail and news are Tesco.net and FreeServe, both of which are offshoots of traditional retail chains.

Still, dotcoms and wannadots, with dotcom-enablers egging them on, represent contrasting styles and face contrasting challenges, both of which I examine in this book. Ask big companies about their goals for the Web, and they are likely to reply, "Cautious experimentation." Ask dotcoms the same question, and they declare, "Total world domination."

That difference in rhetoric and attitude sums up the contrast between those reluctant to let go of the past and those hurtling into the future at warp speed. For companies that were not born digital, the big problem is change—when to change, how to change, and how to prepare people to live with the consequences of change.

Wait a minute! Before we rush off the cliff into the future, let's catch our collective breath and pause for perspective. Many discussions of the New Economy take place in a historical vacuum. Mention the Internet, and intelligent people sometimes act as if they have had a portion of their brain removed—the memory. (That's why I called this introduction "The New Economy Lobotomy.") As we search for the new and different things that occur in the wake of revolutionary communications technology, it is also important to recall what can be learned from previous waves of innovation. In earlier decades, television was going to replace radio, teaching machines were going to replace teachers, and *Sunrise Semester*, a set of televised lectures, was the first sign that mass media were going to replace college classrooms. The broad reach and interactivity of the Internet are much greater than that of television or other media, and so is the potential for displacement. But history demonstrates that new channels tend to coexist with old ones and sometimes even join them.

New Economy rhetoric is often extreme, at both ends of the spectrum of love-the-Web or hate it. Not since the Marxists roamed the earth has the word *revolution* been used so freely. Evangelists urge companies to "blow up your business model," while critics decry the "toxic excesses of capitalism" in the Internet boom. In both cases, people feel free to fling around provocative slogans without thinking about what they really mean or examining what is really happening. Media critics have faulted journalists for reporting financial news with little perspective on its meaning and little analysis of the business models of the glamorous companies they lionize. In 1999 and 2000, the press swung from being overly bullish, featuring young millionaires on magazine covers who never made a dime, a critic said, to being overly bearish after the spring 2000 market downturn.[2]

Because the United States was the launch site for the world's journey into cyberspace, I suppose this lack of interest in history is understandable. To tell someone they are about to be "history" (as in "You're history!") is an Americanism for impending elimination. *Legacy* has become a negative term in the information technology community, referring to traditional systems that now impede progress. It has long been a hallmark of American popular culture to look for the fresh face, and it has long been a tenet of American entrepreneurship to value the fresh start. The late great anthropologist Margaret Mead once claimed that America was the first culture in which the young taught the old instead of the other way around. She was referring to the children of immigrants' children who learned the language first, and then taught their parents. Today, that observation could be made about the Internet.

The Internet economy exaggerates antihistorical tendencies, offering a premium for new ventures and new ideas deliberately detached from tradition—witness the higher market valuations placed on dotcoms that separate from their parent companies. How many years a company has been in business and what its track record has been counts for less in some marketplaces than whether it has the newest, latest offering. History not only seems to matter little, but also may be seen as an encumbrance, or a sign that the company is stuck in the past. Even recent experience—"What have you done for me lately?"—is less important than "What do you promise to do next?"

As I was beginning the work for this book in 1999, popular exhortations to leaders to "forget everything you know because the Web overturns every accepted business principle" filled the air. So I tried to approach the e-world by assuming that I knew nothing. Before designing my massive research venture, I sat at the feet of twenty-year-olds and asked them to teach me. (My Harvard Business School MBA students were already influenced by their work experience; I was looking for the truly fresh new thoughts.) One weekend a set of four college students, aged nineteen to twenty-two, brought laptops and flip charts and industry statistics to my country retreat and talked through new business models. (They were then vetting business plans for a venture capital firm, while trying to find time for their college courses; one had started a Net business he sold eighteen months later.) When I suggested to a young magazine founder, who was tempted to leave the print magazine in the dust in rushing to the Web, that the print magazine was an asset that the Web wouldn't eliminate so fast, I was stung by his retort that "you're not twenty-five," so I redoubled efforts to shed preconceived notions. (P.S. I was right, as the founder has since acknowledged; the print magazine is the biggest single driver of traffic to the website and the vital lure for advertisers.)

My virtual lobotomy was illuminating, but a little went a long way, and my memory started returning to normal. I started to see that cyberspace is full of reinvented wheels. Yes, the technology is revolutionary, network economics are different, and all the wheels must turn a lot faster, but the problems of leadership, organization, and change are similar to those we have experienced for decades. So even though this book breaks new ground in examining a set of big new challenges, it also rests on a foundation of enduring truths about people and organizations—a foundation that serves as a springboard for an evolutionary leap into a new, networked age.

The research that led to *Evolve!* is both broad and deep, involving not only the United States but also on-the-ground investigations in Canada, Europe, and Asia carried out by my research team at Harvard Business School and augmented by conversations in Israel and Latin America.

(See the Credits for the names of my terrific team, led by Daniel Galvin and Michelle Heskett.) Three pillars were used to develop and test hypotheses:

- A global print and online survey included responses from 785 organizations of all sizes and types, primarily from North America and Europe but including Latin America and Africa. Survey respondents included Global 2000 companies that belong to the World Economic Forum and emerging fast-growth companies in the Inc. 500 and Young Entrepreneurs Organization.

- My Harvard Business School team conducted over 300 interviews in nearly eighty companies and other organizations in North America, Europe, and Asia, using both a structured guide to identify the dimensions of e-culture and an open-ended search for best practices and object lessons. We included prominent and newborn businesses of all types, as well as a sprinkle of professional firms (law and consulting), schools, and trade associations. Interviews were augmented by e-mail dialogues and a discussion forum on theglobe.com.

- Over two dozen companies from three continents were examined in depth through multiple interviews and richly detailed case studies. These included Abuzz, AlliedSignal, Amazon.com (and partners), Arrow Electronics, barnesandnoble.com, Blackboard.com, Cisco Systems, CNBC.com/NBC, Digitas and clients (Bausch & Lomb), Earth-Web, eBay, Hewlett-Packard, Honeywell, IBM, iSteelAsia, iXL, Lucent Technologies, Mainspring, Razorfish, renren.com, Reuters, Sun Microsystems, Tesco, and Williams-Sonoma. IBM's Reinventing Education initiative and Bell Atlantic's partnership with a New Jersey school system were included to extend the research beyond business to public education. For several of the United States–based companies, we interviewed at international as well as American locations. (See Appendix A for company descriptions.)

The result of all this work is reflected in the lessons of this book. I show that the Internet and its associated network technologies play two primary roles. The World Wide Web is both the stimulus for a new organizational culture (making it necessary) and a facilitator of that same culture (making it possible). I call that new way of working *e-culture*. E-culture defines the human side of the global information era, the heart and soul of the New Economy. People and organizations everywhere must evolve to embrace this business culture of tomorrow—no matter where they are on the continuum of Internet use.

Taking full advantage of the potential of the Internet Age requires leaders to lead differently and people to work together in new configurations. Consider these truths of e-culture as the new truths for success in general:

- *E-culture is about creative destruction.* It means getting serious about continuous dramatic change, even if it destroys your own already-profitable business.

- *E-culture is like living in a glass house under a huge spotlight that's always on, 24/7.* Mistakes are immediately visible and magnified. And no one wants to hear excuses. They only want to hear about what's new, what's next.

- *E-culture is superficial—in good ways.* Communication is the core of e-culture. Internet time requires fast, cryptic communication among strangers who cannot take the time to interpret subtleties or build a deep relationship based on intimate knowledge.

- *Done right, e-culture protects against armed combat.* It fosters a spirit of cooperation because the network requires it, despite battles over screen space or brand image or merchandizing decisions. There is no time to fight it out, no time for thorough debate. People need to get on with it. They have to learn to collaborate.

- *E-culture is made up as you go along.* It involves emergent strategies, improvisation in response to opportunities.

- *E-culture is full of paradoxes.* The e-world is highly decentralized and hard to control, but it forces organizations to become more integrated—even centralized. New media rely on old media that they claim to displace to promote use of the new media. The value of unproven companies can increase with the rate at which they lose money.

- *E-culture can be a lot of fun.* Companies compete for talent by staging the goofiest games, sponsoring the most exotic trips, and stocking the most lavish snack bars.

The messages of this book derive from the deeper implications of those simple statements. *Evolve!* consists of insider stories and lessons about effectiveness drawn from organizations at all stages of Net change. It describes role models and best practices: how life is lived and work gets done in companies that lead the pack. It tells cautionary tales: why change is fumbled or resisted in those that lag behind. And it includes practical conclusions that readers can use to ensure personal and business success in their own ventures and workplaces. *Evolve!* explores the readiness of companies to embrace e-culture, the capability of leaders to lead within it, and the willingness of people to commit themselves to it.

The Way to *Evolve!*

It is common in the business world, and increasingly wherever busy people are found, to provide an executive summary at the beginning of documents. In this book, I am providing two. One of them is conventional—the verbal tour through the contents of the book that comes next. The other one is the result of the hours I spent in dotcom offices that had music on all the time—it's the song whose lyrics are found just before the table of contents.[3] Take your pick.

PART ONE. SEARCHING, SEARCHING: THE CHALLENGE OF CHANGE

The three chapters in the first part of the book set forth a variety of challenges. First are the ways that the Internet affects all of us, like it or not. In chapter 1, I argue that e-culture derives from basic principles of community: shared identity, sharing of knowledge, and mutual contributions. Online, community is a metaphor. Offline, the spirit of community is required to implement the changes that the Internet makes possible—to give customers more choices, citizens more voice, educators more capacity to improve children's learning, and businesses greater market reach and internal efficiency. Understanding the dynamics of community is also required to respond to the changes the Internet forces on us—whether they work in your favor or represent communities of opposition and protest. The Web represents opportunity for some, an enormous threat for others.

To some people, it seems that only the young can master this new, bewildering environment. It is no accident that young people of the Net generation are disproportionately represented in dotcom companies. Are those youth and those companies pointing the way to the future? Dotcom culture is described in chapter 2, along with the reversal of generational roles when the younger mentor the older. There is a distinctive dotcom workplace style that my team found everywhere in the world. But that style by itself is not enough to create a viable business. In chapter 2 I introduce some young companies with the substance to succeed—that begin to reflect elements of a new culture. But it's not youth that leads the way, it is new ideas executed with discipline and traditional values.

New companies do have one advantage: the fresh start. Wannadots, in contrast, can be inhibited by their size and organizational legacy from incorporating the Internet successfully, as chapter 3 shows. They face numerous barriers to change, and they are tempted to let those barriers stop them. Some wannadots are laggards, moving slowly through predictable stages en route to the Web—denial, blame, and insignificant cosmetic change. Others, however, are pacesetters that exhibit organizational curiosity and the desire to innovate. These pacesetters share many e-culture characteristics; along with the best dotcoms, they serve as models for the future.

PART TWO. IN THE GREEN: THE ESSENCE OF E-EFFECTIVENESS

"In the green" means "all systems go," and it also suggests financial viability. The four chapters in the second part of the book analyze the implications for business of the advent of the Internet and identify best practices in implementing e-culture principles. Each chapter covers one of the four big things companies—and organizations of all kinds—must do to achieve excellence:

- *Treat strategy development as improvisational theater (chapter 4).* When outcomes cannot be known in advance, the action itself creates the goal. Instead of following a script, e-savvy companies run an improvisational theater. A general theme is identified to get the actors started. Then the actors try out different scenarios, develop the story as they interact with each other, and create a different experience with each round. Because it is impossible to know which model, which standard, which concept will prevail, it is unwise to follow a script written in advance of the action; it is better to launch many small experiments and learn from the results of each—a hallmark of improvisation.

- *Nurture networks of partners (chapter 5).* In the Old Economy, partners were an afterthought or a relabeling of existing transactional relationships with a vow to treat each other better. The New Economy builds networks through multiple partners—important not only for online links among dotcoms but also for offline links among dotcom-enablers who need complex multilateral partnerships to build the technology for cyberspace.

- *Reconstruct the organization as a community (chapter 6).* The outlines of the "new organization model" are familiar: flatter hierarchies, more fluid boundaries, more team oriented, an emphasis on processes over structure. But often that model led to decentralization, one of the fashions of the late 1980s and 1990s, as the pendulum swung toward divisional and departmental autonomy. The Internet is a recentralizing force in that it makes more urgent the need to present one face to the customer, link separate systems for seamless integration, and meet the demand outside and inside the organization for full connectivity. But because of a legacy of decentralization, many of the battles inside wannadots ("dotcombat") involve turf and territory. This chapter deals with two overlapping issues: (1) how to get best business proposition on the Web—the face to the *outside*; and (2) how to work together differently because of networks in order to get the benefits of the technology and implement e-culture *inside*.

- *Win the battle to attract and retain the best talent (chapter 7).* Is commitment an outmoded concept in a world of mobility, or are there new ways to build bonds between people and organizations? In chapter 7 I describe culture-building at the workplace level—how to treat people as volunteers who renew their commitment periodically through the three Ms of mastery, membership, and meaning.

Part Three. Morphing: Leading Fundamental Change at Internet Speed

The final three chapters offer a practical guide to change—how to move fast to transform a whole organization, how to lead change, and how to cultivate the human skills required for an Internet-enabled world.

Let's say you like the idea of a new organizational culture but don't know how to get there—or that you're on the road and want to make sure you're headed in the right direction. Chapter 8 is a working chapter for people responsible for big changes, especially a major overhaul and comprehensive shift to e-business and e-culture. It focuses on overcoming the common barriers we have encountered throughout the book and successfully implementing systemic change. It shows how to ensure that the organization has been transformed to a new way of working that will permit continuing successful change. It addresses comprehensive change activities—not single projects, but building the entire organizational platform. A step-by-step practical roadmap is included.

Change is not a decision; it is a campaign. So chapter 9 is for leaders—appointed, elected, or self-appointed. The stars of this chapter are entrepreneurs and innovators of all stripes—in independent ventures or within already-established organizations—who have appeared earlier in this book as the forces behind successful e-ventures and change efforts. Change in the e-world involves mass mobilization, resembling a political campaign or community organizing. Change involves shaking up thinking (like shaking a kaleidoscope), communicating with internal and external audiences, staging pep rallies and other events, and building support within and outside the organization. This chapter pulls together leadership lessons about the skills required at every stage of a change process.

In chapter 10, I encourage all of us to stand back to put e-culture in perspective. What does all this mean for individuals and society? Are we on the verge of the next stage of social evolution—a great leap forward to shared consciousness? The advent of the Internet, if guided by leaders who understand its full potential and deeper implications, can help connect people in powerful ways that build human community. But there is also the danger that unless offline communities nurture social interaction, the Internet could become an isolating force, and children could grow up without the very skills that the Internet requires to run. The best online businesses have a community element; the best e-culture companies operate like communities internally and serve the external communities in which they live. Those individuals who will be most successful in the Internet Age will exemplify this possible evolutionary leap toward shared consciousness: They will be more collaborative systems thinkers, excellent communicators, and great members of improvisational theater troupes able to make quick adjustments as they interact with their multiple audiences of users and partners.

OVERALL, THEN, this book is about change—what to change and how to change. It is about a new culture, e-culture, that involves better ways of leading, organizing, working, and thinking. Through *Evolve!*, I hope to help readers prepare to evolve—to be leaders who can make the right decisions in an uncertain world and execute them quickly and effectively. This involves deep systemic change, not cosmetic change, and a deeper emphasis on human skills that build meaningful community out of mere connections.

Part One

◆

Searching, Searching
The Challenge of Change

1

---◆---

ONLINE COMMUNITIES AND OFFLINE CHALLENGES
How the Internet Affects All of Us

I thought people would simply use the service to buy and sell things, but what they really enjoyed was meeting other people.

—Pierre Omidyar, Founder, eBay

The Internet is the uninvited guest that crashed the party.

—Pete Blackshaw, CEO, PlanetFeedback.com

SEARCHING. . . SEARCHING. . . reads the message at the bottom of my screen. It seems emblematic of the state of the world. Everywhere I turn, I find people who want to know what the Internet really means for their future and what they must do to succeed.

The Internet is a revolutionary technology that cannot be ignored or avoided. New economic and organizational forces stemming from the rise of the Internet affect more than just those people and companies whose work centers around the World Wide Web. These forces have an impact on workplaces of all kinds, reaching non–computer users as well as avid techies. The Internet has the potential to transform every economic and social institution, from business to education to health care to government.

The power of the Internet goes well beyond the simple question of whether businesses should engage in e-commerce. Internet phenomena reshape markets, but also reach far beyond them to society itself, in several ways:

- *Network power.* Everyone is potentially connected to everyone else. Network reach is more important than the size of individual components. There is a greater reliance on partners in order to get *big everywhere fast.*

- *Transparency and direct communication.* Information access is rapid, open, direct. There is greater exposure and visibility.

- *Fast feedback, easy protest.* Competitors can become partners, but there are opponents lurking everywhere that can mobilize quickly.

- *Constant change and reliance on new knowledge.* There is fierce competition for talent with the newest skills. New knowledge earns a premium. Rapid innovation creates the need for still more change.

- *Large audiences and crowd behavior.* Messages reach wider audiences. To coordinate complex networks, larger groups must share information and spread it further.

To master this environment requires evolving to a new way of working, a new way of doing business, a new style of human relationships that together constitute e-culture. The Web rewards organizations that are nimble and innovative, with a freer spirit of creation, ones that can move quickly because all the right connections are in place. That need for agility has been noted frequently. What has not been examined is the Web's hidden secret: that it provokes a shift toward more collaborative work relationships, ones that resemble open, inclusive communities more than they resemble secretive, hierarchical administrative bureaucracies.

Community might seem a strange word to use in conjunction with the ever-expanding virtual world. But one of my most robust findings about e-culture is that it centers around strong communities, online and off. The community-forming potential of the Web presents both the greatest opportunity and the greatest threat to organizations and their leaders, as I will show in this chapter. One company's loyal community of empowered users is another one's biggest nemesis. One company's exciting opportunity is another company's death threat. Recognizing the revolutionary potential of the technology is a first step toward successful change. Recognizing the ways that it intersects with social institutions and human relationships on the ground is even more critical.

This poses three challenges to everyone engaged with the Internet:

1. The Internet can greatly empower and connect people, but it can also isolate and marginalize them.

2. The Internet can enable user communities to form and grow, but it can also use them to attack and deny.

3. The Internet can help build businesses and communities, but it can also destroy them.

No wonder everyone is searching for answers. But perhaps they are searching in the wrong place. As I will argue throughout this book, the answers lie not in cyberspace but on the ground, where real people make real choices.

The I-Paradox

Internet propositions scream Me, Me, Me. There are thousands of domain names beginning with "I" (iVillage, iflowers, I-traffic), with the implied triple entendre of the Internet and I, interactive. It is possible to read only MyNews downloaded on my machine with no concern for what anyone else is reading, or to visit websites called mytown, myhealth, mycar, mydog, and mycomicshop. The Web is personal, marketers tell us. It breeds intimacy with end users, and so offerings must be customized to fit them perfectly. Business buzzwords such as *one-to-one marketing* further reinforce individualism. Critics fear that the Internet breeds head-in-the-sand isolation. Media tales of dotcom billionaires make it seem as though individual greed powers the Internet.

Yet the hidden paradox of the Internet Age is that rampant individualism destroys the potential to derive economic value from the technology. When members of a network do not cooperate, do not pass on information, the network itself slows down. Having too many ideas, unchanneled by a common theme, impedes innovation and instead invites time-wasting, energy-draining conflict. Companies dominated by individual incentives for unit performance ("every tub on its own bottom") are slower to succeed on the Web than those with collective consciousness, as reflected in both the global e-culture survey findings and my case studies in later chapters.

It is individuals-in-community that create the greatest value—strong individuals in strong relationships. The worst of individualism involves isolation and separatism that is dysfunctional for the wired world. The best of individualism involves strong individuals with a strong sense of responsibility to others in their community. On the Web, *community* is an analogy more than an emotional reality. The term is often used (incorrectly) as an equivalent for an audience with the potential for interaction, but not every website that claims to form a community fosters much interaction or connects users to one another. Community is sometimes a distorted analogy because many so-called communities are just excuses for making money—attracting people for page views and then "monetizing" their "eyeballs." But the community metaphor does suggest a different attitude toward customers and users, namely, that consumers have changed from passive members of an audience to more active members of a community.

Within organizations, community must become an emotional and operational reality. Operating as a community permits speed, releases human energy and brainpower, engenders loyalty, and reaches across walls and beyond borders to include volunteers, partners, and unseen audiences. Speed comes about because people value their connection to everyone else and know how to work together to permit seamless execution or rapid mobilization. Human energy and creativity are released because of the motivational potential of feeling like a member, not an employee or a subordinate. High performance and even loyalty are engendered, even in an age of job hopping, because people are connected to the community in multiple ways beyond economic transactions—as member, citizen, helper, and recipient of help, as well as buyer, seller, or worker.

Seven elements are contained in the community ideal (even though they are not always present in reality):

1. *Membership.* Customers, users, partners, employees—when they are members, differences disappear, and connections transcend the role-of-the-day. People feel an obligation to fellow members that they do not feel to, say, fellow customers. Membership implies a kind of citizenship, with the right and obligation to speak up.

2. *Fluid boundaries.* Communities are loose aggregations. There may be a formal core that is organized and firm, but around that core are people who come and go, move in and out, and become more active on some occasions and less active on others. Possibilities are open ended, and ties extend in many directions and for time periods after

people have left the center (e.g., alumni associations). People can belong to several communities at once.

3. *Voluntary action.* It seems odd to talk about volunteers in the same breath as businesses, but there is a voluntary quality to the actions taken by community members. They do more than their jobs, because they want to. Leaders with new agendas are dependent on above-and-beyond contributions. Change is like community organizing, like political campaigns or mass mobilization. Leaders get people to vote with their feet for change.

4. *Identity.* Community is an idea, not a geographic location. A community exists because many people think it does and define themselves as part of it, whether it is a professional community, a community of interest, or a birthplace. The relationship of community identity to physical places has gradually weakened as communication media extended human bonds. China is a place; Greater China is a community. An idea—call it a "brand"—is the basis for identity as a community. (Even nations are getting into the branding game, seeking simple images to convey their attractions: Cool Britannia, New Zealand as the source of green products, and Massachusetts as the dotCommonwealth.)

5. *Common culture.* Shared understandings, a common language and disciplines, permit a relatively seamless interchangeability of one for another, or a relatively seamless passing of the torch. Some say that this commonality of approach is what sets the outer boundaries of community.

6. *Collective strength.* Communities tap the power of the many. The empowered individual consumer is a myth unless many consumers are empowered simultaneously and can push back. People bond to each other and to the community when there is a greater cause that uses their collective strength. Perhaps this is why there is so much change-the-world rhetoric surrounding entrepreneurial ventures.

7. *Collective responsibility.* Service to the community as a community can be a unifying force in addition to its pragmatic benefits as a workforce motivator, talent attracter, and brand builder. Becoming big everywhere often means becoming an insider everywhere, a player in many communities—real ones as well as virtual ones.

Localization, not globalization, is the term Internet companies use for creating operational bases in countries outside their home base. They are already global via the World Wide Web, so what they need is to look local to local users. Contributing to local causes produces community embeddedness to ensure on-the-ground influence.

The community analogy has limits and downsides, of course. A bad business proposition trumps all aspects of internal culture, as I will make clear throughout this book. Communities can turn into cults, closing minds instead of opening them and stifling innovation instead of encouraging it. Some ties can be broad but very shallow, making self-declared communities just fly-by-night gatherings. Superficial "community-building" bells and whistles, from parties to dress styles, may deflect attention from the serious substance of a venture. Thus it is important to distinguish *community* as a label from the underlying principles that make community integral to e-culture: sharing of knowledge, mutual contributions, smooth coordination, easy border-crossing, and responsibility for a shared fate. Let's turn to some unlikely bedfellows that illustrate this ideal: eBay and a set of public schools.

Dot-Communities

Online, community is only one of the three Cs said to be associated with e-business success: community, content, and commerce. Offline, the spirit of community is required in order to benefit from the changes that the Internet makes possible, such as giving customers more choices, citizens more voice, educators more capacity to improve children's learning, and businesses greater market reach and internal efficiency. Understanding community dynamics makes it easier both to create change and to live with the changes others create. The success of eBay, the world's largest Internet auction site, illustrates the interplay between online and offline community-building.

From Online Commerce to Offline Community: eBay

In June 2000, eBay reported 12.6 million registered users, four times the number fifteen months earlier, and a huge increase from its 88,000 registered users in the first quarter of 1997. By the first quarter of 2000, annualized gross merchandise sales were about $4.6 billion, and 4 million items were listed for sale in 4,300 categories. Key to eBay's success, analysts agree, was creating a passionate, almost cult-like, community of users.[1]

Building community was a goal from eBay's beginnings. Founder Pierre Omidyar launched Auction Web on Labor Day 1995 because his girlfriend (now wife) wanted to trade Pez dispensers and interact with other collectors over the Internet. A self-described "anti-commercial" software developer, Omidyar believed that users on his site, soon renamed eBay, should be empowered to safeguard it themselves and develop their own solutions to problems. He wanted as few rules as possible, valuing empowerment and trust.[2] Generally eschewing advertising revenues (except on co-branded sites, such as a March 1999 AOL deal), eBay relied on listing fees and a percentage of the final sale price of each item sold. The company took pains to foster a close-knit feeling on eBay and not to appear too corporate or slick.

Ironically, that community strength gave eBay stickiness rarely found in cyberspace. CEO Meg Whitman contrasted it with other online auction sites, saying "OnSale's view of the world was auctions and economic warfare. This isn't about auctions. It's about community commerce."[3] Many users purchased their first computer specifically to buy and sell items on eBay, according to marketing vice president Steve Westly, and eBay spawned many small businesses from users' living rooms.

Scoop 98 is one of those living room businesses. By day, Berta Maginniss is a mild-mannered executive (senior vice president of the Greater Washington Board of Trade, a prestigious business association). By night, she turns into Scoop 98, selling second-hand clothing on eBay from her home in Aldie, Virginia, forty-seven miles west of DC. (eBay's draw makes her the largest postal customer in town.) In late 1998, Maginniss, with no retail or technical background, offered Scoop's first item: a pair of Ferragamo shoes. By July 2000, Maginniss listed thirty-five to fifty items per week. "eBay makes you feel like part of the 'community' from the very beginning. The sell/buy process is efficient and safe. Each product generation is better. Service issues have been handled efficiently and honestly. Instructions assure success even if you are not a 'techie,'" she enthused to me by e-mail. "My business is global from a small room in my house. It couldn't be easier or more fun!"

Meg Whitman describes eBay as "of the people, by the people, for the people."[4] Empowerment and trust show in many ways. Users rate one another based on the quality and reliability of their trades or sales, with ratings appearing on-screen. Volunteers among eBay users form "neighborhood watch groups" to guard against abuse—an example of online community policing. Users are involved as the company makes adjustments, updates, and changes to its website. "eBay has changed time and time again, but in a very comfortable way and with the input of the user," Maginniss commented. "The 'new' homepage is the fifth that I remember. Each time, we, the community of users, had the opportunity to live with it in a beta area for several weeks and to offer comments and suggestions. By the time it is introduced on the screen, the change is seamless." Users even became employees. During its first two years, eBay hired respected users for customer support; these users responded to e-mails and answered questions posted on bulletin boards from home. (As eBay grew, users were augmented by professionals in San Jose and then a dedicated service group in Salt Lake City.)

To users, eBay is more than an auction site. "I thought people would simply use the service to buy and sell things," Omidyar said, "but what they really enjoyed was meeting other people."[5] Online features (including category-specific chat rooms, bulletin boards, a monthly newsletter, e-mail, and the opportunity for users to create their own home pages free of charge) make eBay a 24/7 forum for trading, talking about trading, and discussing common interests. An official eBay magazine was launched in May 1999. As eBay grew, special-interest groups emerged, and personal relationships developed offline. There were reports of eBay users holding picnics, taking trips, working together, and assisting each other in the real world—even helping with home repairs. Executives frequently compared this to the growth of a small town. "People on eBay feel like mayors of their own little cyber towns," Westly said.[6]

eBay wants employees to understand the importance of community as a social value, not just as a way to extract economic value from aggregating an audience. Trust, respect, and empowerment are expected to extend offline within the company as well as online among users. In choosing Whitman as CEO in March 1998, eBay board members liked not just her brand-building skills but also her quick grasp of community values. Her initial changes responded to the needs of a growing organization: segmenting sellers by type and frequency, and clarifying internal responsibilities now that it was no longer possible for everyone to be involved in everything. But eBay still tries to foster a feeling of community among its paid employees. Whitman encourages them to be collectors themselves and to think like customers. Most desks at eBay corporate offices hold a collection of some sort—a reminder of eBay's origins as the site started selling big-ticket luxury items such as cars and yachts. Whitman and Omidyar speak about the company's values at employee orientations.

Remaining a community governed largely by users is difficult when growth requires controls. After a New York City Consumer Affairs investigation of fraud on eBay in January 1999, the company announced it would toughen up its antifraud measures with its SafeHarbor program, which consisted of a twenty-four-member team who worked to remove illegal items and suspend users for inappropriate behavior. Such changes had to be made with a light touch, because internal staff and users would bristle at any seemingly top-down or heavy-handed corporate changes in rules, including safety measures. When eBay decided early in 1999 to eliminate all auctions of guns and ammunition, the move was applauded by analysts and investors, but opposed by some in the eBay community. One user wrote on the bulletin board, "I am DISGUSTED."[7]

Members of the eBay community generally deal directly with each other, with eBay as a facilitator; they rarely deal directly with the company. Omidyar mused, "So how do you control the customer experience? We can't control how one person treats another. We can't say, 'you're fired' or 'go back to training.' The only thing we can do is to influence customer behavior by encouraging them to adopt certain values." Sharing values in an online community is difficult enough, but added to that is the challenge of exponential growth—more *new* people using the service in a quarter than the *total* number of people who had been using the service in the previous quarter. "In the past, those values [of the community] were communicated person-to-person; most users would come on as buyers and interact with an experienced seller. But as more new people interact with one another, they have no basis on which to communicate values," he said. So eBay relies on tangible signs of intangible values, with offline community service as the visible manifestation of online community values.

In June 1998, eBay used pre-IPO stock to establish a foundation to ensure that "people are not only empowered to do business in a trusting environment, but they are also respected for what they contribute to the community," as its website said. A volunteer committee of eBay employees set priorities and made grant decisions, guided by quarterly themes. The first two grants were for organizations near eBay's home base outside San Francisco. By January 2000, under a Global Impact theme, the eBay Foundation gave grants for food security, workplace mentoring, antipoverty initiatives, and services for the blind in Florida, Washington, Michigan, and California. The foundation declared itself to be "clever, unique, passionate, and eclectic," just like eBay itself, but what really set eBay apart was not corporate giving but a truly unique user initiative, the Giving Board.

During the 1998 holiday season, eBay introduced the Giving Board, a bulletin board on its site for posting stories about people in need. Users were known for their generosity. At one point, a group of doll collectors tracked down another collector after she disappeared from the site. They discovered that she had lost her computer in a divorce and could not afford to buy a new one. So they pooled resources and bought her a new machine.[8]

Response to the first Giving Board was so enthusiastic that users formed a committee of volunteers to coordinate a permanent one on eBay. The charitably minded could surf through messages and find an appealing cause. Requests for help in July 2000 included books for a lending library serving low-income parents, costumes for a youth drama group, and personal pleas—*"I am a single mom of 2, husband left when youngest (7mons) was born w/Pfeiffer Syndrome and was not perfect. Now father is not paying child support & we live on youngest's SSI."* Auctions in the general section of the eBay website can elect to contribute to a specific Giving Board request by donating 10 percent or more of their receipts, posting the notation ^i^ to indicate that it is an "angel" auction for a specific cause.

The only official guideline is "common sense," instructions on the board explain. "The members who assist with fulfillment of requests are individuals with families and obligations of their own. We are unfortunately, not equipped to solve monumental problems. If you have found yourself with an emergency (layoff, illness, surgery, accident, death), then we would invite you to let us know how we can help make your life a little less stressful, and to put things back in order." The instructions also admonish people to be honest, because "there is no way to know if a request is a scam." Though it is nearly impossible to track donations, 325 people reported donating to at least 1 of over 1,600 requests for help in early 2000. The numbers are small, but the symbolic value to eBay people is huge.

The eBay community saga illustrates many of the conditions for e-business success that form the core of this book: frequent, rapid upgrades with user feedback; a network that is stronger and stickier because it is based on multidirectional connections among all members and not just one-way ties to the company; and a set of values that unite employees and help them avoid turf battles. eBay operates both as a business with management controls and as a self-regulating, helping community of independent entrepreneurs that empowers its members while enriching its investors. It sounds almost too good to be true, and perhaps the model will prove unsustainable at larger size, with bigger commercial partners and more high-ticket luxury items.

Still, the eBay story makes clear that when the community metaphor online can reverberate offline, it improves the business in the process. What about the other direction, from offline to online? Let's examine the role of the Internet in building high-performance communities in an unlikely setting, public education in troubled urban districts in the United States.

From Offline Bureaucracy to Online Community: Public Schools

It's not the computer that creates community, it's the human connections. The relationships that electronic networks enable can potentially transform social institutions in powerful, beneficial ways. Consider the experience of public schools that have begun to use networks to forge new connections among teachers, parents, and students. Most people still imagine that technology in schools means computers in classrooms, but that is the least important, lowest impact, and often most counterproductive application of technology, fostering individual isolation. Networks, on the other hand, can build community and raise educational performance.

In the once-failing inner-city school district of Union City, New Jersey, a partnership with Bell Atlantic for Web access in the early days of the Internet transformed relationships. And those relationships transformed education. Then-Mayor and state Senator Robert Menendez (later elected a U.S. congressman) had envisioned making Union City the first wired city, with the schools at the center of a community network. Starting in 1992, the Bell Atlantic partnership wired a just-opened middle school for high-speed communication and put computers in the homes of inner-city students and their teachers to connect with that school.

I remember sitting in the tiny library at the Columbus Middle School on my first visit in 1997 and being startled by how few books those few shelves could hold, for all those students. But the Web helped overcome the physical limitations of library space and book shortages. Classrooms became team-based collaborative learning centers, with the Internet a research tool and a way for students to work together outside school as well as inside. High school teachers such as Marian Secudas and Agnes Colinari changed their styles. "I was a good teacher within the confines of a book," Secudas said. "But when you open up the whole world on the Internet, it's very scary." She stopped lecturing and started facilitating students' Web-based research projects—morphing from the "sage on the stage" to the "guide on the side," as teachers put it. Colinari used Web-savvy students to teach fellow students—and herself—new skills. Through Parent University, teachers and children taught their parents technology skills that improved family fortunes. The Union City public libraries were linked to their schools as part of the community web, and school children created websites for community organizations. Academic performance and school attendance shot up.[9]

Consider a second, more systemic, example. IBM's Reinventing Education initiative, launched in 1994, took this model even further. Working collaboratively with teams from K–12 public schools in twenty-one sites in the United States (including cities, counties, and the states of Vermont, West Virginia, and New York) and eight other countries, IBM experts created solutions to remove barriers to excellence identified by the school districts themselves. This initiative was emphatically far more than computers in classrooms; in fact, IBM had to turn away schools who thought the program involved computer donations. Wired for Learning, a communications network connecting schools and parents, was created first in Charlotte-Mecklenburg, North Carolina; a data warehouse, with all information on one easy-to-access system, originated in Broward County (Ft. Lauderdale), Florida; electronic portfolios of students' work, designed to display much more than final grades or test scores, started in Vermont.

In some ways, schools were once like prisons—individual teachers were isolated in individual classrooms in schools that didn't communicate outside their own walls. Schools need to become better-connected communities. Once IBM helped them to achieve this connection, teachers and parents alike are empowered to help children learn. Parents can view their children's work on the Web, compare it with models, and stay in e-mail contact with teachers instead of waiting for yearly conferences. Teachers can use the Web to create and share lesson plans, get mentored by experienced teachers, submit lessons for peer review and posting, schedule training days and find substitutes who can fit right in, or tap into e-learning programs offered outside the school district. Members of the school community can create their own home pages, to present themselves as they wish to be known and get to know everyone else more fully.

Certain education fundamentals haven't changed. Teachers still look students in the eyes every day in physical classrooms. But backing them up is a virtual community of mentors, supporters, and involved parents. Ann Clark, principal of Charlotte-Mecklenburg's Vance High School, reflected, "Probably the 'ah-hah' moment for many of our teachers came when they had the opportunity to go online and see what teachers in West Virginia were doing with math, or what teachers in Vermont were doing with writing portfolios, and to really look at lesson plans and ideas. We had a line backed up at the copy machine to make copies of those plans." Electronic connections to parents stimulated other real-world changes: The building stayed open to 10 P.M., and the graduate center was made available to parents. "Technology as an enabler has redefined the hours that our school is in operation, the way we teach, the way students learn. That's how we set ourselves apart from other high schools," Clark said proudly. Two rounds of evaluations revealed that changes such as these improve educational outcomes.[10]

The Global Town Meeting

Empowerment has two faces. The same forces that can create community in the interests of businesses and other organizations can also create communities to oppose them. When users feel like they are part of a community, they feel entitled to protest changes, just as they did at eBay, and they can use the company's own technology against it. That's the second major challenge the Internet presents to everyone. It is like a continuous 24/7 town meeting in which the whole global village can participate whenever they feel like it. Here's the good news: Some of the less helpful aspects of traditional organizations could disappear because of the Web.

No More Mushrooms

Fast, open access to information and the ability to communicate directly with nearly anyone anywhere sets e-culture apart from traditional environments. Businesses, schools, and other established organizations must stop treating people like mushrooms. "Mushroom management" is the philosophy that it is best to keep employees in the dark, cover them with manure, and when they ripen, can them. It was tempting to operate that way in big bureaucracies because hoarding information was one way managers expressed their power—"I know something you don't know."

Bigger, more complex audiences for every action make organizational behavior more transparent, however. It is harder to hide problems or hope that customers, employees, or bosses won't notice transgressions. When asked what's different about selling through the Internet, executives say that it is a less tolerant and forgiving medium. Leaders at U.K. supermarket chain Tesco noted that online sales brought them new customers and new buying patterns (less frequent but larger orders) but also that customers did not tolerate errors in online shopping, even if the mistakes were their own fault. Lucia Quinn, a Honeywell marketing executive, observed, "E-business is like a giant lens you give your customers. If the rest of your business is broken, e-business just magnifies it."

Transparency is the new rule. More data are disclosed about more things in more places to more people faster—and to strangers in audiences of unknown composition as well as to friends and neighbors. There are more conversations, more exposure, and even more mischief when information is false or seized by opponents to use to do damage.

Voluntary critics and self-appointed watchdogs (such as Corpwatch.org, an activist-sponsored site tracking corporate ethics issues) find the Web a convenient town meeting or a place to become a town crier. There are complaint communities, such as customerssuck.com, on which customer service representatives commiserate about having to put the customer first, and flame sites, designed to be inflammatory, such as northworstair.org, started by a disgruntled customer in March 1999 and claiming 160,000 hits over the next year. A May 2000 Netscape search for *sucks.com turned up 57,000 webpages, from chasebanksucks.com to walmartsucks.com. Milksucks.org, meatstinks.org, and vegnow.org are just a few of the sites that link seamlessly to each other in a family of related causes. There are even sites for watching other sites. For up to $137,000 a year, depending on use, eWatch.com tracks online activity and reports to companies; for an additional fee, its Cyber-Sleuth service can dig behind screen names of troublemakers.

Under the everything-direct principle of e-culture, leaders must learn to spread information everywhere fast, rather than hoard it. Mediated communication is increasingly distrusted when it is possible to go directly to the source, or when e-mail distribution lists make it easy to copy everyone on everything. As companies "go direct" to customers—not just selling to them directly but also enabling them to track the progress of their orders—they must also communicate directly with employees and partners. Cascade models in which one level passes on information to the next are too slow and indirect. Why get the big boss's message from your boss, for example, if there are easy ways for the big boss to communicate directly to you? And why think in terms of levels in the first place, when everyone on an e-mail list can see the same thing?

This is one more revolutionary, subversive aspect of the Internet, and revolutionaries take advantage of it. In a conservative wannadot, the e-commerce group made a breakthrough when they posted the CEO's name and e-mail address prominently on the company website and asked his administrative assistant to make sure that each e-mail was responded to within five hours regardless of his location. This risky move paid off. He heard directly from customers about their needs and how the Web could help them, instead of getting feedback filtered through a sales force biased against the Internet. "We now have a tremendous ally in the CEO's chair," an insider said. Direct communication stimulated change.

CYBER PROTESTS AND E-ORGANIZING

Throughout the world, e-organizing makes it harder for establishments to maintain control—not an entirely bad thing, given the traditional tilt toward too much establishment control. Consider examples from three continents:

- *Europe*: In October 1998, Italian Internet users set up a website to protest plans by Telecom Italia SpA to increase the cost of local calls and thus the cost of Internet access. Newspaper publicity directed users to the website, which invited them to access TI's site en masse to paralyze the site, and then to follow up with an e-mail campaign targeted at TI executives and regulators.[11] Italian telecom authorities decided not to raise local rates for Internet use, though they raised rates for voice services. In June 1999, user groups from fifteen European countries organized a Net strike (no connections to the Internet for twenty-four hours and campaign literature on their websites) to protest high, metered rates charged by Internet service providers (ISPs). Three Greek political parties issued statements, and France Telecom proposed a flat rate.[12]

- *Asia*: "Cyber protests are proving very effective for enhancing consumer rights because response is very quick," a Korean activist said. "Consumer-related organizations and NGOs all run to the Internet first these days when an issue comes up. Some say they learned how to use the Internet just to join online protests."[13] In the April 2000 South Korean elections, as many as fifty of the leading candidates were defeated because of online debate and publication of damning information about some candidates' records that did not appear in the traditional media. An umbrella website enabled about 600 grassroots citizens groups to exchange information and views, turning them into a national force.

- *North America*: Key organizers of the December 1999 protests in Seattle against the World Trade Organization, such as Juliette Beck of Global Exchange in San Francisco, worked largely by e-mail. Online coordination by the Direct Action Network linked disparate independent groups, who were free to pursue their own tactics, to some common goals. Even before the live protests, a group of "hactivists" called Electrohippies attacked the WTO's website in November. Though Beck preferred face-to-face organizing, she also said her group could not do its work without the Internet.[14]

Sometimes business is the target, and sometimes it is the instigator of protests against other institutions. Joseph Sweeney, a founder of Asia Online, reminisced to us in the summer of 2000 from his new post at the Gartner Group in Hong Kong about the 1995 protests that gave his business a boost and caused the government to back down. At the time, Sweeney ran Asia Online's "Department of Blue Skies" (product development), which guided its evolution from community site to Internet Service Provider (ISP). In 1995, the Hong Kong police raided seven ISPs, including Asia Online, confiscating equipment and jailing the principals for failure to hold the correct licenses. The Hong Kong police asserted that the shutdowns were intended to help capture a hacker, although the search warrant stated lack of compliance with regulatory standards. Victims suspected that the actual cause was political, namely, that a government-linked entity did not want competition. Pressure was put on the government, Sweeney said, by getting 10,000 indignant subscribers who suddenly found themselves without Internet service to help shine the world media spotlight on the incident. At an Asia Online rally, chairman Philip Wong held up a copy of the book *Internet for Dummies* and suggested the government should read it. A few days later, the police returned the computers and allowed service to resume, quietly dropping proceedings against the service providers. "Trying to bolt down the Internet and hold it back was what drove it into the public consciousness," Sweeney recalled. "That whole fiasco actually thrust our business into the limelight."[15]

Empowerment by the Web can enable even single individuals to move mountains or mammoth corporations. In June 1999, a Japanese consumer, upset with inadequate repairs to two allegedly defective Toshiba VCRs, created a website about Toshiba's postsale service, telling the story and demanding a formal apology from Toshiba (plus $26 to cover his shipping costs). The site included audio recordings of customer service representatives: "I'm not going to apologize for being impolite, why should I?" By August, the site had registered more than 7 million visits and generated extensive press coverage. Copycat sites with similar tales sprang up, some calling for a boycott. On July 19, Toshiba issued a public apology, withdrew a lawsuit against the site, and sent a vice president to make a personal apology for rudeness.[16] But site use continued.

Companies are often unprepared for the speed with which opposition to their actions and offerings can mobilize. In the fall of 1999, e-Toys filed a lawsuit and got an injunction in U.S. courts to bar a Swiss artists' cooperative called etoy from using the name they had used since 1995. e-Toys's users, accessing etoy, had found offensive material, but etoy refused e-Toys's offers to buy the name. After e-Toys went to court, Slashdot.org, a "resource run by Geeks for Geeks" that has over a million daily page views, ran an article about the situation that caused concerned readers to set up a website, toywar.com. In toywar.com's first two days online, 700 volunteers surfaced to lead protests in support of the artists over the business. The offline art world held a press conference at New York's Museum of Modern Art. ®Tmark, an online anticorporate site, helped orchestrate virtual sit-ins (volunteers plagued the e-Toys servers with enough repeated requests to bring them down) and posted the suggestion that protestors bombard investor message boards with negative news about the company. At its peak, the etoy/e-Toys battle involved an estimated 10,000 to 20,000 protestors.[17] Ultimately, e-Toys backed down, dropping the suit.

"WORD OF MOUSE"

Cyberspace seems to have invented a new law of physics: Bad news travels faster than good news. The technology lends itself to guerilla tactics such as the rapid spread of unconfirmed rumors or fast publication of leaked documents. In May 2000, Silicon Investor said that it received about one subpoena a day for chat room records because of the viral impact of rumors on financial markets.[18] "Consumers are often more willing to believe the sources in their e-mail address book than an unknown company spokesman who's trained to save face," said Pete Blackshaw, CEO of PlanetFeedback. Warnings have spread among e-mail correspondents about everything from kidnappers in mall parking lots and stolen kidneys to allegations that antiperspirants add to the risk of breast cancer. People pass these warnings by "word of mouse" to their e-mail list of friends and family, feeling they are doing a good deed. My own in-box recently held false tales about Neiman Marcus chocolate chip cookies, anti-Semitic books on Amazon.com, and offers of payment from Intel for forwarding chain letters.

Some rumors are relatively benign and even charming, such as this e-mail joke declaring that Sony was replacing Microsoft's impersonal error messages with Japanese haiku notices on new PCs:[19]

> *First snow, then silence.*
> *This thousand-dollar screen dies*
> *So beautifully.*

> *A crash reduces*
> *Your expensive computer*
> *To a simple stone.*

> *Three things are certain:*
> *Death, taxes, and lost data.*
> *Guess which has occurred.*

But rumors and protests can wreak havoc as they ripple through an industry. Agriculture biotechnology companies lost the battle over genetically modified foods in the United Kingdom and, it soon appeared, nearly everywhere else, as their opponents mobilized public opinion despite government support for crops grown with their seeds. They were zapped by new media campaigns. The critics' unedited messages and calls to action spread farther faster than anyone inside those companies could have imagined, drowning out information from reputable scientists.

The Online Whine

Every problem presents entrepreneurial opportunities. Infomediaries have turned protests, rumors, and complaints into businesses, thereby encouraging more people to complain more easily more often. Bitchaboutit.com promises to help resolve complaints for a community of people seeking better service, better government, or even better behavior from individuals, through legal assistance (under the banner "I want to sue! Where do I sign?") or collective action (under "Mad as hell and not going to take it anymore! I want to join the boycott!"). eCaveat.com and eComplaints.com offer access to databases of complaints; Epinions.com has reviews on over 100,000 products. Other websites, such as Feedback Direct and ugetheard, offer complaint resolution services that empower consumers (for free) and inform companies (for a price).

PlanetFeedback.com is a new leader in this field. The company seeks to be a positive, constructive force, and investors are betting heavily on it. Think about PlanetFeedback as a self-fulfilling prophecy: The very existence of this company guarantees that consumers will complain.

"The Internet has put key influencers on steroids; it's the uninvited guest that crashed the party," PlanetFeedback CEO Pete Blackshaw told me at a Silicon Valley gathering of Harvard Business School (HBS) alumni running dotcom companies. Before HBS, Blackshaw had worked for the California legislature as a legislative aide on consumer issues, and after getting his MBA, he co-founded the interactive marketing team for Procter & Gamble (P&G). PlanetFeedback bridges Blackshaw's worlds of consumer activism and corporate marketing. Founded in late 1999 in a loft above a microbrewery seven blocks from P&G headquarters in Cincinnati, it immediately began to record its history on www.startup-tv.com. The site went live on February 17, 2000, to turn "the voice of one" into "the power of many." On this consumer-to-business site, consumers can create rants (or raves) directed to companies and cc'ed to Congress or others who should know. Within two months of launch, Blackshaw said the site had several thousand regular users (on their second and third letters) and was beginning a first wave of "escalation" with companies that did not respond to the feedback.

Those most likely to be vocal about either a positive or negative experience with a company are the key to viral marketing, Blackshaw learned from his P&G experience. He had tracked the phone calls to P&G about an inaccurate e-mail rumor linking tampons and asbestos. P&G received about 100 calls a month, representing perhaps a million people receiving the message that month. One month it shot up exponentially, he recalled. "There's just a point at which it gets all this traction on the Internet and takes off. And you don't know when it's going to die and how to stop it." Blackshaw's team found that the best way to "fight fire with fire" was to find their own key influencers ("viral sandbaggers") and communicate with them. And that led to the model for PlanetFeedback.com. The data from individual consumer feedback are used to create valuable information for companies: benchmarks for consumer education and identification of trends and influencers. PlanetFeedback.com functions as an early warning system for companies about emerging feedback fronts. At the end of May 2000, PlanetFeedback's business model received a vote of confidence when investors added $25 million in a second round of financing, at a time of dotcom disfavor. The next step is to go wireless for real-time on-the-spot feedback.

A Swiss flag hangs in PlanetFeedback's office, signaling that it is neutral territory for both consumers and companies. But the initial reaction to the PlanetFeedback model of friction-free feedback is often alarm, Blackshaw said. "Smarter companies may say, 'Hey, we're sitting on top of a focus group here.' Others may say, 'Just more bad news to manage.'" Either way, the ability of people to whine online through PlanetFeedback, through other sites, or on their own means that there will be more direct pushbacks requiring greater responsiveness.

IBM set the tone for corporate responsiveness when it turned on a dime to reverse a decision on a new pension plan after just a few days' flood of e-mails and Web protests from employees. All companies must listen and react fast. A Yankelovich survey in late 1999 found that 60 percent of the nearly 600 CEOs polled worried about negative information about their companies appearing on the Web. Top concerns included Internet-spread criticism of the company by unhappy customers (40 percent), ex-employees (28 percent), and current employees (25 percent), and the use of company e-mail for company-bashing by current employees (25 percent).[20] But the survey questions as framed seem narrow, and the response mild in light of the growing power of the Internet to shape the agenda itself, exposing companies to large new audiences who are no longer passive consumers. The World Wide Web is becoming the town meeting—or the town crier—for the global village. The discussion that occurs there directs the fate of corporations and nations.

Death Threats and Other Reactions to Change

As we have just seen, one company's loyal community is another company's nemesis. One organization's revolution is another organization's death notice. The third major factor shaping responses to the Internet is whether it appears to threaten existence itself.

Nearly everything can be offered directly to end users through the Internet. Airlines can bypass travel agents and sell their tickets directly to passengers; they can eliminate preparation of a paper ticket and send purchase records directly to check-in agents. Manufacturers can bypass wholesalers and retailers to sell directly to consumers and business customers. Mixtures of products and services can be offered in a package to customers, as a kind of assembly system in cyberspace; MyPlant.com, a Honeywell website, allows customers to create their own process control system, order it, and purchase it directly on the Internet, without the need for expensive engineers who would charge their time to configure the system. The Web blurs industry distinctions, allowing those successful in one field to cross into many others, threatening businesses far outside of their industry—such as Japan's 7-Eleven convenience stores trying to add a virtual bank. And consider the gigantic but amorphous threat to the recorded music industry from Napster, software that enables anyone to share personal musical collections with anyone else, making it possible to find on the Web and download instantly almost any piece of recorded music through a network of thousands of small sites that the industry cannot easily find, let alone control (although they are going to court to try).

When one company moves into e-business, new requirements reverberate through the supply chain; traditional partners must change their behavior or step aside. Handling the complicated logistics of online ordering and rapid delivery requires sweeping change in many relationships simultaneously and requires dramatic changes in how each partner does its work. Working out the relationship of e-commerce activities to existing lines of business is one of the most difficult problems encountered by Internet pioneers. Existing groups or departments within the company worry about losing their customers or clout. Internet models shift the center of gravity or eliminate steps, and every step they eliminate can wipe out a department or a business.

Channel conflict—the term for the fights among channels of distribution (e.g., store sales or direct sales over the Internet)—seems an awfully polite way of describing the skirmishes, which have often involved verbal blows and bitter fights. Faced with the demise of their business because of the new online channel, some offline organizations say, in effect, "If I go, I'll kill you first." This happened to Steve Rothschild, founder of Furniture.com, in 1996. For Rothschild, the Internet resuscitated his family's declining bricks-and-mortar furniture store, but the rest of the industry didn't applaud his entrepreneurial medicine. Once his online direct-to-consumers cyberstore went live, furniture distributors went ballistic. Rothschild received hate mail and a death threat. Distributors attempted to get factories to boycott Furniture.com by complaining about his methods. He and Furniture.com stayed alive—but this was literally doing business under the gun. By fall 2000, he had left and the firm folded.

"Handy Gadgets" (HG) also faced death threats, and some of them seemed to work. (The actual organization and industry have been disguised because the battles are still raging as I finished this book.) HG was a $1 billion, low-margin, troubled manufacturing business within a multibillion dollar corporation when its leaders decided that e-business might provide a cure. Newly appointed e-business head "Craig Lebolt" focused on the do-it-yourself consumer (30 percent of the total U.S. gadget market). In the fall of 1999, HG launched "GadgetsPlus" and "GadgetsPlus.com." Consumers could use the Web or a 1-877 telephone service to place orders and receive technical advice online or by phone. HG's sales teams had been provided with key messages for distributor and retailer customers ("The Internet offers a way to reach potential customers who want but can't get Gadgets products easily"; "We're not looking to compete with our current customers"; "All our business partners benefit from a stronger Handy Gadgets"), which HG thought would calm any fears.

How wrong they were. The week after launch, Lebolt and his boss, division head "Michelle Hellman," attended the annual Gadgets tradeshow. They ran into a storm of protest from their traditional distributors, including inflammatory voicemail messages in their hotel rooms and jokes about contracts (implying both agreements and violence). The bottom line: Many distributors said they did not want to deal with a manufacturer selling directly to end users. Hellman had expected retailer concerns about losing sales to the Web, but the intensity of distributor reaction was a surprise.

Hellman and Lebolt returned home to manage the crisis. They offered distributors the opportunity to buy through GadgetsPlus, but they were not interested. To win them back, HG had to turn the 1-877 customer service hotline into a referral number that let customers buy directly from distributors. HG survived the death threat but was left with an expensive campaign that primarily benefited distributors. Meanwhile, online e-tailers wanted to partner with HG. "Our advertising gave exposure to our brand in this market, and now they're clamoring for us," Lebolt reflected. Now HG had "to manage the risk. The short-term risk of losing our traditional customers is too high." At our last conversation, HG leaders were still wondering what to do.

The disruption of traditional relationships is particularly difficult when those relationships have been geographically based, such as local businesses with franchises for particular territories in physical communities who are threatened with bypass by virtual communities for which geography doesn't matter. What happens to car dealerships, awarded to dealers by geography, when Greenlight.com sells cars online, or when the manufacturers decide that they might as well sell directly? In the spring of 2000, the discussions raged about whether the auto companies should sell not just cars but whole dealerships to dotcoms; CarOrder.com, owned by software maker Trilogy, was vying to buy a dozen dealerships. Even nonprofit organizations are affected by these debates. Every Girl Scout troop once had its territory for selling Girl Scout cookies, but enterprising troops with Internet merit badges who offer cookies over the Web "could blow a hole the size of Greenland in that setup," Kevin Maney predicted in *USA Today*.[21]

The car dealer/Girl Scout problem is exactly the one faced by cosmetics company Mary Kay Inc., a territory-based direct sales organization. The Internet posed a death threat to the tried-and-true Mary Kay model. But instead of defending old turf, Mary Kay evolved, creating a dot-community. This is particularly interesting because leading the charge were senior citizens and women, groups supposedly last to embrace the Web.

By mid-2000, Mary Kay Inc. was forming hundreds of independent dotcom businesses weekly, managed by its independent beauty consultants (BCs) with support from Mary Kay. "A company that always believed in word of mouth now believes in word of mouse. We believe the Internet will blow up business-as-usual. Especially our direct selling business-as-usual," proclaimed its long-time vice chairman Richard Bartlett, age sixty-five. With only 3,200 employees on the corporate payroll but over 620,000 beauty consultants worldwide, Mary Kay is a market leader in direct sales of cosmetics and the most active in e-commerce. A hefty portion of its revenues come from the Web (in 1999, 50 percent of total U.S. wholesale sales of almost $1 billion), and the Internet was expected to produce exponential growth.

Between September 1999 and April 2000, 34,000 independent women-owned businesses went online with websites linked to marykay.com. The old territory-based business model, one that involved face-to-face demonstrations and hands-on makeovers, was evolving. Leads coming in over the Web, like those from the 1-800 telephone line, were allocated to BCs within a geography on a random, rotating basis. Online opportunities attracted new customers among younger women and tempted a new breed of women interested in running dotcom businesses to join Mary Kay's dot-community.

Hope Pratt was an unlikely Internet enthusiast. In 1982, as a young mother in Cleveland married to a coach for the Cleveland Browns football team, Pratt wanted a home-based business and found Mary Kay. In 1987, when Mary Kay's computer department called to ask her to computerize her operation, Pratt had never even seen a keyboard and had to ask where the space bar was in order to follow the directions she was sent. A dozen years later, she became an example for her peers, running her e-commerce website, teaching software classes, and using Mary Kay's e-learning system for online training. "At the Mary Kay conference in Dallas every July, they say, 'This is the woman who didn't even know about the space bar,' or 'Here's Hope, if she can do it, there's hope for you!'" she enthused. In July 2000, her business home was Valrico, Florida (near Tampa), her husband coached for the Kansas City Chiefs, and she led over thirty independent beauty consultants while handling 650 loyal, repeat customers in twenty-seven states herself.

The Internet made it easier for Pratt to retain her clients when they (or she) moved out of her territory, but harder for her to compete with local Mary Kay franchisees offering fingers-to-face demonstrations. "I had to do everything in my power to make it appealing for that woman to stay with me rather than buying from someone else down the block. I told them that if they e-mail me by 9 A.M., I'll get their order out by 1 P.M. and they'll get it the next day or the day after, depending on where they live," Pratt said. Her postage bill grew but her phone bill dropped with the advent of the Web. In a business that people go into because they like working with people, the human touch is still central. She periodically phones her long-distance clients just for the greater intimacy of voice contact. Although e-mail became an essential communication tool, Pratt thought of it as "just a bunch of words" (though hers are bubbly even on-screen: "What a fun, exciting year! Hugs from Hope" read one of her e-mails to my Harvard office).

It is almost too coincidental that Dick Bartlett steered us to a woman named Hope.

Bewitched, Bothered, or Bewildered

Who are you, as you read this chapter? Are you an empowered consumer, an enthusiastic entrepreneur, or an embattled executive? Are you a viral sandbagger spreading information, or a frantic leader wondering how to contain it? Locate yourself on my attitude spectrum (borrowed from an old song title):

Bewitched? Then you are mesmerized by the Internet, a true believer, unwilling to hear any negatives about the Web. You still think cyberspace is the road to riches (even if you lost money by investing in anything with the dot).

Bothered? You could be in a field threatened with displacement by the Internet, worried for yourself. You could be a concerned citizen unclear about the Web's social impact or worried for your children. New technologies are disturbing not just because of personal threats but because their effects are unknown and uncontrolled. (And when the dotcom financial bloom faded, dotcom death was fair game for social backlash.)

Bewildered? Join the crowd. My e-culture project's interviews reflect the confusion surrounding the emergence of e-business. There is clarity about the back-room, within-the-enterprise side of e-business—electronic procurement, employee information networks, and customer service connections—but confusion about the economic and social implications of the Web. Even the most sophisticated Net evangelists talk of immense uncertainties and unexpected turns in the road ahead. Most find the whole topic bewildering. The Internet changes so many things, we were told. Yet many people were hard pressed to articulate exactly what it *does* change, beyond elevating techies and geeks to the status of cultural heroes. Nearly everyone said that this is only the beginning.

Having an online presence does not make people feel less bewildered, we found. Heads of some smaller companies, including dotcom pure plays, expressed anxiety and insecurity about what will happen next. An early Web-based fine art vendor was taking advantage of the moment, doing well as an intermediary in a fragmented market. But in the future, the CEO said, what will prevent customers from leapfrogging her site and going directly to other dealers who finally go online? Another dotcom amalgamated a range of repair and support services for small business customers, but the founder worried constantly about what would happen when customers got smarter about searching for themselves, or when companies from unrelated industries, such as banking, added these services to their sites, or when some other still-unforeseen event occurred.

The Internet thrives on imagination and visualization, like the Microsoft commercials asking "Where do you want to go today?" But just because we can visualize a way to do something does not mean that the technology is there to make it come true. Imagination runs ahead of the ability to execute. There is an unevenness about all the changes associated with the Internet. Networks move fast, but many users are still in dial-up mode. Consumers who buy online might find better service over the telephone than over the Internet—and so some dotcoms tout their live service, with real people. "If you can dream it, you can do it" is not always literally true. The Web promises more, but it can also disappoint more. A savvy user said, "When I log on, I have higher expectations. I want all that I see, and I want it now. So it is a bigger disappointment if these expectations are not fulfilled."

"The Internet can make a small company like mine look just as big as the competitors I'm going after," said the founder of a website for local home services. Though his dotcom had only one full-time employee, several part-time people, and a volunteer working out of the founder's house, his website had the look of a large and sophisticated company. Meanwhile, those large companies and their enormous sales forces can be reduced to mere midgets on-screen. In the children's classic *Through the Looking Glass*, Tweedle Dee and Tweedle Dum take Alice to a house with one door labeled "the world's smallest giant," and the opposite one marked "the world's largest midget"—the same thing viewed from different angles.

That's how I have come to think about the Internet. Depending on the angle, it is both friend and foe, tool and driver, death threat and fountain of youth.

It's not enough to embrace the Internet in theory. Living with its consequences is more challenging. There are new requirements for leadership, organization, and careers; there are new skills and new sensibilities.

Success strategies in an e-business environment require radically different approaches. It is not enough to decide to use the Internet, develop a website, and craft an e-business strategy. There are deeper implications, from the emergence of community as a positive organizational model to the potential for communities of opposition. The challenge that leaders face is to manage the next step in a cultural revolution that began even before the Internet became a household word. And for everyone, the challenge is to form and join communities that elicit the economic and social benefits of the technology.

Being a member of a community creates a very different relationship to an organization than the by-now clichéd stakeholder image suggests. The Web affects people as individuals because it enables them to exercise their views and to influence results in any direction they choose. If that were all it did, we would be right to worry, and we would be wise to protect ourselves against its misuse by creating technological and legal restraints. Happily, the Web also yields a much more optimistic prospect of enhancing human and social values and the relationships that contribute to them through the growth of a universally accessible community. Thus it is both decentralizing and integrating at the same time. The outcome is not preordained; it is our choice.

In the chapters that follow I will try to deprogram the bewitched by dousing them in reality, to comfort the bothered, and to show the bewildered what to do.

2

♦

ALICE IN TOMORROWLAND
Will the Young Lead the Way?

Here, you see, it takes all the running you can do, to keep in the same place. If you want to get somewhere else, you must run at least twice as fast as that!
—Red Queen to Alice, in Lewis Carroll's *Through the Looking Glass*

Whether old economy or new economy, the rules still apply. No brand wins without a defensible, distinct brand positioning that adds value for the customer and is defensible. No company wins unless the math works, delivering earnings growth and increasing shareholder value.
—Jeanne Jackson, CEO of Walmart.com

IN THE WEB'S EARLY YEARS, dotcoms seemed to live in a different universe, one full of fantasy and easy money. This land seemed to rewrite old rules, turn business wisdom on its head. And a distinctive culture suited to young people emerged. The office becomes home, with the kitchen at the center of the office. Employees are temporary, but external partners have long-term deals. Newcomers with little business experience get free rein to direct a company's future. The young teach the old.

It's like Alice in Wonderland walking through the looking glass into a world in which everything is reversed, except that in Tomorrowland (the fantasy world of cyberspace), she can't ever walk, she must always run.[1] The speed of change resembles Alice's croquet game, in which everything is alive and moving quickly: Her mallet is a flamingo, the ball is a hedgehog, soldiers bend over to form the hoops, and it is futile to get any of them to stand still. Internet time is said to be seven times faster than ordinary time, but sometimes I wonder if it isn't even faster than that. New companies start faster, acquire earlier, go public sooner, and have their first downturns and layoffs at breathtaking speed, all well before established companies reach the middle of a five-year plan. Dotcoms go from birth to old age (and, in many cases, death) before a traditional firm is out of the starting gate on a new strategy.

Does it take an Alice—an imaginative youth still in touch with wonder—to navigate through Tomorrowland? Dotcoms may know that cyberspace is fraught with surprises, tough rivalries, and death traps, but they seem confident they are headed in the right direction and playing the right game. In my global e-culture survey, 88 percent of representatives of pure Internet units strongly agreed with the statement that "the Internet will completely transform every aspect of business in the foreseeable future." Young dotcom leaders are not feeling confident inside, as they face market conditions few will survive. But those with solid business models project strong belief as they seek the biggest prize of all: Total World Domination.

Abuzz Technologies is one of those youthful dotcoms, and *Total World Domination* is the name of the film Abuzz commissioned to celebrate the release of its first big Internet offering. If Abuzz were not a real company, I would have had to invent it. It has every characteristic of an ideal dotcom. It is a pure Internet business offering a service that would not be possible without electronic networks. It has built a community at work as well as communities online, and because of this it enjoys an unusually high retention rate for its highly skilled staff. Abuzz's engineers, designers, and marketers are team-oriented perfectionists with a track record of delivering solutions to complex problems on deadline at breathtaking speed. As a measure of Abuzz's achievement potential, it executed a successful sale to the New York Times Digital (NYTD) group of the venerable New York Times Company. In its short life, it has invented and improvised and executed many 180-degree turns. And all this while looking just like other youth-oriented dotcoms: a communal kitchen, 24/7 workforce, casual dress, pets in the office, music on all the time, revolutionary rhetoric, and a desire to impress Mom and Dad.

Our tour begins with a detailed look inside Abuzz to convey the things that make the dotcom world distinctive. Abuzz represents the young in two senses: the youth of the company, and the youth of the founders and staff. But note that it has a wise parent, wise enough not only to learn from Abuzz but also to steer it in sensible business directions. After deep immersion in the culture of Abuzz, we will return to the question of whether the young—young people and young dotcoms—lead the way to the future.

Abuzz: Chronicle of a Young Company

I first met Abuzz through an unusual route. Abuzz was an unexpected addition to a Boston Chamber of Commerce program at which I spoke about what businesses could contribute to improving public education. I was charmed by Abuzz's youthful exuberance and distinctive Internet proposition (Abuzz was not just another look-alike e-commerce company), and I was impressed that tiny Abuzz showed up at all for something that usually attracted only big businesses. The following year, I put Abuzz on my interview list for the e-culture project. We were hooked after one long probe and wanted a deeper look. We signed nondisclosure agreements (NYTD was considering an IPO), and Katherine Chen from my research team returned repeatedly for interviews and conversations, including with NYTD and partners. We sat in on meetings. Katherine attended Abuzz events. An Abuzz gang of six came for dinner at my home. (Little did I know then that I would have a chance to play a modest role in their dreams, but that's a later story.)

GREAT TECHNOLOGY, NO MORE SUITS: THE FIRST BUSINESS MODEL

Abuzz was conceived in the summer of 1996 as an Internet venture by three partners, then all in their mid-twenties but with relevant work experience under their belts. Andy Sack was a former venture capitalist who had been a co-founder of Firefly Network, subsequently sold to Microsoft. Andres Rodriguez was a Venezuela-born software developer who merged his fledgling company with the new entity. Shaun Cutts was a computer scientist fresh from research on the Human Genome Project in Europe.

One of Sack's motivations, shared by his partners, was to work in a setting where he would never again have to wear a suit. (One staffer said she worked at Abuzz for six months before she saw Rodriguez in long pants instead of shorts.) The first offices were in Rodriguez's attic.

The founders' initial idea was to run information auctions that matched buyers and sellers of expertise. The space seemed to be open, and the idea of auctions was still there for grabbing (eBay was then in its infancy). Cutts was credited with the Abuzz name. The image of social animals, maybe social insects, seemed to best reflect the concept of knowledge sharing. But should they be apes? (Simian Software was an early thought.) Bees? Ants? Sack took a clipboard to South Station (Boston's big train station) seeking opinions from strangers about animal names. Bees were the winner. Then Cutts decided that an adjective was better than a noun, and after a computer search, he chose Abuzz. Friendly images just started to flow: beeline, beehive, names for the servers like "I'llbeeback." Later, the additional advantages of being first in the alphabet became clear. The name was a winner. Rodriguez admitted, "At the time I didn't know the power of the name. I thought it was fluff. Today, the name is probably the second most important asset this company has. After the people and before the technology."

Let's look at the people first. Early hires mixed social activism with their techno-savvy. John Capello, then twenty-two, was employee number 2 (after the founders and their first hire). A Harvard College roommate of Rodriguez's brother, Capello had been working with at-risk youth and trying to start a cybercafé in Harrisburg, Pennsylvania. Jess Brooks had worked both on Wall Street as a trader and in a nonprofit organization for battered women before starting at Abuzz, first as a volunteer. Their combination of technology and social values attracted others like them.

The immediate challenge was to find the right business model in which to use the collaboration technology. "We probably switched directions more than we had to because of a lack of self-confidence," Cutts reminisced. By February 1997, Abuzz had moved away from an information auction model, Beeline, designed to connect people to content, to another model, Beehive, designed to connect people to each other. They found that other companies were in the people-to-content space; Boston neighbor Firefly was getting big. Even with the switch to Beehive, by the late summer of 1997 they had another "cold feet moment." The word on the street was that the Internet was dead; Firefly was closing down their million-user community website to go after tool development. Abuzz's

Internet pitch was fizzling, and nothing was built. The three founders were convinced that startups had to demonstrate profitability in order to attract investors (this was just before the time when American investors' free-wheeling Internet optimism made profits, let alone revenues, unnecessary for obtaining capital).

What to do now? A business colleague of Sacks's, Jonathon Glick, then at iVillage, helped Abuzz get a consulting contract for technology development with Sony. The Sony experience, plus a few other consulting contracts, convinced Abuzz to move to an enterprise model. "This big company has bought our technology, and we've delivered," an insider recalled feeling. There was a market for Abuzz's technology among large companies. Companies had elaborate information systems, but no way to help people with questions or expertise to find one another. Moreover, companies would pay for the systems.

So Abuzz developed an enterprise consulting model and received $4 million in venture capital from Flatiron Partners, Softbank Ventures, Draper Fisher Jurvetson, and others. In October 1998, Abuzz launched its beta program for Beehive software, which could capture corporate employees' tacit knowledge through a collaborative adaptive filter that posed questions and answers through e-mail. Honeywell Hi-Spec division was an early beta site.

Reversing Direction: A New Partner and the Internet

The enterprise model was just underway, with beta tests in eight companies and feelers from Microsoft and Lotus about partnerships, when Abuzz made another dramatic turn, one that unexpectedly restored the founders' original vision. Glick, the patron saint of the Sony deal, was now working for The New York Times's Internet ventures, about to be renamed New York Times Digital, and he told his colleagues about Abuzz. In the winter of 1999, NYTD sought Abuzz as a contractor (it was also looking at Orbital Software, a Scottish company), and then offered to buy it for an undisclosed amount if it would steer its technology to the Internet. Rodriguez, then vice president of engineering, was reluctant at first, and work on Abuzz's enterprise software continued. Repeated requests from Capello and others eventually convinced him to sell.

Abuzz turned upside down. "We had just finished a product that was dead," recalled product design chief Jay Brewer. Jess Brooks, then in sales and later head of communities and affiliates, commented, "It was a weird period. We had just staffed up for the enterprise product with a client serv-ices department. The first enterprise software was released April 30. In May we were starting to sell it to customers. Then in July we were bought by The New York Times, and we had to suddenly shift to an Internet product."

Despite the turmoil, there was also relief that Abuzz was not going to become a software subsidiary of Lotus or Microsoft, as intended by one of the founders during 1998–1999. With those partners, Abuzz would prob-ably have continued in its knowledge management enterprise model and possibly lost its often-admired character and relative independence. Its leaders had watched Microsoft assimilate Firefly and felt they "ripped it to shreds," one Abuzzer said.

The Internet model turned out to be a powerful energizer. Suddenly, the ambivalence some social activist Abuzz staff had felt about going cor-porate and selling to businesses was resolved. It was "almost a conversion experience," Brewer said. Despite having to displace nearly 20 percent of the staff, "Everyone believed in doing this for the world, bringing this to the world. We were doing something good for a change. We felt that someday, even though this was awful now, people would realize that this is a really good thing." Brooks agreed: "We were trying to figure out what's so good about an Internet product. Then someone says, 'because my Mom can use it.'"

The company was heading into uncertainty again, and people had to recommit. Rival companies immediately tried to recruit Abuzz talent. Abuzz's leaders had to make it clear that not only was the new Abuzz business concept stronger, but also that Abuzz now had the money, pres-tige, brand, and security of a Fortune 500 company watching over them. Believers in this new future soon emerged. Marketing VP Liesel Pollvogt said, "Their vision is big. We're at the heart of it. We're not going to be just newspaper.com." And Capello: "They're not just about producing news-papers. They're about ensuring a social good. They have a history as a company that's all about vision."

GREAT EXPECTATIONS, GREATER EXECUTION

The contract with NYTD involved delivering the first release of a Web-based product in two months, by the end of August, and the second release by November. To accomplish this mission that some felt was impossible, Abuzz chartered two different teams. A small team worked on release 1, staying on to support it, while another team went for release 2.

Deploying the technology on the Web posed new challenges, besides sheer scale—for example, how to get people who don't know each other to share knowledge.

An established Abuzz principle is to always deliver on time. Andres Rodriguez said that from the beginning "The attitude in the company was 'you can do whatever you want, don't come into work, come in late, leave late, we don't care as long as you never fail anything that you tell somebody else you are going to have ready. Never, ever be late.' We were harsh on that. If you missed a deadline, you were never put back on a project. I think we demoralized a few people with it, but we created this phenomenal culture where the peer pressure is to deliver exactly everything on time. This team will go nuts if they feel like they are going to miss the delivery." Brewer described the last-minute scramble to perfect the product before undergoing an audit that would not cover the same level of detail: "We made the job harder for ourselves. It was so incredibly stressful. We wanted to do so well. It was the A+ student problem."

How does Abuzz move so fast? Abundant communication and teamwork. Brewer contrasted the Abuzz approach with the style engineers reported in their previous companies: "Before we commit to a deadline, the engineering team sits down in a room—20 people and more. You're going to build this. How long will it take? Not just the managers. It's the people who will do the work, committing to each other. Design details are taken to a level where everyone is a lead and has to make a public commitment. There is a sense of ownership for the schedule. The engineers say that other companies don't do it that way." While phasing out relationships with former clients and restructuring the company's divisions and personnel, Abuzz reconfigured its Beehive software to encompass a highly scalable community of users on the Internet. "We turned around the company, changed the model completely. Of course we'd pull it off. I never doubted it," an insider said.

The youthful team benefited from good parenting. Martin Nisenholtz, head of NYTD, wanted to keep Abuzz people happy through the transition: "My goal was to send the signal to the folks at Abuzz that while we were going to start to do a whole range of new things together, I was not going to come in and manage the company. I took a very light touch, almost to a fault. This was not going to be about Martin sending his people in to manage this company or to manage it himself. It was going to be about the Abuzz folks finding their own way inside of our company."

In December 1999, Andres Rodriguez commissioned a movie called

Total World Domination to show off the Web design to the whole company and NYTD. "Mr. Brewer," he said, according to Jay Brewer, "we need an Apple-like keynote to launch release 2. We'll make them believe like we believe." The result: a professional-quality demo film of the website spliced with military takeover imagery and martial music. (It continued to run periodically on Abuzz TV, an always-on flat-panel display screen that showed what was happening on the website as well as other important items.)

In January 2000, Abuzz launched its public Internet website, competing with Keen.com, ExpertCentral.com, Ask Jeeves, Deja.com, and others. Abuzz users could participate in question-and-answer circles organized by topic (e.g., health, work, technology, extracurricular activities, regional areas, international news). There were over a million transmissions in the first few weeks; within just a month, there were already 20,000 active users. Abuzz, like eBay, created an online self-regulating community. "When we first started we thought we were going to have to be very vigilant," Brooks reported, "[but] for the most part the community actually monitors itself."

Later, after evaluating the high costs of developing name recognition for an Internet firm compared with the New York Times brand, Abuzz shifted to an affiliate model, serving users routed from other NYTD properties (NYTimes.com, NYToday.com, WineToday.com, eGolfDigest.com, and Boston.com), with the goal of capturing a quality network of well-educated users with an interest in travel, wine, and other activities dependent on disposable income.

How Abuzz Works: The Culture

While focused on building the website, Abuzz's leaders did not neglect building the company culture. They wanted a work environment that emphasizes offline as well as online community, with all the features of the new dotcom world that mixes work with play.

Office as Home. Abuzz in 2000 consists of almost a hundred people working in the Brickyard, a converted factory in Cambridge, with others at remote locations. Signs of the Abuzz culture appear on entry: bicycles, paintings by staff, stuffed animals, and cutouts of *Star Wars* characters. The office is a place to live as well as work. One product developer worked two ninety-hour weeks, sleeping on a couch in his office rather than renting an apartment (since his home was a long commute away). Abuzz's twenty-four-hour ethic goes especially well with being an Internet company instead of a software installer; the Web is live at every moment. "It's definitely Internet time," an Abuzzer said. "Here you can work as much as you want, which is not always good. People are always e-mailing each other at midnight or on the weekend saying, 'Get offline.' 'No, you get offline! Like stop working!'" Another observed, "There's always something fun going on in the office, but there are also always people here at work." Jess Brooks recounted waking at 3 A.M. one night at home, unable to sleep because of ideas in her head that she had to get out. Arriving at the office at 4 A.M., she found Shaun Cutts there; he had come after dinner at 11 P.M.

Music All the Time. In addition to watching Abuzz TV, employees can listen to Abuzz Radio. People load the server with MP3 tracks from their CDs. They can request specific songs and listen to broadcasts that include fake Abuzz radio spots. This is a voluntary project started by Russ Miner, a recent graduate who wanted to continue the fun of his college radio show. "When you're here from early in the morning till late at night," staffers felt, "it's nice to have a little music playing."

Pets in the Office. Next to one computer is a glass aquarium with a heat lamp aimed at it, holding George's gecko. George moved her from Portland, Maine, but couldn't get landlords to accept this innocuous pet. In George's second week on the job, Andres Rodriguez stopped by to say hello. He okayed the gecko at Abuzz if other people didn't mind. (The only problem was crickets escaping before being eaten.) Crickets are the only insects. There are no live bees, but there is a dog. By mutual agreement, two directors, Jay Dunne (member services) and Jess Brooks (communities and affiliates) share an office with Grizelda, a large, friendly German shepherd. Grizelda has a corner of the office to herself, with a blanket, dog food, water, and a chew toy.

Brooks described the reaction of Martin Nisenholtz, CEO of NYTD, on his first visit to Abuzz after the acquisition: "It was obvious that he was not used to the informal feel of meetings at Abuzz. People were calling out questions to Martin, and each time people clapped at his answers, Grizelda would bark, which startled him. Eventually he barked back, getting into the spirit of things."

Communal Kitchen. Food is very important at Abuzz, and the kitchen is one of the most important rooms, featuring a large open meeting space. Food is one way Abuzzers bond and get to know the person behind the job title. An early practice was for nearly the whole company to have lunch together every day. As it got larger, the habit of communal lunches continued, but in smaller groups. There are Friday afternoon margaritas (replacing beer), a Dolce Vita lunch club (monthly informal gatherings at various restaurants), and a morning coffee group. A decision was made to have only one coffee pot, so everyone would have to come to the kitchen.

Community Events. A semi-monthly free lunch (usually pizza) features an Abuzz innovation called a Cool Talk. Anyone can lead a session describing his or her passions and nonwork activities. An April 2000 Cool Talk on music featured Jess Tardy, a Harvard-educated jazz singer who joined Abuzz after realizing that she couldn't support herself on gigs, and John Capello, recently named general manager and hence the boss. Tardy, a striking redhead, was attired in evening wear with high heels. Capello, who had brought his bass, wore a dark blue shirt with a martini logo. Tardy reported that she used to perform with Capello until he got too busy with Abuzz. They performed three numbers (the third one joined by another employee jazz singer), and then talked and answered questions about the music business.

Weekly company meetings are well attended and considered an important form of communication. "Instead of trickle down, everybody gets the message all at once," a leader said. A silver chime announces the start of the meeting. People sit on tiers of a small amphitheater, in bean bag chairs or on the floor. A playful atmosphere is balanced by serious content. There are slide presentations mixing business updates (number of registered Abuzz users, products, marketing), announcements (a retreat with "more food for you all" at the end of the month, a new way for employees to access the Abuzz network from home), introductions of new employees, and social diversions (who is going to a Boston Red Sox game). ("Abuzz loves to play!" declares a memo on company history.)

Open Communication and Teamwork. People at Abuzz go out of their way to attend meetings and stay informed. In the Internet space, Abuzz faces the challenge of "making sure the right people know about things as they're happening because they're moving so quickly; making sure that communication isn't sacrificed for efficiency or speed to market," a leader said. So a storyboard presentation for an upcoming release in the fall of 2000 was voluntarily attended by nearly the whole population in the building. Russ Neufeld, Chief Technology Officer, and Jay Brewer presented plans for the Abuzz spaces that users would create by selecting specific people and content. There were constant references to

Abuzz's focus—collaboration and community-building—and to the user experience, which told them to minimize and simplify the interface.

Another communication facilitator is the product manager, a powerful cross-functional role that coordinates among engineering, marketing, and other business groups. John Capello once played that role. His replacement came from Amazon.com, not for the money (he probably took a pay cut) but for the Abuzz culture and the chance to have broader opportunities to contribute than in a narrower job at Amazon. Teams, such as an architectural review team, also keep information flowing. All the people building and updating the site, regardless of function, have weekly meetings, prioritizing what they should build next. But Abuzz leaders are careful to distinguish communication from decision making. The emphasis is on keeping people informed, not on throwing everything open to vote.

Online and Offline Community Service. People often draw parallels between Abuzz as a work community and the online communities on its site. "We're participating in the experience we're creating," marketing director Christine Mohan said—for example, how do new people come into a group that has already been active? Rodriguez echoed the image: "It's very much like a community. It's a community with a purpose. It's not like a neighborhood. As an overall purpose, we would like to think of making money. But I think the company operationally has two purposes. One is to build the coolest technology that anyone has seen for collaboration, for communities, and the other one is to take care really, really well of the people who are part of the external community, our customers." The emphasis on helping people learn online is also echoed within Abuzz.

Community service reinforces Abuzz values. Soon after she joined Abuzz, Jess Brooks had a conversation with one of the founders in which she described her interest in volunteering with schools. As a result, Abuzz made a long-term commitment to the Dante Alighieri Elementary School, a public school in a disadvantaged neighborhood in East Boston. Abuzz employees contribute computer expertise to teachers and students, helped network the school's patchwork of computers, and built the school website—in the process building stronger bonds throughout Abuzz. Over a quarter of the company generally gets involved—designers, system administrators, engineers, and customer support staff—and reports on the school are a regular part of the all-company meetings. Community service has expanded to other schools closer to Abuzz's offices, such as an art project with the Cambridge Friends School. Abuzz wants to make community outreach one of NYTD's core values.

TEACHING THE PARENT

David Thurm, COO of NYTD, commented on the unexpected bonus that came with Abuzz: "Our main purpose was to buy an application. We are certainly still very enthusiastic about the application. But as we've gone forward, we've benefited in addition from Abuzz's culture of innovation. That innovative spirit washes over the rest of the company, which I think is really helpful."

Abuzz's emphasis on teamwork and communication made its experience central to an NYTD culture committee that has representatives from each affiliate. Jess Brooks and Christine Mohan represented Abuzz (until Mohan moved to NYTD in August 2000—another indication of what the parent got from Abuzz). On one committee conference call, everyone seemed interested in Abuzz's emphasis on openness. One committee member asked, "Jess, why do you think anonymous communication gives people bad vibes?" "You feel like a child," she replied. When another affiliate said that "talking to someone here is just not part of the standard way of business" and that Abuzz could communicate so widely because it was smaller, Mohan wondered if "They're just using size as an excuse."

Early in Abuzz's history, the founding team discussed success and how they would know they had achieved it. They covered the walls of a conference room with yellow sticky notes, each one with an aspiration for any and all to see, customers as well as new hires: *Billions of dollars. Maintain respect. A mention in the* Wall Street Journal. *Live our values. An article in* Wired. *A Harvard Business School case.* (That last dream I could help with.)

Is Abuzz sustainable and scalable as an organization? Let me put it this way. It has a good shot at effective growth because its e-culture foundations are in place. Giant Cisco Systems, still growing at record-breaking speed from its 1999 revenue base of about $13 billion, shares cultural features with Abuzz:

- War stories about on-time delivery and expense control. (Cisco Systems CEO John Chambers likes to tell one about his rejected expense report for airport parking.)

- Emphasis on communication to the largest groups possible. (At Cisco, 700 managers in live strategy sessions webcast the next day to everyone. Employee information networks get 10 million hits a month, and every executive is a skilled presenter who can speak to crowds without notes.)

- Leverage of even-larger partners (for Cisco, that's IBM).

- A significant commitment to public education. (Cisco Academies teach networking skills.)

- A crusade to become the biggest and best ever. (Total World Domination, anyone? But that's my phrase, not Cisco's. They prefer the phrase "end-to-end solutions.")

The hands-off stance of Abuzz's corporate parent toward the young company it adopted reflects an understanding that, in this case, Abuzz's culture might be better suited for the e-world ahead than corporate routines inherited from the past. The New York Times did not claim that its 150-year-old history gave it all the answers and the right to mold a dotcom in its image. NYTD changed Abuzz's advertising agency (which met with hearty approval by Abuzz staff, happy to have access to even better resources through its new parent) but was light-handed with demands. Instead, the "elders" at NYTD show every sign of being willing to learn from Abuzz, in a kind of reverse mentoring that is becoming more and more common in the Internet Age, as young people and young dotcoms appear to be the tour guides to Tomorrowland. (The stress is on *appear*.)

From Diapers to Dollars: Dotcoms as Youth Movements

Are only the young able to change quickly enough to succeed in cyberspace? They are certainly overrepresented in the dotcom world. The number of teenagers in Internet-related work is growing rapidly; the U.S. Department of Labor estimated that the number of people aged sixteen to nineteen in the computer and data processing industry increased from 5,000 in 1994 to 29,000 in 1998.[2] Some youthful entrepreneurs drive Internet businesses before they can drive cars—we can call them infantrepreneurs. By twenty-two, they are considered seasoned veterans. Ryan Zacharia, the teenage owner of Stockpickz.com, was featured in *The New York Times Magazine* shortly after his sixteenth birthday in April 2000. "This generation is growing up in a revolution," he said. "We offer knowledge that other people don't. Someone that lives on the Internet can foresee what's going to be popular." (But he also said he probably wouldn't hire teenagers himself.)[3]

Antony Yip, already considered a pioneer in China's Internet market at age twenty-one, started MyRice.com in 1998 (before turning twenty) as a Chinese portal, building it through investments in a collection of Web properties. With a mushrooming number of student-founded Internet companies on campus, Harvard University, my own parent institution, updated its stringent rules against students running businesses in their dorm rooms. Among the dotcoms already founded on campus were Chipshot.com, a multimillion-dollar site selling golf equipment; Collegebeans.com, for textbooks online; and Datesite.com.

Sometimes executives in Internet companies are startled themselves at the youth of their staff. A vice president of Allaire, a successful e-commerce software company, stood in front of 400 employees in a movie theater Allaire had rented for a corporate conference and joked, "When did we start recruiting from kindergarten?" She was kidding and the laughter was loud, but a point was made. Even the boards of Internet companies are youth oriented. Search firm Spencer Stuart found that an "astonishing" one-quarter of inside directors of Internet company boards in 1999 were under forty, "an age group that would barely be represented on S&P 500 boards," and outside directors of Internet companies tended to be ten years younger on average than those of the S&P 500.[4]

Age is far from the only variable in Internet leadership. My research findings show that people in their sixties and beyond have embraced e-culture enthusiastically and effectively—and that youth, of the company itself and of its staff, can have drawbacks. Still, the dotcoms have to be viewed as another example of the age dimension in adopting new technology: The young seem to do it more readily, and they are prevalent in new-technology occupations. Low barriers to entry make it relatively easy to get started, whether in a garage or a dormitory room, but that cannot be the only reason for the youthful cast to dotcoms. Nor is it that the young are specializing in marketing to other young people, although my research team found that music propositions were a favorite among budding young entrepreneurs worldwide. I think the reason is simple. There is something about revolutionary new technology that matches the appetite of the young for revolution. Across a wide range of dotcom startups, I found striking similarities in rhetoric and style to youth movements of the 1960s in North America and Europe.

The rush to start Internet businesses has the quality of a social movement, not just a business change, and that has always been the territory of the young. Many dotcoms say that they are on a crusade to change the world. (And indeed, flanking the dotcom millionaires are nonprofit organizations and social activists that want to use the Internet for social change.) They are populated with true believers who plunge in wholeheartedly, ready to risk everything—as only those who do not yet have obligations associated with "adult responsibilities" can do.

This is not new. Throughout history, the young have led revolutions. For the past few decades, there has been a youthful cast to high technology. A stream of declarations has issued from Silicon Valley and other entrepreneurial outposts about world-changing technologies and companies. In the late 1970s and early 1980s, Apple's youthful founders proclaimed that they were creating bicycles for the mind that would democratize access to computer power, declared war on IBM on national television, and presented themselves as the advance force of a revolution. They were right, even if they were eventually humbled by the IBM PC and spent another decade-plus fading in prominence until their no-longer-boyish co-founder returned to restore creativity. Digital Equipment Corporation's average workforce age hovered in the late twenties for its first two decades; as Digital's graying founder, Ken Olsen, lost touch with the market and new technologies, its age profile increased, and then it too lost ground, only to be swallowed by Compaq.

When Youth Lead Their Elders: Intergenerational Tensions or Reverse Mentoring?

Because the young are considered the Internet experts, the early days of the dotcom boom showed a bias toward the young and the newcomer over those with long experience in the company or the industry. A Silicon Valley venture capitalist was widely quoted as saying that he wouldn't invest in any Internet company started by anyone over twenty-six. The twentyish founder of a successful Internet consulting company told me that his ideal new hires have a few years of work experience but not more than three. "We want to get them before they are brainwashed by the McKinseys or the Andersens," he said.

That bias for youth angers many mature adults. In 1999, young dotcom millionaires became a major topic of conversation among their parents' generation, the baby boomers. Everywhere I went, it seemed, successful professionals—lawyers, physicians, consultants with high billing rates—

complained that it was unfair that people so young were getting so rich so fast. Instead of feeling satisfied with all they had accomplished, many boomers expressed frustration that they had devoted their work lives to something that seemed to get them nowhere; some wanted to throw over their professions and find a dotcom to join.

Even more upset are older job-seekers. Public debates surfaced in newspaper letters columns about whether young people deserve their opportunities because they are the only ones capable of leading the Internet revolution. One angry exchange refuted a writer's assertion that younger workers show a wider range of daring and experimentation with newer technologies. The rebutter challenged the first writer's assumption that over-forty workers haven't stayed current on technology and can't learn anyway.

Within companies, intergenerational tensions abound. Older professionals are angry that younger ones won't listen to them. The conflicts in one e-commerce company divided on age lines. "We're a very young management team," a youthful insider told us. "We bring a lot of people from the retail world who tend to be ten years older, on average, than some of the Internet and marketing teams. There are some gigantic battles because of that. They insist they know what makes for a good catalog layout or a good retail store, but we have to fight them, because their knowledge doesn't translate onto the Web." The problem with those who resist learning from the young is that they equate youth with inexperience, and that's a mistake.

Young does not necessarily mean inexperienced. At twenty-four, when he founded brandnewmusic.com in London's pop music center, James Toledano was a veteran with seven years of experience in Internet businesses. He had a global perspective (he knew he should stay away from the U.S. market, going instead for Latin America and Japan), a deal with Smart Card Axis in Europe for its smart cards (especially important in the Latin American market, where his audience doesn't have credit), and a big-league partner in Apple, on whose website brandnewmusic.com was a fixed channel ("As a very, very small company this is quite cool for us," Toledano exclaimed). He knew his own limitations as a manager and was conservative about spending investors' money, stretching a six-month investment into a year. He learned what not to do from watching the rise and fall of his previous employer, Web Media, the United Kingdom's first Web design house.

We found characteristics of other dotcoms in Toledano's startup: flexible schedules, a dressed-down hip young style ("This is the first time I've worn a tie in months because I'm meeting someone from Harvard," Toledano confessed to us), music on all the time, and the promise of equality ("Everyone's like the CEO"). But Toledano tried to combine the virtues of youth ("Because we're all young we create our own environment") with the value of experience ("I've got investors who are 50 times more senior than I am").

In short, experience still counts, as should be expected, and the smarter of the young dotcom founders are willing to tap the assets that the older generation bring. Young entrepreneurs make good press, but there are often experienced hands behind youthful dotcoms, such as Tim Koogle at Yahoo! Declaring that "this is not a 29-year-old's game," an early investor in Women.com insisted that a two-decade veteran of high tech, Marleen McDaniel, be hired as CEO, replacing the founder.[5] Stephan Schambach founded Intershop in the former East Germany in 1992 at age twenty-two with two older partners. Intershop became one of the world's three largest e-commerce software companies by 1999, based in both Germany and San Francisco and supplying software running over 40,000 online storefronts. Schambach's youthful impatience was balanced by the maturity of his partners, a *Wall Street Journal Europe* reporter observed.[6] In October 1999, Schambach lured former Compaq CEO Eckard Pfeiffer, age fifty-eight, to become chairman.

But seniority does not rule the Web. Mature executives, even those with big names, are often not expected to take over the reins. Their history is not always valued. They are often expected to unlearn what they previously knew, suspend disbelief, and take direction from the less experienced. When distinguished editor Michael Kinsley moved to Seattle to start Microsoft's online magazine, *Slate*, he was startled to take orders from a boss almost two decades younger than he and to discover how many of his previous assumptions did not fit the Internet.

Older managers must get younger in spirit to fit in, and they must be willing to be mentored by those who are their juniors in every conceivable aspect. Veterans hired for their experience find themselves influenced by the youthful environment—and indeed, must learn to act younger. Blackboard.com's veteran, graying temporary CEO, who was recruited by the company's twenty-seven-year-old co-founders, talked about his job as a learning experience, not as an application of what he already knew. George Conrades, hired as CEO for Akamai, a high-flying Internet technology company founded by an MIT student and his professor, brought a wealth of experience from IBM and Bolt Beranek & Newman, developer of Arpanet, the Internet's precursor. Akamai is like Conrades's fountain of youth. His love for sports cars, motorcycles, and rock music—all dotcom appropriate—became more pronounced and visible.

Reverse mentoring is more common everywhere. Consider these role reversals:

• *Students teach the teachers.* In the public school system in Union City, New Jersey (introduced in chapter 1), Parent University computer classes run by the public schools are staffed by the schoolchildren. Computer-savvy eleventh grader Jonathon Loor earned $50 an hour teaching the teachers about new technology. "Jonathon knows ten times as much as I ever will about a computer," said teacher Agnes Colinari.

• *Novices guide big investments.* It is not new to find bright, enterprising college students running businesses while in school; what is startling is to see large institutions handing them responsibility for financial decisions. A group of four college juniors were hired by venture capitalists to screen business plans. Then they were hired by their own university (a large distinguished one) to make investment portfolio recommendations, complete with office space on campus and a faculty adviser who was never asked to advise.

• *Children hire their parents.* After launching a successful music website in Sweden at barely twenty, Ola Ahlvarsson founded Result Venture Knowledge International, a dotcom incubator, in his mid-twenties, persuading his father, a former deputy mayor of Stockholm, to run one of his ventures. Microsoft's Bill Gates also hired his father, to head the Bill and Melinda Gates Foundation.

• *Children rival their parents.* At twenty-three, fresh from Stanford University, Richard Li, son of Hong Kong magnate Li Ka-shing, started his own communications technology empire. Pacific Century Cyber-Works, which he established in 1993 with the billion dollars he received for selling Star TV to Rupert Murdoch, is already one of the world's biggest Internet companies—a satellite-based broadband Internet network built through acquisitions, joint ventures, and venture capital investments. In a few years, he built a net worth almost equal to his father's lifetime accumulation. And after the elder Li launched an Internet venture, Tom.com, in early 2000, observers speculated about potential embarrassment as son and father became business rivals.[7]

Inside organizations, learning from those with fresh new knowledge is an essential part of e-culture. John Chambers, legendary CEO of Cisco

Systems, employs a teenager in the office of the CEO to keep Cisco in touch with young technology users. Whether companies hire those with new knowledge or merely use them as consultants, they are likely to find assumptions of hierarchy turned upside down. Juniors guide seniors, subordinates lead teams with their bosses on them, newcomers with no internal experience determine external offerings, and consultants take over and run corporate functions. Corporate executives grumble to me about ceding control of their Web proposition to twenty-year-old designers or to firms that have been in business less than two years, but some feel they have no choice. The young have the knowledge, and they don't.

Wait a minute. That's only one side of Tweedle Dee and Tweedle Dum's house. Did I mention that Tomorrowland is part fantasy? The young may be disproportionately represented in the dotcom universe, they may have a distinctive style, and they may even have fresh new knowledge to teach their elders. But reverse mentoring doesn't wipe out the traditional kind. Success in the New Economy stems from some of the same values and management lessons as success in the Old Economy. Even when children's startups depart wildly from the experience of their parents, there is something to be learned in both directions.

When Mentoring Works Both Ways: Building the New Economy on Old Economy Roots

The case of Internet pioneer Jack Hidary, founder of EarthWeb, and his father illustrates many intergenerational issues of style and success. Yet it also captures the continuity of values that elders must never neglect transmitting to the young, even when the young monopolize technology know-how.

Jack Hidary's New Economy New York of Silicon Alley's multimedia companies stands in striking contrast to his father's Old Economy New York, the garment district. EarthWeb's Park Avenue offices are in a modern high-rise, with staff working in open cubicles and sharing a spacious kitchen. Several blocks away, on West 33rd Street, are the offices of M. Hidary & Company, the apparel company that Jack's grandfather built and his father David now heads. M. Hidary occupies more traditional, closed offices, with a suite of conference rooms bedecked in current apparel lines.

Jack founded EarthWeb in 1994 at twenty-five with his brother Murray and their friend Nova Spivack when their earlier business creating websites revealed a frustrating lack of resources for developers on the Internet. In 1999, EarthWeb was the third fastest growing company of *Business Week*'s Info Tech 100. By mid-2000, EarthWeb's 350-plus employees ran fifteen online resource websites for information technology (IT) professionals (an audience estimated at 15 million people), including over 150,000 technical resources and hundreds of proprietary tutorials. EarthWeb, which went public in November 1998, expected to top $60 million in revenues in 2000, doubling its 1999 performance, and, according to analysts, expected to become profitable during the first half of 2001. EarthWeb owns dice.com, the largest online IT jobs portal (with 175,000 high-tech listings), as well as online certification programs such as MeasureUp and the e-learning site CCPrep. Dice.com, whose paid listings provided 51 percent of EarthWeb revenues in 2000, is at the center of content and marketing agreements, such as one with Yahoo!Careers. Another 32 percent of 2000 revenues came from banner ads and sponsorships, and 17 percent from premium products and services. EarthWeb e-mail newsletters reach over 1 million subscribers.

Jack and his younger brother Murray had been expected to join generations of Hidarys in the family garment business. Jack came to the M. Hidary offices all right—but used them as the launch pad for a new Internet business that taught Jack's father things he had never imagined.

Fascinated with computers from an early age, Jack progressed from computer camps to revamping computer systems as a Columbia University student. After graduation, he conducted research using computer brain scans as a fellow at the National Institutes of Health in Washington, while trying his hand at a few entrepreneurial ventures. He even honored family tradition by importing fabrics. But in 1993, in the early days of the Web, Jack saw the Internet as a greater opportunity. He started a business creating websites in his apartment, called GoToNet, and considered numerous ideas, such as selling tickets for sports events. Friends in Boston and New York helped him, especially co-founder Nova Spivack.

Jack decided to return to New York because it was becoming an Internet center. He set up in his father's offices. His father recalled: "We gave him some space. We have extra desks here and there. We can just squeeze them around. Nova came up with him also, and the two of them were working literally around the clock. They used to stay up late night doing projects for quality name accounts. Retail stores. Electronics. For the Metropolitan

Museum of Art, they put a virtual museum on the Internet. You could walk through and see the art."

Soon younger brother Murray also switched his interest from garments to the Web, and the apparel company offices became the center of an expanding Internet business. David Hidary was struck by the different culture: "They were hiring all these young guys, computer programmers, computer graphics people—a different breed. They've got ponytails and jeans. Earrings, you know, that kind of stuff. They don't get dressed up in ties. We're looking around, what's going on here? A different culture altogether. . . . And we have maybe a dozen people here at one point and we're putting them over here; putting them there. We'd get another table and another phone and computer. They would just collide all over the place. And we would leave here at 5 or 6 o'clock at night, and they'd stay until midnight. If they had a project, they'd stay all night. . . . But it was fine."

After six months, with a revenue stream flowing, Jack's venture moved to its own offices. The name was soon changed to EarthWeb, and eventually the business model changed too, from building websites to providing career development resources and technical expertise for the world's IT professionals. David Hidary, who learned about the New Economy from watching his sons, was catapulted into a different world. "They had this dream, and they really worked very hard," David Hidary said. "People believed in them. The venture capitalists believed in what they were doing. And then they went public a couple of years later." The son's IPO was a high point for the father; it was a thrill for him to see the opening of trading in the investment bank's offices. "And, thank God, they're doing OK."

Despite the generational role reversal, Jack Hidary maintains close ties and a continuity of values. He lunches with his father regularly. His office sports an old family picture of his grandfather surrounded by the five sons. More important, Jack honors the family tradition of community service. Two nonprofit organizations, MOUSE (Making Opportunities for Upgrading Schools and Education, which provides technology resources for public schools) and Trickle Up (microlending for disadvantaged women), are Jack's other passions. When I first met Jack in December 1998 (at Renaissance Weekend in Hilton Head), he was almost more excited to talk about MOUSE than about EarthWeb. "I grew up in a family, in a community, where service was just what you did," he said later. "Almost every week, every other week there were various functions in my house. I knew growing up that my grandfather was very involved in the community—head or co-head of many of the organizations." Jack finds opportunities for others at EarthWeb to get involved in social causes, and he is admired as a leader for his community commitments.

The best mentoring works in both directions. Technology may be a young person's game, but values are created from parents' and teachers' and bosses' examples. Arguably, EarthWeb's success comes from the combination of values-based leadership and technological savvy. Abuzz is in an earlier stage than EarthWeb, but is building on the same foundation.

E-Culture or E-Cults?
How to Tell the Difference

Companies such as EarthWeb and Abuzz, along with eBay in chapter 1, reflect both the style of youthful dotcoms and the substance of e-culture. There is a great deal of strategic, organizational, and technological substance important to Abuzz's success at laying a foundation for future business growth. Abuzz uses technology to provide a service unique to the online world. Its teams bridge the technology/marketing/content divide. Abuzz employees have deep know-how in specialty areas but a willingness to learn things from other areas. There is abundant redundant communication, professionalism, and a dedication to meeting deadlines. Like the best companies of any era, Abuzz has a customer/user focus and the ability to innovate quickly. Its partnerships with other media companies ensure broad reach.

But there are all too few EarthWebs and Abuzzes. Unfortunately, many dotcoms have only the style parts—communal kitchens, dress-down codes, pets, music, game rooms, revolutionary rhetoric—and not the substance. Many dotcoms resemble an e-cult rather than defining a more generalizable e-culture. Of course, most Internet companies are small and new, and that alone gives them a special flavor. But strip away the chaos of a startup—working out of boxes, doubling up in offices, tripling the staff every few months—and they still seem different. They are often like fashion-oriented youth groups.

The style part is half the fun for some members, who are happy not to be among "the suits" (but whose all-black outfits or baggy pants have their own air of conformity). Not since the youth movements of the 1960s has so much long hair on young men been so visible. The earrings-and-ponytail look on young male techies extends even to conservative Switzerland, where serious Internet startups take names like Fantastic. After a young New York Internet company made its first acquisition, leaders were widely quoted as disdaining the acquirees for their uncool khaki pants. Rudy Chan, brought in at age thirty-eight as CEO of hongkong.com, the region's largest portal, laughed when he recalled his introduction to the staff: "And then I turned around and see all these kids . . . in worn-out jeans and T-shirts."

For many youthful dotcoms in my e-culture project, the kitchen is the most important room, and food the most important part of bonding. Employees bring sleeping bags to work and take pride in pulling all-nighters that resemble communal living in the office. They are convinced that they will change the world and that no one over thirty can be trusted. They spend venture capitalists' money as though it were allowances from their parents. One senior staffer of a successful Web design firm enjoys gaining credibility with corporate clients despite his purple hair. A twenty-two-year-old who is one of the top leaders of a fifteen-person Internet startup complains secretly that his boss, a forty-two-year-old former investment banker who founded the company, does not really understand the Internet because the boss still insists on wearing a tie to work. A Boston dotcom begun in a dorm room by recent college graduates just hired its first "token adult." In some circles, hiring experienced professional managers for Internet startups is referred to as getting adult supervision. An incubator in Silicon Valley is known as a day care center for entrepreneurs.

Young workers in dotcoms sometimes convey a sense of entitlement derived from inexperience. A dotcom executive who had worked in several e-commerce companies and was barely out of his twenties himself commented on this. "It's an interesting dilemma for any employer right now—the expectations of junior level people in the workforce for less than five years," he said. "They have no experience in a world where dotcoms aren't on every newsstand, and tales of instant wealth aren't everywhere. Their expectations are very unrealistic about what they should be paid, how hard they should work, how quickly their rewards should come, how good they really are at what they do. You find their resumes on Monster Board and they list their expertise in HTML and Adobe Photoshop, expert, expert, expert, expert. I want to say to them, 'Do you really think you're an expert in those things? Because I've got news for you!' I've had people who have worked at a company for less than 60 days at a very entry level position come and ask for a 40% raise because now they're actually doing Web production work. There are a lot of unrealistic expectations among entry level players."

A similar air of unreality clings to some students with dotcom business plans. Because an early wave of these dreams came true, everyone else became convinced that they too could get rich quick based on little more than an imaginative Internet idea. I met with a group of twenty-year-olds who had a very creative idea for a website that would use streaming video to bring shoppers to tour real places. Among them they had excellent design and programming skills, salesmanship (required to bring stores on board), access to an enthusiastic summer workforce of college kids, and the ability to spout statistics on Internet use. But it was all theoretical, the stuff of Web surfing. They had never been to the places that the site would feature. Worse yet, they didn't really want to do the work. They wanted someone to buy their idea so they could get a cash payment, equity, and a consulting contract—and then finish school.

Hubris like this extends to numerous Internet land grabs. New companies claim a territory even if they have no expertise to deliver value once they are open for business. They figure they can always buy the expertise later. Some e-strategy consulting firms have public relations engines that announce their superior solutions before they hire the skilled staff to produce them.

In London, we met with the twenty-something founders of therumour.com. Chris Mair (the business head) and Rob Pawlowicz (the technical guy) were roommates at King's College, along with their third partner, Omar Ali (finance). My cultural scene observer, Dan Galvin (twenty-three), noted that they had a cool, trendy look: unshaven, edgy, loose. The partners' first idea was a new payment mechanism for the Web. After spending a great deal of time hand-copying market research reports out of the city library, they hit upon the idea of an online community for teenage girls, enlisting Mair's seventeen-year-old sister to do informal market research on her friends to validate their business proposition.

Animated as they energetically told their story, they jumped in and finished each other's sentences. Their first name, agreeablenotion.com, just didn't have the right ring. When they chose therumour.com, they had to convince the domain name's owner, a woman in Palm Beach, Florida, to lower her price, and found that their negotiation skills were lacking—so instead of using their business titles, they used Mair's girlfriend's e-mail address and name to buy the domain name for considerably less.

As their business concept grew, the three young men tried to get venture capital in Britain but were unsuccessful. They disdainfully recalled that "traditional VCs were definitely still very old-school types. They wanted to see more infrastructure and they were very unwilling to take the leap of faith and invest in 22-, 23-year-old graduates." The three men considered incubators to help build out their idea, but decided that "we want to be entrepreneurs, we want to be businessmen. The incubators we spoke to were demeaning in their approach and called us 'cubs.' We said we're not cubs in any way, shape, or form. Ultimately, it came down to the fact that they were the wrong people for us." Mair's girlfriend worked at an exclusive nightclub that attracted some big players, and she introduced Mair to a group of investors who "took a liking to us." Acting as a financial advisory board, the investors who signed on to help therumour.com would be able to veto major strategic decisions.

When we spoke with the founders they had just moved out of their apartment (where they would work in their underwear) to offices populated with other employees and owned by their major development partner. Their challenge: to move from management by argument, possible among friends, to taking a leadership role with strangers.

Is there any hope for therumor.com? Not likely. Startups like this will die quickly because they are all style, with no substance.

Style versus Substance

The e-culture project compared dotcoms such as EarthWeb, eBay, and Abuzz that had all the signs of endurance and success with a group of others (some of them well known) that are terminally ill—high turnover, valuations near zero—or already dead. The difference is whether substance or style is emphasized. The dotcoms most likely to succeed want to be successful long-term businesses, not just stock sellers; they create professionally run organizations that function as integrated communities. Problem-ridden dotcoms, in contrast, have all the glitz and flash and fun without the underlying business fundamentals. That's why I am so skeptical about startups like therumour.com, unless it evolves. Its founders know little about their user base; they have no unique use of technology; they lack a network of experienced partners; and they rejected adult supervision.

Consider these differences between dotcoms that have only the style and those that work on the substance first:

Style Dotcoms	Substance Dotcoms
"Spend" mentality: Grab space, and revenue will somehow follow	"Earn" mentality: Have an early money-making proposition, something users will pay for
Uneven knowledge of users: Limited experience in content area, few similarities between founders and users	Deep knowledge of users: Many similarities to users, content experience
Ad hoc changes: Business model drifts, appears fuzzy	Thoughtful changes: Each version of business model is clear and focused
Main audience: Capital markets	Main audience: Users/customers
Arrogance: Know-it-all attitudes, "no one's ever done this before," failure to watch competition	Willingness to learn: Confident about ability to absorb knowledge, paranoid about competition
Technology: An afterthought; dominated by marketing/PR	Technology: Balanced with marketing, content
False equality: Appearance of camaraderie but founder control, cult of personality, cliques, invisible hierarchy	Abundant open communication: Inclusiveness, involvement of those with something to contribute
Casual: Relaxed style extends to deadlines, many time-wasters and little coordination	Flexible: Many choices of when to work but work gets done, clear discipline, deadlines must be met
Forced fun: Seems mandatory, interferes with work, imposed from top, resembles everyone else's	Genuine fun: Reward for hard work, emanates from below, reflects unique characteristics of the group
Utilitarian: No interest in anything but the business	Ethic of community service: Bonding through giving

The style-versus-substance distinction reflects the nature of the Internet itself. There are two Internets. One is a utilitarian, workmanlike, get-the-job-done Internet. This Internet roughly corresponds to the back end, the stuff that the technology dotcom-enablers sell under product names and descriptions that the general public cannot understand. It is less glamorous than front-end appearances on computer screens, but in many ways it is where the real promise of the Internet lies. And then there is the Web of imagination and fantasy—the vehicle for creating any persona, for pretending to be anything you want to be in cyberspace. Part of e-culture is an attraction to fantasy—the mystery and the possibility of the Internet. The front end is largely about style.

Style without the substance is all glitz and hype and game playing. But technology without a culture of play and rituals and communal kitchens can be boring and unmotivating. Substance comes first, then style can support it.

Fireflies, Popcorn Stands, or Cyberspace Pioneers

Because a certain amount of Internet hype revolves around image, appearance, presentation, and style, seasoned business leaders sometimes look askance at the dotcoms. They view them as evanescent—likely to disappear once established companies embrace e-business. IBM CEO Louis Gerstner called the independent dotcom businesses "fireflies before the storm." General Electric's Jack Welch called them "popcorn stands." A Williams-Sonoma executive argued that established retailers like his company would soon take back the Web from youthful startups. "There needs to be a website called AmateurHourIsOver.com," he declared. By the middle of 2000, when average dotcom stock prices plummeted, it appeared they were right. Many fireflies lost their glow, new popcorn kernels failed to pop with investors, and amateurs were no longer valued over professionals.

So will the young lead the way? Do whole generations have to die off in order to get change? In the Judeo-Christian Bible, it took forty years for Moses to lead the Israelites through the desert to the Promised Land—just long enough to replace two generations. But replacing generations is not the answer. The dotcom death rate shows that young companies are not yet a model for the future, especially not in their superficial aspects such as dress style or office-as-playground. The right age profile is not the essence of e-culture.

The real grain of truth to be learned from companies that are born on the Internet involves improvisation, quick learning, community feeling, and passion for the mission—to change the world, if not to attain

Total World Domination. The fresh start that dotcoms represent illuminates the barriers that established companies face. The imagination that the youthful companies display and the speed with which they move presents a strong contrast to the inhibitions of older, larger organizations. Large bureaucracies have the substance but neglect the style, creating tense and grim work environments.

The young do point the way in a certain sense—toward rejuvenation. They encourage companies, bureaucracies, and people of all ages to become younger in spirit. To seek reverse mentoring, absorbing what the young person and the newcomer can teach. And then to integrate that new learning with enduring values. Without forgetting history entirely, companies and people can become more youthful. But that does not come about through the use of cosmetics; it involves deeper interior changes.

3

$\blacklozenge$

Lipstick on a Bulldog
Why Cosmetic Change Doesn't Work

Had there not been resistance, I don't think we would have been as successful
as we have been. That being said, I hated that resistance.
—Patrick Connolly, Executive Vice President, Williams-Sonoma

E-BELIEVERS ARE CONVINCED that the Internet rewrites the rules
of competition, overturns conventional wisdom about how to run an
organization, and offers limitless opportunities to grow new businesses
and create wealth. But there's another group that feels cyberspaced-out
and wants to declare E-nough. They think that the Internet is overhyped,
that e-commerce promises more than it delivers, and that e-mail and
Web surfing consume too much time, draining productivity instead of
increasing it. The dotcom death toll confirms their skepticism.

Companies populated with skeptics want to do as little as possible,
spend as little as possible, change as little as possible. They tack on a website or two and feel that their work is done. "The teenage son of the
finance director comes in on a weekend and designs them a website,"
commented Cheryl Shearer of IBM Global Services in London, reflecting

her experience with companies in this early stage. "They don't link it to any cash flow system, they don't realize they're going to need to operate 24/7, they don't think about whether they should rebrand themselves or change any processes. And uniformly, they are gloomy and disappointed." Superficial add-ons, with no change in how the company operates, do not produce Internet success. Indeed, one corporate giant discovered that it had spent over $100 million in a three-year period on over 1,000 websites representing its many product lines, divisions, market groups, and internal units—and then could not identify incremental revenues or cost savings associated with its multiplicity of sites.

The way many wannadots try to conduct business through the Web has been likened to "putting lipstick on a bulldog."[1] That kind of makeup job is extremely hard to do. Worse yet, it doesn't work. The bulldog doesn't suddenly become beautiful because it is forced to wear lipstick. Nothing else about the bulldog or its behavior has changed. And the use of cosmetics just covers up problems that still exist under the makeup.

A company is not transformed simply because it creates a website; that might be only a cosmetic change. Success requires a more complete makeover, namely, rethinking the model for how to organize the work of the whole organization. It requires challenging traditional assumptions about relationships with customers, internal and external communication, decision making, operating style, managerial behavior, employee motivation and retention—and then defining a new way. That's a human problem, not a technological one.

Whereas pure dotcoms are born to Internet style, wannadots have to morph into it. Everything in their structure and history pulls them in other, more traditional, directions. So it is not surprising that some of them let their customers, suppliers, or competitors determine their fate. While Raytheon's marine products division was still debating whether to go online, inhibited by concerns about conflicts with the current channels through which its products were sold, an Internet company launched a marine website featuring a dozen Raytheon products.

Leadership offline does not predict innovation in cyberspace. The transition to the Internet can be hard for even the best companies. Success requires systemic change, a shift in the organizational way of life. That's the chore that's hardest for wannadots. That's why, in the early days of the Web, the pure dotcoms' fresh start looked like a permanent head start.

Laggards versus Pacesetters: Who Is Prepared to Change?

My e-culture research project sorted offline established companies into two main groups, pacesetters and laggards, based on survey and interview responses, and then examined how they evolved (or didn't) with respect to Internet use.[2] *Pacesetters* are companies that are faster and earlier than their competitors to move core business processes to the Internet and are more satisfied with their progress toward accomplishing clear goals. Both first movers in the industry and fast followers were grouped in this category. *Laggards* are slower to move, more limited in their use of the Internet, behind their competition, and dissatisfied with their progress.

Pacesetters embrace the Internet as an opportunity for questioning their existing model and experimenting with new ways technology could improve the business. They are more likely to consider the systemic consequences of their Internet propositions. They do not wait to have a plan that springs full-blown from the heads of top management; they improvise through multiple experiments until finding the approach that seems right. They then establish senior-level guidance to ensure that the approach is strategic, that related initiatives are integrated, and that the rest of the company is cooperative. They work hard to balance autonomy for an e-venture with appropriate integration that will create synergies between the online and offline offerings. They start with curiosity and questioning and then move into experimentation and innovation, linking that to culture change—to how the business and organizational model will now be different.

Laggards, in contrast, pass through a different set of stages on the road to systemic change. They begin with denial. Instead of asking questions about the potential of the new technology, they dismiss its importance, certain they can ignore it or do the minimum to use it. Instead of exhibiting organizational curiosity about what might be different about the new environment, they let past successes blind them into believing that they can approach it the same way they do everything else. Sometimes denial is accompanied by anger and blame. As IBM's Cheryl Shearer said, "They badmouth the whole experience, they say it doesn't work, but it can't be me that's wrong, it must be It"—or that universal scapegoat, "Them." *If we are falling behind, it must be someone else's fault. "They" are playing unfairly. "They" should be stopped.* That's when death threats and protest movements kick in, or their politer business equivalent—lawsuits. Of course, blame consumes energy and rarely stops the target of the rage.

A second phase for laggards involves cosmetic change: putting together a side venture as an afterthought, an add-on project that is still entangled with the mainstream business and unable to break free of traditional assumptions and conditions and thus unable to tap synergies with the mainstream. Cosmetic change sometimes involves imitation and conformity rather than creativity and innovation—following fashion with the right shade of lipstick rather than creating a new look. It can also include an obsession with the main rivals. Small victories over competitors become more important than making internal changes. So while pacesetters are experimenting and innovating, laggards are copying someone else's last move.

The struggle for laggards is to move from cosmetic change to a complete makeover. Laggards are rarely successful with their cosmetic changes, which are too little, too late, and too costly. But sometimes the new look offers a convincing demonstration to move skeptics out of denial into commitment. And a pilot venture can make clear that deeper systemic change is required to take full advantage of the potential of the new technology. In the companies my e-culture team studied, only when decision makers realize that e-business was important and financially viable are they finally ready to admit that the mainstream organization needed systemic change.

Even fast-moving pacesetters need a mind shift to understand just how different the network-enabled world is and how much greater the challenges of interactivity. For example, Sun Microsystems was among the first computer makers to tie its fate to the Internet, and it became a favorite of Internet service providers. Sun had always designed for networks, and it billed itself as "the dot in dot-com." Yet Sun itself underwent a wrenching two-year conversion of internal IT systems to run on its own networks. Sun faced jarring new business assumptions as it partnered with Internet companies (e.g., that developers expected free software, cheap hardware, and to pay Sun with equity). It took nearly a year to convince all its business unit heads to give full support to online sales. Sun's efforts to "eat its own dog food," in Silicon Valley lingo, involved demanding, multiple changes.

If dotcom-enablers find Web makeovers challenging, imagine how much harder systemic change is for wannadots light years away from Silicon Valley. Consider the example of "FashionCo," a chain of luxury apparel stores in the United States (given a pseudonym at their request).

FashionCo's first reaction to the Web was to dismiss it as trivial. Decision makers thought they could afford to ignore it. Then they decided, without much consideration, to put their catalog online. That was an easy step because it was viewed as just another form of communication—e-mailing orders instead of faxing them. A committee was assembled from around the company to oversee a casual website project. When FashionCo got more serious about e-commerce and hired a leading e-strategy and website design firm to help, its managers were still not sure they wanted advice on things such as driving traffic to the Web or improving look-to-buy conversion ratios, because they felt merchandising was their field of expertise. "They initially started out thinking, 'OK here's how we do business today in the physical world, how are we going to apply those systems or process to the online environment?' That's always the first assumption at a very senior level, it's their comfort zone," the lead consultant said.

But as FashionCo tried to keep the change merely cosmetic, managers encountered disturbing differences all over the map that suggested the company might need a bigger culture change. Some differences were simple and practical, such as photographs of the merchandise. FashionCo was accustomed to using analog photography with expensive, high-quality film for high-end fashion shoots. To make images suitable for the website meant taking the time to rescan and retouch them. This raised the question of whether to switch to digital cameras for the Web but retain analog photos for store ads and catalogs. Should they treat offline and online as two separate businesses with separate requirements? Should they shoot photos for them separately, try to do both when photographers, models, and studios were booked, or simply convert images from analog to digital later?

Product descriptions were another simple area with complex consequences. Traditionally, these were internal documents put on the computer for buyers, merchandisers, customer service staff, or other internal users. But putting internal information on the website required a clean-up process for content and consistency (e.g., abbreviations, capital letters). Should FashionCo require that all internal material be Web ready? People in departments unrelated to the Internet were drawn into heated debates about photos and writeups as policy choices affected their own areas. And for the website launch, many people assumed unfamiliar roles in order to move quickly. Senior people rolled up their sleeves for nitty-gritty tasks, from copy approval to cleaning up legacy systems to optimizing images.

FashionCo was not content to use the Web just as an electronic catalog, because those sales were the low end of FashionCo's business. Its challenge was to create a distinctive Internet offering that would be true to its high-end brand and use the distinctive potential of the technology. The innovative solution was a virtual studio online based on an actual store. Simulating a store visit, the camera could zoom in and look at details, and the customer could place an order, all online. This strategy was more exciting and potentially much more lucrative—but also more demanding of large-scale systemic change. It required unprecedented collaboration throughout the entire organization, such as managing inventory across stores or getting hundreds of warehouses to cooperate.

"Their biggest challenge is to understand the interactive space and see that it is inherently different than the way that their traditional business is run," FashionCo's consultant reported. "They have buy-in at the highest levels, realize the potential of the online space, and view it as strategically important to their future business. The question, though, is how much are they really prepared to change?"

That's the right question. But is the answer sufficient? Alas, the answer for too many laggards among the wannadots is that they are not really prepared to change. They appoint an e-commerce or e-business vice president, ramp up their website, and let the new unit flounder unsupported. It is as though laggards were following a set of instructions for putting lipstick on the bulldog—how to minimize commitment, keep all their options open, and ensure that change is only cosmetic. I imagine that they are reading a manual that tells them the exact opposite of what is required for success—a set of "anti-rules" for avoiding change.

My imaginary guide to How Not To Change would be funny except that it summarizes the experience of too many companies. The problem with cosmetic change is that it is all about appearances and not about deeper substance. It is driven not by a desire for innovation to serve customer needs but by the wish to look good without much effort. And when that happens, even great companies stumble, as we are about to see.

How to Use Cosmetics to Cover Up Problems: Instructions for *Avoiding* E-Business Change

• Sprinkle Internet responsibilities throughout the company. (A little website here, a little brochureware there.) Let them all go forward, as long as they stay small and hidden. If any of them look as though they have bigger potential, raise skeptical questions about them at executive meetings, and repeat frequently that the Internet is overhyped.

• Form a committee to create a new corporate Internet offering. Staff it with people from unrelated areas who are already doing five other things, and don't release them from their regular jobs. Give the leadership role to a bored executive as a reward for his years of loyal service. (Never mind that he has no Internet business experience; he surfs the Web, doesn't he?)

• Find the simplest, least demanding thing you can do on the Web. Go for "copyware" that looks like what everyone else is doing. Instead of a "killer app," create a "yawner app." (That way, you can cross the Internet off your To Do list quickly.)

• Choose vendors to build the site who are the most critical of your traditional business (they think you're dinosaurs). Then hand over the technical work to the vendors (that way nobody inside has to learn anything new), but refuse to take their advice (after all, you're the industry experts). Use more than one firm (that way you can have the fun of watching them slug it out).

• Duplicate your traditional business assumptions online. Make sure what you do on the Web is exactly the same as what you do offline. Change as little as possible. (After all, the Internet is just a tool, isn't it? So why change for a tool?)

• Insist that an Internet venture meet every corporate standard: cost controls, quarterly earnings, recruitment sources, compensation policies, purchasing procedures. Allocate just enough resources to keep it alive but not enough to risk its becoming an innovator, because that would require *more* investment.

• Under the banner of decentralization and business unit autonomy, reward each unit for its own performance, and offer no extra incentives to cooperate in cyberspace. (Maintain your belief that conflict is a healthy spur to higher performance.) Keep reminding divisions that they are separate businesses because they are different, and that's that.

• Compare your performance with your traditional industry competitors in the physical world. (That way you will always have someone to whom you can feel superior.) Dismiss online competitors as ephemeral fads. And don't even consider whether companies from unrelated industries could steal across the borders and poach your customers by using the Net. (Why worry about the hypothetical?)

• Celebrate your conversion to e-business by giving the rest of the organization tools they are unable to use and that require changes they are confused about making. Schedule training classes at a distant location. Then watch as the new tools and processes take too much time and make it harder to get the work done, and then punish people for resistance to change.

• And never forget that the company, not the customer, is in the driver's seat. The Internet is an opportunity for *us* to communicate with *them*.

If you actually want to succeed at e-business change, just reverse these rules.

Cosmetics or a Systemic Makeover?
The World's Most Famous Case

When Barnes & Noble first approached the Internet, culture change was not on its agenda. Barnes & Noble was a stunning success in the physical world. Leonard Riggio bought a New York icon in 1972 and built it to a thousand-store chain by 1995, when Amazon.com (founded in 1994) launched its online store. So why not use the same leaders and principles to win in cyberspace? By 2000, Barnes & Noble was also big on the Internet—with perhaps the most successful site launched by a traditional bricks-and-mortar retailer in terms of audience size—but not as big as Amazon.com. (And in mid-2000, both were losing money and stock market favor.)

Did any literate adult miss hearing about the rivalry between Amazon.com and Barnes & Noble? It became a cautionary tale oft cited by companies about the risks of underestimating new online competition. Barnes & Noble set the industry standard offline, and it beat traditional bookstores handily on the Internet. If Barnes & Noble lagged, its bricks-and-mortar competitors such as Borders were so slow that they were hardly in the race. Borders was late to move to e-commerce despite pioneering the use of information technology to improve customer service and inventory management, and engaging in early discussions about distributing computer floppy disks that customers could use to order books from home. Borders.com, launched in May 1998, generated $4.6 million from online sales that year, a pittance compared with barnesandnoble.com's $63 million. But Amazon.com's $610 million over the same period dwarfed everyone.[3]

To get behind the headlines and test my hypotheses about pacesetters versus laggards, we interviewed a range of former Barnes & Noble employees who were in on major events. We steered away from those who were disgruntled, picking instead ones who said positive things such as "I had the greatest job in the world. I really had a blast for that period of time." Or: "I had an image of them as a corporate chain, but it's really a great entrepreneurial story. The company was just super aggressive, really lean, and totally willing to spend what at the time seemed like enough money to win the online book wars." We saw that founder and CEO Leonard Riggio and his younger brother Stephen were much admired by employees. But we also learned about the problems created when a new channel and new technology were approached in old ways. The passage from denial through cosmetic change to grappling with systemic change can be difficult without full commitment to change.

Denial

In the beginning, denial reigned. The innovators who created book superstores could not believe at first that upstart Amazon.com, founded in 1995, would make a dent in the industry that Barnes & Noble dominated. Dealing with Amazon should be like swatting a fly. So in 1996, when Stephen Riggio convinced his CEO brother Leonard that Barnes & Noble needed an Internet presence, Stephen became part-time head of a spotty effort based on the assumption that the Internet would market the physical stores. Barnes & Noble thought that its existing brand, wide distribution, and deep pockets were good enough to outcompete Amazon. After all, an online bookstore lacked features such as couches and coffee bars that the Riggios believed essential to destination retailing. The Internet could be handled with casual attention, infrequent meetings, minimal investment, and existing employees.

Throughout this first phase, Barnes & Noble tried to apply its store experience to the Internet, duplicating online what had worked offline. The first website, launched in March 1997, was designed by an agency with a print background, so it looked like a newspaper. (And it went live before the external firm thought it was ready.) A former manager observed that the first website was treated as an online literary magazine that happened to sell books. As a retail outlet, Barnes & Noble was known for couches in the store enabling people to hang out for hours; therefore, senior management invested in message boards, online author chats, and places to hang out virtually on the website. "It was interesting that the two things that Barnes & Noble spent the most time focusing on in the early days were things that Amazon just flat out didn't do, and people didn't care about," an insider reported. "Our research found that less than 5% of users were interested in reading reviews by Barnes & Noble editors or author chats, but that got 50% of the company's attention."

As Amazon.com continued to grow, denial was spiced by anger and blame. Seeing the threat posed by its online competitor, Barnes & Noble sued Amazon for unfair business practices over claims in Amazon's slogan that Amazon, not Barnes & Noble, had the world's largest bookstore. The title "World's Largest Bookstore" was granted Barnes & Noble's Fifth Avenue flagship store by the *Guinness Book of Records*. The parties reached a settlement several months later, but Amazon's slogan, "Earth's Biggest Bookstore," remained intact. Meanwhile, public temper tantrums were unlikely to help Barnes & Noble win customers, especially among the hip young crowd of early Web shoppers. And attention was deflected from ways in which barnesandnoble.com had actual advantages over Amazon, such as having more books available faster through its warehouses. It was "hard to overcome the image of being a store company," another former employee recalled. "Somehow the perception was that because they were a virtual company, they would deliver faster."

Three other challenges finally convinced Barnes & Noble that cyberspace was different. Decisions that made sense in the offline world, such as Barnes & Noble's traditional tests and slow rollouts place to place, did not make sense on the Web, where *big everywhere fast* was the rule. Adapting the corporate brand identity to the Web proved difficult. The website had five or six different names, logos, business cards, and branding campaigns in under three years—all driven by the simple fact that one cannot put an "&" in a URL. Barnesandnoble.com could not match Amazon's discounts if the site was linked to physical stores, because then Barnes & Noble would have to charge local sales taxes. This was another factor encouraging the website to cut loose from the stores—and to move toward greater independence from the parent corporation. The e-venture would not be leveraging the brand, but at least it would get room to grow.

So denial was over; cosmetic change was beginning.

ATTEMPTS AT CHANGE

In late 1997, barnesandnoble.com moved to its own space on the eleventh floor of the Port Authority building on Manhattan's West Side, with its own dedicated leadership and a new Web design firm. But under this arrangement, it still did not move beyond stage two, cosmetic change.

Having once denied Amazon's virtues, new COO Jeff Killeen encouraged his team to become obsessed with Amazon and ritualistically imitate its features. In early 1998, a reporter wrote, "Killeen told the staff, 'You're not just here to sell books. You're here to annihilate the competition, to kill it dead!'"[4] The new aggressiveness led to some clear wins, an insider recalled. "We surprised Amazon because we started consistently beating them out for deals. The company was very aggressive, fast-paced, all about high growth. How could we go faster?" The affiliate network grew from a zero base to 100,000 member sites, but that quantity masked the fact that Amazon had locked up some of the biggest portals first, which drove traffic to Amazon.

Barnesandnoble.com was still putting lipstick on the bulldog. The unit produced a better-looking site, but one that was not well differentiated from Amazon. Its independence from the parent company meant that it couldn't get brand synergies, and it was reported that senior management still swooped in to micromanage. Former senior managers said that what was missing was clarity about the customer experience. One told us, "I think senior management didn't know what to focus on and tried to do too many things before doing the one or two things that customers really cared about the most, which was, 'Is the site really fast and simple, and when I place an order on the site, do you get me the book in 48 hours?'"

Killeen lasted about a year. By his exit, the company had already spent an estimated $100 million.

As the company moved into 1999, still another new leadership era began. This one initially held the promise for culture change, in which both the website and its parent company would work differently. Through a joint venture in October 1998 with the German giant Bertelsmann, involving several hundred million dollars in new investment, barnesandnoble.com was spun off as a separate company with its own CEO (Jonathon Bulkeley, a veteran of the AOL-Bertelsmann European JV) and allowed to chart its own course, focusing once again on synergies between online and store marketing. (By the spring of 1999 the website URL began to show up on store receipts and bags.) Barnesandnoble.com was floated in an IPO in May 1999; the partners kept a 41 percent stake, while Barnes & Noble maintained operating control. (One impetus for the IPO was the need to separate the online company as a legal entity so that it did not have to charge sales tax on online orders, as it would if it were linked to Barnes & Noble's physical stores). Barnesandnoble.com rose to fourth on rankings of the most-visited e-commerce sites (Amazon.com was number one) and ranked in the top thirty most popular sites on the Web overall. The new barnesandnoble.com (also known as bn.com) started to explore electronic book publishing, and Barnes & Noble CEO Leonard Riggio indicated that he was rethinking the nature of a bookstore in light of the advent of the Internet, a sign that finally he saw how technology challenged traditional business assumptions.

Offline Barriers to Online Success

The e-venture continued to stumble over barriers to change, including internal rivalries and spillovers from the offline world. A former leader recalled, "It was still a tug of war between editorial and merchandising people who were thinking about the aesthetics of books and technologists who weren't thinking about aesthetics of anything, really. Nobody was thinking about, 'How do people use the website?' This is a holistic experience on the site. It's not just about the content, about the books, it's not just about the code behind the scenes. It's about how all those things fit together and that's what the company didn't have." Barnesandnoble.com created a product development team as a bridge between the technologists and the business strategists (the Riggios and the new CEO, who saw themselves as booksellers), staffed with strong people who could speak both languages.

Barnesandnoble.com still carried baggage from the retail world. Time was wasted redoing things that the dotcom inherited from its parent. Barnes & Noble's back-end legacy IT systems were not built to bill direct to the customer nor built to the scale of an Internet market. "Bn.com got big in all of the wrong ways," said a former employee. "The company was less than three years old, and we had a lot of frustrating legacy issues." There were also some successes. A dotcom customer fulfillment system was designed that was also adopted by the stores, for use when customers wanted books sent to their homes.

Particularly disturbing to many employees was a clash between bricks-and-mortar retail culture and Internet culture. One observed that "In traditional retailing, you're not a member of the senior management team until you've done your time, and that time is usually 15 years, so there wasn't an opportunity for people from the Internet generation. Compensation and responsibility at barnesandnoble.com mirrored that of the retail side, weighted to the super senior management team of ten people. But you have to manage 400 dotcom employees differently than you manage 25,000 retail store employees."

A trickle of turnover in the summer of 1999 soon became a flood. CTO John Kristie left in July 1999 to co-found Online Retail Partners (ORP), a new company that incubated e-commerce businesses in partnership with established consumer-branded companies. ORP soon recruited over twenty-five former barnesandnoble.com employees and contractors. In January 2000, bn.com CEO Jonathon Bulkeley announced his departure (with $11 million for his stock options). Stephen Riggio was once again acting CEO. Between

March and April 2000, the company lost its vice president for technical infrastructure (who went to Saks Direct), at least eight technical employees, and others in corporate communications, community services, and marketing.[5]

Former executives give the company credit for being courageous. "Bn.com was at the front line of change. They made a lot of mistakes but did a lot right, too," one said. "They had a lot of vision and took risks to make the culture different. They have been walking that fine line, that tightrope, of adding the dotcom to their business. Everyone else watches with amazement as the guy gets up there and walks the tightrope. When the guy stumbles and falls, everyone laughs and points fingers. But they don't have the guts to get up there on that wire." By September 2000, there were signs that Barnes & Noble's offline assets were finally bringing major online advantages. Barnesandnoble.com replaced Amazon as a featured merchant on Yahoo!, with new joint Internet offerings to be promoted in 551 Barnes & Noble physical stores.

Being at the front line of change implies a need to work harder to master it. Think about the ways barnesandnoble.com fell just short of the four elements of the e-culture ideal that will be described in the next four chapters. The e-venture used too many imitative strategies instead of innovative improvisations creating waves of raves. It waited too long to tap a partner network; even though it eventually attracted many partners, some of the best were already taken. Internal rivalries and tensions between the new venture and the mainstream prevented seamless operation as an integrated community. And high turnover prevailed, instead of a culture that holds people.

But the story is ongoing. Barnes & Noble is learning, and I don't want to make any of this seem easy. Wannadots face numerous obstacles because of their size and history, especially in comparison with startup dotcoms, and it is tricky to see how to convert legacies into advantages. Even the most successful company cannot buy its way to change by altering its appearance; it must be willing to change more fundamental aspects of its way of life. That means confronting the barriers to change.

Confronting the Barriers to Change

What are the most common barriers to e-culture and e-business change? And what difference does age make? I identified a set of seventeen barriers to productive use of the Internet and tested them in the global e-culture survey. I then compared the frequency with which barriers were encountered in the 390 companies responding to the survey that were over twenty years old (i.e., founded before the modern information era began around 1980) versus the reports of barriers in the 395 younger companies, founded since 1980 (see the table).

Note that the older companies said they faced slightly fewer marketplace or technology barriers than the younger ones, but many more internal barriers—from decision-maker uncertainty to employee resistance to divisional rivalries. Indeed, in interviews most wannadots reported multiple barriers. For example:

- *Financial services executive:* "It starts with senior management ignorance of technology. This attitude has changed in the past two months; now there is an imposed urgency from above to do everything. But we have internal opposition from parts of the organization that are threatened by the Internet. The sales force is obviously not keen on deploying the Internet with channel partners which means reduced sales to them."

- *Retail executive:* "Because the Internet flattens the hierarchy, we have management that is uneasy with this change in focus and power that is leading to a team-based approach to work. Our company has been very hierarchical in its 50-year existence, and the sweeping changes that the Internet brings are unsettling to many. In addition, the company has had bad previous experiences with new technology, and is thus now more risk-averse."

- *Transportation executive:* "You can't just go out and ask the customer to communicate with you on the Internet if that's not how they do things. You just become more difficult to do business with. Internally, we give people a lot of tools that they use very poorly, and that makes their work a lot more difficult. We outsourced our IT area and have very little in-house expertise; we never bothered to learn. We're not a very high margin business, and constantly changing technology is a major investment challenge. We started slowly, put our website in the wrong hands, and had no sense of what we needed to be doing. Our e-commerce site is being run by public relations people, so the business heads ran off to meet their individual needs; now we have one person in charge of e-business, they have to pull in the reins of all the individual initiatives and figure out how they go together. We have no overall vision."

Barriers to Change in Older and Newer Organizations

Percentage of Respondents

All (n = 785)	Organization older than 20 years (n = 390)	Organization younger than 20 years (n = 395)	Barrier
38	48	27	The unit does not have staff with adequate technical or Web-specific skills.
37	37	37	Customers and key markets do not want to change their behavior.
35	33	37	There are more important projects that require existing resources and time.
34	31	36	Technology and tools are inadequate, unavailable, or unreliable.
31	29	32	It is hard to find the right partners to work with.
28	27	29	Suppliers are not cooperative or are not ready for electronic business.
25	29	20	Employees are not comfortable with change.
21	30	12	Leaders are not sure where to begin; they don't understand how to make the right choices.
16	22	10	Top executives do not personally use computers and are not personally familiar with the Internet.
15	22	9	Rivalries or conflicts between internal divisions get in the way.
13	15	11	It is hard to find capital for new investments.
12	17	7	Managers fear loss of status or privileged positions.
10	14	6	Employees fear loss of jobs, or unions and employee groups fear loss of membership.
10	10	10	Government rules and regulations get in the way.
10	12	8	The company is successful as it is; leaders see no need for change.
9	10	8	The company had a bad previous experience with new technology.
4	5	2	It is a waste of time or money; it is not relevant to the business.

Excuses, excuses. Some companies faced practically all of the barriers to e-business change and surmounted them. Williams-Sonoma is an excellent example of the path around the obstacle course to e-business success.

Williams-Sonoma: Getting Cooking on the Web

With Williams-Sonoma's successful dual-channel strategy of retail stores and catalogs, and its huge warehouse in Memphis next to Federal Express for direct marketing fulfillment, it should have been a breeze for the company to embrace the Internet. In 1998, when the company first dipped its toes in cyberspace, it operated 163 Williams-Sonoma stores for quality cookware, 96 Pottery Barn stores for home items, 33 Hold Everything stores, and 6 outlet stores. About 60 percent of its catalogs were mailed to areas where retail stores existed, to create brand awareness. The Pottery Barn catalog alone reached over 6 million homes per month—a circulation claimed to be larger than that of the five largest upscale home magazines combined. Its total database included over 19 million households.

But Williams-Sonoma (W-S) struggled first to get on the Web at all, and then to make sure that its changes were more than cosmetic. Check off all the barriers the company's e-commerce advocates faced. Just for starters: *CEO skepticism. A legacy of failed technology ventures. Belief that customers wouldn't use the channel and fear that if they did it would dilute the brand. Limited capital and tough ROI requirements for new ventures. Uncertainty about what model to pursue.*

Once e-enthusiasts worked through those problems, and CEO Howard Lester lent his support, additional change issues surfaced: *Problems finding the right development partners. Too few internal people skilled in the new technology and an exodus of key talent. Divisional rivalries between retail and catalog that kept slowing things down.*

Once the first site was up and running, and a dedicated team tackled the Web, more challenges surfaced: *Retraining frontline workers who didn't like change. Determining which division got credit for sales. Getting functional departments to change their habits. Coping with high turnover in a tight market for Internet talent while making sure insiders felt they had opportunities, too.* And the champions of e-business had to convince the whole organization—riddled with concerns about cannibalization—to work toward a common goal.

Patrick Connolly, long-time senior direct marketing executive, reflected: "I thought that adding a third channel would be easy, since we had so much experience and success with two channels—the retail stores and catalog. Nonetheless, there were lots of conflicts. There were these incredible tradeoffs. Howard Lester, our CEO, is a big proponent and has a very sensible view of the Internet now—an additional channel to reach and serve our customer and build our brands. It was very difficult to sell him. But the end result was that we had such a tight plan and such a commitment to do it, that had there not been resistance, I don't think we would have been as successful as we have been. That being said, I hated that resistance."

A SLOW WALK TO THE STARTING GATE

Let's go back to the beginning. In 1997 and early 1998, dotcom startups were appearing everywhere around Williams-Sonoma's San Francisco home base. There was a buzz in the air about the Internet throughout the company. But when Connolly began to suggest a serious look into expanding to the Internet, Howard Lester was skeptical. "I just can't imagine that people are going to sit in front of a computer screen and buy our merchandise," insiders heard him say. "Right now, I think it is way overhyped."

Other reasons for foot-dragging stemmed from memories of earlier failures at technology-based marketing. In the mid-1980s, W-S participated in an early kiosk test by putting catalog merchandise on a CD-ROM in kiosks in stores and airport lounges; "we got about 20 orders out of that one," Connolly mused. In 1995, Williams-Sonoma was approached to sell catalog merchandise on cable channels through Time Warner's DreamShop. It seemed a no-brainer; the venture was well funded, and it required little financial outlay from W-S. But as one of the first e-commerce websites, its functionality was less than ideal. Navigation was cumbersome, pages were static, and changes hard to make. The low-risk W-S investment became a big time drain. Deciding it was not "on-brand," W-S pulled out. A year later, W-S declined a proposal by a big consultancy to build a demonstration e-commerce site nearly free, because it was focused on recovering from an earnings slump.

Despite his colleagues' initial negativity, Connolly persisted. He assembled a task force of several vice presidents who shared his optimism about the Internet and solicited the assistance of Prophet Brand Strategy, a Silicon Valley e-commerce strategy consulting firm. Connolly charged the task force with writing a compelling business proposal to convince the executive team to fund an Internet initiative. The consultants suggested a low-cost, low-risk pilot approach—a website that offered twenty Williams-Sonoma products for Mother's Day 1998. The site did not generate significant revenue, but it proved that Williams-Sonoma customers would buy products online. Lester and other leaders remained unconvinced. Now brand integrity was the reason. Williams-Sonoma had labored to create brand consistency across its two channels; for example, the "open-shelf" style of displaying products outside of their packages used in retail stores was replicated in the catalogs with a simple, elegant layout.

Lester's conversion began with students to whom he spoke at the University of California at Berkeley, where he had endowed an entrepreneurship center. The students' positive response to the Internet made him reconsider his initial opposition. He chartered a task force from across the company to work part-time to create a bridal registry website, wsweddings.com, under the leadership of Cathy Halligan, a direct marketing executive. The ground rules: that it make money and be integrated with the rest of the company. Lester did not want to create an Internet spin-off. In October 1998, requests for proposals (RFPs) were solicited from fifteen Web development firms. One was chosen for the back-end technology infrastructure, another for the front-end creative design. Prophet Brand Strategy would also continue working on the project.

Then came the first glitch. The back-end vendor had considerably underestimated development costs and submitted a new proposal that was three times the initial price. (Surprise, surprise.) This exacerbated the task of convincing leaders that this was not going to be a losing venture. "Howard [Lester] was up in arms, no one believes the task force, no one trusts them. Cathy is pulling her hair out; she has no idea what to do," an insider recalled. Lester had funded the initial architecture validation study, but the wsweddings.com team was otherwise operating on vastly limited resources. The revised bid forced the team to revisit revenue forecasts and investment figures, push back the launch date to late May, and enter into a new round of negotiations with top management. The team needed greater expertise, additional funding, and a firm commitment from the CEO to create an organization around the Internet concept.

Meanwhile, Williams-Sonoma faced online competition. Cooking.com was launched in early 1998 and quickly established partnerships with Internet giants such as AOL. Digitalchef.com went online in the fall of 1997, with kitchenware added a year later—and $10 million in venture capital. Williams-Sonoma people had a growing feeling of falling behind.

One afternoon in mid-November 1998, members of the Internet team vented their frustrations over lunch, and a member suggested running another pilot test. Why not use an outside vendor and simply put some products online for the holidays fast? The catalog division had just mailed out a catalog of twenty-four last-minute gift ideas—why not offer those products online as well? The orders could be received by the vendor in Los Angeles, faxed to Williams-Sonoma's call center in Las Vegas, and processed like mail or telephone orders. Buying the vendor's "cookie cutter" application could simplify the process and allow Williams-Sonoma to have a more significant test of the Internet without seriously disrupting the flow of activities during the holiday peak time.

In the best spirit of improvisation, the team decided to go for it. Customers went for it, too. "Customers started buying products faster than we had speculated. Our biggest difficulty was getting new merchandise in when it ran out," recalled Kerrie Chappelka, Creative Services VP. "We all just laughed because all of a sudden we're on the Internet without a total commitment to it—it's like eloping after you're not willing to get engaged."

Getting Serious

Once the team created a business model that could be profitable quickly, funding was authorized. After wsweddings.com, the next goal was to bring a full assortment of Williams-Sonoma products online in the fall of 1999. In January 1999, the Internet team was made official. Halligan became the head of e-commerce. There were five dedicated internal people, primarily from the catalog division; a similar number from Prophet Brand Strategy; a technology team; and some part-time volunteers from other functional areas of the company, whose willingness to help reflected widespread enthusiasm that the company was finally going online.

W-S had organizational capabilities that they could use for the Internet: a call center, customer service reps, order fulfillment, demand planning for mail order promotion cycles. But to launch and support the new channel, new business processes were required. Each of the key functional areas (merchandising, inventory management, call center, distribution center, database marketing, and financial reporting) sent liaisons to coordinate closely with the Internet team to ensure that the mail order systems, retail systems, and Internet site were in synch.

Traditionally, the catalog and retail divisions had operated independently. Although roughly 70 percent of the products were the same in the catalog and in the stores, each division owned its own inventory and had its own merchants. Although both utilized the central warehouse in Memphis, the retail and catalog divisions had different P&Ls. Employees were compensated largely on their own division's growth in sales. The divisions maintained separate distribution centers, systems, buyers, and points of contact for vendors. Despite the sharing of customers who shopped through both channels, there were two internal cultures. Catalog people had the direct marketing experience, but retail had the merchandise. Bridal registries were traditionally a function of retail stores—and retail was a world unto itself, accustomed to functioning independently. E-commerce team members from the catalog side had to get retail buy-in to get merchandise, "but it was not a priority for them," a team member recalled. "And you can understand their point of view—why am I going to help you take away business from me? Initially, they didn't necessarily believe in the concept—but they believed in the cannibalization."

It soon became clear that Internet sales would require change in the way in which many people did their jobs throughout W-S. For example, retail products were not generally shipped in consumer-ready packages—they were mailed in bulk to the retail stores. Vendors and employees at the distribution center were unaccustomed to breaking up bulk shipments into individual mailings or to wrapping gifts. New training was required in many areas. In the call center, customer service representatives needed to be comfortable with the website and able to respond to e-mail. In the stores, associates would have to inform customers about what the website could or could not do.

By mid-February 1999, several important, conflict-ridden questions still needed to be answered by the executive team. Which division would get credit for online sales? Would there be a separate P&L for e-commerce, or would it be rolled onto the mail order or retail P&L? Who owns the inventory, and is any inventory dedicated to e-commerce? A key executive retreat in Memphis near the central warehouse finally changed the atmosphere from contention to cooperation. Discussion of a focused proposal for tight execution received leaders' support. Connolly reported: "When [Lester] finally put his full support behind this, the entire company galvanized around the issue and said we're going to make this work. There was so much passion about proving that we made the right decision. I mean, people would have died before they let this thing fail."

Then another crisis threatened to derail the effort. A few weeks after full and firm executive buy-in at the retreat, e-commerce head Halligan and two other key people resigned unexpectedly to join a well-funded luxury goods dotcom. "All hell broke loose," people recalled. Connolly called Scott Galloway, Prophet Brand Strategy CEO, who promised to lend his firm's president, Michael Dunn, as interim vice president of e-commerce the following Monday. Dunn had an awkward role as both outsider and insider, but he quickly developed a coalition of supporters within W-S. He scrambled to convert crisis into a sense of urgency. He created an Internet War Room at headquarters. Adorned with posters and paintings and a large calendar, it stood in stark contrast to the elegant, sedate offices that featured high-end product samples and a beautiful view of the San Francisco Bay. The War Room calendar counted down: *87 days to launch, 86 days to launch. . . .*

Online on schedule on June 1, 1999, wsweddings.com did not meet its aggressive sales plan but was very well received by the stock market. The company got a bump in its stock price. Even more important was that Howard Lester was pleased. In July 1999, he approved funding for a williams-sonoma.com website to be launched in November.

Williams-Sonoma was still barely out of the cosmetics stage. Although e-commerce had become an accepted business strategy, the new processes required by the new channel were not yet integrated into the larger organization. Operational confusion surrounding wsweddings.com demonstrated a real need for an operations head dedicated to the e-commerce division. Inventory and merchandising questions still remained with regard to future product offerings online. And the e-commerce leadership position was still being filled by a consultant, who was looking for a permanent head. Dunn recommended Shelley Nandkeolyar, a former Levi Strauss e-commerce project leader, for a new position as vice president of e-commerce. After confirming that the company was serious about e-commerce through close to twenty interviews, Nandkeolyar accepted.

From Cosmetics to Inner Beauty: Tackling Systemic Change

Now systemic change could begin. Dunn and Nandkeolyar designed a new e-commerce division that would bolster some of the organizational weak points revealed by wsweddings.com and clarify roles and responsibilities. Dedicated personnel from e-commerce were relocated a half-mile from headquarters to a separate Williams-Sonoma building where most of the technology personnel were located. Marketing, creative services, and technology staff could work together to define the customer experience for the website. The group designed technologically elegant features; for example, to ensure that customers' selections were still there when they finished their shopping and were ready to check out, the system automatically decremented the inventory when items were put in the online shopping cart.

Nandkeolyar focused on integration: building goodwill in the rest of the company and smoothing the way for seamless links between the Internet, retail, and catalog divisions. Patricia Skerrett became operations director to resolve conflicts across channels. Skerrett created an operations task force that met weekly. Liaisons gathered data from their divisions to report to the task force, and then reported back to their divisions about the task force meetings. Nandkeolyar consolidated front-end and back-end technology responsibilities in one external firm and sought new developers for the technology team. He sprinkled his staff with insiders in order to give current internal employees the opportunity to work on the Internet as well as use their brand experience and relationship networks. Since many members of the MIS division wanted to be involved with the e-commerce operation, a careful transition plan was put in place to avoid stripping the existing MIS organization. And Nandkeolyar emphasized communication, insisting that his group stay in close touch with the other business units and functions. He met regularly with leaders in the retail and catalog divisions to maintain consistency across the channels, ensure that items looked identical, and protect the customer experience.

Williams-sonoma.com launched on schedule in November 1999. Advertising for the launch included posting the URL of the new site in the windows of stores during the first week. Store associates wore badges that read "Williams-Sonoma Now Online." Postcards and e-mails were mailed. A print campaign announcing the launch of the website ran in major dailies in key Internet markets. The catalog printed the URL on every page, and an advertisement for the website dominated the back cover of the catalog. Soon after launch, williams-sonoma.com entered into portal partnerships with two online sites considered compatible with the Williams-Sonoma brand: epicurious.com, a comprehensive culinary website, and WeddingChannel.com (formerly Della.com), an online gift registry; they helped direct 11 percent of the transactions to Williams-Sonoma's website.

In the first twenty-two days, the website brought in $1 million, and another $2 million in the next fifteen days (the average physical store generated $2 million to $2.5 million in yearly sales). Between Thanksgiving and Christmas, williams-sonoma.com was running an 8 percent conversion rate from traffic to transactions, a figure significantly higher than the industry standard of 3 to 4 percent, and roughly 30 percent of its customers were new. Of 70 percent of online customers already in the W-S database, 40 percent were multichannel buyers who had shopped in the store and through the catalog and now were shopping on the Internet. About 10,000 catalog requests a week came through williams-sonoma.com, confirming multichannel synergies—an important issue. "We've got to demonstrate that you can drive sales in the other two channels with the Internet," Patrick Connolly said. "We've got to use this as a tool to build and extend our brands. If we can't generate incremental sales in our retail stores and in our catalogs using the Web, then this whole exercise has been a defensive reaction, and an expensive one at that."

By the middle of Williams-Sonoma's peak season, the new website was performing above expectations, with a total for the fourth quarter of $8 million in online sales (catalog and retail sales were $530 million), and breakeven was expected within a year. But forecasting online demand proved to be tricky. On March 6, 2000, the company announced that fourth-quarter profits would fall about 13 percent below analysts' estimates because of overstocking of goods for the holiday season. Despite the earnings shortfall, Williams-Sonoma announced "across the board success for its e-commerce site" after six months in cyberspace. Williams-Sonoma was named the best entry into the Internet by a bricks-and-mortar company by *Internet World* magazine and was recognized by ZDNet as one of the top ten best examples of e-commerce over the 1999 holiday season. Williams-Sonoma's wedding and gift registry was relaunched in January 2000 and was an immediate success, recording an 87 percent increase in total registries companywide, which would pay off over the entire wedding season as couples began directing their wedding guests to those registries. One more dramatic statistic: the online customer acquisition cost was tiny by Internet industry standards—less than 15 percent of sales.

SUSTAINING SUCCESS: ADDITIONAL E-CULTURE CHALLENGES

E-commerce was looking good for W-S, but was the rest of the company cooperating with its makeover? Resistance from retail stores was still considered a problem. One e-commerce leader was frustrated by the contrast with gap.com, which plastered their URL everywhere, whereas she suspected that Williams-Sonoma stores put the window displays concerning the website in a window facing a back alley. Nandkeolyar wanted to control merchandising and inventory management as well as the content of the website, but no one in the traditional units wanted to cede territory. Meanwhile, many dotcom startups competing with Williams-Sonoma were now staffed by former Williams-Sonoma employees, including Cooking.com, digitalchef.com, and BabyCenter.

The e-commerce leaders believed that if employees continued to do interesting work and were challenged, they would stay, "but if they start to feel like they're not a part of the solution, they will leave." One way to keep them interested—and make the rest of the company feel included—was continual training. Every Friday, the e-commerce division held "e-school" sessions for other employees; buzzwords were explained and concepts taught—personalization, collaborative filtering, customization, whatever they did not understand. But Nandkeolyar knew that compensation issues still needed to be addressed, such as the need to offer higher scales in the Internet division to compete with dotcoms and the need to change the overall reward system to encourage cooperation rather than a focus on each division's own results.

"We're still a cute and cuddly kitten without the fangs," Nandkeolyar said, anticipating friction with other parts of the company now that W-S was on the Web to stay—especially when the non-Web people saw that they still needed to change their own work styles, address compensation issues, and share stardom with a new set of people who did not come from retail backgrounds. Now the even deeper work of systemic change could begin.

Williams-Sonoma is a great example precisely because it had such a hard road to travel from initial denial to its first round of successes. There are numerous lessons it offers. The CEO was converted from skeptic to sponsor through two pilot ventures that were improvised quickly. The first one, the holiday website (which I consider a light application of lipstick while the bulldog temporarily stood still), involved a simple, inexpensive trial involving no change and no commitment, just to see if customers would buy anything at all. The second pilot, the wedding registry, was different and more creative; it demonstrated that Web technology could create entirely new opportunities for reaching new customers in new ways. So the first lesson is: *When in doubt, create small experiments. Pick one loaded for success that doesn't require much change and one that demonstrates the virtues of changing. Don't bet the company, and don't waste time. Just act, simply and quickly, to have something concrete and positive to use to convert skeptics.*

Having passed both an easy hurdle and a harder one, Williams-Sonoma Web advocates could build support among top executives for a complete e-commerce site. The working group moved from part-time volunteers (the lipstick stage) to a full-time dedicated team when they presented a solid business model showing a relatively rapid return on investment. The support they earned through effective prototypes and a responsible business plan helped them weather crises, such as vendor problems and loss of key people. Committed sponsors would not let them fail. Lesson number two: *New ventures need dedicated teams, given space and autonomy. But venture teams also need to be responsive to business realities. And they need to have sponsors in the wider organization to back them up, because so many things can go wrong.*

The appointment of an experienced vice president who understood both technology and organizational politics ensured Williams-Sonoma's success. The new leader brought together insiders from all parts of the company to develop the design for the website, using proven expertise. Sensitive to change issues, he worked on creating positive relationships with every other function and division, persuading them gently to accept the changes brought about by the addition of the Internet channel. He deployed someone they respected to work with them on how to change. The third lesson Williams-Sonoma offers: *Recognize that e-business requires systemic changes in many ways of working. Connect new e-ventures to the company mainstream. That's where the synergies are, but that's also where the obstacles are. Without good relationships, without diplomats who can negotiate across all parts of the organization, the obstacles will never be confronted or overcome.*

A Foundation for Change

Wannadots are propelled into e-business and e-culture changes more easily when the promise of new technology converges with other big strategic change goals, so that e-business is not just an afterthought on the sidelines while the main action is elsewhere. The experience of pacesetters shows another, more effective, path to change. Instead of beginning with denial, they start with curiosity about the future. Instead of fooling around with lipstick, they go right for a makeover. It can still take time to get the business model right and remove barriers, but the results tend to be bigger and bolder actions on more fronts, laying the foundation for bigger returns.

For Honeywell, a global company in controls and aerospace, the Internet was seen as important to shifting the company from a manufacturing to a services focus. This big strategic goal was supported by a culture that encourages looking to the wider environment for change opportunities: vehicles for improvisation and innovation, experience with partnerships, and a desire to work across organizational walls. But change, as we'll see in this case, is not a one-time decision; it is an ongoing campaign. And change continues; in October 2000 General Electric announced its intent to buy Honeywell.

Among industrial giants, Honeywell was an Internet pioneer. Before most large manufacturing companies jumped on the business-to-business (B2B) bandwagon, Honeywell was winning awards. In early 1999 it reached number 5 on *PC Week's* list of the top Internet Technology Innovators in North America, cited for its internal worldwide Internet steering committee; a website that offered not just information but online processes that customers, suppliers, and employees could use to get work done; and e-commerce offerings over the Internet that augmented Honeywell's already extensive electronic data interchange through private networks. Via the Internet, Honeywell reaches new and different customers, such as thousands of small companies that would not have been found through its traditional distribution system.

Honeywell's CEO Mike Bonsignore, known for the significant amount of time he devoted to customer visits, set a personal example of Honeywell's outward focus and commitment to customer-driven innovation. "We could do new things for customers if we started listening to them," he told me. "Customers didn't want to buy products from us, they wanted us to solve their problems." Over a five-year period, Bonsignore put in place several mechanisms for innovation. One was a corporate venture capital system encompassing two kinds of ventures: "grow programs" for good ideas within a business unit that were not funded in that unit's plan, and "home run programs" for technology ideas that had no other way to get supported. Vision 2005, started in 1997, asked thirty-three top talent employees from around the world to envision the world in 2005 to 2010. Their ideas, generated over the course of a year, were honed to six, culminating in three themes that received funding and appointment of a venture team: "agile pharma" using biotechnology; "aviation enterprise," integrating the air travel system in the air and on the ground; and "asset management," for the protection of valuable assets in a dangerous world.

Honeywell had brought together a set of small, entrepreneurial software acquisitions to form the Hi-Spec Solutions division of the Industrial

Controls group (a $3 billion business). The mission was to focus on solutions and engineering services rather than selling hardware-based control systems. The search for cutting-edge technology outside as well as inside the company led Hi-Spec to Abuzz in 1998, and Honeywell became Abuzz's first beta site for the enterprise-based knowledge sharing system that Abuzz was then developing, as I described in chapter 2. Hi-Spec developed a suite of virtual testing tools that could be downloaded from its website and used to improve manufacturing performance through faster, more frequent adjustments run by the customers themselves—for example, heat exchange tests, process control loops, and "user alerts" for plant operators.

MyPlant.com was one of Hi-Spec's key initiatives. Launched on the Web in June 1999, its potential was accelerated a few months later when e-business leaders at Honeywell decided it should be grown aggressively as a stand-alone business—an e-hub for the manufacturing industry, with its own president and the freedom to "think like a dotcom." As a first mover in this vital B2B space, MyPlant.com links solutions providers (such as industry consultants, software application vendors, engineering and construction firms, equipment providers, and academics) directly to end users (such as plant engineers, managers, operators, technicians, planners, schedulers, and purchasing agents). Customers can enter in an RFP or a request for information, run product demonstrations, participate in live interactive seminars, run Web-based software applications, and make electronic business transactions. Honeywell's relationships with major corporations are big advantages for MyPlant.com, ones that independent dotcoms would have trouble duplicating. One such advantage is the willingness of customers to link Honeywell's extranets to their intranet sites, tapping through the customers' firewall.

While MyPlant.com was getting underway, Honeywell announced its merger with AlliedSignal to form Honeywell International. In October 1999, the soon-to-be-joined companies formed a corporate e-business council, consisting of eighty heads of e-business for each AlliedSignal and Honeywell unit. Most of the AlliedSignal e-business heads were new hires, because AlliedSignal had started its move to the Internet later than Honeywell; Honeywell already had many in place. Bonsignore pushed the e-business group to be more innovative. He called the hundreds of projects currently underway in AlliedSignal "bunnies"—they were small, cute, and didn't eat a lot. What the new company needed were "tiger" projects that could create new markets and transform the business.

MyPlant.com had already shown tiger potential. The corporate e-business council believed MyPlant.com represented a model for how to build additional online propositions in other business units at Honeywell. Russel McMeekin, Hi-Spec president, was appointed corporate e-business president. He looked for other units within Honeywell that could build e-hubs similar to MyPlant.com. By the first corporate executive council meeting of the newly combined company in January 2000, McMeekin had cultivated widespread support for the e-hub strategy and for two new e-ventures, myFacilities.com and MyAircraft.com. MyAircraft, in partnership with i2 Technologies and United Technologies, was envisioned as the first comprehensive open electronic marketplace for the $500 billion aerospace industry. Online aviation customers would be able to buy, sell, trade, and manage parts and services; utilize supply chain services such as demand forecasting and inventory planning; access technical experts; and view online publications. E-hubs, Honeywell thought, would ultimately transform their industries—and Honeywell's virtual marketplaces would be at the center of the transformation.

MyPlant.com grew rapidly; in 2000 it had over 6,000 registered members, over 300 third-party companies participating as solution providers, and 42,000 logged user sessions. A co-branding partnership with TrainingNet allowed MyPlant.com to offer 600,000 Web-based training courses; a strategic partnership with Microsoft allowed MyPlant.com to increase traffic from users of Microsoft's Web properties and Internet services from MSN. By the spring of 2000, MyPlant.com had been incorporated as a separate legal entity, moved into a new location of its own, and was exploring an IPO. But online competition was heating up, because the B2B space was the new darling of the capital markets. To become the e-marketplace of choice, Honeywell had to move fast to sign up partners—but competitors were thinking the same thoughts.

Internal issues were equally challenging. Honeywell's e-hubs faced the same balancing act as all new ventures in established companies: how to manage the delicate balance of growing the e-hubs as independent businesses while leveraging the domain knowledge, resources, and organization of Honeywell International. Along with the presidents of the e-hubs, e-business head McMeekin cultivated relationships with functional heads and other important resources within the larger organization, explaining the strategy as well as why the e-hubs needed exemption from corporate traditions. He had to convince successful units responsible for revenues and profits about the virtues of providing attention, support, and expertise to tiny startups that might eat their existing businesses—exactly the same problem faced in every wannadot. An e-business leader explained: "The challenges are, oh my god, I'm going to cannibalize my traditional business unit. My peers are asking, Who funds this? Who gets the revenue, how do I count it? Do you own my customer, do I own my customer? Are you going to screw up my channel to market?"

People in the mainstream businesses wanted Honeywell to be a top Internet player, so there was willingness to embrace the new strategy and consider the new questions. Top leaders stressed their firm commitment to changing the way the organization worked to provide the necessary resources for the e-hubs. But applauding an aspiration was one thing; changing behavior was more difficult. MyPlant.com president Tom Galanty had to convince some of the larger, more established functions (human resources, legal, and finance) that his thirty-person unit had needs "way beyond" other groups. Attracting dotcom talent required changes in recruitment and compensation, let alone stock options. "We're trying to change the culture inside our organization," Galanty explained, "and a lot of people internally are not familiar with what's happening in the e-business world. I think you have to be willing to take a lot of risks with a big company like Honeywell and push every boundary that needs to be pushed. You have to be professional about it, of course, but you also have to break rules."

James Cudd, a Honeywell strategy vice president, reflected top leaders' commitment to e-business: "Any time an organization encounters anything as fundamentally transforming as this, the scariest issue is, what is our timeline? How fast do we have to move? What is our level of urgency? Is it a fad, or is it fundamentally transforming, and if it is, what long-term benefit or damage do we do to ourselves proceeding at whatever rate we proceed at? And the leadership is really wrestling with that. Our sense is this is a crisis. It's essential. We have to move faster than we've ever moved before." McMeekin observed, "There are a lot of incredible issues surrounding the internal organizational piece. The executive team is due a lot of credit, because they have said, we don't have all the answers, but we believe in this, we're going to go for it, we may make mistakes, let's manage this in a practical manner, but let's keep moving."

That desire to keep moving is one of the distinguishing characteristics of innovators. A foundation for change doesn't guarantee success (in late 2000 Honeywell had widely reported business and leadership problems and a sale to General Electric was imminent). But it does ensure that the action will start faster, problems will surface earlier and be faced (not denied), leaders will maintain the momentum, and a new culture will emerge.

Organizational Curiosity and Desire:
Wannadots Have to Want That Dot

It is a stretch to attribute emotions to organizations. But some of the differences between laggards and pacesetters boil down to the emotions reflected in key decisions. Whereas laggards are mired in denial and anger, pacesetters exhibit curiosity and explore opportunities. Whereas laggards show ambivalence, pacesetters are filled with desire. They may not use the rhetoric of Total World Domination expressed by dotcoms, but they are eager to get rid of the barriers to change.

Pacesetter companies often have a base of innovation to begin with. (The vice chairman of an industrial services giant told us that one barrier his laggard company faced was that there was no tradition of R&D expenditures in their business.) Instead of trying to do as little as possible, leaders reach for potentially big ideas—Honeywell's tiger projects. But because there is a great deal of uncertainty and the right models are not yet known, they set broad themes and let specific ideas emerge from a period of experimentation. Their ideas emanate from intimate knowledge of customer needs, not from a scramble to match a competitor. They are innovative, not imitative—no copy-ware for them. They seek to use the technology's potential—to do things they couldn't do without it—instead of trying to duplicate or force-fit traditional models to the Internet. But they also seek to maximize the advantage that established companies potentially have over pure dotcoms: the multichannel synergies that come from leveraging their brand, their customer relationships, and their backroom logistics experience.

By the time they undertake a systemic culture change, successful companies operate differently, too. They dedicate resources to their e-ventures, giving them a clear identity and appropriate autonomy—the flexibility to adjust policies and procedures to fit their situation as ventures that are both new and different, operating in Internet space. Top management is involved and supportive without micromanaging, keeping the themes clear but leaving the details up to the venture team. The top group also encourages cooperation across the rest of the organization. The effort itself features a mix of inside and outside people to balance industry experience and ties throughout the organization with fresh perspectives and new technology skills.

Pacesetter companies have a head start at operating "in the green"—

in the go-ahead zone, near the money. They are already closer to the four key elements of e-culture mode:

- treating strategy as improvisational theater,

- opening themselves to a network of partners,

- turning cell-like organizations into integrated communities, and

- creating a culture that attracts and holds the best talent.

PART TWO

✦

In the Green

The Essence of E-Effectiveness

4

◆

WAVES OF RAVES

Strategy as Improvisational Theater

There is no profit in operating in the realm of the widely understood.
—Robert Shapiro, Chairman, Pharmacia

The scripted life is orderly but sterile. Living off the wall, hanging loose, and being open to chance can bring unexpected delights.
—John Powers, *Boston Globe Magazine*, May 7, 2000

All the world's a stage,
And all the men and women merely players;
They have their exits and their entrances,
And one man in his time plays many parts.
—William Shakespeare, *As You Like It*, Act 2, Scene 7

A SINGLE GREAT PERFORMANCE that gets rave reviews from its audiences does not guarantee a successful long run. In the fast-paced Internet Age, people and organizations need to generate the capacity to create a series of hits. They need waves of raves.

The drama of management was once like traditional theater. Each season's run involved a series of plays following predetermined scripts, whether new offerings or revivals. Actors were assigned roles, and words were put into their mouths that were expected to come out pretty much the same way every time. Boundaries were predetermined, and mavericks whose interpretations went too far beyond those bounds had to contend with vicious critics. The action led to an unvarying endpoint, the same way, every time. After each play had a good run, new scripts would be written.

Some companies still want a perfect plan before the action begins. For them, the cardinal rule is no surprises—but that attitude is exactly what creates cosmetic change and stifles the creativity necessary to succeed in a new channel such as the Web. E-business environments are full of surprises. An executive in a retail wannadot commented on the contrast between traditional planning and Internet speed: "Our traditional culture is predicated on the model of perfecting everything, then releasing it. In our old business, extensive consumer research is conducted, and it takes 18–24 months before a new product reaches retail. In the online division, we need to do it differently. In Internet time, we need to move much faster, and while this is hard for many in the company to deal with emotionally, we need to just do it, fix it later, and know that the launch will never look worse, always better."

Instead of following a script, e-savvy companies run an improvisational theater. A general theme is identified to get the actors started. Then the actors try out different moves, develop the story as they interact with the audience, and create a better experience with each round. Soon the performances of many troupes accumulate to take the organization in a new direction.

Pacesetter companies establish themselves on the Web without waiting for the risk-free plan; they just start improvising. Tesco, a top player among Britain's largest grocery retailers, vaulted to Internet leadership with Tesco.com, grabbing 66 percent of the U.K. online grocery market and serving as one of the country's most popular portals for e-mail and news. But Tesco didn't head directly for the Web. In late 1995, Tesco tried home shopping in a few trial stores as Tesco Direct, using phone, fax, and Internet orders. A small team of six, given direct access to the CEO, started a home shopping service in a housing cluster. Another exploration involved mail order sales of gifts, flowers, and food baskets. A parallel set of projects explored the Internet. In 1997, Tesco dropped CD-ROM discs in targeted neighborhoods in affluent areas, but they had low rates of adoption at first. There were numerous fits and starts. Poor customer service led to a temporary halt in rollout and a focus on service improvement. Eventually Tesco Direct joined Tesco.com for a big push, and the combination of Internet orders and home delivery of goods picked in the stores was a hit. In mid-2000, knowing that they could not count on staying ahead without constant innovation, the actors were exploring new scenarios. Unattended delivery? Filling orders from stores at night? New products first via the website? Tesco has already received rave reviews, but it is still improvising.

Innovation through improvisation is at the heart of e-culture. Plans are often just best guesses. Strategy emerges and is revealed through action, because when outcomes cannot be known in advance, the action itself creates the goal. Sense-and-respond, not make-and-sell, is the primary operating mode in Internet companies, as my Harvard colleagues Stephen Bradley and Richard Nolan explained.[1] A decision-making hierarchy is replaced by an internal marketplace of ideas. Innovators initiate and sell projects, and then attract others to their ventures.

All innovation has an improvisational aspect. Decades of research show that innovation combines the discipline of skilled players with serendipity and chance; and even strategy formulation can be discovery based.[2] Innovators create value by working on things that are not yet fully known. Periods of technological change have always involved numerous creative experiments followed by shakeouts and establishment of an industry standard. Times of uncertainty call for improvisation. Whenever it is impossible to know which model or concept will prevail, it is unwise to make one big bet; it is better to launch many small experiments and learn from the results of each—a hallmark of improvisation.

The idea of improvisation in business has an honorable history. When others have used this image, however, they have generally had musicians in mind. John Kao likened innovation to the common practice among jazz players of "jamming." Shona Brown and Kathleen Eisenhardt used the Grateful Dead as an example of how to strike a balance between structure and rules (the original tune) and chaos (variations, free-form playing).[3] But the Internet Age propels business beyond the dynamics of interaction among the performers themselves to the bigger issue of turning the whole organization into a theater for innovation that has multiple dramas on several stages, some well inside the organization and some involving the external partner network.

Inside-out and outside-in improvisation are two complementary ways to move at Internet speed, and later we'll see how both of them work.

Some companies improvise primarily from inside out, encouraging legions of internal entrepreneurs to try out new directions. Top leaders serve as sponsors, sometimes starting the action by assigning a project, sometimes supporting projects that innovators initiate; external partners are side players involved on an ad hoc basis. As the results of the innovators' projects accumulate, a new strategy takes shape—new clarity about what to do. So far, that's a familiar drama of innovation, common among the best Old Economy companies.

The second approach, improvising from outside in, is a rising model well suited for the Internet Age. Today, many small, independent companies are the source of new concepts and new technology, rather than corporate giants with large development staffs. So in the outside-in model, a company builds relationships with independent troupes of actors, each of whom is figuring out something new, something promising but unformed and embryonic. The company's own leaders serve as talent scouts, patrons, and directors of a production company that develops the connections between improvisers and company strategy.

Later in this chapter, I'll bring to center stage two top performers illustrating each model: Sun Microsystems, starring in the inside-out approach, and Reuters Greenhouse, starring in the outside-in model. But first, let's assemble the elements that both kinds of companies need before they can improvise.

"I'll Know It When I See It": Six Elements of Improvisational Theater

Innovation is inherently improvisational because it is impossible to know how people will react to something they have never seen before, something that has not yet been invented, or something that has not yet happened. They can love the initial idea but hate the execution, or hate the idea but like what starts to emerge from it. I call this the IKIWISI Effect. *IKIWISI* (pronounced ick-ee-wis-ee) stands for *I'll Know It When I See It*.[4] We may not always be able to describe the perfect fulfillment of our needs or the perfect solution to our problems, but we certainly know it when we see it.

If the play can't be described in advance, it must be performed often in order to take shape from the reactions of those coming to understand it. That's why the best improvisers include members of the audience in a series of quick performances, taking account of each round of reactions to shape the next round. *Rapid prototyping* is what this process is called in the technology world. Each prototype is a demonstration of possibilities that are difficult to articulate before you see them.

It is hard to convince other people of the power of a vision without concrete demonstrations in a series of specific projects or events. Even top decision makers might not always know what they want until they see it. For Williams-Sonoma, it took two demonstrations (the first one thrown together hastily to see if top leaders knew it when they saw it), guided by few instructions other than IKIWISI to show the company the way toward an e-commerce strategy. For some IBM Reinventing Education sites, the play started without clear plans or budgets, as IBM partner Doug Walker, of the Vermont Department of Education, indicated: "I guess we'd be completely paralyzed if we weren't willing to act not knowing the end of the story, or not knowing where all the resources were going to come from. And maybe it's risky, maybe it's crazy, to start things not knowing how you're going to get it resourced." But once there is a tangible performance, decision makers know it when they see it, and improvisers can gather support for the next round of innovation.

Strategic improvisation takes shape out of six elements: a theme, a theater, actors, suspense, audiences, and successive variations.

THEME

Improvisation is just chaos and messiness if there is no clear theme—a topic, a headline, a domain, a direction. Themes can be statements of direction from top leaders ("Let's find our best niche in e-commerce") or topics of interest ("Let's explore technologies that could put us out of business"). What's important is that they provide a focus to get the action started and ensure that it won't be just random motion.

The theme has to be broad enough to encompass a range of possibilities and focused enough to create the potential for depth. Breadth permits flexibility as alternative paths are pursued. When one doesn't work, try another. Otherwise, the effort is doomed to premature death at the hands of one wrong factor. (The CEO of a Canadian bank saw a study showing that a high proportion of Canadians wouldn't use their credit cards over the Internet and immediately wanted to close a fledgling e-commerce venture because of this single issue.) At the same time, focus sets some rough boundaries indicating how far to wander before the venture falls over the edge.

The theme permits communication without destroying creativity: Everyone is working in the same arena, but in different ways. Themes can also include values, such as eBay's unique sense of community. An e-tail executive admired Amazon.com for picking a good theme and sticking with it as the basis for innovation. "For the first three years of their existence as a company, they did one and only one thing. They were a Yahoo! for books, and they managed to ship those books on-time to the right address, accepted the returns properly, and answered the phone and e-mail consistently. The other brilliant thing about starting with books is there are 1.5 million SKUs, so if you master that, you can fairly easily add music—50,000 SKUs—or video—80,000—or hardware—50,000."

THEATER

You can't create the future in a structure designed to repeat the past. Innovators need a place to stage the action, to develop the play—an organizational room of their own in which to rehearse and perform, freed from constraints that stifle the creativity of improvisation. Once called *skunk works*, the new theaters are now more likely to be incubators and internal venture capital funds supporting breakthrough projects and fledgling ventures occupying their own space on the organization chart, even if they might be in the same building as the mainstream parent. Honeywell had two kinds of corporate venture capital and Vision 2000 teams improvising on futuristic themes, as we saw in chapter 3. Even dotcoms need places for improvisation; Women.com set up an e-commerce skunk works to convince a skeptical CEO to add product sales to a community site.[5]

After spin-off from AT&T in 1995, Lucent Technologies created a New Ventures Group (NVG) to build new growth businesses around promising ideas from Bell Laboratories that weren't being pulled to market by mainstream business groups. Entrepreneurs-in-residence at NVG's offices were like a repertory company, ready for a variety of plays. NVG's first venture, elemedia (Internet telephony), stopped Krishna Murti from leaving Lucent for a Silicon Valley startup. "I'd had 12 years at AT&T, and that was enough," he said, but as elemedia CTO, he had equity plus corporate job security. Elemedia CEO Joe Mele was told to "assume that you will have all the freedom in the world to break the rules or tell people to get lost. Ignore all the corporate kinds of things. You have a license to kill." Removal of constraints helped elemedia to win a development race with Netscape and Microsoft; seven months after startup, Netscape was a customer. In

1998 and 1999 elemedia was named Internet Telephony Product of the Year and made *Interactive Week*'s list of top ten companies to work for. In June 1999, elemedia, still led by Mele and Murti, was integrated with Lucent's Switching and Access Systems as a core part of its strategy.

The NVG was a halfway house for corporate types not ready for the leap to independent entrepreneurship, as Steve Socolof, NVG vice president, joked. Lucent needed more theaters like it. Though $38 billion Lucent was the industry leader, Cisco was often cited as the company to watch. Lucent's per employee revenues of $250,000 and operating margin of 16 percent in 1999 lagged behind Cisco's $650,000 in revenues per employee and 25 percent operating margin. So business units created their own venture groups, asking the NVG for tips. Lucent Venture Partners was chartered to make outside investments in more traditional venture capital style. And Bell Labs created "breakthrough projects" (about fifty in early 2000) to bring new technologies to market quickly. (But in mid-2000, lagging financial performance made this look like too little, too late.)

Without a degree of separation, improv troupes can be bombarded with requests and demands that start restricting and then killing creativity,[6] not to mention taking time away from the intense task of development. (At one lagging dotcom, the technology team would "come in in the morning and find who knows what new project on their plate. And there was always something on the periphery that has the potential to distract the company."

Actors

Outstanding improvisation can demand more of actors than traditional roles. To pull it off takes highly skilled and disciplined actors. They must be willing to take on unfamiliar roles, think on their feet, pay attention to several things at once, walk into situations for which they are not prepared, and ad lib. This is no job for amateurs. Many analysts point to the risk-taking spirit of entrepreneurs who start things, but fewer chronicle the self-discipline and team discipline required to actually produce innovation (e.g., the engineers at Abuzz snapped to deadlines for big design feats). Or the confidence required to step out of familiar territory to do something new. (To launch FashionCo's website quickly, senior people rolled up their sleeves for new tasks, from copy approval to cleaning up legacy systems to optimizing images.)

Improvisers must be willing to commit to actions without full information. A leader in a dotcom-enabler reported his experience with a bold venture: "When you're on a freight train like this, with a well-defined schedule, you don't have the luxury to get as much information as you'd like. In fact, the information isn't out there anyway, because this venture is a first for the company. When you've got 60% of the information you're going to need, you have to go ahead." A marketing executive at eBay described talking with his team about a design he saw the previous day that he felt the site needed. Half the people said "yes," half said "no," some said "retool it," and he said "just do it."[7]

Improv actors are not unguided; they have producers and directors. But leadership often emerges from among the actors as they start performing. Who volunteers extra time? Who has the idea that is right for the moment? Who earns the respect of peers? The key roles in improvisations cannot always be captured in advance assignments or job descriptions.

DRAMA AND SUSPENSE

What will happen onstage? If the ending is predictable, or we've seen it before, then by definition it is not original, contains little innovation, and looks like the same old thing. Improvisation, like all good theater, always contains an element of suspense, which is resolved as the ending comes nearer. The conclusion—our strategy, our direction, our approach—becomes clearer and clearer as the action proceeds. Sometimes it is not revealed until the end, when the strands come together to reveal the strategy that lay under the surface all along. What adds to the suspense of improvisation, what keeps the audience on edge waiting for the next move, is that no one has done this before.

Strategists look smart after the fact, but they may have no idea of the right direction at the beginning. The Internet was a priority for television broadcaster NBC even before General Electric CEO Jack Welch, NBC's corporate boss, announced a major push into e-business. NBC was ahead of the curve when it started exploring paths to interactive television in 1993; only Time Warner was pursuing similar technologies. Insiders credited NBC President Bob Wright's focus on new business models. Marty Yudkovitz, now president of NBC Digital Media, described to my team (in fast-talking, colorful Hollywood agent style) a series of dead ends and side streets as NBC improvised its way down the Information Superhighway. The realization that media interactivity would not start with the television set but rather with the PC led to a 50-50 joint venture with Microsoft to create cable channel MSNBC and website MSNBC.com, launched in July 1996. CNBC.com was relaunched in 1999. A series of investments in a range of Internet startups eventually shaped a strategy for NBC Digital Media.

Bold new strategies often spring from dramas that have the audience on the edge of their seats, wondering how this will ever be resolved. It takes imagination to enter a theater where the action is improvised. It takes courage to invest in developments with unknown outcomes, developments that require IKIWISI—knowing it when you see it, but not knowing what it will be until then.

AUDIENCES

Audience interaction is an important component of improvisational theater. There have always been multiple audiences for business dramas, outside companies and within them, but now those audiences are Web empowered, so they include more constituencies in more places who get more information faster and speak up about it. Companies have always had to think about their customers, suppliers, employees, investors, regulators, partners, critics—though maybe not as quickly and simultaneously as the Internet demands.

The e-world makes sensitivity to multiple audiences even more important, and it shifts the emphasis from the narrower concept of customers to the wider concept of audiences. In the complex business models dotcoms favor, it is not always clear who the paying customer is. Is it the consumer of a product, the user of a service, the advertiser or sponsor getting space, the partner getting click-throughs, the investor providing the cash? Not all are customers in the traditional sense, but all are certainly audiences. There are also important audiences inside the company that can make or break a drama: decision makers, immediate bosses, peers.

Outside the company, the audience can be diffuse and unbounded, containing critics as well as fans, as we saw in chapter 1. The audience that reacts might not be the one that the company was hoping to attract. Monsanto has languished and shrunk as a company because it paid attention to its customers (farmers who bought genetically modified seeds) and even its customers' customers (food processors) but failed to notice the growing audience of environmentalists who were mobilizing opposition to genetically modified ingredients—opposition that caused consumers to turn away from food containing them and British stores to ban them.

Improvisers must do more than watch audience reaction closely; they must invite the audience into the action. Customers can become design partners, users the best source of the next move, and potential critics the commentators on each unfolding version.

SUCCESSIVE VERSIONS AND VARIATIONS

Sense and respond, launch and learn, try and trash. . . . E-culture involves creating a rapid sequence of ever-improving versions that incorporate critical reactions.

Rapid prototyping helped IBM's Reinventing Education project teams create breakthrough new technologies for K–12 school systems, such as voice recognition tools based on children's voices to teach reading, and software to allow flexible scheduling of high school courses based on students' learning needs. Teams were based in the schools, not in IBM laboratories, so they could interact with teachers every day, if necessary, and create variations incorporating their feedback. The spirit of improvisation means tolerating false starts and wrong moves, as long as feedback is rapid and changes are made. At eBay, a no-penalty culture allows people to admit they had a dumb idea and move on to the next thing.

"To improvise, you take a group of people and enter a situation with their collective knowledge, with the best information you have to date, knowing that the second you enter, change begins," Robin McCulloch e-mailed me. Toronto-based actor-turned-consultant McCulloch teaches improvisational acting to companies under the name Corporate Agility. He uses group exercises to teach clients (e.g., Ontario Hydro, Icom Information, Maple Leaf Sports) such skills as positive listening, focusing on others, discovering the shifting form of a group, building a risk-taking environment, supporting intuitive responses, and understanding how getting into the action changes it. But most important, he said, is reducing fear of making mistakes and of "making the use of 'yes' mandatory." Katie Goodman, leader of Improvisation for the Spirit in Bozeman, Montana, concurs. Improvisational theater involves "winging it in a secure environment," she says, pointing to the importance of trust among a team of actors.

Go up a level from trial and error in groups, and consider the ways that companies moving to the Web must create successive versions not just of their products but of their business model itself. Technology companies have always reinvented themselves every few years; today's dotcoms often change business model every few months. Rudy Chan, CEO of hongkong.com, traced the evolution of his business and its name in under three years: from WebHK to cover local elections; to Corner.com, a city guide; to a shopping site with some e-commerce added; to hongkong.com, which includes entertainment and online services (e.g., e-mail and home-page building). Chan wanted the company to be open to multiple services as they evolved; hongkong.com partnered with I-Silk.com to add a trans-lation engine allowing users to shop in French, Japanese, and other lan-guages. James Toledano, founder of brandnewmusic.com, said that he felt emotionally distraught at first when he had to change his business plan, as though change were a sign that he couldn't stick to what he knew; but the marketplace was moving, and he had to change with it. Or recall the experience of Abuzz from chapter 2. Abuzz began as a software company creating CD-ROM–based knowledge management systems, became enamored of the Internet, but then decided to sell its applications for cor-porate intranets and had beta tests in eight big companies. Abuzz was about to make a deal with Microsoft or Lotus when The New York Times entered the scene, offering Abuzz a chance to morph its system for the Internet, so action shifted to a new arena. All within a two-year period.

Treating business development like improvisational theater can lead to bold new directions and stimulate successful new strategies. Let's start in Silicon Valley with Sun Microsystems's method for inside-out improvisa-tion—dazzling the marketplace because of continuous improvisation by internal entrepreneurs and innovators. We will then take the show on the road, going to London to view Reuters's outside-in improvisational model.

From the Inside Out:
How Sun Became a Dot in Dot-Com

Project-by-project improvisation, creating a series of hit performances, makes it possible to reinvent the organization constantly, without the trauma of a sudden bloody revolution. The critics who don't like one play can watch others, because new ones are always unfolding. An inno-vator at Sun Microsystems quieted skeptics trying to stop his venture by rattling off serial strategies that kept the company in front of change: "We were just generic desktops, then we became CAD desktops, and then we became small commercial servers. Now we're larger commercial servers. Now we're getting into storage. Sun will learn it. If we execute, Sun will expand its expertise."

In 1982, when Sun Microsystems was founded, the network age was a visionary notion. Back then (many generations ago in Internet time), the new thing was having a personal computer that plugged into the wall, not into the phone jack; you didn't dream of talking to anybody else's computer. But Sun's focus on network computing ("Network computing is the heart and soul of this company," CEO Scott McNealy declared) was destined to pay off. By the late 1990s, while the rest of the world was catching on to the possibilities of e-commerce, Sun was riding high by improvising on its networking theme.

Sun's products and services constantly changed in successive waves of innovation. It introduced the world's first workstation in 1982, and offered free licensing on network file sharing (NFS) technology in 1984. In 1986, Sun extended its NFS technology to PC users. In 1987, Sun formed an alliance with AT&T to develop the UNIX operating system as the foundation for business computing. Exceeding $1 billion in revenue in 1988, Sun consolidated its networking leadership with a series of innovations: the SPARCstation system, Java, Solaris, Jini. By 1999, the year of the Gold Rush onto the Internet, Sun was a $12 billion leader in network computing with more than 25,000 employees, offices in 170 countries, and a single, driving ambition: "to dot-com the world" by supplying systems and software to drive the electronic marketplace. "We're the lumberyard for the Internet," President Ed Zander said. In a world where cars, TV sets, refrigerators, microwave ovens, and more could all contain computers connected to the Web, a Sun leader envisioned inserting Sun technology "into the billions of devices that are going to be network-connected over the next 10 years."

McNealy is restless about complacency and insistent on change. This is more than a message or a set of speeches. It is reflected in a constant shuffle of the deck: reorganizing the formal structure, changing people's assignments, moving people into special projects and assigning job titles that would disappear once the project was finished. Although some long for more stability, most recognize that this Hollywood-style model of assembling actors for a shifting series of projects makes Sun what it is. "We manage to Scott's philosophy that if you're doing the same job with the same direct reports in the same geography with the same boss and the same peer groups and the same customer sets for three years, that's a red flag," a leader said, adding that the goal was to ensure that "the magic genie inside is fresh." Changing the structure frequently, even when things are going well, means that roles cannot become so rigid that they impede the search for innovation. And people find that their experience broadens dramatically; they can understand multiple facets of the business and know people throughout the company well enough to play off them every time the curtain rises on a new performance.

Despite its size, Sun retains much of the culture of the four computer guys who started it. A new product still gets its highest blessing when Scott McNealy—or, as he is called in the company, just plain Scott—takes over a demonstration from the presenter at a board meeting and gets excited ("geeked up") about it. An insider said, "It's always refreshing at Sun that our executives take a new idea and go absolutely wild. If you can get past the middle quagmire, the top level is totally supportive of innovation."

Sun depends on the initiative of leaders at many levels throughout the business to identify new opportunities and act on them quickly. Streams of independently conceived entrepreneurial activity converge to create Sun's next big wave. The thirty-two Sun leaders my team interviewed included a wide range of innovators. Many started with only a theme, not even a specific goal, and it was their improvisation that shaped the performance. We saw particularly striking examples of improvisation and IKIWISI—that leaders could not describe what they wanted until they saw it. That happened to Albert Ormiston, leader for e-Sun and Sun.com. He told us in June 1999 that a year earlier top management couldn't say exactly what they wanted e-Sun to be, even though it was endorsed by the board, "but each month over the past year it became clearer to them what they wanted done. Management supported 'it,' but no one in the beginning could clarify what 'it' was. Then each quarter, they got closer to the goal. Now if you asked at the top level of Sun, you'd get an incredibly crisp answer." That's strategic improvisation.

Together these projects and many others shaped Sun's strategy; they made it possible for Sun to stake claims to "the dot in dot-com." Yet, ventures were often hatched independently by innovators taking advantage of opportunities in their neighborhood. Two who figured in parallel innovations that I am about to describe—Philip Nenon and Bob Gianni—met each other for the first time at my Harvard Business School class in February 2000.

NETRA AND THE BILLION DOLLAR BET

Sun's willingness to bet on the Netra project, despite enormous uncertainties, gave it an unexpected strategic advantage with new kinds of customers. In mid-1997, the Network Systems Group, led by Vice President and General Manager Neil Knox, inherited a small Sun acquisition based in the United Kingdom that made fault-tolerant computers applicable in telecommunications. This could be Sun's opportunity to expand its network presence from the periphery into the actual network infrastructure and help to define a new industry for Sun, but it required startup-style entrepreneurship with no certainty about the plan. Knox's team went to the board of directors with the idea that they could build a huge incremental business for Sun—they called it a "billion dollar bet"—if they could get funding to work with the acquisition to expand their portfolio from one product to a number of products and make them part of the mainstream Sun product line. The board saw this as a natural evolution of the Internet. Within a matter of weeks, the project was funded and on its way.

The project's mission was tweaked over time. A flexible implementation plan allowed room to accommodate an evolving marketplace and customer feedback. A significant amount of management courage was required. "We had to give up a number of other technologies to other product groups," Sales Director Nenon explained. "We had to give up engineers and give up projects people had worked on that were in the development stage, in order to execute on this product plan. That's very tough to do. We had people saying they didn't understand why we were changing where we were going."

The group worked closely from the beginning with its audiences—customers such as Cisco, Lucent, and Nortel—to modify each wave of new Netra products. Sun first had to convince these potential customers that they were serious about building a network computing business. "Some of them were doubters. Some groups were quicker at talking with us about what they thought they needed from a supplier like us, or one of our competitors. We had to run at them a number of times before they opened up and actually started having quality communications." Lucent and Cisco verified that Sun would be on the right path "if we produced a platform that met their requirements and incorporated the traditional Sun technologies of SPARC, Solaris, UNIX, and built-in networking," Nenon reported.

Knox's troupe took customer requests for additional features and functions to staff meetings with engineering and marketing. The actors changed the tune to fit audience response but repeated their chorus of "We've got to find a way to do this" every time the functional groups said it couldn't be done. Time was tight; the team was trying to do this twice as fast as the usual project, and Sun was targeting an evolving marketplace with very stringent standards. "If you've ever seen a bid response from

Lucent, or you ever go through a quality check with Cisco—I mean, they are excruciating," Nenon said.

There were times when the marketplace challenges and the internal resistance were discouraging. "It's a tribute to the management team here, especially Neil Knox and Bob Howard Anderson, our VP of engineering, that when implementation issues came up, they did not freak out. They got closer to it. They got directly involved when it was needed, instead of just trying to stick to a hierarchical, authoritative management style, and gave it both the attention and support that were needed for us to execute." The product's key customers served as its consultants—and also helped pull it through the difficult phases of development. "The customers said they'd stick by us while we bring this thing to marketplace, instead of pulling away when we had some product challenges in finishing the development," Nenon explained. "We got even closer to key customers."

The applause started coming. One customer quickly went from a trial to deploying hundreds of the products worldwide as a fundamental part of their wired and wireless networks. The group showed Netra at Sun's annual "technology fair" as part of its leadership forum—an internal meeting of all directors and vice presidents across all functional groups. McNealy, Zander, and other top leaders spotlighted the product and drew attention to it. McNealy announced it before launch at a service provider event.

From a set of legacy products with revenues under $25 million a year, the group created new products for new customers (such as Lucent and Cisco) that were bringing in over $150 million a year less than two years later and were headed for a projected billion dollars of annual revenue within three years. Netra expanded Sun's role from a peripheral to a central partner in building the converged network infrastructure that was the buzz in the industry by 1999 and 2000. "We didn't wait for the buzz," Nenon said. "We were talking to customers and working on this for a couple of years now. If we had not made the decision back then to get into network infrastructure, we would be missing a vital part of the dot-com communications link, and we would be either fighting Microsoft on the desktop or fighting IBM in the data center."

THE NETWORK COMPUTER

Robert Gianni's project was another vital link. A group at Sun labs under a distinguished engineer, Dr. Duane Northcutt, had a concept for a new generation of network computers (NCs) aimed at bringing workstation performance to the desktop at a lower cost. In 1998, Gianni, an engineering director who had been with Sun eleven years, became NC product development director. The network computer located file storage, print facilities, and other applications on a centralized network, thus lightening the amount of hardware and software put on every desktop.

The idea wasn't entirely new. Several manufacturers, including IBM, Cisco, and Sun itself with its Java station, had already introduced products described as network computers. Despite predictions that a million units would be sold within two years, only some 200,000 were shipped. "They weren't that much cheaper than PCs in terms of the on-going maintenance, and they had limited functionality," Gianni explained. By 1998, improvements in Ethernet technologies made it feasible to deliver the network to the desktop; ten times as much bandwidth was available in a switched rather than a shared system.

Gianni's first challenge was to find a patron and a theater. "This product clearly straddled a lot of business units," Gianni explained. "It wasn't a desktop workstation. It wasn't a server. It wasn't a purely software thing, so it didn't quite fit in any particular place. And so a new area needed to be carved out for it." The idea was shopped around and picked up by a vice president who recognized that it fit his business, a fairly new organization serving customers interested in network computing. Then he hired the actors. The troupe grew from eight engineers to about forty-one or forty-two performers attracted by the creative ideas. "Although it wasn't kosher for us to raid other groups or steal from ourselves, people who knew us and our reputation learned what we were up to, and they wanted to come work with us. They were excited about the product, too, when they saw it." (There's IKIWISI again.)

Gianni likened the work to "concentric rings, like when you drop a pebble in a pond and you get rings of knowledge." At the center of the concentric rings—the core group of knowledge—were the product developers. This team had a "synchronization point": a meeting every Monday morning at 11 o'clock to discuss last week's activities and next week's plans. All the bits and parts were represented—hardware, software, mechanical; at least twenty or thirty people would be in the room, and sometimes over forty. The next circle was a product team (a Sun tradition) that brought a few engineers together with representatives of a dozen or more other functions—technical writers, operations, the service group, power supply, reliability testing, quality assurance, compliance testing. At the outer ring was a business team, consisting of senior managers from marketing, engineering, operations, and services. Frequent feedback from these freeform audiences guided each round of improvisation.

Gianni taught his engineers to become better performers in the presence of critics. Internal skeptics saw the NC as a throwback to the old days of the mainframe terminal when nobody had computers on their desks. It would not act like a PC, they argued; a user couldn't run software or load a CD directly—it wouldn't be "your own little private PC domain." Some customers also doubted it would work, or expressed frustration that they had just finished installing their network and couldn't change. The team kept rehearsing and refining the way they presented their message, getting more applause as the product progressed. When the NC was ready for global launch in the spring of 1999, the troupe took the show on the road (call it "The Network Computer Hits Primetime"), staging key events for Sun sales and service organizations in major geographies.

Learning through Improvising

Sun encourages its innovators to do whatever it takes to make a project successful, but doesn't provide much in the way of formal tools, processes, or disciplines for doing so. "Sun really does leave it up to the individuals to go off and figure out how to implement." I heard many Sun innovators express a wish for more order and discipline (meaning that other people should fall in line for their project, not that they should lose their own freedom). But improvisation is the main source of learning.

Innovators developed some tricks of the trade. Setting aggressive deadlines, they said, helped move action forward: "You know, 'On January 1, the curtain will rise.'" They also stressed the importance of playing to a wider internal audience and getting them onstage, into the action: "It's no good just to try to localize a change in one area if it impacts lots of parts of the organization. You need to make sure that they are all with you as you are driving through the change. Even if one of them doesn't perform or doesn't buy into it, it could potentially put the whole thing into jeopardy," an innovator observed. Nenon added, "I personally learned about following your gut instinct. If you think there is an opportunity and you believe it's the right thing for the company, the right thing for your group, and the right thing for customers, go with it. It taught me about innovating like a startup, but at the same time, building consensus and teamwork."

Leaders of Sun's improvisational troupes go right to the audience for ideas about how to shape their plays. A Sun innovator explained how this interaction speeded the development of a set of technologies called Java TV: "We formed expert groups to help us define where the products should be going; we engaged the best and brightest people at customer companies to make sure that we had a good view of where things were going. One of the technologies we targeted involved extending Java as a technology base for television sets. Of course, Sun is not in the TV business. So we pulled together a very broad set of companies: cable TV, the broadcast networks, developers of TV shows, advertisers. Over the course of about a year we had customers directly engaged in helping us to define the shape this technology should take for the television industry." Java TV technologies came on the market in mid-1999.

Sun's Internet mail server was another venture that "lived and breathed with the customer," observed Stuart Wells, senior vice president of infrastructure products for the Sun/Netscape alliance. "Customers were very demanding. They needed unique software architecture." The mail server project's funding needs (in the tens of millions of dollars) had been underestimated, but feedback from prime customers such as Pacific Bell convinced groups around Sun that it was worth keeping it going. Rapid prototyping with customer input paid off. Sun began in April 1997 with just an idea, shipped its first Internet mail server in November 1997, and released its Solaris server for ISPs in February 1998, partnering with Netscape. It reached a number 2 position in the industry, with 15 million mailboxes sold the first year, Wells reported.

The toughest audience is often the people within Sun. "You can put together a proposal," an innovator explained. "You can go up the chain and sell it, and let's say somebody way up top says, 'OK, this is a good idea, let's do it.' But that's all that happens. Your work starts right then all over again, to really get it done. And that's a big challenge. You start all over again with a whole different set of characters to try to convince them one at a time." Effective improvisation requires constant communication. It takes great actors, star performers: "If you don't have a visionary, dynamic person who can get out and sell the thing within the company, it just fizzles because there is no real provision to make it happen." Once people demonstrate their own strong and unwavering commitment, however, the support is there: "At the end of the day, whoever speaks louder at Sun, and whoever has more perseverance, ends up prevailing. People keep coming back at you, trying to see if there are any chinks in the armor. You have to be 100% convinced."

A Sun norm requires that people commit to projects after they are argued out, even if they do not necessarily agree. "Disagree and commit" is common parlance within the company. "We have a saying about this: 'You agree and commit, you disagree and commit, or you get out of the way.'" Another: "We will argue vehemently over whether something is the right thing to do, but once people make the decision to commit, we're committed. There is no going back. We don't feel like we have the right of infinite appeal. People don't necessarily have to agree, but we do like them to say 'I will support this.'" Disagree and commit is community glue for a company that fosters individualism.

"We do a lot on gut feel," one innovator noted. "We do a lot of fire hose things where there's just so much that we want to do, and there's so little time. All of us, I think, define the speed of execution as success." A Sun product development head, who had worked for a competitor that was now losing business to Sun, contrasted the "aim, aim, aim" style of his former employer to Sun's preference for "fire, fire, fire," saying that Sun takes more risks and is better at self-correcting. People are quick to point out the ways in which Sun is not perfect: silos and territoriality, battles about change involving "blitzkriegs" and "helmet bumping," the need to develop stronger process disciplines, and the danger of complacency setting in to middle ranks because of Sun's success. Still, a leader said, the company will keep innovating: "We know we have to do it. We have the fortitude, we're willing to pay the price of the 20-hour days and the driving people to change because of where we want this place to be in three years."

From the Outside In: Silicon Valley Plays London

Sun's home territory in Silicon Valley is eight time zones away from London, one-third of the way around the world. But Reuters, a venerable media company faced with the threat that the Internet would wipe out its core business, brought Silicon Valley to London. In 1999 and early 2000, Reuters's CEO Peter Job announced a series of new strategies aimed at putting the Internet at the center of the company. "Reuters is undergoing a fundamental transformation," a Credit Suisse First Boston analyst exclaimed. "It is morphing into a CMGI-style hybrid, combining a cash-generative operating company with a flotilla of new media growth assets. Reuters has a track record of nurturing growth second to none in the publishing market."[8]

Morphing sounds instantaneous, but in fact, Reuters's ability to change from an Old Economy company to a New Economy company is the result of years of improvisation that eventually created a new script. One of the lead actors—and he is often theatrical—is John Taysom, founder of the Reuters Greenhouse Fund. The mission of the Greenhouse is to imagine the future of the business information world, to find the companies that are creating that future now, and to support their growth while giving Reuters access to technology with the potential to put Reuters out of business. "We dream our worst nightmares and then invest in them," Taysom said.

Reuters traces its history back to some pigeons. In 1850, Paul Julius Reuters used carrier pigeons to transport stock market news across a seventy-six-mile gap in the telegraph line between Berlin and Paris. Once a complete telegraph link was established, Reuters moved from pigeons to cable, eventually using the underwater wire under the English Channel to transfer information between the London Stock Exchange and the continental exchanges. Reuters's product offering later expanded from telegraph-based international exchange of general news and financial information to carrying private telegrams and financial remittances. Radio further transformed Reuters's business, adding broadcasts of commercial price quotations and exchange rates. By the 1970s, Reuters had developed the largest private communications network in the world.[9] In the early 1980s, Reuters developed technology to permit bidding and selling over its network—in essence, creating the first virtual foreign exchange market trading floor and B2B online exchange.

London's Fleet Street, a center of journalism, still has a lot of pigeons outside, but inside Reuters's headquarters the information flow is virtual. Employees call Reuters the world's oldest online company, because it provides its services over proprietary networks without printing or distributing any tangible products; its only bricks-and-mortar asset is its London building. In 1999, Reuters had annual sales of £5 billion, over 16,000 employees worldwide, and a market value of $25 billion (U.S. dollars).

REUTERS'S TALENT SCOUT

In 1982, John Taysom joined Reuters as a salesman and was sent to Bahrain, where he sold Reuters's services to banks and insurance companies. But the customer base for Reuters's products in Saudi Arabia was limited by government regulation. "All you could do was exploit technology," he recalled. He began using his understanding of technology to help transform Reuters's infrastructure into what would later become an open, standard-based transactional network. By the time the Internet began growing in prominence in the mid-1990s, Taysom had become a resident expert in the areas in which Reuters's proprietary network and the public Internet were technologically similar: caching hierarchies, edge caching, and proto-XML systems. Navigation, security, and performance were still better over Reuters's network, but if the Internet caught up, Reuters would be in trouble. Why would customers need a proprietary network if they could get what they needed over open public networks?

Taysom had been commissioning small technology firms to build projects for Reuters, but he began to see that small technology development projects (on the scale of £50,000 to £100,000) were distracting for the small companies, stifled their potential to innovate, and generally gave Reuters yesterday's knowledge. He observed that innovative Silicon Valley companies were run by "serial entrepreneurs" and "compulsive innovators" who jumped from project to project in search of the next best thing. Instead of telling technology companies what to do (through contract work), it made better sense to follow startups toward the next discovery (through investment)—and do it fast. "If somebody got to one of these companies before we did, invested and locked us out from the new technology, that would be a huge risk to Reuters," he explained. And he didn't want the companies' last thing, he wanted their next idea. "It isn't what they're doing, it's what they intend to do, that's the secret. The secret is don't talk about what they're doing—the old rock star thing—talk to them about what the next thing is."

To get closer to center stage, Taysom moved to Silicon Valley in 1994. David Ure, Reuters executive board member, and Buford Smith, head of Reuters's new media business, had purchased Teknekron Software in Palo Alto, California, for Reuters in 1994 for $124 million; Teknekron supplied information management systems to financial trading rooms. Smith, Taysom's boss, was also a visionary who agreed with him that the Internet would fundamentally transform Reuters's business. But dedicating Taysom to the Silicon Valley scene was seen as little more than a networking job, of little relevance for Reuters. To convince Smith to move him to California, Taysom found out what flight he was going to be on from London to New York and purchased a ticket for the seat next to him. Every time Smith tried to fall asleep, Taysom pitched him about the idea. Despite shared views, convincing him was "painful, painful stuff. But we got the job," Taysom recalled.

Once in Palo Alto, Taysom kept his eyes open, hung around, and met the future rock stars. Grabbing pizza one day, Taysom found himself sitting next to Marc Andreessen, co-founder of Netscape Communications. Another time, Taysom read an article in the Stanford University student newspaper about two young entrepreneurs who were running a search engine/Web indexer called Yahoo! from a space on Stanford's campus. Taysom had used the online service and saw that Yahoo! could produce one of the major threats to Reuters's business: improved navigation over public networks. He telephoned Jerry Yang and David Filo to suggest that putting Reuters news on their index would create stickiness—and to explore a marriage.

Yahoo! didn't want to sell the company, and at first, Reuters's London decision makers didn't want to invest. "When we started to talk with Yahoo, there was nothing," Taysom recalled. "They had no process. They didn't own the code. There was no agreement with Stanford. They were two guys still at university and no staff. They used to do a night shift, so they'd be sleeping on and off for four hours until they got the work done." Taysom argued potential benefits from a deal with Yahoo!, including a possible new business model, as Reuters had never earned revenue from advertising. (Reuters sold content to some new media companies such as AOL and CompuServe, but both were private ISPs, and the revenue stream was similar to Reuters's old media business.) In November 1995, he finally won approval from the Reuters board for a $4 million investment, but Yahoo! accepted only $1 million.

Taysom assumed an advisory role on Yahoo!'s board and worked out of an office at Teknekron. Taysom observed that Yahoo! wanted to build a custom finance feature for its online users, and suggested that Teknekron would make a great platform for the new service. Yahoo! was interested, and a deal was struck. Teknekron reconfigured its product for the Internet, growing a new business selling its application infrastructure to other major portals and online players. (Eventually, Taysom convinced Teknekron CEO Vivek Ranadivé to spin off the software half as TIBCO.)

Suddenly, the unfolding story took a dramatic turn. It was almost *Death of a Salesman*. In early 1996, Taysom was fired. Yahoo! had yet to go public, and Taysom's networking was not producing tangible results. "It was not regarded as a money-making scheme, it was a getting to know people and getting to understand it scheme," David Ure said. Taysom recalled: "They called me to New York and said, 'Look, John, you're a nice guy, but you're very expensive, and you're out there in Palo Alto and there's no revenue coming out of this, so I'm afraid you're fired.' My wife was in crisis, my nine-year-old son was at school, our house in London was on a two-year let so we couldn't go back to it, and we couldn't stay where we were because we had no green card. I'll tell you, life was pretty bleak."

Feeling defeated, Taysom boarded a plane back to California. "I arrived in Palo Alto, and the phone rang. It was one of the guys from London, who said, 'Look, old chap, about this firing thing, you know, a bit of a mistake, really, and we'd like for you not to be fired, really, if you wouldn't mind?'"

The Greenhouse Fund:
Theater for Staging Improvisations

The next act resolved the crisis. Taysom stuck with Reuters, and the Reuters Greenhouse Fund was born. Soon Reuters's investments began to pay off handsomely.

Yahoo!'s IPO in April 1996 brought an $848 million market capitalization the first week. TIBCO went public in 1997, raising $110 million, and by 2000 it had a $20 billion market capitalization. Increased traffic on the Internet brought Reuters revenue for its content. As Yahoo! grew, so did other online portals seeking Reuters news, and Reuters news found itself available on about 900 websites, viewed by an estimated 40 million users a month. Brand recognition followed. Until Yahoo!, Reuters's news service was not well known in the United States; not long after the deal, a Reuters London executive visiting Palo Alto was impressed that his taxi driver recognized Reuters as a media company. Advertising revenues were a more tangible benefit. "We built a whole new business from the germ of an idea," Taysom remarked.

The Greenhouse's focus on navigation continued beyond Yahoo! with an investment in Infoseek (automated navigational tools). Next up was VeriSign in December 1996. Taysom had lobbied to get VeriSign to work in areas essential to Reuters (technology for authentication on the Web) even before its founding in May 1995, holding out the promise of possible investment.

Taysom returned to London in 1997. By the start of 1998, the Greenhouse had invested in eight companies, and five had already gone public (including Yahoo!, SportsLine, Infoseek, USWeb, and VeriSign), giving Reuters £10 million from a partial sale of stock. Reuters's executive board began to give Taysom and his growing team more and more freedom to improvise. For 1998, the Greenhouse generated £26 million in realized profits; now, it was significant enough to be reported separately from the rest of the Reuterspace division in which it was housed. The first half of 1999 brought as much as the full year of 1998 (10 percent of Reuters's total profit), and by the first half of 2000, the Greenhouse had brought in 17 percent of Reuters's total operating profit—more than the whole of the Greenhouse's 1999 realized profits. The fifty-two portfolio companies in mid-2000 included fifteen IPOs, six trade sales, and no write-offs.

As California opportunities became expensive and promising technologies sprang up elsewhere, the Greenhouse looked globally, to Asia, Israel, and Europe. Taysom found the Fantastic Corporation in Zug, Switzerland, and was instantly reminded of California. "The CEO is bouncing all over the place, he's irrepressible. You walk into their office, out in the boondocks, and there's this bit of Silicon Valley, with people doing wacky things and wacky colored chairs." In April 1997, Reuters agreed to sell its content to Fantastic and enter into a strategic partnership, taking an equity stake in March 1998. (Fantastic went public on the Frankfurt Neuer Markt in September 1999.)

Reuters made minority investments of $1 million to $7 million and forged a marketing agreement with each company. Reuters maintained an option (like Most Favored Nation status) to adopt the new technologies for its own products. The Greenhouse invested in themes important to Reuters's future. In addition to navigation, Reuters targeted security (Entegrity in Sweden), performance (Fantastic Corporation in Switzerland, for multimedia distribution software), mobility (Phone.com in California), and unique niche content around which to build new product (SportsLine in the United States). There were small investments in key portals (Yahoo!, StarMedia, GO/Infoseek), investments in companies whose technology helped Reuters provide rich e-mails, and investments in companies that provided added functionality to enhance Web content (VeriSign for authentication). The companies were to operate independently, even if Reuters owned a majority share. In 1999, Reuters acquired 100 percent of VentureOne, a provider of online venture capital information. Reuters supplied daily news to VentureOne for redistribution over the Web, but stayed out of daily management. "The thread that runs through all this," Taysom said, "is to turn the risk of technology into opportunity by being the first there."

The Greenhouse "works on long-term transformational horizons that are probably on a 10 or 15 year basis, which is way beyond our normal planning horizon," said Keith MacBeath, Reuters's director of strategic planning. Time frames are only one difference between the Greenhouse troupe and its mainstream Reuters audience. So Taysom brought the executive audience into the act.

In 1997, Taysom began a yearly tradition of flying Reuters's top management to Silicon Valley to interact with portfolio companies and potential ones. Startup CEOs from about thirty companies educated the executive board about new technological possibilities over two days. Taysom called it boot camp for the executive board and reported that they loved the presentations and the fun. David Ure dubbed the California retreats an "intellectual health cure": "If my colleagues never go near Silicon Valley and only read about these things in the newspapers, they think that financial markets exist without the benefit of technology."

Playful activities were mind-expanding. At one of the first events, Taysom borrowed electric cars from General Motors (not yet released to the public) and took the board to a parking lot at TIBCO, where some of the executives raced the cars. They saw how fast the cars went, but understood that they were still too expensive because they were held back by a lagging technology (in this case, batteries). At another one, a portfolio company CEO gave a presentation about technology in the financial industry, surprising members of the executive board with the depth of his insights. When he finished, "he was seen headed for the lavatory to change out of the suit that he had changed into for his speech," Ure laughed. "He made a tremendous impact on the more stodgy members of our team."

The Greenhouse's unfolding technology dramas were increasingly visible to the Reuters mainstream. Associates traveled through Europe giving speeches to Reuters employees, such as sales managers in Geneva, generating excitement about the Greenhouse. A daily online briefing kept senior executives informed. And when InterTrust went public in July 1999, the tenth Greenhouse company to do so, Reuters took over London's National Portrait Gallery for a big cocktail party. Invitations read "Reuters Celebrates its 10th Greenhouse IPO" (though the newspapers got it wrong, headlining "Reuters' 10 years of investing"). Following that celebration, Reuters began discussions with merchant and investment banks about the viability of floating the Greenhouse as an IPO (while still emphasizing technologies that serve Reuters's core business).

Greenhouse staff operate informally and collegially. Weekly pitch-and-decide meetings by videoconference include everyone in Greenhouse offices in London, San Francisco, Paris, and Singapore. The meetings are designed to get people to challenge one another and to make decisions fast. "It's a small team which is very distributed," Greenhouse CTO Marc Goldberg said. He enthusiastically described the Reuters culture as one where "if you want to do something of value to the company, you can do it. People have an incredible amount of freedom—more than in any big company I've worked for or heard about. As long as you can make a sensible business case, anybody can do what he wants. It's very unique in that regard. It's very organic. Each of us can do stuff, can mutate, and experiment." The Greenhouse exhibits qualities of the dotcom culture I described in chapter 2. Lights are on at the Greenhouse almost all night—most employees stay until around 9 P.M., some until midnight.

Every Greenhouse staffer must ask of every potential investment, Does this fit Reuters's theme? In the tradition of improvisational theater, tangents and digressions are permitted as long as they make sense in the end. Investments must be viewed as potentially useful to either a Reuters product or the company's future growth, so there is encouragement to find a customer within the mainstream business for portfolio companies.

One example of the importance of being on theme is Persistence. The Greenhouse was approached in 1997 by Persistence Software, a San Mateo, California, startup whose caching technology to transfer data between back-end computer systems and the user interface promised to decrease lag time in online transactions. Taysom found the technology interesting, but risky. He told Persistence to find a customer within Reuters, to ensure the technology was relevant and valuable. Persistence began speaking with Reuters's Instinet division and forged a strong relationship with Duncan Johnston-Watt, Instinet's development head for global fixed-income markets. After six months of due diligence and product trials, Johnson-Watt asked the young firm to provide additional functionality for the Instinet core product. For Persistence, adding synchronization capability strengthened its products. Instinet fixed income went live quite successfully, using Persistence for maintenance and support.

The Persistence relationship was a first move toward a new approach. It departed from the Reuters tradition of handling development in-house and buying only finished products from outside vendors. The story of Persistence and Instinet was publicized internally, and other Reuters groups began to adopt this development model. Reuters Television incorporated Virgage's technology to catalog and search video content as well as make it interactive over the Internet.

The Greenhouse funded projects to jump-start incorporation of new technologies in the Reuters mainstream, for example, paying for a project using Digimarc to watermark sports pictures on the Web to prevent copyright infringement. Taysom said, "Every time we make an investment of five million bucks, I put aside about $50,000 for Reuters to work on a pilot to demonstrate use of the technology. If you invest in VeriSign and do nothing, nothing happens. But if you show that it can be used for journalists when they're filing stories from the war front to authenticate the author, that's powerful."

In 1999, CEO Peter Job announced that Buy, Don't Build would become Reuters's new strategy, the result, in large part, of Greenhouse activity. The idea is to stimulate even greater use of technologies on which Reuters has an option. Instead of doing everything themselves, Reuters now partners with cutting-edge technology firms. This is a way to "avoid the turkey farm," a Reuters staff member said, referring to a story Sun's Scott McNealy liked to tell. The story describes the leader of a large high-tech company who proposed to horizontally integrate a turkey farm in order to reduce the costs of Thanksgiving turkeys for employees. (Any turkeys at Reuters are disappearing like the pigeons.)

The Internet is now at the center of Reuters. In early 2000, Job announced that Reuters would "make the Internet work for the financial services industry." Many developments are underway, including a personal portal development with Microsoft dubbed the Reuters Digital Dashboard, targeting the financial services sector; Microsoft's treasury department is an early user. The Greenhouse, which has already helped spawn two Reuters's businesses, Reuterspace (because of the Yahoo! connection) and TIBCO, is accelerating efforts to help the rest of Reuters utilize portfolio companies' technologies. Security authorization, personalization, real-time data, and streaming news are being moved from Reuters's private network or infused with Internet-based thinking. "Internetization" of Reuters's product lines began with milestone-based 100-day and 200-day projects, a set of short-cycle quick wins and rapid prototypes.

By July 2000, the Greenhouse had become a promotional tool for the mainstream organization. Job, a strong supporter from the beginning, regularly calls Greenhouse staff to ask how he can open doors for them on his trips to Scandinavia and elsewhere around the world. Taysom spins future scenarios for the executive board and others, about Reuters's role as the "adrenaline in the Global Digital Nervous System." He offers visions of daily e-mail wake-up calls to customers around the globe, with a professional broadcast cooked to order through e-TV, and then the ability to make a transaction immediately based on the news.

"The Greenhouse has been a kind of beacon, a symbol of hope. John has been a maverick, a pioneer," reflected Reuters's chief strategist MacBeath. "At times in the past five years, that spirit has been difficult to find elsewhere in the organization. That's changed now."

Keep the Raves Coming: Options on the Future

A culture oriented toward tomorrow is a culture of improvisation. What we've seen at Sun and Reuters is e-culture at work. Improvisers inside Sun and from outside Reuters invented strategy through exploration and action, betting in different ways on the network technology theme. Sun's theater is the company itself, its development labs and culture of entrepreneurship; Reuters's theater is its investment fund. The culture of experimentation is similar, however. In both cases, there has been plenty of suspense, and not just because no one knew how the technologies would turn out—John Taysom was almost fired. Both companies' improvisers know how to involve their audiences; for Sun, these are their customers and partners, for Reuters, the mainstream core business. Both companies have profited handsomely from their rapid bursts of innovation and have exercised their options on the future ahead of the pack.

Improvisational theater suits the Internet. The technology itself stimulates rapid changes. New ideas spread quickly, like viruses moving and replicating without human agency, giving rise to viral organizing and viral marketing. In complex interactive systems, leaders cannot wait to get everything aligned before they permit action to begin, for two big reasons. First, they are unlikely to control all the relevant people, some of whom will do what they please anyway. Second, delays are costly. Network economics (first mover advantages, winner-take-all races) tell us endlessly that if you don't get in early, you can't get in—or at the least it will cost you much more to enter later. So any action is better than no action as long as there are rapid adjustments. Speedy response is more important than early perfection.

Thus, companies and their actors must shed attitudes and behaviors that stop the action. They must eliminate the most common action-stoppers: expecting the perfect plan; waiting for full information; fear of making a mistake; defensiveness about previous commitments; rigidity about the right way to do things; arguments that drag on endlessly, even after decisions have been made; interruptions and distractions that sidetrack the venture; and knee-jerk no's, especially for anything not clearly articulated or well understood.

E-culture speed, learning, and change is aided by the opposite—attitudes and behaviors that are action-accelerators:

• Act on a promising theme, even without a full script.

• Get going and keep moving before you know everything.

• Tolerate a few false turns, and recover from them quickly.

• Embrace goals for tomorrow, letting go of attachment to yesterday's commitments.

• Experiment with new ways to do things that are different from how it's always been done.

• Surface disagreements quickly but then commit to action.

• Stay on course, swerving around obstacles.

• Be comfortable with uncertainty and think IKIWISI—"I'll know it when I see it."

Pacesetter companies allow small groups unfettered by mainstream constraints to try out new scenes that confront the threats to their business—their worst nightmares. They are not so much figuring out how to make money today as looking to be where the money will be made tomorrow. Pacesetters evolve quickly because they start earlier, and that gives them the appearance of morphing instantly. But even "instant" success takes time. Many creative experiments, small and large, flow together to make a new strategy possible. The best companies are prepared for change because they are always preparing for it. That's what helps them create waves of raves—not just one success, but imaginative leaps and bold transformations.

5

❖

CONNECTING THE DOTS
Nurturing Networks of Partners

Because getting big fast is the watch-word on the Internet, there's a huge premium on getting new deals done. It's like there's grab, grab, grab, grab, grab, grab, and worry about making it work after the fact.

—Ron Sege, Executive Vice President, Lycos

You have to build trust before you have the right to ask to create unique things in the marketplace with your partner.

—A Hewlett-Packard global alliance manager

MANY PEOPLE HAVE WRITTEN ABOUT the rise of dynamic networks of partnering relationships on land and online. But not many have recognized the extraordinary shift of consciousness it takes to live in such a world. The sensation is like improvisation for diverse audiences in several places who are watching multiple performances, with each set of actors needing to react simultaneously to all of the audiences. You're part of one drama but must be alert to opportunities in all of the unfolding stories, because any one might change your own play for the better or for the worse. It is *Alice in Wonderland*'s croquet game on several planets at once. The array of changing configurations is dizzying. Anything can be connected to anything else anywhere in the known universe (and beyond), and the race is to get *big everywhere fast* by maximizing as many connections as possible.

The promise and power of the Web is the opportunity to create new possibilities by joining forces. Startup dotcoms use partnerships to scale quickly. Wannadots envision themselves as hubs for new kinds of marketplaces that will transform competitors into partners. Front-end partnerships extend on-screen links, opening vast worlds of information and activities that make every entry point a portal, a doorway to the new universe. Back-end partnerships provide the best and latest technology to keep the network humming. Financial partnerships create portfolios of companies that can benefit from shared resources or collaboration. Outsourcing partnerships connect organizations to a new pool of capabilities.

There is already a dictionary's worth of new names for Internet Age networks of partners: *b-webs, e-hubs, e-partners, ecosystems, eco-nets, netglomerates, e-form organizations.*[1] But it is hard to define and catalog something that consists of complex overlapping relationships in constant motion and change. Some business networks have been called by the Japanese term for collections of intertwined companies, *keiretsu,* but unlike the Japanese version, most are neither long term nor exclusive, nor are the boundaries sharp. For example, williams-sonoma.com partners with gift registry Della.com, and Della partners with Amazon.com, while Amazon's kitchen store competes with williams-sonoma.com. We are watching not fixed forms but a universe in formation, with new planets and new ways to group them visible through our telescopes every night. Cyberspace is as much a frontier as outer space.

Collabronauts: Explorers of the Evolving Partner Universe

The explorers and guiders of the universe of connections are departments of a new sort, charged with the search for collaborative advantage: offices for strategic alliances, business development, communities and affiliates, or partner relations, just to name a few. Staffing these new groups are a range of deal makers, ambassadors, and diplomats who can make or break partnerships. They are known by prosaic corporate titles, such as Hewlett-Packard's global alliance managers, and sometimes they are merely glorified account managers, just one step beyond sales representatives. But they are at the vanguard of a new role and a new function. They journey from their home organization to forge new alliances and to explore creative opportunities, like leaving their home planet to bring back knowledge of strange new worlds and new civilizations. I call them *collabronauts*.

The best collabronauts are good at making connections, both human and intellectual. They are constantly on the lookout for new ways to benefit from combining forces with partners. They venture into unfamiliar territory, make deals, and return with knowledge that transforms their home world. They bring organizations closer together, introduce people, and build relationships among groups that can initially seem like aliens to one another. They work out complicated dealings between and among partners, manage rumors, mount peace-keeping missions, and solve problems. They use personal friendships and powers of persuasion to sell people on the importance of helping a partner. They convince their colleagues to forget the old rules and try something new, something that comes with having partners.

Let's follow collabronauts on a tour of their universe—the three major types of networks of partners that are most relevant for the evolving Internet Age. The first can be thought of as a solar system: a set of planets and moons in orbit around a single blazing star, a company that provides energy for its satellites but also exercises enormous power over them. The second type is looser, and there is no clear center of control; it is more like a galaxy, in which many entities operate independently but can be connected by a smart company that sees how to get value from many possible connections among them. The third type resembles a space station: an assembly system for launching other companies into cyberspace, in which complex but shifting multipartner collaborations produce end solutions.

Consider this tour the continuation of the strategy drama we began in chapter 4. We will stop to see some actors we've met before—Amazon.com and barnesandnoble.com, Reuters Greenhouse, Sun Microsystems—and watch others in action. And we will derive lessons from the challenges of collaboration that can apply to all sorts of business and nonbusiness partnerships. Cyberspace gives us a particularly clear view of how to connect the dots, because that is where the actions of collabronauts can make or break the business.

A Star Is Born: Creating and Managing
the Amazon.com Solar System

In just a few short years, Amazon.com created a network of partners bound by its strong gravitational pull. For dotcoms such as Amazon, such partnerships are essential parts of their business model from the start. Amazon gets high marks for great partner deals, but it took time for the company to learn about the nurturance of partners once they were in orbit. The deal is not the relationship, and that's the first lesson for collabronauts. That said, we'll begin with the deals.

"Choosing a network is like choosing a mutual fund: some are better than others," a California dotcom executive said. "You don't want to be left standing alone, but you also want to secure the best partners you can and avoid being pulled down by someone else's poor partnering. You can have a high level of confidence that Amazon partners will be desirable ones."

With about 18 million unique items for sale and nearly 20 million customers, Amazon.com is the star able to form a solar system. Founder and CEO Jeffrey Bezos claimed in February 2000 that Amazon had passed a tipping point: "When you reach a certain critical mass of customers, you very quickly have a long line of people who want to associate with you" (and, the reporters added in their own words, will "give you boatloads of money for nothing more than a few square centimeters of your Web page").[2]

Amazon's mission was to become the ultimate online shopping destination—the place to find anything. After its 1997 IPO, Amazon inked deals with portal and online communities (e.g., Yahoo!, iVillage) to acquire customers; paid commissions to thousands of associates selling Amazon products on their sites; and bought companies such as PlanetAll for services (address books, calendars), Junglee for technology, LiveBid for live event auctions, Back to Basics Toys for expanding its toy offerings, and Tool Crib of the North for building its tool business. By mid-2000, Amazon made money not only through its flagship book store, but also its online stores for music, DVD and video, electronics, software, toys and video games, tools and hardware, and lawn and patio supplies (all shipped from seven U.S. distribution centers) as well as a set of marketplaces that included auctions and z-Shops. Through z-Shops, small retailers could sell their wares from a tab on Amazon's website on a nonexclusive basis for a monthly fee ($9.95 and up, depending on placement within z-Shops) and a percentage of each sale. Such opportunities made the Amazon.com network a platform for building new businesses. Operations Vice President Jeffrey Wilke declared, "I want to have people lining up out the door begging, begging, begging us to fulfill their operations."[3]

AMAZON COMMERCE NETWORK: THE DEALS

Amazon.com's retail engine includes strategic partners, called the Amazon Commerce Network (ACN), in which Amazon holds an equity stake. ACN partners are American dotcoms, generally in product lines that required special regulatory knowledge and licensing (such as pharmaceuticals or wine) or a different distribution infrastructure (such as furniture or cars). Some promised to pay handsomely for valuable real estate on Amazon.com's home page. Big deals that Amazon closed in the first months of 2000 theoretically represented about $500 million in potential revenues over the next five years, most dropping to the bottom line— but only if the partners can survive; to pay Amazon, partners must grow in a tough market for dotcoms. (The international sites, Amazon.co.uk and Amazon.de in Germany, did not yet include similar partnerships.)

A strong customer focus is among the most important criteria for Amazon's choice of partners. This is reflected in numerous company stories. "Two weeks ago a new partner was signed, and when the management teams met, the top Amazon executive said, 'if anyone *ever* thinks we are not focusing on the customer in a given decision, call me and tell me,'" an Amazon manager told us.

Drugstore.com was the first such big e-commerce equity partnership. Amazon took an initial stake in 1998, before drugstore.com even went live; Amazon was then selling only books and CDs, an easy pick, pack, and ship process. Silicon Valley venture capitalists at Kleiner Perkins Caufield & Byers were investors in both companies.[4] Amazon business development staff told us that drugstore.com was considered a perfect partner because of its minimal overlap and maximum leverage. Particularly valuable was drugstore.com's partnership with Rite Aid, consummated in mid-1999, for fulfillment through its 3,800 bricks-and-mortar stores and access to the 50 million customers covered by corporate pharmaceutical benefits plans through Rite Aid's benefits division. Drugstore.com even located in Seattle to work closely with Amazon during its prelaunch phase. The drugstore.com relationship, as Amazon's first partnership of this kind, caused Amazon to start identifying liaisons—a relationship manager from business development, a marketing contact, technology liaisons, and some ties in operations.

In January 2000, Amazon expanded its equity by $30 million to bring its total to a 28 percent ownership of drugstore.com. At the same time, drugstore.com agreed to pay Amazon $105 million over a three-year period in a marketing deal that included a tab as Amazon's health and beauty store, activated in April. Other big deals consummated in the heady days before the spring 2000 stock market downturn involved equally large payments. They included Audible (downloads of spoken word programs, such as radio shows and audio books). The Audible relationship reflected numerous synergies; Amazon customers bought books with the same cultural, informational, and entertainment content as Audible's audio programming. "We'd like those customers," Audible founder Don Katz said to us. Living.com paid the most: $145 million over five years to get a tab on Amazon.com's home page, and an Amazon equity stake of 18 percent in living.com, with warrants to purchase 9 percent more. But the fees never materialized, and living.com closed its website and filed for bankruptcy in August 2000. Amazon also had minority equity stakes in a variety of other e-commerce companies, including Pets.com (now defunct) and online gift registry Della.com.

By late summer 2000, ACN relationships involved online promotion and hot links, but not shopping integration yet. Partners explained on their websites how their policies differed from those of Amazon.com. Although a tab on Amazon took health and beauty customers to drugstore.com ("a trusted partner") and Amazon backed purchases from drugstore.com, items could not be put in the same online cart or purchased with one click. Even without full online integration, there were considerable benefits to operating in the Amazon.com solar system. Amazon drove traffic to partner sites and promoted them through e-mail campaigns and in-box swaps (promotional materials included in Amazon shipments). Amazon had a conversion rate up to twenty times that of portals such as Yahoo! or AOL, because Amazon's customers went online to buy, not just surf. One analyst cited a 20 percent to 30 percent increase in e-commerce traffic almost immediately after a major deal with Amazon.

Outside observers wondered, however, why drugstore.com had to ante up another $105 million to get on the tab in January 2000, after having already given up almost a third of the company to Amazon. The initial terms of the deal with drugstore.com and other ACN partners were signs of Amazon's might as the blazing star exerting enormous gravitational pull over many planets. We consistently heard in confidential interviews what others said publicly: that Amazon knew its power and wanted deals on its own terms—"they-win" instead of "win-win," one insider said. Others said that Amazon promised huge marketing benefits informally, sometimes beyond the characteristics enumerated in the contract, leaving the possibility that some partners might let their expectations go unchecked and imagine help that might not be forthcoming.

Amazon had learned from early experiences that flexibility was important and that contracts should be open to renegotiation and reinterpretation, company representatives said. A good example was Amazon's decision in August 2000 to restructure its agreements with certain ACN partners, accepting lower cash payments because of the perilous finances of some dotcoms. Internet property evolves and takes on new functions, so valuations fluctuate. In a business arena taking shape through improvisation, some things could not be known at the beginning. Amazon's deals included an understanding that companies would work together on how any evolution changed a partnership. Market conditions in late 2000 made it unlikely Amazon would get paid unless they helped their partners.

Amazon insiders said that flexibility worked both ways. Amazon did not restrict partners' product offerings, even if they competed with Amazon's own shops. Living.com and Amazon's kitchen store both sold microwave ovens. The decision not to limit what partners sold through the tabs on Amazon.com (up to some limits of too much competition) was a result of the focus on customers, to make it easy to buy, and was also considered a way to help partners succeed. Some partners were grateful for the freedom to link to Amazon competitors, but they were not happy to see z-Shops and auctions listing products in their category and going online for a tiny fraction of what they had promised to pay.

Amazon's Collabronauts: The Execution

When contracts are not set in stone and things are in flux, relationships take on increased importance. That's when collabronauts enter the scene.

Top-level interaction happens as needed at Amazon; Jeff Bezos or another senior executive sits on the board of some partner companies, although there are no guidelines for when Bezos talks to which partners. Below Bezos, a large department is dedicated to every aspect of partner relations. Mark Britto became vice president of strategic alliances in June 1999 when Amazon acquired Accept.com, which he had co-founded. Two business development officers, Doug Boake and Owen Van Natta, are responsible for both customer acquisition and retail partnerships. There are parallel partner management teams for portal partnerships, such as AOL, Yahoo!, or Excite (about seven account managers handling two to three relationships each), and for the ACN (about nine partner product managers). After the deal, partner managers work with cross-functional teams to implement site connections. A large technical team supports ACN; other areas throughout the company, such as fraud or accounts payable, are pulled in as needed.

ACN managers track partners to ensure that they meet performance expectations, and they look for new ways to develop existing partnerships. Amazon marketers work with partner marketers for co-promotions. Partners are treated in some ways as insiders, but they are not invited to Amazon meetings.

Todd Edebohls, a veteran of Beyond.com and Pointcast who came on board in October 1999, calls himself "Owen's boy" (referring to Owen Van Natta) because his job is varied and difficult to pin down with one title. "The current system has been in place for about 30 minutes and will continue for another five minutes," Edebohls joked. Reflecting dotcom style, he said that Amazon has no bureaucracy, titles do not mean much, people take on broad roles and float among tasks (he did projects for Britto or Boake), support staff are tapped as needed, and there are no traditional secretaries.

Edebohls handles perhaps 8 percent of the work for big partnerships (such as those with drugstore.com or living.com) and all facets of the deal with next-tier relationships, such as a link to 1-800-flowers on the first screen of Amazon's gift ideas page. He also reviews incoming plans. (When we spoke, he was about to decline a proposal for a Web-based hot coffee delivery service.) Other groups within Amazon approach him for help with finding, valuing, and structuring potential partnerships. He has become a mentor to other collabronauts.

After initial due diligence, partner quality control is done through objective measures such as "four nines," or 99.99 percent uptime (though Amazon's four nines during fourth quarter holidays set a precedent most companies couldn't match). Strategic partners are given firm metrics, with some third-party evaluations and online reporting. Dialogue in regular meetings is expected to work out problems before they reach a critical point. There are "serious repercussions" if partners do something that might compromise Amazon's image with customers, we were told.

Monitoring is important, because partnering brings risks. Outages reflect negatively on Amazon. Customers clicking through Amazon to a site that goes down think of it as an Amazon outage. Amazon alarms go off when a partner site goes down. When a partner does not have the resources to fix it fast, Amazon uses its own backup systems. But Amazon staff then go to the partner to make it clear that it is unacceptable for Amazon to have to fix customer problems on its behalf.

Negative press for any links could also stick to Amazon. Despite posted policies prohibiting sites that encourage violence or criminal activities from becoming associates, in 1998 one reporter found that the neo-Nazi Utopian Anarchist Party was an Amazon affiliate, with the Amazon logo placed next to the group's black-gloved fist on its home page. Public airing of partnership woes is also a risk. After the debut of the sothebys.amazon.com site in November 1999, the result of a ten-year partnership agreement, the elite auction house became embroiled in controversy and operational problems that sunk its stock (and the value of Amazon's 2 percent stake, which slid from $45 million to $16 million in less than a year). *The Wall Street Journal Europe* reported that the working relationship was "choppy. Several senior Sotheby's employees weren't given access to the co-branded site while it was under construction and weren't told the launch date until about a month before the site went live. There has also been tension over whether Sotheby's is saving the best material for its own site." Still, both partners told the reporters that the relationship was working well.[5]

Direct relationships among partners in the Amazon network are "more organic than prescribed," insiders said. Everybody talks informally, but there are no big partner gatherings. Nor is there formal partner training or online training resources. But Amazon is often very helpful to partner companies as issues come up. Edebohls estimated that he received phone calls from business development teams at partner companies about once every two weeks, with questions about a company or a strategy.

In the early years, much of the communication occurred by phone, but e-mail was also used, and there were pivotal face-to-face meetings. One partner's leadership group appreciated Amazon's mentoring on website priorities, technology architecture, and marketing approaches. For Bonnie Neulight, senior director of business development at Pets.com, visits to Amazon for training were a benefit. She was given an office for the day, and eight or nine people came in and out to run her through processes, templates, and economic models, with offers to review her plans later. This helped the Pets.com partnership. (Even Amazon's assistance could not keep Pets.com alive; it died in the fall of 2000.)

SOLAR POWER OR SUNBURN?

In mid-2000, when jitters over the future of business-to-consumer dot-coms pervaded the media and the markets, partners publicly praised Amazon's marketing clout, and analysts applauded the bottom-line contributions from the partnerships—while waiting to see what the company did to tap potentially huge advertising revenues and achieve profitability (in the midst of speculation that Amazon would turn out to be a shooting star, not a permanent fixture). Privately, partners were wondering how they would fare in the e-commerce shakeout and whether they would derive their full value from the partnership. Amazon's promotions tended to support what Amazon owned in full. This was a good business decision in Amazon's short-term interest. But if the network was important in the long term, could Amazon afford to have any worried partners? We heard speculation that Amazon's gravitational pull could weaken if there were any alternative universes to explore, or that the network could spin out of control if Amazon continued to be stretched too thin to nurture key partners. But others said that Amazon had learned to create long-term relationships. And Amazon's willingness to restructure deals in August 2000 was a hopeful sign for cash-strapped dotcoms in the Amazon orbit.

Successful partnering requires a shift of perspective from the individual company to the community—from what's good for me to what's good for the network. Each strong two-way partnership fits my classic "8 I's that Make We,"[6] and each rift derives from a shortfall in one of them. Apply the I's to Amazon, and we see a pattern of formal strengths and a few informal weaknesses:

- *Individual excellence:* Amazon gets high marks for being and choosing the best.

- *Importance:* The top tier of partners were more strategically important than others, but sometimes not always treated that way in terms of time, attention, and resources.

- *Investment:* Amazon and its key partners invested in each other, especially financially.

- *Interdependence:* Some partners competed to sell the same things. Would they need each other long term?

- *Information:* Performance measures were in place, but in some cases, such as the Sotheby's incident, there were concerns that not enough strategic information was shared. Future business-building opportunities could be missed without a spirit of open disclosure.

- *Integration:* Joint marketing was carried out, but Amazon was still working on operational integration with its key partners. Communication among various levels of partner companies was still just informal.

- *Institutionalization:* Relationships were governed by contracts, and collabronauts were assigned to watch over them.

- *Integrity:* No one questioned Amazon's integrity, but there were concerns that deals and activities were always skewed in its favor. Was there enough trust and mutuality? Amazon demonstrated concern for its partners when it lowered payments it would accept, but was that deep concern or a recognition that they might not get paid at all if the partners failed?

Amazon has the forms in place for deals, while its partner nurturance is still evolving. Before the dotcom bust, it could operate by the "golden traffic rule." Lycos Executive Vice President Ron Sege defined this for us as "he who has the most traffic on the Internet rules. So the biggest players drive the hardest bargains, which might be win-lose deals." This gap provided an opportunity for Amazon's nearest competitor to mobilize its own collabronauts for a cyberspace battle. As the dominant player, Amazon could afford to throw its weight around with partners; barnesandnoble.com had no choice but to develop a collaborative approach.

Star Wars: Attracting New Planets by Innovations in Partnering

Question: Where does an 800-pound gorilla sit? *Answer:* Anywhere it wants to. But if you're number two and a lot lighter, you try harder—and compete hard to be a better partner.

Amazon.com was already a Web giant by the time barnesandnoble.com was launched in March 1997. It was becoming clear that portal partnerships were valuable for bringing traffic, and both barnesandnoble.com and Amazon sought them. Barnesandnoble.com became the exclusive online book store for AOL members in February 1997, but Amazon landed deals with the top portals Yahoo! and Excite in May 1997, followed by AltaVista, Netscape, and AOL.com (AOL's public site). "Amazon had already staked out many of the largest partnerships," an executive from barnesandnoble.com reported, "so when we started going after partner-ships, we had to target the next tier."

Because it was a subsidiary of an offline company with no ability to tap the capital markets, barnesandnoble.com did not have the capital that post-IPO Amazon.com had to make deals, and there were concerns that it was falling behind. "We lost Netscape in head-to-head negotiations. We were never even pitched AOL.com because they knew we wouldn't pay much for it, because we were already on the proprietary network," another insider recalled. "So we went on a tear signing big deals." Barnesandnoble.com partnered with Lycos, gaining links to every Lycos property. Eventually it became the exclusive bookseller for many other major content sites, including MSNBC, CBS SportsLine, TicketmasterOnline, iQVC, GoTo.com, NYTimes.com, CNN.com, and Blue Mountain Arts, and it partnered with ISPs such as Earthlink and Mindspring (which later merged) or AT&T WorldNet.

To gain an advantage against Amazon when negotiating with potential partners, the business development team created innovative partner nur-turing practices. Dedicated account executives were told to "own" the partnership and be responsible for managing and improving the rela-tionship through collaboration and other innovations. "Instead of my signing the deal and throwing it over the wall to some support group," a former manager reported, "if I signed a deal, then I had to manage that deal." Barnesandnoble.com was able to show potential partners that the attention it would give to the relationship would be greater than that which Amazon.com could provide.

Barnesandnoble.com's business development team met on a regular basis to discuss the company's partnering strategies and new ways of nur-turing their partners. A coordinated effort with specific goals helped the collabronaut team stay focused and efficient. Communication and inno-vation were key. "If you just put up your logo on your partner's site, or just put up a banner, it's not going to work. You have to be working these relationships," one team member explained. "We were constantly thinking about how to integrate e-commerce into our partnership relationships. For example, now, if you type in 'cooking' on Lycos, the results page that is returned to you has a button that reads 'For more information on cook-ing, go to barnesandnoble.com.'"

As other innovative ideas blossomed, barnesandnoble.com started beating Amazon for deals, even when Amazon offered more money. Barnesandnoble.com partnered with Be Free, a provider of performance marketing technology, to become the first to monitor the traffic and transactions of users. Barnesandnoble.com could thus provide its partners with robust reporting of online activity, a leader said. "We could see that the link we put on a partner's site generated 3,000 clicks yesterday. Lycos could see that too. You could then tell whether the customer actually bought the book after coming directly from Lycos. Partners could see what people were doing, from the impressions on their site all the way through to what they bought. Over time, our reporting technology made deals more effective because it changed the way our partners looked at advertising."

A website, www.affiliate.net, served the barnesandnoble.com network from the first day of its affiliate program (a series of links similar to Amazon.com's e-tail partnerships). Affiliates could access the online reporting system, generate links, get barnesandnoble.com logos, and get advice on everything from graphic design to how to optimize a page for search engines. When the barnesandnoble.com team realized they were spending too much time answering the same ten questions from their various partners, they added a FAQ (frequently asked questions) service to affiliate.net. By utilizing the partnership website to handle more of their work, the collabronaut team was scaling itself, virtually. They were thus able to maintain strong relationships while spending more time seeking future opportunities.

"We were always looking for ways to be a better partner, to do things that were not so obvious. We were trying to stay in front of the curve and be creative. If all you do with your partner is put on a logo, it's very easy for them to swap you out and put someone else in, but if you do more to integrate yourself into your partner's business, then it's harder for them to swap you out," an executive explained. Meanwhile, collabronauts at barnesandnoble.com heard industry buzz that "Amazon was an arrogant company; they didn't return phone calls or e-mails. When partners compared us and Amazon, they saw that we were responsive and had an affiliate network. Amazon saw this. Eventually, they put up online reporting and changed their partnership program to look like ours," one recalled. Amazon, for its part, could write off this criticism as sour grapes from a lagging competitor.

The online bookstore Star Wars began to look like a never-ending daytime drama, in which partners change places with each peak or valley in the capital markets. In September 2000, Amazon parted company with Yahoo! by mutual agreement, so that Amazon could focus instead on its AOL relationship. Yahoo! announced that barnesandnoble.com would become a featured merchant on its site and its partner for a free Internet service, in a deal that was said to surpass the one with Amazon. But Amazon retained a prominent position on Yahoo!'s properties outside of the United States. Meanwhile, each worked hard for Most Favored Partner status.

Imagine that. Here are two fast-moving Internet companies competing to develop the best ways to nurture partners: more communication, more attention, more ways to embed themselves in each other's business, and the use of the Web for routine matters in order to free time for face-to-face exploration of strategic possibilities. This is indeed a new mindset. But it is still only the simplest form of partnering.

Note that the Amazon and barnesandnoble.com model involves a central star attracting partners one by one. Collabronauts must also know how to leverage an entire network by strengthening connections among a whole galaxy of independent systems. That's what some of the galaxies known as netglomerates are trying to do, and that's what Reuters Greenhouse has accomplished. If Amazon demonstrates the power one company can wield over its partners, Reuters shows how to build network value without having much power at all—a masterful example of what collabronauts can accomplish when they work on the relationships, not just the deals.

Galaxy Quest: Finding Connections to Strengthen Networks

In June 2000, CIBC World Markets initiated coverage of *netglomerates* as a new kind of entity—an interconnected network of independent companies that share something beyond the same funding source.[7] One of CIBC's picks was CMGI, owner of 83 percent of AltaVista and investor in over seventy Internet companies (including Lycos, Engage, and Furniture.com), but the list could include other incubators and strategic investors trying to build a business network, such as Softbank's Hotbank Incubator, divine InterVentures (featured in *Red Herring* as a model for new economic networks, or eco-nets), or Cambridge Incubator (my personal favorite because of its "startup hotel" near MIT that features exercise and sleeping facilities for a 24/7 lifestyle, and its commitment to community service). Reuters Greenhouse wants to outperform all of them.

We met John Taysom in chapter 4 as a master improviser; here we continue the story in his starring role as one of the world's first card-carrying collabronauts. Network principles were embedded in the Greenhouse approach from the beginning. Although individual investments had already paid off for Reuters during the hot IPO market, even-greater long-term value could come from combining technologies for Reuters and the marketplace. John Taysom felt he had to grow and strengthen the entire network fast.

One-by-one connections brought first-order advantages to each Reuters partner, such as the Yahoo! deal. But network power doesn't come just from bilateral relationships between a focal company and its allies, one by one. That system is too easy to break apart, because partners can be picked off individually. Real network power comes from strong ties among every partner in the system—a multiplicity of links reaching in all directions. The Greenhouse wanted to enhance the value of the whole network, not just make money from individual investments. This is a competitive advantage that is as difficult to create as it is to duplicate.

NETWORK ADVANTAGES:
LINKING PARTNERS TO EACH OTHER

By early 2000, more than half of the companies in the Reuters investment portfolio were dealing with each other. They were under no obligation to do this. It was an opportunity, a benefit, created by Greenhouse collabronauts through persuasion and contact making. And network value was part of the sales pitch to attract companies to the Greenhouse: there were fifty-two companies in the portfolio that could access Reuters, Reuters customers, and each other.

Greenhouse collabronauts brokered relationships across companies. The biggest triumph was the May 3, 2000, announcement by three portfolio companies, Persistence, Adero, and Equinix, in collaboration with giants Cisco and Sun, of the launch of a joint product, Dynamai, to run the Internet faster, in direct competition with stock market favorite Akamai. Taysom explained that this was not an accidental synergy: "Although we don't know precisely how the bits will fit together, we can see that they are building blocks. And if we can see that, they can usually see that in each other. We are trying to maximize the intellectual capital they create, whilst minimizing the financial capital that gets deployed."

Senior associate Norman Fiore had handled the Adero deal himself. "The fact that they're working together without us is cool. They're doing something bigger already, just by combining themselves," Fiore said. On his next trip to California, he paid a visit. "When I invested in Adero, they said that they could create this product, and now they needed Persistence for what they promised that they were going to do anyway. So I asked if they had been lying to me," Fiore laughed. "No, they weren't lying. They were planning to use a different partner. When they found out what Persistence could do, they decided to forget the other partner and work with Persistence."

Such partnerships among portfolio companies not only strengthen the network but also offer preferential access for Reuters because of its relationship with all the involved companies. Fiore said of the Persistence, Adero, and Equinix partnership, "Those guys are making a huge play. If they need a content partner or a financial partner, well, all three companies are Greenhouse companies, all have a great relationship with Reuters. Who are they going to pick?"

By the end of 1999, network multiplier effects were starting to emerge. New companies were attracted to the Greenhouse because of the portfolio, and newcomers, in turn, made the network even more attractive. In the spring of 2000, Reuters became Forbes's first outside investor in its long history as a privately held media company, and now Reuters had a relationship with Forbes.com that was valuable to portfolio companies that transmitted content. A new investment in Zapper Technology, a small Israeli company with bases in Tel Aviv and New York, could benefit several other portfolio companies, so collabronauts convened meetings of technology heads to explore new ties. Such instant partnerships would speed Zapper's business development to everyone's benefit, dramatically reducing partner search time.

SKIING AND SCHMOOZING

Convening network members for face-to-face meetings is an important step in building personal commitment to network value. In March 2000, Reuters put on its biannual InfoWorld conference, a by-invitation event in Geneva, Switzerland, for over 3,000 customers and prospects. Leaders from about fifteen portfolio companies stayed all two weeks to meet executives from around the world. Then the Greenhouse took about twenty of them to Megeve, France, for skiing in the Alps. Rides in horse-drawn sleighs to the opening dinner were the starting point for two days of relationship building. "This may sound very soft, but we deliberately had no agenda for that meeting," Taysom reported. "We were informal about it. We made no presentations. We arranged some ski guides. We got everyone to introduce themselves and their companies the first day. It was up to them to figure out how to find each other."

One of the biggest surprises to Taysom was that everyone seemed to like each other, since there could have been friction among outspoken, individualistic entrepreneurs. "Once I got to meet the other CEOs and founders in Geneva, I was so impressed with that group," recalled Carla Gardepe, founder and chairman of Harmony.com. "I was amazed when I realized how much synergy existed." The CEOs got along so well that a number of potential partnerships emerged from the mere fact of being in one room, in one place. The idea for a Persistence partnership with Adero and Equinix, for the Dynamai venture to run the Internet faster, was seeded on the ski slopes.

The Greenhouse team provides the links for the network in all of their activities. Seats on the boards of portfolio companies provide not just a way to watch investments and help the companies develop long-term strategies, but also a vehicle for connecting companies with one another. Taysom is considered a consummate matchmaker and network builder. Fiore praised Taysom's skills: "I've seen him in action. It's amazing. John gets at least 10 or 15 companies into every single conversation. He's always selling companies. If he's on a board, you can be sure that, at every board meeting, he's cross-pollinating companies and giving phone numbers, giving names, saying you should talk to this guy, you should talk to that guy." Fiore followed Taysom's model, playing network connector for the companies on whose boards he sat. Generally, the Greenhouse gave the board seat to whoever did the deal, knowing that it would jeopardize the relationship with a portfolio company to switch representatives after the deal was consummated.

Compared with network connecting, mentoring is a minor task, but Greenhouse collabronauts try to help with operations or finance where they can. Taysom's own job ("and God knows, it's a tough one," he said) is to mentor some of the CEOs. Startup companies were more receptive to mentoring after the devaluation of Internet and technology stocks in the spring of 2000; before that, Fiore claimed, they wouldn't listen. "Last year they didn't need nurturing, it was enough to have a business plan, get the money, and off they go," Fiore recalled. "Some of the biggest trouble I had among my boards was to tell these guys to stop talking about the bloody IPO. They had no sales, they had no performance, and all they wanted to talk about is the IPO."

More naïve portfolio companies were steered to the more experienced for direct mentoring; for example, Carla Gardepe taught some of her fellow portfolio companies about raising money, at Taysom's request. "As he sees different talent sets amongst his portfolio teams, he shares that around," she said. In early June 2000, the Greenhouse took a further step toward connecting the network via a website for communication among portfolio companies.

We asked repeatedly whether anyone worried that Reuters would find itself out of the loop and losing control as portfolio companies connected directly with each other. Everyone in senior Greenhouse positions gave variations of the same answer: Reuters could not lose control, because it never had control in the first place.

That comment about control (or rather, its absence) is worth emphasizing. The goal of a network is not for one part to maintain control but to maximize the power of the whole, the value that can come only from interconnections. Reuters is just a minority investor in each company, so it has to work through persuasion, dangling enticing opportunities. More important, the whole point of the Greenhouse is to create a network that can get stronger and stronger on its own. It could even rise to threaten Reuters's core business. "Bear in mind that we're investing in companies whose technology in some sense is a threat to ours. If you combine those technologies, you can create large components of Reuters' infrastructure. It's potentially quite subversive," Taysom said. But as part of the network Reuters itself had spawned, Reuters would own the future either way.

The Greenhouse's connected galaxy evolved from a mere financial portfolio to a synergistic network. It could do this because of explicit attention to enhancing relationships, from social events to the search for opportunities to make connections. It shows that humanity, not technology, powers strong networks of partners.

Cyberspace Stations: Master Builders of the Network Universe

The third kind of network acts more like a space station, because companies assemble the components that together provide end user solutions. The dotcom-enablers whose platforms, systems, services, and solutions are the biggest space stations in cyberspace are also the vanguard in collabronaut best practices. Giants such as IBM, Cisco, Hewlett-Packard

(HP), and Sun, as well as numerous software and professional firms, are inventing new kinds of multipartner networks.

For any particular Internet or technology venture, the set of partners might be entirely different. The fluctuating links I see among companies remind me of the combinations in the board game Clue: Rolls of the dice put random groupings together ("Mr. Green in the library with a knife"; "Miss Scarlet in the kitchen with a candlestick"). Getting to know one company inevitably leads directly to the others (except for arch-enemies Sun and Microsoft), as I discovered from numerous cross-references and intercompany dealings sprinkled through my team's fifty-five-plus inter-views in three major computer companies alone. IBMers respect Hewlett-Packard for HP's leadership in deploying global alliance managers (GAMs). HPers envy Sun Microsystems for Sun's aggressiveness in attract-ing some of the best partners first. Everyone admires Cisco Systems—and Cisco is IBM's biggest partner and model for its other alliances.

Complicated multipartner activities reflect an Internet Age shift in power from hardware to software to services. End solutions are more important than which company's name is on the bits and pieces of components, and all must connect seamlessly for users. "You cannot afford to be in only one network. You have to be in many to satisfy the needs of the marketplace," declared Towney Kennard, IBM vice president of strategic alliances for the Cisco relationship. "Customers want the very best of the very best; they demand that you work together. That makes it much more difficult. Because on any given day, your ecosystem partner can be your customer or your hated enemy. Who would have thought that you'd see IBM and Sun standing on a stage together, getting an award for a joint solution?" (Or that IBM would have a team dedicated to Microsoft applications despite direct com-petition with Lotus, IBM's software star.) "E-business has made these types of partnerships more necessary and more critical to everyone's success."

An exploration of best practices in this kind of network resonates with lessons from Amazon.com, barnesandnoble.com, and Reuters Green-house to provide a job description and how-to guide for collabronauts.

The Collabronaut's Role:
Competing through Collaboration

In new dotcoms, collabronaut jobs are often highly desirable because of a heavy emphasis on deal making that can bring enormous resources (as in Amazon's relationship with drugstore.com). Win one of those deals and you too can be a hero. In large established companies, however, the job is not always desirable: big responsibility, little formal power, and shared glory because so many people have to get involved with the partners.

Hewlett-Packard staff know how difficult it is to shape the role. Alliances are important to HP's future, as computer group president Ann Livermore told us emphatically, and its GAM force of global alliance managers is an industry model, evolving from high-level salespeople trying to push HP hardware to diplomats brokering new business initiatives. But new CEO Carly Fiorina inherited a program in need of fixing; in mid-1999, HP's global alliance program had shifting objectives, confusing performance measures, and an exodus of staff frustrated by lack of support.

Powerful sponsorship makes a difference in whether collabronauts succeed, because they are not only cultivating partners but also are competing, like barnesandnoble.com was, to get the most attention from them. HP was slower than Sun to partner with Internet companies, our informants at both companies told us. One HP alliance manager had suggested as early as 1997 that Internet service providers could become important partners for HP, but the company took nearly two years to act on this idea; by then, it was almost too late because many of the ISPs had already built their businesses on competitors' platforms (Compaq for Windows NT and Sun for UNIX). Sun's Douglas Kaewert told us how Sun did it. Kaewert had left HP for Sun in the mid-1980s (as employee number 73), rising to vice president of market development and developer relations by the mid-1990s. He valued HP know-how, he said, but at Sun he received high-level support for fast action.

Kaewert's team was responsible for recruiting independent developers to create software solutions on Sun's platforms and for supporting them through the process. In the past Sun looked at these developers as customers, selling them compilers at a profit. In 1997, Kaewert kept running into venture capitalists who would tell him about interesting little companies that could use network delivery systems. After a dozen or so company visits, Kaewert and his bosses, CEO Scott McNealy and President Ed Zander, saw a trend Sun could capitalize on. "Some of it is just fortunate timing," Kaewert recalled (though HP was also a Silicon Valley powerhouse surrounded by the same possibilities). "The ISP community was growing, Sun had products for network environments. A lot of people, including venture capitalists, were pointing ISPs to Sun. We were eager to work with them, because we saw them as the future." Sun quickly established partnerships with many ISPs, giving them development software for little or no cost in order to be their platform for cyberspace. And that's one way that Sun could stake claim to "the dot in dot-com" while HP was still picking a strategy.

By mid-1999, HP had launched several e-services partnerships. Millennium Commerce, for example, incorporated HP and Cisco hardware, as well as software from multiple vendors, to provide a solution for Internet service providers; ISPs could offer their small and mid-sized business customers a complete electronic commerce package, including website, order-taking ability, and credit card processing, without the need for purchasing all of the hardware and software components. But Sun continued to move aggressively to establish alliances. In mid-1999, Sun announced a Preferred Integrators Initiative, developed by Sun in alliance with Netscape, to implement e-commerce solutions for client companies. Five major global system integrators—Andersen Consulting, CapGemini, Computer Sciences Corporation (CSC), EDS, and PricewaterhouseCoopers—would participate; CSC and EDS issued their own press releases noting that they had been named in this program. This list included some of the same partners HP was counting on for its e-services strategy, and others with whom HP had had difficulty partnering. Judi Hirsch, Hewlett-Packard's GAM for CSC, tried to stay close to CSC during this period, arranging numerous meetings between CSC and HP experts to talk about development possibilities. But Sun kept moving. In early 2000 it announced a new kind of partnership with e-integrators, stimulated by its relationship with e-strategy consulting firm iXL, to offer end-to-end e-business solutions.

This brief tour of a few Sun and HP relationships sounds like the announcement of a contest: *Sun's ahead—no, HP's pulling even—no, there goes Sun again.* But as I dug into the inner workings of companies who are all among the best in the world at what they do, it became clear that keeping score minute by minute or even partner by partner is not the way to assess the performance of networks. The race to line up partners is won not just by the swift but by the caring. It is won by those who do the best job of nurturing their networks. Five lessons emerge from the experiences of the most effective collabronauts.

LESSON 1: FOCUS ON THE FUTURE AND BE OPEN TO DISCOVERY

The value of networking derives not just from today's deal but from the promise of greater discoveries tomorrow—the premise behind Reuters

Greenhouse. Decisiveness helps a company grab partners, but trust helps them leverage partnerships.

When relationships involve explorations of new possibilities, they are necessarily open ended. IBM's alliance with Cisco was so big that it received four months of U.S. Justice Department scrutiny before it could take off in January 2000, yet the formal contract was relatively loose. It listed activities and mutual investments but was "still pretty open to allow us to flow with the market," IBM's Kennard reported. Nondisclosure agreements covered technology still in the research stage, but the IBM stance is to be open with strategic partners. Joint development teams were launched early in 2000 to work in four or five key areas to leverage Cisco and IBM expertise and technology, with six-month to two-year time horizons. "You're sharing your company's strategy for that marketplace, you're sharing what you have on the product pipeline," Kennard said. "And if you both modify products based on what you've heard, you'll have a knockout punch in 12 months. If you don't share data you could wake up a year later saying, 'I wish I had known your product was going to do that, because I would have done this.'"

Loose contracts without trust and without a commitment to mutual exploration can simply frustrate partners. For many dotcoms, the "win" is often the deal itself, signing a particular partner, but that's not the real payoff. The big multipliers come later, after joint innovation.

Trust derives from people honoring commitments to other people whom they know on a personal basis. Face-to-face meetings with no formal agenda can help build relationships that foster trust. In the spirit of improvisation, such gatherings permit unscripted conversations that lead in surprising directions, such as the major Internet venture seeded at the Reuters Greenhouse ski trip. HP global alliance managers frequently arranged dinners, golf outings, and other get-togethers. Social relationships by themselves are not enough to sustain a partnership. But they can serve as "an enabler and a catalyst for the access, trust, and information needed to create a joint vision of real customer impact and value," said Feyzi Fatehi, head of alliances for the Asia Pacific region. One HP sales executive, "a real deal guy," gave another GAM a hard time about the money she spent flying across the country for face-to-face meetings, until he was questioned by a CEO about why they got together only when there was a problem. "You have to build trust before you have the right to ask to create unique things in the marketplace with your partner," another GAM said. "Because we've walked on coals for them since August, they're willing to recommend us even though this project hasn't come through yet. So there's residual payback from having built this relationship."

Collabronauts can point to many wins for trust-based space station alliances. The IBM-Cisco partnership got big fast. In the first four months of 2000, IBM had booked almost ten times the business done with Cisco in all of 1999. Customer wins had big revenue consequences for both, and IBM's Kennard said that customers feel they get better end-to-end solutions because IBM and Cisco are partners. Sun's Kaewert pointed to design wins and to happy new customers committed to Sun, because of Sun's ISP partnerships. For example, Bidcom, which serves the construction industry with Web-based management tools, moved from a Microsoft Windows NT platform to Sun's. "When they dump your arch competitor and install you—it doesn't get more gratifying than that," Kaewert exclaimed.

But how does one quantify return on trust? HP can track how much hardware was sold through system integrator partners that also served as hardware resellers, but there is no way of knowing whether the hardware would have sold anyway, or how much leverage the alliance team creates for HP. Is HP's Global Alliance Program just marketing overhead? Unless the partnership creates a unique product or joint venture, it is difficult to know whether marketing activities, or even joint sales presentations, lead to hardware sales. Multiple partners make this even more complicated; whose actions bring the revenues? And internally, how can HP apportion credit to alliance diplomats who nurture the relationship compared with sales reps who are deal closers? "Because results are difficult to measure, it becomes a leap of faith to support the alliance program. There's only so much a company is willing to invest on gut-feel," commented John Fogarasi, an HP Asia-Pacific GAM. But visionary leaders see the value; HP's new CEO Carly Fiorina showed immediate support for the Global Alliance Program as part of HP's innovation strategy.

Lesson 2: Devote Resources and Pay Attention

This sounds like a no-brainer, except that too many companies (and people) fail to do it. Nurturing networks of partners is not an idle task, nor can it be a diffuse general obligation. It begins with dedicated collabronauts—an investment of company resources in the partnership's future—who then ensure that other people pay attention to the partner too.

In mid-2000, the IBM-Cisco alliance had fifteen people on the IBM side and about forty-five people on the Cisco side dedicated to nothing but each other. They also could draw on bigger pools of talent throughout both companies. IBM's Kennard divides his team into three groups. A marketing and new business development group is responsible for driving new business between IBM and Cisco. A maintenance services group monitors IBM's ability to maintain Cisco products sold by IBM in any part of the world (162 countries, Kennard said), taking into account different processes used by each company. A small operations team ensures that things work smoothly and puts out fires when they don't. Beyond Kennard's team, dedicated liaisons in other departments (such as Legal or IT) are knowledgeable about the relationship. Cisco's IBM alliance office dedicates an even larger number of people to joint development opportunities with IBM. And the two companies' alliance offices have weekly conference calls.

Internet startups that race for deals sometimes forget two things— that the relationship must be nurtured, and that nurturing uses up a lot of bandwidth. There is no substitute for high-level attention, and that comes with human limits. It takes time to pay attention to the needs and the plans of partners. (Just add up the hours the Reuters Greenhouse staff spend in board meetings, not to mention private meetings and other gatherings, when each one is responsible for five or six companies.) But let's say everyone gets someone to watch over them; who is that someone? Strategic partners do not want to be courted by a powerful executive and then handed off to a lowly account manager. High-level executives—corporate vice presidents—are in charge of IBM's and Cisco's alliance teams, with large staffs under them. A company can title all of their alliance managers vice presidents, or even senior vice presidents, but then partners wonder who gets to see the *really senior* senior vice presidents and the CEO.

Sun's partner iXL was singled out by Gartner Group as one of the best at alliances because of the attention devoted by senior people throughout iXL to partners; iXL helped Sun design its e-integrators and iForce initiatives and received Oracle's "newcomer partner of the year" award. "We are changing the way people view and measure alliances," said Lorin Coles, iXL's senior vice president of worldwide alliances. His matrixed team of twenty-eight high-level people representing all parts of iXL is there to ensure that partners get attention on a daily basis, not just when being courted for the Big Deal.

Even a large company can run out of bandwidth or fail to give key partners special attention. HP relationships were nonexclusive in 1999, and HP offered the same services and benefits to any company that could meet alliance criteria. Some of its most important partners disliked finding that their competitors were getting the same attention and deals. HP computer sector president Ann Livermore, a strong sponsor of alliances, called this a way to be fair, to offer a level playing field. But other people felt that an emphasis on fairness had kept HP from making the strategic choices it needed to make. They complained that HP had become the "Switzerland of alliances," a neutral country that would welcome anyone. One executive, eager for change, declared that "fairness is way overrated. Because we've spread ourselves too thin, we've been outgunned by the competition." Some were concerned that HP was not making the investments it needed to make with its partners. One alliance manager said: "We are not aggressive enough in loaning technology and transferring expertise, providing strong joint marketing programs and awareness. We talk a lot at the management level and have very good relationships there with all of our alliance partners. But at the pragmatic, project manager, sales representative level, we are not as strong as our competitors are. We don't provide enough real sales tools and support."

Lesson 3: Get Embedded in the Partner's Business

The race is not just to implement together but to improvise together, to become embedded in partners' offerings. This means getting close enough to partners to become a part of their business and then to help them succeed, which ensures a return on the investment in intimacy. Collabronauts are like live hot links among companies in a network. That's why HP's global alliance managers travel about 40 percent of the time and communicate all the time.

Sun collabronauts work with both technology and the commercial leaders of Sun's Internet and software partners. On the technology side, they help get Sun products built into partners' plans. On the commercial side, they help create demand for partners' products on the Sun platform through joint sales and joint marketing. Some are linked to Sun's PR bandwagon to give them credibility. Kaewert stressed the importance of both formal activities and informal communication: "We need to get relationships set up so that we are integrated into their business. One thing that I remember from HP is management by walking around. It's incredibly valuable just to show up and ask somebody, 'How is it going?' Then they know they're important. You can reinforce the things that we think are important."

HP alliance veterans felt that a secret of their success is *multithreading*—using many threads to tie many people together throughout partnership networks. The HP global alliance organization included long-service senior people with networks of personal relationships within HP, people who were skillful at finding the right people within partner organizations. One GAM said that "the key to success is not just a single person or alliance manager, it's technical people, marketing people, sales people, feet on the street. It's the collection of all of them coming together to create the impression that HP is the best partner. Then, later when facing a tough decision, the partner can easily say, 'Let's go with HP. They're our friends, and they're there when we need them.'"

Multithreading weaves a web of relationships connecting the companies. The Sun-iXL partnership is a good example. "Sun Lunch and Learn" events help iXL professionals meet local Sun staff over a meal. Sun competency centers within iXL spread knowledge and offer training on Sun technology. Sun and iXL executives meet for joint planning, and both partners attend each other's technical and business events.

The ultimate form of leverage is a small group of collabronauts getting enormous things done by mobilizing a network. Towney Kennard is an IBM vice president who managed 1,500 people worldwide in his previous job, and now manages just 15 in the Cisco alliance office—but he can drive much more business with 15 than with 1,500. His team can tap many groups within Cisco and leverage Cisco in other parts of IBM. E-business, Kennard said, forces managers to get over the ego trip of counting the people they own and focuses them instead on ways to help others succeed.

IBM collabronauts work on creating the right personal connections and the best online connections. The personal side begins with CEO Louis Gerstner's regular conversations with Cisco CEO John Chambers, which often include a few of their senior vice presidents. Technology helps, too. IBM developed a website for the Cisco alliance, covering rules of engagement, who to contact, and examples of successes. External sites connect customers with either IBM or Cisco, demonstrating the embedded nature of the relationship. Because websites facilitate information sharing, a smaller number of people can keep the threads moving through a larger number of partners, a function also served by barnesandnoble.com's affiliate.net and Reuters Greenhouse's extranet.

LESSON 4: EXERCISE DIPLOMACY

In contrast to the easy mouse clicks that link one site to another in cyber-space, the offline networks supporting those seamless connections can be riddled with tensions. Extraordinary diplomacy is required to handle the politics of partnerships.

Dealing with the challenges of *coopetition*—the fact that the same companies can both cooperate and compete[8]—is a big part of collabro-nauts' diplomatic portfolio. The word is hard to say, and the concept is even harder to execute. Not only can any one partner also be a competitor in some fields, but the connections of partners to bigger networks makes it highly likely that both a company and its partners will be working with each other's competitors. "The thing that causes the most heartache is when we announce partnerships with each other's competitors in the same space," IBM's Kennard said. "Cisco has partnerships with KPMG, Cap Gemini, Arthur Andersen, and we have partnerships with Lucent, Nortel and Alcatel. That's been the sorest point. The funny thing is that both of us will say 'well, you have partnerships with our competitors,' and we will say, 'yeah, but we don't want you to have one with that one.' You find that some are more sensitive than others. We don't have that worked out yet."

HP's alliance managers spend a great deal of time sorting out rela-tionships when partners feel that HP is crossing the fine line between friendly unrelated competition and attempts to drive them out of busi-ness. HP's software group developed alliances with some of HP's hard-ware rivals, including Sun Microsystems and Dell, while the hardware group formed an alliance with Computer Associates, which had an offer-ing that competed directly with HP software's leading product. When HP moved into the services business, Judi Hirsch had to spend the next few months trying to calm the fears of service provider CSC that HP was moving into its market space; then she had to do it again when HP changed the name of its services organization to HP Consulting.

Collabronauts monitor their own organization as well as the partner's for signs of trouble and intervene on behalf of their partners if competi-tion gets out of hand. Before their collaboration agreement, IBM and Cisco were "bitter enemies," Kennard said. Now that they are close friends, he continued, "Someone generally forgets that the war is over, and they mis-behave in the field. That happens on both sides. When you have two aggressive sales teams, you butt heads from time to time." One example of conflict: The IBM 2029 and the Cisco Metro 1500 were competing switches for high-speed networks, such as those used on Wall Street. When things got tense, Kennard convened meetings with internal groups involved with the technology, and then with Cisco. A technology comparison uncovered some differences in the switches, and a communique was issued to the field about when to lead with which product—and, when in doubt, whom to call. "That doesn't mean everybody's happy with the answer. But at least we know the rules of engagement," he said. That's a typical IBM problem-solving method: Gather facts, try to solve a problem through discussion with peers, take it up a level if necessary, and then communicate the resolution to the wider organizations, using the Web as a tool. The faster the communication, the less likely that rumors will circulate.

Rumors are a constant risk in partnership networks. The rapid changes on Internet time, and the ease with which information can spread, means that collabronauts are constantly explaining rumors or interpreting events for both partners and concerned members of their own organizations. Judi Hirsch's CSC contacts within the partner company had told her that CSC was planning the Sun announcement in a few days. By knowing this before public release, she could do advance work within HP to soothe ruffled feathers and maintain support for HP's own alliance with CSC.

Collabronauts are deployed on a wide range of peace-keeping missions. Some seem trivial, like the debates about the shape of the conference table and seating arrangements that delay summit meetings between countries. When one of HP's larger system integrator partners learned that they would be sharing the stage at an HP event with two small up-and-coming integrators, they decided to send a middle manager to the event instead of one of the company's top team, as they had originally planned, and the alliance manager had to sweet-talk them into sending the top person after all. Other issues involve more complicated diplomacy. For example, an HP sales representative in Asia called a GAM upon learning that her partner company was doing some consulting work for a customer it had been cultivating for a major hardware purchase. The sales rep was upset because now it seemed that the partner (the consultants) would influence the hardware decision as part of their consulting engagement. The sales rep wanted the GAM to get the consulting partner to push an HP purchase, but the partner wanted to appear nonbiased. The GAM had to smooth tense relations between the sales rep and the consultants.

Sometimes diplomacy involves saying No. Collabronauts must explain to partners why they cannot get something they want, without creating hurt feelings or damaged business relationships. Partners are not all things to each other—which is why they are part of a wider network in the first place—and their organizations are not a match for every occasion. At IBM, e-partner company A, which is strong in the United States but not in Europe, might ask for business opportunities with IBM in Europe. The IBM rep for company A would fly to Europe to talk to the executive responsible for that marketplace. If the IBM Europe executive said that IBM already works with company B, which has dominant market share, the IBM partner advocate would try to talk company A out of their hopes for an IBM Europe deal without jeopardizing the American partnership.

Without excellent diplomacy, partners can feel they are not getting everything they're entitled to, as we heard from some Amazon partners. As trusted partner advocates, collabronauts can also manage partner expectations.

Lesson 5: Master Internal Change

Collabronauts don't work on partner projects themselves; they mobilize virtual teams—often large global ones—for network initiatives. "The worst mistake that IBM has made with a partner," Towney Kennard said, "is when expectations go unrealized. That's when you think you've agreed at the top level, but when you go to execute, it falls apart." Things fall apart when they hit organizational barriers.

Sun's Kaewert encountered "antibodies at lower levels in the system" that had to be fought in order to get changes through for Sun's Internet partnerships. "You've got the top guys in the company—all of them— nodding their heads saying yes, yes this is what we want to do. But then you get down into implementation. There are thousands of people in this company; you've got to get many of them to understand and to change their practice." Kaewert's team had to interest people in the wider organization in helping Internet companies that were aliens in every respect: not exactly customers, instead beneficiaries of giveaways, paying Sun with equity, promising uncertain future gains. "The standard goaling mechanisms in the sales organization are at odds with what you want to do in the ISP community, which is get them hardware and software so they build their cool stuff on your platform," Kaewert said.

The further from headquarters, the harder Kaewert's challenge. "There is nobody in Asia Pacific who believes it's their job to implement things like this. They all have other priorities there, and we can't do it from here." The only way was to deploy more collabronauts to make connections throughout Sun and communicate like crazy. Kaewert's best persuader was a key marketing staff member comfortable dealing with engineers on technical matters. "You can't anticipate everything," she said. "There are bound to be questions. You've just got to go out there to meet with them, review everything, and let them ask away."

HP's alliance managers also have to convince people outside the alliance group to work on partner initiatives. It takes a strong personality and an ability to make friends to sell such people on the importance of the partners. Not everyone who controls purse strings understands the value that the partners can bring to their work. A global alliance manager reflected, "I think a smart GAM who has a strategy and a vision can get almost any resource within HP. The challenge is getting buy-in for what you want to do." That challenge is exacerbated by geography. "Distance creates opportunity for people to say no or just not reply. It's a lot easier for someone on another continent to not play along. You can't sit in front of them to convince them. Out of sight, out of mind," another GAM said. In a decentralized yet consensus-oriented company, getting input from people in many places makes it hard to operate at Internet speed.

It is often easier to entice partners to join a network than to convince the rest of the home organization to play along. One of HP's most dramatic successes eventually reached an insurmountable barrier and collapsed. The success follows the pattern I have already sketched—from trust to becoming embedded in each other's business. But the collapse is a cautionary tale that shows what happens when a collabronaut has a willing partner but unwilling colleagues and rigid walls inside his or her own organization.

For a time, HP's model alliance was its multiyear, trust-based relationship with German software giant SAP. In the early 1990s, SAP wanted to develop a minicomputer version of its enterprise resource planning (ERP) software, with Oracle as a partner for database infrastructure, and had approached both IBM and Digital for hardware before coming to HP. Hewlett-Packard won the deal because of its willingness to invest in the relationship. HP held frequent summit meetings with SAP Vice Chairman Hasso Plattner and CEO Dietmar Hopp to discuss strategies. A joint development center in Waldorf, Germany, enabled engineers from SAP and HP to work together on innovations that made the new R/3 product a breakthrough. HP helped SAP move to the United States, hosting SAP's American operations at their California offices until SAP could find space. HP and SAP created another joint engineering coordination center in the United States and worked together to land a deal with Chevron.

The relationship was trust based, recalled Peter van der Fluit, then HP GAM for SAP: "This is all about people making commitments to people. We started without a written contract. Eventually California forced us to write one. So we did—and immediately put it in a drawer." To honor SAP's trust, HP did not undercut sales of SAP's old product by urging customers to wait for the new HP version.

The partnership was so successful that SAP put a German HP executive on its advisory board, and HP promoted its SAP alliance team members (van der Fluit became worldwide marketing manager for alliances). Then the relationship was lost. HP's NT division (working on Microsoft Windows NT for desktops) didn't see an opportunity for SAP enterprise solutions on NT, so SAP went to Compaq, which soon became the number one SAP player on NT. R/3 had been developed by a UNIX-based group at HP. There were internal fights over UNIX versus NT software, which were handled by two different HP units, two different vice presidents, two different report cards. Years later, we were told, SAP leaders were still upset.

The SAP relationship was not the only one to fall through the cracks of HP's decentralization. In 1999, each of the major business divisions had separate alliance teams. Coordination across these teams was an additional complexity because divisions differed in goals and performance measures. And the GAMs didn't help, because the role of the GAMs was to maximize their own partner relationships. One said, "My job is to find the right decision makers in HP to support my partner. Personally, I don't care about the others." This separation sometimes led to decisions that were good for a division, but less than optimal for HP as a whole—for example, a services sales rep uninterested in helping with a big hardware partnership because it was too small a deal from his perspective.

Here was HP, mentioned by IBM's Kennard and numerous others as one of the best at alliances, struggling with internal change. Sometimes the biggest barriers to being successful in cyberspace lie at home, within one's own organization. To nurture and leverage networks of partners, companies must be open to changing themselves. (The same thing seems true of all strong human relationships.)

Becoming a Star Partner

There are many stars in the sky. Collabronauts connect the dots that turn those twinkles of possibility into recognizable constellations. Networks of partners are essential to success in the Internet Age. So leaders must spread awareness of collaborative advantage, and they must heed its lessons:

- Focus on the future.

- Emphasize discovery.

- Invest in relationships.

- Build trust.

- Devote resources.

- Pay attention at high levels.

- Get embedded in the partners' work.

- Weave many threads of human ties to strengthen the network.

- Exercise diplomacy.

- Remove internal organizational barriers to collaboration.

And then bask in the sunshine of close and strong connections.

6

◆

FROM CELLS TO COMMUNITIES
Deconstructing and Reconstructing the Organization

A community is like a ship. Everyone ought to be prepared to take the helm.
> —Henrik Ibsen, *An Enemy of the People*, Act I

Management fighting for its God-given territory . . .
> —CEO's response to interview question about the biggest barrier to change

THE SCENE WAS A CONFERENCE ROOM on the California coast filled with twenty senior executives of a large multichain retailer I'll call Brand E. To open discussion of future business challenges, I posed my favorite icebreaker question: Describe the sport that most resembles running this company. The first woman up said, "Gymnastics. We are all really strong and talented people. We practice and perform alone." The man on her right changed the game to a relay race: "We each have to be fast but then hand the baton to the next one in line." Finally, the head of global distribution begged to differ, naming the Olympics: "All of us represent our flag to big audiences, with lots of competition, so we'd better pull together."

Brand E is successful and widely admired, known for aggressive marketing and strong financial performance, and even for early bricks-and-clicks achievements. Yet its leaders are uncertain whether they were playing individual sports or coordinating a complex enterprise. Powerful external forces, from the Internet to globalization, are calling for a unified one-company response from Brand E. But getting every division to cede even a little bit of control seems nearly impossible. People are isolated in cells, the cells are stuck in silos, and it is hard for the cells to unite to become a powerful organism.

Like many others, this company embraced decentralization because of advice about how to be lean and speedy, focused and performance oriented. Less than two decades ago, management thinkers proposed a "new organizational paradigm." The outlines of the new model are familiar by now, even if less common in practice: flattened hierarchies, open boundaries, horizontal orientation, an emphasis on processes over structure. In the 1980s, that model encouraged a pendulum swing toward decentralization. Indeed, federations of nearly sovereign divisions were considered an improvement over centralized bureaucracies.[1] Technology from the same era reinforced the decentralization thrust. A PC on every employee's desk was considered empowering, even if each set of silos had different systems and different information and could not communicate with each other.

Then along came the Internet as a revolutionary integrating force, and the problems of excessive decentralization became apparent. In a global, high-tech world, organizations need to be more fluid, inclusive, and responsive. They need to manage complex information flows, grasp new ideas quickly, and spread those ideas throughout the enterprise. What counts is not whether everybody uses e-mail but whether people quickly absorb the impact of information and respond to opportunity. The Web creates an expectation of being able to find everything easily in the same place. E-business cuts across every organizational process. It can touch every function, affect every product. It can magnify mistakes and turn them into opposition of unprecedented magnitude, as I argued in chapter 1. For already-established companies, the Internet makes more urgent the need to present one face to the customer and link separate actors and actions for seamless integration. The Internet isn't just another channel; it is a medium that demands connections to all the other channels. When companies are embarrassed because they cannot accept returns from online sales in their physical stores, or when customer data residing in different corners of various silos cannot be retrieved to the frustration of those customers, it is clear that existing operations must be reconceived.

Companies pose organizational questions at two levels of sophistication. The narrow question: How do we structure our e-business unit? The broader question: How do we change our whole organization? The first is oriented toward presenting the best face to outside audiences. The second recognizes that the biggest challenge is inside.

Companies that are successful on the Web operate differently from their laggard counterparts. On my global e-culture survey, those reporting that they are much better than their competitors in the use of the Internet tend to have flexible, empowering, collaborative organizations. The "best" are more likely than the "worst" to indicate, at statistically significant levels, that

- Departments collaborate (instead of sticking to themselves).

- Conflict is seen as creative (instead of disruptive).

- People can do anything not explicitly prohibited (instead of doing only what is explicitly permitted).

- Decisions are made by the people with the most knowledge (instead of the ones with the highest rank).

Pacesetters and laggards describe no differences in how *hard* they work (in response to a question about whether work was confined to traditional hours or spilled over into personal time), but they are very different in how *collaboratively* they work.

Working in e-culture mode requires organizations to be communities of purpose. Recall the elements of community sketched in chapter 1. A community makes people feel like members, not just employees—members with privileges but also responsibilities beyond the immediate job, extending to colleagues in other areas. Community means having things in common, a range of shared understandings transcending specific fields. Shared understandings permit relatively seamless processes, interchangeability among people, smooth formation of teams that know how to work together even if they have never previously met, and rapid transmission of information. In this chapter we will see how the principles of community apply inside organizations and workplaces, sometimes facilitated by technology but also independent of it. And I will examine the challenges that have to be overcome to create organizational communities.

The greater integration that is integral to e-culture is different from the centralization of earlier eras. Integration must be accompanied by flexibility

and empowerment in order to achieve fast response, creativity, and innovation through improvisation. Web success involves operating more like a
community than a bureaucracy. It is a subtle but important distinction.
Bureaucracy implies rigid job descriptions, command-and-control hierarchies, and hoarding of information, which is doled out top-down on a
need-to-know basis. Community implies a willingness to abide by stan-
dardized procedures governing the whole organization, yes, but also voluntary collaboration that is much richer and less programmed.
Communities can be mapped in formal ways, but they also have an emotional meaning, a feeling of connection. Communities have both a structure and a soul.

In youthful dotcoms, the search for community finds its most important physical manifestation in the communal kitchen—a nice carryover
from the traditional role that sharing food has always played in community spirit and religious rituals. But the barriers to community also have
a physical symbol: the political and cultural walls that divide cells and
silos in established organizations. Before reaching the ideal of community,
people must tear down the walls of the past. And they must be careful
not to erect new ones when they start e-ventures.

The Walls of the Past: Divisional Dotcombat

People unaccustomed to seeing the world outside their silos have a problem understanding that distinctions and separations appropriate for physical space disappear in cyberspace. Some companies get it; others don't.

For example, Kraft's products, such as coffee, cheese, or gelatin
desserts, are lodged in separate divisions because of great differences in
sourcing, processing, storing, marketing, handling, and consuming; only
cheese bears the Kraft brand name. Yet, with the help of e-strategy marketing firm Digitas, Kraft linked all its brands on the Web using a Kraft
Kitchen concept—over protests from some of the business units, whose
autonomy was reduced. When a manager from Nestlé in Europe
approached me to discuss how online grocery sales in Europe might affect
Nestlé, I suggested an approach similar to the Kraft Kitchen, such as a
Nestlé dessert boutique. "We could never do that," he replied. The divisions were too separate, they didn't talk to each other, and brand names
for the same product differed across countries.

"Many, many organizations have independent business units not used to seeing the big picture," Digitas's Sheila Malkin observed. "People have various interests and they are unable to reach agreement. Time and again, deadlines get missed and action is prevented." Opponents do not even have to express overt hostility; they can nod politely in meetings and then engage in passive resistance through foot-dragging and minimal cooperation.

Decisions about e-business expose organizational fault lines, and their emergence can cause earthquakes. Joe Sweeney, a consultant with Gartner Group in Hong Kong who had run the "blue sky department" at Asia Online, felt that this was especially true of Chinese businesses: "E-business crosses so many boundaries. The business managers think that if they don't grab hold of it that they will lose their power position in the company. And to be honest, they're probably right. Greater China businesses are extremely political by nature. They're very deep hierarchies. E-business cuts through that so I think that they react with terror. Either control it or hide from it, there's no middle reaction."

But my e-culture team uncovered concerns about loss of power everywhere, even in some of the most innovative American companies. Almost 41 percent of the 108 big-company respondents to the global e-culture survey (those with over 20,000 employees) identify rivalry and conflict between divisions as a barrier to Internet effectiveness, and 26 percent of them indicate that "managers fear loss of privilege and status." The CEOs we interviewed noted repeatedly that a pervasive barrier to leading their companies to the Web is "management fighting for its God-given territory," as one put it.

Highly innovative companies that once thrived on decentralization and internal entrepreneurship find that the Internet forces an unfamiliar degree of integration and communal sharing. In 1997, Sun Microsystems was not yet fully using internally all the networks and Internet applications it sold to customers. In chapter 4 I listed the e-Sun initiative as an example of improvisation at Sun Microsystems. But because of organizational silos, this success almost didn't happen. Let's dig deeper into this case.

It was Sun President Ed Zander's idea to create e-Sun out of the ashes of SunExpress, an after-market, tele-Web-based operation that had sold Sun products in direct competition with other Sun units. Market analysts as well as customers were asking Sun to follow Cisco's lead and walk the talk, to eat its own dog food by using Web technology itself. Albert

Ormiston, who became vice president and general manager of e-Sun, recalled, "Our ads say 'We're the dot in dot-com' and customers are saying to us 'How are you dot-comming yourself?'" E-Sun was envisioned as a unified e-business portal—a partner to the rest of the organization, not a competitor. That was the theory, anyway.

Ormiston set to work to get "buy-in to integrate the whole front office, the back office, the supply chain, across all of the company." Because the new processes cut across traditional functions, everyone was affected, but it seemed (at first) that few wanted to change. An underlying reason was an absence of trust. "You find yourself right in the middle of some horrendous historical relationships across silos," observed Kenneth Sauter, Vice President of Sun Online, who worked with Ormiston. "Sales hates Operations. Finance doesn't talk straight to Sales. Finance doesn't talk straight to Operations. They all screw around with each other. They don't talk honestly with each other. And because the silos are driven so deep, they don't talk about the business anymore. When you move in with a change like this across the functions, you go in with a fresh message about the business, but that's totally foreign to a lot of these folks. They're like, 'What are you talking about? And who are you to come to me and talk about this?'"

It is not surprising that the sales force was the most resistant, but loss of commissions to the Internet channel wasn't the main reason. Sun could figure out how to compensate its sale force for online sales, just as partners such as Oracle had. Rather, e-Sun would force them to join the community, and there was little community spirit in sales. "There was a certain macho-ness about the sales organization," another Sun leader said. "We had always pushed the notion that you take care of yourself and make as much money as you can, and you will have served the company. Ten years ago, the direct sales organization was an independent entity. They could get things done without having any partners or anybody else involved. They could just push it through with brute force. In today's world, they can't do it. It's just impossible. You need internal support, from enterprise services, from the service organization, from professional services, from all the groups that are supporting our partners, our system integrators, resellers. And you need help from them on specific projects that we're dealing with in the commercial world."

Sun needed to develop greater internal cooperation so that it could mobilize quickly and efficiently to meet the needs of customers, and not just through the Web. The challenge for Ormiston and e-Sun was to get people to care about contributing to something that was not included in their immediate list of responsibilities. "We don't have any way to get anyone to pull together and say, 'Yes, we could get a major win with a new customer if we deliver a large server in five days, let's get it there in five.' Immediately the first 10 people step forward and say, 'We can't do that'—and by the way, they don't care. Because their job doesn't involve getting anything to that customer."

Sun's legacy of decentralization and entrepreneurship meant that it was impossible just to force change on the organization by top-down edict, as more hierarchical companies tried to do. It took a year of demonstration projects and constant communication, but Ormiston and his team eventually prevailed for a successful launch of Sun.com. To get people out of their cells and into a community, they borrowed techniques from community organizing: one-on-one persuasion, a lot of coalition building, and when there was enough evidence that this was the wave of the future, getting e-Sun mentioned at every top management meeting. The longer process of buy-in turned out to be a community-building activity, as more and more isolated Sun cells started thinking about their connections to the larger whole. And by 1999, Sun was an e-business star.

The Danger of New Walls: Newstreams versus Mainstreams

The second issue in deconstructing and reconstructing the organization is relevant primarily to established companies: exactly how to organize around e-business itself. Should there be a unit dedicated to e-business? A venture or two focused on e-commerce or other new business opportunities? Where should they be located? How much independence should they have?

This is a classic problem of all new ventures in established companies—the tension between newstreams and the mainstream.[2] Once wannadots get beyond the cosmetic stage of part-time, casual attention to new e-ventures, they sometimes swing in the opposite direction, setting up an independent unit that has total autonomy and few synergies with the parent company. Until the devaluation of Internet stocks in the spring of 2000, some rushed to create quasi-independent dotcoms of their own in response to the capital markets in order to unlock valuation, raise cash for acquisitions, and compensate employees with stock options, just as the Internet pure plays did.

Tesco, a leading British grocery chain and online first mover, grappled with finding the right organization and the right degree of separation. In September 1999, Tesco combined Tesco Direct and a new business development unit which explored opportunities beyond groceries. This was one effort to move beyond the mainstream emphasis on groceries to become a broad portal for online shoppers. (Tesco was already an ISP and an e-mail provider.) Eight months later, Tesco announced the formation of Tesco.com as a separate, wholly owned subsidiary with its own P&L, accountability, and objectives. The separation would help Tesco.com focus as it competed with other strong brands seeking portal status, such as Virgin.net and FreeServe (a spinoff from Dixon's). But the advantages of staying close to the Tesco mainstream were also apparent, as an insider indicated: "We don't intend to be disintermediated from our customers . . . FreeServe could not offer Internet grocery shopping without partnering with someone else." The announcement of Tesco.com ended the debate about spinning off an organizationally separate venture. The opportunity to raise cash for investment that the bricks-and-mortar mainstream would never consider was appealing, but managers were also aware that "online is simply the next evolution of Tesco, and is integral to the whole company." One demonstration of the close ties: When there was a delivery problem one Christmas, e-commerce and mainstream employees packed baskets in stores, piled them in managers' cars, and delivered them personally on Christmas eve. The relationship between mainstream and newstream could not have been clearer.

Ironically, some e-business enthusiasts who want to unite the organization around the Web behave in ways that push the organization away or create new barriers between newstream and mainstream. Those in the newstream flaunt their differences in style or privileges, and then wonder why they engender resentment instead of support. When I am asked questions by embattled e-commerce heads in laggard companies that amount to "Why doesn't anyone like us?" I throw the question back at them: "Why don't you like any of them?" Convinced they are the vanguard of the revolution, they are scornful of the traditional business and isolate themselves from it, confining themselves to their own cells rather than helping other groups move out of theirs.

It has to be a two-way street. Managers on the traditional side must cede some control in order to attain the full potential of the Web. At the same time, those in new Internet ventures must build connections to the mainstream organization. To create an organizational community of purpose, both groups must let go of identities that divide rather than unite.

The problems on both sides are captured in the sad story of an internal Internet entrepreneur at a global bank in Hong Kong. I'll give him the pseudonym "Nigel Brown" and call his employer "Empire International Bank," because he was already punished enough for trying to do the right thing. Empire, a British-led Asian bank, had swung the pendulum toward decentralization in the early 1990s and now enjoyed all the power bases that entailed, spread across dozens of countries. Empire's Web presence was a Tower of Babel of hundreds of offerings that could not communicate with each other. In Asia alone, there was a Singapore consumer banking Internet product with little in common with a Singapore treasury Internet product and nothing in common with a Hong Kong consumer banking Internet product. Hong Kong had an e-mortgage service not used anywhere else in the bank. And experienced technology people were beginning to jump ship for dotcom startups.

In 1999, Nigel Brown was a temporary hero. His Hong Kong team had developed a successful Y2K website for international use. It was so user-friendly that it became the first step in a campaign Brown undertook to Internet-enable the bank. He created another project. He negotiated across territories and across power bases. Then a delegation from the central IT group in London came to audit him. Because he had started to work on Web projects against their wishes, they froze his budget. Brown suspected it was because he was successful, and "London" did not want to be seen as subordinate to him.

No sooner did he survive his suspension (he had other supporters and another source of funds) than his Web skunk works decided to flaunt tradition. The group spent endless time on how to distinguish itself from a buttoned-down British bank. "Part of the discussion we're having is how different do we make ourselves?" he remarked. "Do we come in wearing ponytails, jeans, and things like this? Or do we play the game and look like them? I honestly don't know. We spent a long time discussing how the bank needs to change. We color-coded it. So yellow is old world. Pink is today. Green is tomorrow." Brown was wearing a pink shirt the day of our interview. "I have a lot of bright pink, that's true. Kevin [a co-worker] thinks I'm very 'today' because I use politics and people to get my job done. But if I were truly 'green,' I would come in wearing a pigtail, jeans, long hair and stuff like that because I'd show that I don't care even a little bit about how we do this."

Although Brown's group had not decided how different they wanted their appearance to be, they signaled difference in their actions. Instead of holding meetings in the bank's usual style, complete with PowerPoint slide presentations, they turned the office into an art gallery to show visitors how they could move their functions onto the Internet. These creative thoughts made Brown's group feel good, but it remained to be seen whether members of the mainstream would become more open to change or just dig in their heels. Brown was walking a fine line that could easily widen into a cultural wall.

When the Wall Becomes Real

Sometimes imaginary walls turn into real ones. In the spring of 1999, construction workers arrived to erect a thick, unpenetrable wall of brick and plaster to permanently divide Arrow Electronics's new Internet group from a mainstream Arrow sales unit occupying the other side of the same building.

Here is what led to the wall. Arrow Electronics was the world's largest distributor of electronic components and computer products, with 175,000 big customers, sales of $9 billion, and a track record of profitability. Arrow was already connected electronically to its customers through proprietary electronic data interchange networks, but Marshall Industries had been the first distributor to move to the Internet. Other competitors such as Avnet were also rushing to the Web, along with over a dozen new dotcoms—all trying for a share of a market estimated to be $50 billion in the United States alone. CEO Steven Kaufman was determined to prevent Arrow Electronics from being disintermediated. If online distributors were going to eat into Arrow's business, then Kaufman wanted a part of his own company to be the one to enjoy the meal first.

After executive and board discussions, Kaufman mounted an internal new venture, Arrow.com. Tom Hallam, then Arrow's chief corporate HR officer, took on leadership of the Internet group first part-time and eventually as full-time president in November 1998. Hallam was an MIT-trained engineer who was a PC devotee in the mid-1980s and then became a Web aficionado. He assembled a core team, with a few of them coming from Arrow's MIS and marketing departments, and moved into a building in Hauppauge, Long Island, shared by a branch of Arrow's mainstream sales group.

Hallam believed that he needed to create a flexible, fast-acting culture distinct from the Arrow norm in order to attract dotcom talent and establish new media partnerships. "Steve told me, 'do it any way you want to, and we'll tell you when it causes some problem that we all have to talk about.'" So he emulated the youthful dotcom style I described in chapter 2.

Arrow.com's offices were open cubicles in a large warehouse-like square. Everyone—the president, the marketing team, the webmaster—was visible to everyone else from across the large room. Big windows stretched from the ceiling to the floor across the entire front wall to let in as much sunlight as possible. The walls were painted yellow, and there were only three or four offices with doors, for the occasional confidential meeting. One area on the side of the room was designated a meeting space, with big comfortable leather couches arranged in a circle. A big-screen TV, VCR, CD player, and an assortment of video tapes and music CDs were displayed at the head of the circle, with a glass coffee table in the middle. Behind the meeting space off toward the corner was a kitchen, with a cappuccino machine and cupboards worth at least $35,000. (I'm cataloging the furniture because it became a sore point.)

Arrow.com's hours of operation were loose. A requirement that every employee use a cell phone and a wireless hand-held e-mail pager kept the staff in constant communication. "We've erased the line between work life and home life," Hallam said. "In a traditional setting, you're either at work or you're not. For us, it's not obvious when we're working and when we're not." Anyone could assemble an informal cross-functional meeting or ask a question anytime. The Internet group even worked out the equivalent of a secret handshake—a series of hand gestures and codes to determine whether or not they were on the phone, busy at work, or available to be interrupted.

"That was about as left of Arrow as you could get," remarked Jim Heuther, VP of semiconductor product management. (He added, "The fact that the organization allowed it at all is a sign of how progressive the company is.") It was no surprise that the traditional Arrow branch sales and marketing employees on the other side of the building immediately resented the dotcom. They were quick to point out the drawbacks of the open offices and open style. One exclaimed combatively: "If I was a vice president over there, I would be sitting in a cube out on the floor. Guess what? I'm not going to do that. I don't care if it's old fashioned or not: I want a door. A door with an office, because I don't want it to be a big deal every time I want to have a private conversation and people speculating what I'm working on. I don't want to work out in the open. I don't care if that's the new model, I guess I'll go down as a dinosaur." Hallam retorted, "Our culture is created this way for communication. The fact that we don't have secretaries, we dress differently, we work different hours, frustrates the hell out of the traditional business group."

Kaufman felt that Arrow.com needed to operate by a different set of rules in order to attract dotcom talent. Other executives agreed that the

Internet requires different programming skills and development cycles. But Kaufman also knew that the freedom could make it look like "they are the favored, chosen few." Rather than let the tensions spin out of control, Arrow leaders decided it was too "confusing" to have a door between new-stream and mainstream. They erected the infamous wall instead.

Not only the neighbors—now conveniently walled off—were critical of the Internet group. Many mainstream senior leaders felt that Arrow.com was operating in a vacuum. Jan Salsgiver, president of Arrow's North American business, said: "We felt that they were going off doing whatever they wanted to do; and we were sitting here feeling very self-righteous about Arrow. We wanted to say, don't call it Arrow.com—because that's us. If you want to be something different, then go be something different, but name yourself something different." She confessed, "We got into these pissing contests."

Kaufman described the tensions between Arrow.com and the traditional business group as sibling rivalry stemming from different standards for mainstream and newstream: "If you had to wear a jacket and tie to eat dinner every night while your sibling could come in a sweatshirt—and then he went with one of your parents every night to the baseball game and you couldn't go, but you had to keep dressing up, and you have to keep getting A's, but they were allowed to get C's and they get praised, would you get jealous? Sure you'd get jealous."

But some of the concerns were not just emotional reactions to different degrees of freedom, they were business concerns about being left out of essential discussions—concerns that people in Arrow.com were not seeking the input of business units whose Web fate they might be controlling. The Internet group needed the support of the core business because they depended on the mainstream computer systems for raw data, order entry, and order processing; on the mainstream purchasing organization for access to inventory; and on the mainstream fulfillment operation for product shipments. Customers, of course, didn't recognize the wall that had been constructed between Arrow.com and the mainstream; they tried to use both channels. Arrow needed internal collaboration to sort out whether new customers registering on the Web really were new accounts for Arrow. And important synergies could benefit the entire business. Some of the processes Arrow.com developed for the Web, such as customer order changes or requests for authorization of returns, could be deployed for other customers through the mainstream sales organization.

Kaufman, an experienced leader under whose guidance Arrow reached new heights of profitability, was not rattled by the battles. "Arrow is a pretty open culture, and while people grumble a little bit, it is not horribly political," he said. "If it gets horribly political, if the time ever comes when the core group is actively working to hurt the Internet business, then I'll have to step in with a little more intervention. But at this point it is more the grumbling that, 'oh Christ, here they come again, they want something tomorrow, just like always, don't they know we have real work to do. Well, let's see if we can help them because if we don't, they are just going to go whining to Kaufman and he's going to come in and say why can't you help them, so let's just help them and get it over with.'" He felt there was too much to do to get bogged down in politics. His tactic was to stand firm and repeat his explanations of why Arrow.com was important, the strategy behind it, and why the Internet group needed to work differently.

Another executive said that the problem was "a feeling that the Internet business people thought they could do anything they wanted. And everybody else is abiding by the normal rules, the culture, the approvals. It was almost like they were thumbing their noses at all this. The same people who had been part of our organization who went over there, 'oh, they're so arrogant.' Now they are trying to work with the core business. Some of them are having to mend bridges that they may have burned." (I'll get to some of Arrow's solutions after we take a tour of one more set of walls.)

Arrow's wall divided newstream from mainstream, but embattled new ventures sometimes erect their own internal walls. Barnesandnoble.com's wall created cells and silos within the e-venture itself.

In late 1997, barnesandnoble.com moved to a giant warehouse floor in Chelsea, something like 65,000 square feet of open space. In the middle was a loading dock converted into the network operations center. A window was put into that area to allow passers-by to peer in to observe the activity. Several informants described a similar first reaction: that this was a good symbol for an Internet company—the network at the center, visible to all. But when the renovations were completed, the technology group decided to put a rack mount up against the window. "So then you could see lights flashing but you couldn't see the people in there working on the technology," an insider recalled. "I thought, isn't this ironic? We put technology in the center, we built a window so we can all look at it, and then we put a wall up against it so that you can't really see what's going on. Putting that rack up against the window was a great metaphor for the network group trying to build walls around themselves. To be fair, they were bombarded with requests and demands. But they worked behind walls."

The company's main functions were located in separate quadrants of the building and were clearly demarcated, despite the open space. The rest of technology had one corner, editorial and merchandising was in another corner, the executive and business side was in a third corner, and marketing and customer service was in the fourth corner. People stuck to their own groups. A social wall divided them. "You didn't even know the people," a former manager commented. "So to get things done, you would follow this path up through your chain of command and down to their chain of command, even though the people you needed at the working level were only a few steps away. They were opposite us physically in the building, and we would never talk to them." One consequence of the separation was a disregard for the other functions, the manager said. "Marketing would be humming along a million miles an hour driving people to the website without any notion of what was actually going on there."

Unlike the physical barrier erected by the network operations group, the other walls were invisible, but there were still clear dividing lines. Another former employee described the visual and cultural separation, especially between technology and editorial: "Those two organizations were such polar opposites: the sneakers and jeans culture of programmers and developers versus the all-black clothes, granola, Soho-type culture of the book literati. Those people didn't speak the same language. What was important to one group didn't make any sense to the other, and vice versa. They butted heads."

Climbing over the Walls

It's a hard climb over all these walls unless there are ladders and bridges. Those are often human bridges. Barnesandnoble.com's solution was already common among strong dotcoms like Abuzz: to create a product development team with people who spoke both the language of marketing and the language of technology.

Arrow Electronics used several types of connectors. Its most powerful bridge was an Internet advisory board—in effect, a board of directors—linking mainstream and newstream through representatives of various traditional units. Informally, strong personal relationships helped give people ladders to get from mainstream to newstream. Because Arrow moved insiders to its Internet unit, mainstream employees knew people in the dotcom and could stay connected. Jim Heuther, for example, kept in touch with former colleagues Stephanie Baranak and Theresa Stanson. A formal integrating structure, personal relationships, and a shared belief in the importance of the Internet eventually healed Arrow's wounds of war. By mid-2000, Arrow was acknowledged as an Internet leader and had been named one of the top 100 online companies by major industry trade journals such as *Internet Week, Business 2.0,* and *Electronic Buyers News.*

Similar bridges helped Lucent Technology's New Venture Group avoid the classic problems of new ventures in established companies. NVG co-founder and vice president Steve Socolof recruited experienced Lucent people with ties back to the business units and corporate staffs. He made NVG participation part of a Lucent career path, rotating people through both newstream and mainstream assignments. He stressed communication about the NVG and its companies. An NVG-dedicated PR director placed a steady stream of stories in the media that would be seen inside the company as well as outside. NVG staff went on speaking tours through Lucent, and mainstream people were welcomed at NVG facilities. They kept enumerating benefits to both Lucent and the startups from their coexistence in the big organization.

Using ladders and bridges takes good balance—for example, balancing a clear identity and autonomy for a new venture to chart its own course with collaborative connections to the mainstream to tap synergies and exchange benefits. When she became president of CNBC.com in September 1999, Pamela Thomas-Graham was determined to get the balance right.

As a former McKinsey consultant, Thomas-Graham had observed the mistakes that retail and media companies made in their Web experiments, especially during the "lipstick on a bulldog" stage of cosmetic change. She shaped her job at CNBC.com to ensure that her new venture was neither starved by being treated too casually nor separated from corporate parents NBC and General Electric. She reports directly to the president of NBC as head of a distinct business. At the same time, as a close colleague of CNBC television and sharer of its brand, her dotcom is located in CNBC's Fort Lee, New Jersey, facility and engages in numerous forms of cooperation and collaborative planning. This helped CNBC.com get dozens of on-air mentions a day from CNBC, fast interchange with the MSNBC newswriters deployed to CNBC, and inclusion in the CNBC advertising sales bundle. These benefits came at a price: CNBC.com could not be fully autonomous, break rules, or avoid conformity with GE financial systems.

So Thomas-Graham works with an internal NBC advisory board that helps her get what she needs from the rest of GE.

For Williams-Sonoma, whose successful move to e-commerce was described in chapter 3, formal integrators help link the new e-commerce division to the mainstream. Although the e-commerce group has its own functional teams for application development, merchandising, and marketing for each store brand, Shelley Nandkeolyar recognized the need for a diplomatic operations manager to create more legitimacy for e-commerce in the eyes of the rest of the company. It made sense that this person be an insider with a strong network of relationships throughout W-S. He chose Patricia Skerrett, who had worked both in inventory management and marketing. Her new role, officially called Operations Manager, marked the first time someone in upper management would be responsible for identifying and resolving conflicts across the separate channels of business.

"Two words summarize what I'm supposed to do. Seamless Integration," Skerrett said. "We needed somebody to tie together all of the channels and functional areas. So I deal very closely with the call center, the distribution center, store operations, inventory, and marketing, in order to make sure that first and foremost, people understand what [e-commerce's] direction is, what we're doing in the Internet and how that can potentially impact their areas." Skerrett and Nandkeolyar meet regularly with leaders in the retail and catalog divisions to maintain consistency across channels, ensure that items looked identical, and that the customer experience is protected. Interpersonal relationships are the key to bridging Williams-Sonoma's silos.

From "Knowing Together" to Working Together

Community doesn't just happen to organizations; leaders must explicitly promote it. They can lead by example, select people for collaborative instincts, head off any sign of territoriality, and coach people to work cooperatively.

Michael Robinson's distaste for workplace politics made him determined to lead renren.com as a unified community. Even the name promised inclusion; *renren* is the Chinese term for *everybody*. Renren.com is a growing Internet portal headquartered in Hong Kong that claims to be the first truly bilingual destination site for the global Chinese community.

Founded in 1998 by ex-McKinsey consultants Robinson as CEO and Anthony Cheng as president, renren.com soon attracted name-brand Silicon Valley investors and partners and went live in May 1999, with 7 employees. By January 2000, renren was up to 100 employees, and by May it had 200 employees spread across offices in Hong Kong, Beijing, Shanghai, Taipei, and California. The founders did not want dispersion to result in dysfunctional divisions.

Communication is at the heart of running renren.com as an organizational community. Language is one possible barrier, so it helps that senior people are trilingual in English, Mandarin, and Cantonese and can revert to English as a common international language. Robinson and Cheng look for people who are team players, they said, and remind them constantly that they want renren.com to be a politics-free zone. (A noble, if quixotic, aspiration.) Robinson said, "Everybody knows that Anthony and I are adamant about destruction of any political stuff. Politics leaves such a bad taste in my mouth because I've lived through it with academia. I just won't have any part of it."

Even so, cross-office communication posed a tough challenge that eventually led to a very unusual policy for an Internet company: no e-mail for disagreements or strategic decisions, only phone conferences. In early 2000, there was a heated e-mail argument going on between Shanghai and Hong Kong that really bothered Robinson. The person in Shanghai was upset that hardware equipment decisions were being made in Hong Kong, arguing that he should make that decision on the ground, but indicating in more subtle ways that he didn't want Shanghai to be subordinate to Hong Kong.

"It got to the point that one of them cc:'d me on this e-mail thread," Robinson recalled. "I said, no more e-mails, get on the phone. Just settle it quickly. I told both the guys that things are done based on their business logic, not on any people hierarchy. That's just baloney, so don't go there. I know you're both nice guys and I know you both actually like each other, so just get on the phone. They got on the phone, and within 20 seconds, it was back to normal. They were very embarrassed afterwards." Getting over that hurdle became an oft-told war story—and the source of the "no e-mail for controversies" rule.

Robinson shifted his emphasis from better communication to higher levels of teamwork across offices. "We went from poor interoffice communication to great interoffice communication but poor interoffice working, so now the big theme is cross-working," he said. "We enforce weekly cross-office meetings by phone." For example, the marketing team might have a meeting in Hong Kong, then a meeting in Beijing, followed by a multioffice meeting by phone to make sure that everybody has the latest information, across functions as well as across offices. It became the norm to e-mail documents back and forth so that everybody knew what everybody else was doing. But even those moves were too passive. Just because people were better informed did not mean that they acted on the information or worked together effectively. "They weren't really working together," he said. "They were just knowing together."

The next step was to foster active exchange of knowledge so that groups could quickly move on opportunities presented by other groups. As the personal visits, conference calls, e-mail updates, and follow-up conference calls mounted, wider involvement became the norm. The ultimate sign of community at renren.com was when teamwork became spontaneous rather than directed from the top, and when groups started setting goals together rather than just responding to each other's goals. "Now people in different areas brainstorm tasks together," Robinson commented. "They work together to come up with the ideas. So everybody buys in and is motivated to get it done."

Acting as an organizational community quickly became self-reinforcing. It reduced frustration and made work more successful. Robinson said, "Satisfaction increases tremendously when people take ownership and are proud of something that millions of people will see on the Internet."

Abuzz is a little older than renren.com, and it is further along in internal teamwork, cross-functional collaboration, and frequent abundant communication as I showed in chapter 2. But new companies like these are still just the size of a small village. Can the same spirit of community pervade larger organizations? Let's move up to a thousand people. One pacesetter company responding to my e-culture survey attributed its ability to work as a unified community to having only a thousand employees. "Since we are a relatively nimble and small or tight organization, we are able to function as one big unit, with an underlying culture that embraces change," a leader said. "We have successfully launched a major extranet initiative seeking a wide audience. We took the time to set priorities upfront and create a consensus for a bottom-up focus that enables many participants to feel like stakeholders in the launching process. The enthusiasm for this initiative spurred us to go beyond our original bounds and seek broader scope."

The classic assumption in organization theory was that bureaucracy is inevitable. Theorists long held that coordination becomes more difficult and costly as organizations scale up. Indeed, classic studies showed that administrative overhead generally grows faster than productive capacity. But in the Internet Age, size does not have to limit communication, and a division of labor doesn't have to create permanent class distinctions. Cisco Systems's success is a prime example. Cisco didn't divide into too many rigid territories in the first place, and didn't turn particular technologies into a religion accompanied by priests to enforce orthodoxy. It did not create separate brands with their own pride of place. Cisco emphasizes rapid information dissemination and abundant communication. It has dazzling figures for sales per employee and remarkable feats of speed, such as the ability to close the books every twenty-four hours.

Cisco—which calls itself the world's largest e-commerce company—builds an internal electronic community. It uses its own networks to encourage very large numbers of people to head in the same direction. So does Cisco's key strategic partner, IBM, which could soon surpass Cisco in e-commerce size. But to get there, IBM had to undergo a massive organizational upheaval. The IBM case is complex, but behind the alphabet soup of titles and task forces, this story illustrates how even an $87 billion company can reconstruct its organization to support e-culture.

The Route to E-Business Leadership: Connecting "One IBM"

In 1993, when the World Wide Web opened for business, IBM was an ailing giant out of synch with the market. Its complexity was overwhelming, and so were its silos: 3 million orders, 10 million invoices, 20 disparate business units, 5,000 hardware products, 20,000 software offerings, 1,000+ product announcements a year, 25 major fulfillment systems, 50+ manufacturing floor systems. "We were a beached whale. We couldn't get out of our own way. Wall Street was needling us to break into various Baby Blues," recalled Bruce Harreld, Senior Vice President of Strategy. "We had been taught that as things got complex we created new divisions and more general managers who thought they had a God-given right to create their own everything."

New CEO Louis V. Gerstner, Jr., wanted to go to market as "One IBM," an integrated, global organization, using technology as an enabler and customer focus as the stimulus for change. Two years of internal reengineering centralized HR, finance, and CIO functions. Then in 1995, the focus shifted to customers and suppliers. Recognizing the huge potential of the Internet, Gerstner began to reposition IBM as a world-class e-business. At first this was greeted skeptically by the media. But when Internet applications exploded in 1997, IBM was ready with IT solutions.

Inside the company, however, this very proliferation of its own e-business activities contributed to a fragmented and uncoordinated result. Consider these amazing numbers: By 1997, IBM ran the world's largest corporate website, with over half a million webpages, 50 million hits a week (half of them over the Internet), and a rising annual investment of over $120 million. Over 250 disparate content organizations contributed to webpages, nearly 1,000 people worked on webpage development, and 4,000 servers scattered throughout the company hosted the sites. Most of the sites were not very strategic, and multiple sites targeted the same audience with conflicting messages. Customers had to use different Web addresses to research several types of products. Worse yet, the sites were oriented toward selling to website visitors rather than supporting their buying decision. And even if the customer was interested in making a purchase over the Web, complex site navigation made this hard to do. The internal organization itself was becoming an obstacle to reaching customers.

By mid-1997, Gerstner was losing patience. Too much was still being spent on IT within IBM. Even more alarming as a sign of fragmentation, 128 different people across IBM held the title of Chief Information Officer. Then-corporate-CIO Dave Carlucci issued an edict that things must change. Silo-shattering structural changes were forced on a reluctant organization. Instead of 128 CIOs, there would be only one CIO for the corporation. All the hundred-plus functions these CIOs were running were consolidated into seven clusters. The former business-unit CIOs became BIEs (business information executives) to represent the data needs of their units to the corporate CIO organization. "There were big disagreements," recalled an insider close to the action. "Business unit heads wanted to keep their own CIO, wanted to maintain control of budgets and reporting relationships. And to this day, almost three years later, some of the BIEs still loathe the people who took away their CIO title."

While back-room change was underway, IBM's top leaders embraced the e-business theme, and in 1998, IBM introduced a centralized e-business organization called Enterprise Web Management (EWM). EWM was a new Internet-focused unit that would integrate product development, the supply chain, and customer interfaces, as well as unite employees, in effect taking the reengineered business processes to the Web. Dick Anderson, an experienced IBM marketing executive, was appointed general manager, reporting to Steve Ward, who replaced Carlucci as CIO in early 1998.

Anderson's mandate was to move IBM to a new business model based on "Web governance," a third and more productive stage IBM consultants identified as the ultimate goal. The EWM group was expected to develop consistent, companywide business strategies and work with business units to create "One IBM" on the Web. This involved IT infrastructure tasks, of course, but it also included a significant organizational challenge: wresting control from business units accustomed to charting their own course for their own divisions, brands, and geographies. Losing a CIO was one thing; this next wave of change was even more threatening to the cells and silos.

EWM took immediate control of the Internet flagship, ibm.com, and began to centralize the numerous initiatives under the Web umbrella, including content approval and security standards. Though IBM was known for discipline, even conformity—it was only a few years beyond white-shirts-and-blue-suits-only policies—there were still many battles behind the scenes, insiders reported. But Anderson kept reminding people about Gerstner's focus on customers. Gerstner preached customer focus and modeled it in his own behavior, spending much of his own time visiting major customers. Since customer feedback drove the need for centralization—it would help customers access IBM products and services in faster and simpler ways—business heads had few grounds for resistance, although some tried the "my customers are different" argument. Loss of business unit sovereignty, they were told in response, would be more than balanced by access to new technology, skills, and infrastructure formerly scattered through disparate groups across the vast company and hard to find.

To design a new organizational structure, EWM convened a large, representative task force of senior people from the business units and corporate groups already engaged in various e-business activities (e.g., e-procurement and e-commerce). The task force sought an operating structure that would combine the best of centralization ("One IBM") as well as decentralization (business unit–specific strategies). Their "One IBM" objective was met through directors for interactive marketing and ibm.com. Seven core processes were identified, and each was given the attention of a director and a cross-business Web Initiative Team: e-commerce, e-care for customers, e-care for business partners, e-care for influencers, e-procurement, e-care for employees, and e-marketing communications. Their "best of decentralization" goal was reflected in ownership by the business units of e-strategies that they developed in partnership with EWM but would execute themselves.

To oversee all of IBM's e-business activities, the task force created a two-level cross-functional management structure. At the top, an e-business executive steering committee provided the vision, clout, and final authority. At the next level, translating vision into action, an e-business management committee made corporatewide decisions. EWM teams facilitated workshops within each business unit and developed new tools to permit a common methodology. The "Web-Site-Go" process provided a streamlined way for business units to generate a new Web address or e-initiative, while also forcing them to justify the business case for their investments and initiatives. Unless business units were willing to cede some of their traditional authority, their initiatives could be denied funding.

Compensation tied to cooperation made the new direction real. "By linking individual incentives to IBM e-business success, Lou Gerstner established the motivation for collaboration across IBM—a tremendous lever for us," said Jamie Hewitt, Business Process VP. IBM created a new annual assessment process, called Personal Business Commitments, which included a bonus scheme that reached far down the hierarchy. An organizational assessment was added in 1998 to measure business units on accomplishment of targets for the top four corporate processes and to adjust the unit's compensation pool according to performance.

By the turn of 1999, the central group was gaining control. It had taken some time, but there was a common IBM look and feel on the Web. E-business was gaining momentum, although EWM was still fighting internal battles and running into organizational walls. A dramatic expansion of e-commerce—from around $3 billion in 1998 to a projection of over $20 billion for 2000—made acceleration of progress essential. One challenge was that the front end (the marketing of IBM as an e-business leader) was shooting ahead, but the back end (the capacity to deliver) was lagging. "In 1999, we were still not integrated, and we had to automate; rip and read wouldn't do," indicated Doug Swanson, a director in the business transformation office of the CIO, referring to the manual process of making hard copies of online orders. In short, one of the world's leading technology companies had still not integrated all of its own processes and was filling e-commerce orders the old-fashioned way. The good news was that there were 150 extranets for IBM's top industry accounts; the bad news was that it was still too slow to update them and add functions.

To create offline community to support online commerce, CIO Ward deployed Swanson to support the e-BT (business transformation) group, a biweekly meeting of BIEs (the former unit CIOs), BPEs (executives in charge of each of the four key business processes), and EWM staff, as they tried to hammer out a solution. The group decided they could make the needed improvements for about $65 million, but the question was where to find that money. "We didn't want to go to Lou [Gerstner]," an insider reported. "So we got the business units to re-set their own priorities and chip in." The prioritization exercise involved a common set of questions each business unit could use to make the business case for that project. Some were easy to justify, because they supported a customer. Others were more contentious, such as bets for the future about how much capacity to add. But after six months of large and small meetings every two weeks, using a common discipline and guided by the need to justify separate cells in terms of their contribution to the whole community, the deal was done. By mid-1999, there was for the first time "One IBM" in the technology organization—a set of shared priorities and a $65 million investment by separate silos in the common good.

Successful execution required the rest of the mainstream organization to get involved. To truly operate as "One IBM" required breadth as well as depth, soul as well as structure. Large numbers of people—outside as well as inside the corporation—would need to think and behave differently. That required extensive ongoing and focused communication. So the message was aimed at a large, diverse audience. This was a sales campaign as big as anything IBM had ever done, but what was being sold was an idea for change. People had to become believers.

The goal was to convey a consistent theme to everyone simultaneously through many different media and channels. "The 'One IBM' objective meant that IBMers everywhere had to understand why becoming an e-business was critical to our success, as well as what they needed to do—or not do— to help," said Will Runyon, communications director for EWM. "And for external influencers and the media, it was absolutely critical that we walked the talk when it came to being an e-business ourselves."

The message was broadcast well before all capabilities were in place to deliver on it, and even before top leaders knew what it would mean in practice. In the spirit of improvisational theater, using the model I outlined in chapter 4, setting the theme would force internal constituencies to make sure that they could deliver on the promises. "Certainly the most effective communication vehicle was Lou Gerstner himself, whether he was leading the e-business industry debates, setting the vision for IBM or communicating to all employees," Dick Anderson observed.

A theme is one thing, but how would people know if they were headed in the right direction? EWM developed very specific companywide metrics for the seven clusters of e-business initiatives. For example, the goal for e-care for employees was to increase the use of self-service and distance learning applications. E-care for customers sought to increase web registrations, increase customer satisfaction, and reduce call center costs. Policies addressed three areas: content (e.g., third-party links, acceptable employee use, brand and logo), context (e.g., site navigation, user experience, site design), and infrastructure (e.g., hosting, security, data management). Abundant communication was important here, too. Employees had to be made aware of the dangers of degrading the common look or of posting information that created legal liabilities.

Creating an IBM-wide content model was a critical, yet difficult, step in implementing the desired consistency, and it took nearly two years. Rory Read, Vice President of E-Business Enablement, reported, "The ibm.com content model has now gone through 10 major redesigns. And the redesigns grow as we learn more about our relationships with customers and stakeholders." Like the successive versions important to improvisation, each wave reduced costs, made development faster, and made the site easier to navigate. Nearly every function at IBM, not just IT and marketing, took some responsibility for Web content management. Content managers were trained in consistent frameworks that all business units would use and were given Web-based tools to assess themselves against global corporate requirements.

By 2000, IBM had become very effective at using its own experience in becoming the world's largest e-business to help educate its global customers. Indicators of change were impressive. IBM moved everything possible to the network, including big things such as the sales of PCs (no longer available except on the Web) and small things such as the sign-in process at headquarters in Armonk, New York (visitors type their names on an IBM ThinkPad and their name tag is printed automatically). Over 42 million service transactions and over 29 percent of all employee training are handled via the Web, and IBM is online with 14,000 business partners and $13 billion in e-procurement.

Inside IBM, the Web facilitates far-flung communities of interest, such as cybercafés, to share knowledge throughout the Global Services group. IBM's 300,000 people send about 2 million real-time instant messages a day.

IBM's external community service was focused almost entirely on K-12 public education, and its massive Reinventing Education initiatives in twenty-one U.S. cities and states and seven other countries draw on fluid teams of experts throughout IBM to find technology-based solutions to education problems—in effect, helping schools become e-businesses too.

Elements of e-culture pop up everywhere: a looser style reflected in casual dress, reverse mentoring, improvisational theater, an orientation toward partnering, and an emphasis on speed and teamwork. "Our innovation centers are populated with people that IBMers of the past would never recognize as IBMers: jeans-wearing 'netgens' with long hair who work for the beauty of the finished product," exclaimed Cheryl Shearer, manager of European business partner channels for IBM Global Services in London. *Fast Company* magazine featured an IBM speed team in a spring 2000 issue. Because this New Economy–focused magazine scorned Old Economy companies, this was almost as good as a national prize for transformation. Stories such as the speed team are textbook examples of improvisational theater in action—dramatizing a message to accelerate creativity and innovation.

Sean Gresh, an executive speechwriter at IBM headquarters in Armonk, New York, exemplifies the new all-E employee. In December 1999, he went online to Monster.com to apply for a job at IBM and was called by a recruiter in Raleigh, North Carolina. After a three-day orientation called "Becoming One Voice," he began life as a virtual employee managing his work through the Web. Gresh reported: "I was struck with the fact that literally everything at IBM centered on the Web—registering for a Lotus Notes account, choosing medical and dental benefits, signing up and taking training programs. And the kicker is that I work at home in Massachusetts and travel to my office one day or so a week. Whenever I need help, I access the intranet. If I need a person to walk me through a process, I dial 1-800-IBM-HELP, and someone is there, 24/7."

As would be expected in one of the world's largest companies, there are still vestiges of the old lumbering bureaucracy (especially the closer one gets to Armonk) and too many examples of the right hand not knowing what the left one was doing. But global teams working together across traditional business silos are more pervasive, and they use the Web to get things done faster. In June 2000, EWM declared victory and moved on. A reorganization dissolved the central group. Its activities were handed to a small set of functions (e.g., Dick Anderson became VP of Internet sales and operations) while the two-tiered corporate committees ensured integrated governance. "I don't want to leave you with the impression that our transformation is over," Bruce Harreld said. "We continue to realize that e-business transformation is about looking deep into the soul of a company, deciding what needs to change, and then using the Web to make that transformation happen." Harreld is right to mention a company's soul. That takes longer to change than its structure.

The benefits of IBM's new-found sense of internal community extend to the external community in unusual and powerful ways, and they help reach the soul. After the refugee crises hit in Kosovo in 1999, a global cross-disciplinary, cross-business team of IBMers was mobilized to help reunite children with their parents in the refugee camps. The International Rescue Committee (IRC), which operated refugee assistance centers in the former Yugoslavian republic of Macedonia, needed the ability to set up a data system in the field. Stanley Litow, Corporate Community Relations VP, wanted to help. Reg Foster in New York and Celia Moore in London led a virtual team from Lotus, Global Services, a Minnesota plant, the European geographic unit, and the worldwide Government Industry Solutions Unit. Within three weeks, they developed customized disaster management database software, delivered servers and laptops, and trained local IRC staff. When word of IBM's contribution appeared on its website, hundreds of e-mails filled Litow's in-box, expressing great pride. Service to the external community throughout the world, using IBM's own tools, was starting to reinforce a feeling of membership in "One IBM."

Constructing Community

I said earlier that community has both a structure and a soul. As the IBM story shows, structure is the easy part. A few bold strokes such as Gerstner's and Carlucci's edict, and titles change; or a new centralized EWM group arrives to set policy, and Internet protocols and processes become must-use tools. Traditionally participatory Motorola enforced Web integration by top-down dictate. To put the Internet at the center of Motorola's new strategy, CEO Christopher Galvin closeted himself with his COO and emerged two weeks later with a new organization chart. He combined thirty business units (cell phones, wireless equipment, satellite, and cable modem products) into one large division, removed some managers' P&L responsibilities, and added an Internet group to coordinate all Web strategies.

So far, this doesn't look any different from old-fashioned centralization. But there's more to organizational community than compliance; it requires voluntary collaboration. E-culture derives from the soul of community, its human elements. And that's the hard part. Moving from policies and standards to ongoing collaboration takes time and attention—what Barry Stein and I call long marches.[3]

Structure needs soul to produce effective work communities. Consider evidence from Harvard Business School Professor Jody Hofer Gittell's studies of flight crews and health care teams who coordinate complex activities. She found that the ideal combination for high quality and efficient operations is both programmed routines and human relationships. On the structure side, standard procedures and information systems provide a uniform infrastructure that improves communication accuracy and timeliness and problem-solving speed; without this precision, meetings are a waste of time. But technology and rules don't produce the feelings and emotions underlying strong relationships. It takes people communicating directly with each other to strengthen shared knowledge, shared goals, and mutual respect. Strong relationships, it turns out, are what turn efficient routines into high performance.[4]

Six elements contribute to building organizational community.

1. A balanced governance structure. Formal structures signal importance, clarify responsibilities, and include those whose input will make a difference. Activities that touch every part of the company cannot be managed by committees—someone needs to be clearly in charge—but they can't work without input and linkages to the rest of the organization either. The best combination for the Web is a dedicated e-commerce unit that can operate as a venture with rights to pursue its own destiny balanced by a representative advisory board with the mandate to connect newstream to mainstream—Arrow Electronics's solution.

2. Shared disciplines and routines. Collaboration is nearly impossible without a common vocabulary and common language. It is facilitated by common tools and disciplines that make it easy to do routine things quickly. The extensive use of their own Web-based tools at Cisco or IBM helps any new group to know how to work together—for example, IBM's lightning-fast disaster relief team.

3. Multichannel, multidirectional communication. Communities are communication intensive. They spread more information to more people more regularly through every medium, from large gatherings to the external press. Despite Cisco's reliance on its networks for rapid, routine communication, the company considers face-to-face communication skills vital: Top leaders must be capable of emulating John Chambers's ability to speak without notes to large groups. Then Cisco webcasts key events so the whole company can see them. iXL holds a weekly management call for its dozen worldwide offices. The call is backed up by data transmission, so everybody sees the same numbers; at Atlanta headquarters, the numbers are shown on a cinema-sized screen, observable by anyone who is interested. With many channels, people can use the right one for the occasion—such as renren.com's norm of voice-only communication for strategy or disputes, not e-mail. Abuzz convenes weekly meetings of the whole company, uses Abuzz TV to keep everyone informed of daily news, and welcomes visitors from other areas in functional meetings. A British Telecom manager renamed his IT group the IF unit, for information flow, to change the emphasis from technology to communication.

4. Integrators. Communities are built through networks of people who meet across areas to share knowledge. They can be structured and formal (the product development team at barnesandnoble.com) or loose and informal (diversity interest groups at FleetBoston). Unlike committees, networks are fluid and open ended, but not just spontaneously self-organizing; they work best when actively managed. Network champions hold people together. DuPont made an art of forming knowledge-sharing networks because Parry Norling in central R&D served as network guru. He helped networks form, cataloged them (at one point he counted over 400 at a time), encouraged them, and passed on lessons about effectiveness. Norling-nurtured networks included resource groups on a particular technical topic, such as abrasion or adhesion; best-practice sharing; and task-oriented networks, such as the plant maintenance improvement network, which ultimately involved over 600 people and led to cost savings of several hundred million dollars a year.

Appointing official integrators—internal ambassadors and diplomats—ties cells and silos together. Patricia Skerrett at Williams-Sonoma was the first companywide operations manager, because e-commerce involved all functions and divisions. Ambassadors from one group to another are like wandering minstrels, traveling from place to place sprinkling seeds of knowledge—what's happening in Chicago, what's troubling Frankfurt, what's new in Singapore. They build community not just through tasks but through the folklore and war stories they convey. Just as the Web needs webmasters, e-culture communities need wandering minstrels.

5. Cross-cutting relationships. Personal relationships are vitally important. It helps to have people with strong social skills who are team oriented and collaborative; innovators at Sun Microsystems, such as Albert Ormiston and his e-Sun project, must build coalitions of supporters in order to lead significant change. But this is also something the organization encourages by convening people across territories on every relevant occasion—corporate conferences, training programs, celebrations. A base of goodwill derived from past encounters keeps communication and support flowing. That's why insiders with long service help build community. Williams-Sonoma and Honeywell's successful e-commerce units balanced new hires with insiders who had a history of good relationships throughout the mainstream. Tesco.com appointed a mainstream manager as its CEO. Arrow's wall was bridged because of relationships. Communities are built around people who know each other, understand each other, like each other, and have a shared history.

6. Shared identity, shared fate. Collaboration is not altruism; it stems in part from people identifying with each other and feeling that they share a fate. Incentives that induce cooperation are a starting point. Tesco executives felt that one of their early mistakes was to count dotcom sales outside of local store manager results, even though online orders were picked from the stores, because store managers then had no incentive to promote the website. At IBM, Gerstner linked individual performance measures to corporate business success. A shared identity is fostered, too, by role switching and job exchanges. Career paths can carry people across silos. Task teams can routinely include people from many silos.

Collaboration works best when it is mutual: Each participant gets something out of it. Each feels good about his or her own part in the success of the whole. Pride in collective achievements reinforces a shared identity, as IBM's community service does. Service to the external community can unite the internal community. But that's not enough without pride in each other. Strong communities thrive on trust and mutual respect. People must respect each other's differences without using them to divide, unlike Nigel Brown's actions at Empire.

E-culture pacesetter companies behave more like communities offline and online. This doesn't mean they erase all distinctions or replace hierarchy with democracy—far from it, as the IBM case shows. Nor does it mean that they eliminate individuality and replace it with conformity. The community ideal is about *unity*, not uniformity; *inclusion*, not consensus; and *communication*, not decision rights.

Community occupies an intermediate position on a continuum from bureaucracy to democracy. It is an organizing principle that allows people to collaborate quickly and effectively, facilitated by technology. Formal systems and processes can certainly produce official integration, but community is the behavioral and emotional infrastructure that supports those other organizational processes and makes them effective. Community action and spirit permit speed and seamlessness, encourage creativity and collaboration, and release human energy and brainpower—the essence of e-culture.

7

◆

PEOPLE.COM
Winning the Talent Wars

What will I remember most? . . . The feeling of belonging to a smart set of people spread across the globe. I've seen exponential growth and am continuously awed by our collective knowledge, creativity, and teamwork.

—Website producer at Razorfish, now working at another company

You are on a mission from God.

—Helen Yang's paraphrase of CEO Scott McNealy's message to her Sun Microsystems team

Stuck in a .bomb?

—Recruiting ad on a San Francisco billboard

PEOPLE, PEOPLE, PEOPLE. Ask any future-oriented employer today what their biggest asset is, and that's the answer. Ask those same employers what their biggest headache is, and that's still the answer. Attracting people, motivating people, and retaining people.

Kerry Logistics, an e-commerce fulfillment house in Hong Kong, made an offer to an Internet programmer who promised to resign from his current job to move to Kerry. Kerry's managing director, Max Jones, shook his head sadly as he told the story. An hour after the deal was struck, the new recruit called Kerry to say he could not quit because he had been offered a 55 percent raise. "Why this sudden generosity?" Jones inquired. The candidate replied, "Because they're desperate. I'm one of the last programmers left."

Organizations worldwide face a competition for talent that confronts them with new dilemmas and unfamiliar rules every day. The number one barrier to Internet success, out of seventeen choices, for the 785 companies responding to my global e-culture survey, is that "the unit does not have staff with adequate technical or Web-specific skills." Nearly 40 percent of all respondents, including pure Internet companies, faced this barrier. Labor shortages in the hottest new fields have turned the attention of entrepreneurs and global giants alike to the talent wars. And some act like they are at war as they try to poach their rivals' staffs—sending spies to peek at employee lists or advertising that they welcome defectors.

The Commitment Crisis

Today's global talent competition is fueled, in part, by the flight to cyberspace. Companies must offer great jobs in a great environment with great amenities—and constantly improve on them. Silicon Valley software engineers and Silicon Alley Internet producers alike talk about their desire to work only on cutting-edge projects using the best tools. They are loyal to an industry, to a technology, and to their profession, rather than to a particular company.

Long-term employment in a large and presumably powerful organization no longer defines a successful life. People want financial security more than job security. Now they have more ways to become financially secure, as the idea of stock options spreads from the New Economy to the Old. And should they still want jobs, they have more ways to find them. The percentage of Fortune Global 500 companies actively recruiting on the Web leaped from 17 percent in January 1998 to 45 percent in January 2000, and the top ten Internet job search sites had almost twice as many unique visitors in March 2000 as they did one year earlier—17.4 million versus 8.9 million.[1]

It is clear that people with Internet-relevant talents are not plants that sink permanent roots; they are animals on the prowl for opportunity. Knowledge workers are often knowledge nomads—a term coined by Harvard team member Todd L. Pittinsky, whose research examines mobility and commitment in high-tech workplaces, for those high-tech professionals who move among companies easily in search of the next exciting project, taking with them what they just learned.[2] Stock options no longer hold them in place; the new employer simply matches the offering. Even in an older high-tech company that has long valued lifetime commitment, the pace of change has led managers to question whether they want so many people with long experience. Being around a long time, they say, is a way for people to get stuck in stereotypes and be unable to change.

It is not just engineers who move from project to project, Hollywood style.[3] Knowledge nomads are everywhere my e-culture team looked. A financial expert had worked in three different dotcoms in the five years since receiving his MBA. The head of public relations for a successful dotcom, who was barely in her thirties, had already worked for seven companies, from large corporations to small startups. The head of consulting for a large computer systems company, who had moved there from IBM, jumped ship for an e-business consulting startup where she could build from the ground up and get equity in client companies—after she herself had plucked people from other firms and worried about how to retain her own talent. She hesitated before accepting the offer out of loyalty to her employer but then succumbed. Her mobility, and that of others, did not necessarily reflect unhappiness with the previous job. At a successful startup, a website producer in her late twenties told me, "I'd never leave such a cool company." That is, not until a cooler one came along. She left eight months after our first interview to join the Internet division of a larger company.

The emerging workforce of more mobile employees cuts across age groups, gender, and geography, studies show. An Interim Services/Harris poll found that new-breed employees are more concerned with gaining new experiences and having opportunities for mentoring and growth. Traditional workers, in contrast, are more concerned with job security, stability, and clear direction. The new breed favors high growth (89 percent were seeking this) over predictability (27 percent), whereas traditional employees prefer a predictable job (56 percent). Nearly all employees express a desire for the opportunity to think creatively, but traditional employees also want day-to-day direction (93 percent) whereas the new breed shun it (27 percent).[4] Autonomy and the freedom to roam are Internet-Age values.

The Challenges of the Talent Wars

For many companies, the search for talent is their number one priority, and they look everywhere they can, even when they do not have the means to compete with impossibly high monetary offers. At CNBC.com, for example, new CEO Pamela Thomas-Graham's first challenge was to fill her management team quickly. At her arrival in September 1999, there were 35 people, a number that grew to 65 two months later, with plans to swell to 150 by mid-2000. Although corporate parent GE's budget review had recommended a hiring freeze for all NBC units, CNBC.com got the "Jack Welch thumbs up," as a manager put it, to hire three times as many as had been previously budgeted. To turbocharge recruiting, Thomas-Graham secured all of the time of her human resource head (who had been half time), increased the number of internal recruiters, and changed executive search firms. Aware of the problems of luring people with Internet skills to work for a large corporation, she sought about half the new people from internal transfers from GE and NBC who were excited about working for an entrepreneurial Internet startup.

The external marketplace was more challenging for CNBC.com. NBC was creating an employee referral program that offered current employees $5,000 and two tickets to the Sydney Olympics if they recruited talent that stayed beyond sixty days. The ability to offer GE stock options to high performers was a help, but CNBC.com's compensation structure could not be different from that in effect throughout GE. General Electric had already encountered controversy over compensation for people involved with its Internet deals and internal ventures because of the contrast of its corporate approach with the opportunities in stand-alone dotcoms, whose huge market valuations made their investors and founding teams very wealthy very quickly. The business press speculated about strains at NBC after its Web team quadrupled the value of a portfolio of about thirty ventures bought for a mere $90 million, much of it in on-air ads. Kenneth Krushel, a former senior vice president who left in the fall of 1999 to run an Internet company, told *Forbes* magazine: "Working at

NBC puts you smack at the center of the deal flow, but GE is having a difficult time dealing with the issue of where to draw the line [on pay]."[5]

Still, Thomas-Graham felt that CNBC.com had no problem finding good people by turning the GE connection into a virtue. She said: "We can go after seasoned people. Our value proposition to them is that, unlike a true Internet startup, we can give them sufficient cash compensation to maintain their current lifestyle. Many people would like to work for dotcom companies but can't take a true leap of faith because they have financial commitments. We can offer more cash compensation than other Internet companies, the glamour of the NBC environment, and a career path within NBC or GE." CNBC.com offered a casual, freewheeling atmosphere, close to the CNBC television newsroom in Fort Lee, New Jersey. However, even this did not necessarily provide an advantage. More than one staffer expressed concern about luring people away from New York City, observing that "you can't have power lunches in the CNBC cafeteria."

CNBC.com's balance of internal and external recruiting is a solution hit upon by other wannadots, too. A talent balance makes sense. External hires bring new skills not yet cultivated by the company; internal recruits bring a network of contacts that can help smooth relationships and create an integrated community. Hiring some people from within also shows that the opportunity to be in on the hot new Internet area is open to company veterans. Once Williams-Sonoma's e-commerce division was officially chartered, the unit made a point of mixing insiders with outsiders— enough insiders from technology areas, for example, to create a bridge back to that area, but not so many as to strip the corporate technology group of its own talent.

But that very issue—how many internal people to move to the Internet group—reflects a common dilemma. In the United Kingdom, Tesco.com was concerned about the danger of taking the best managers from the rest of the business, especially since traditional food retailing was still the giant core. Not all retail managers could make the imaginative leap into new frameworks, but the best Tesco managers wanted to work in Tesco.com because it was seen as one of the most exciting areas. So how could they be told that they couldn't move because the mainstream business needed them? Internal people with the skills to move to the Internet side were also in demand in the external labor market. Marketing staff were the most mobile, not only to Tesco.com but also to outside competitors. Training internal people for Internet positions often does not help. Once trained, people have left even companies long considered to be good employers

with loyal long-term employees. L.L. Bean trained long-service professionals to run e-commerce, only to lose them to startups offering stock options.
The first Williams-Sonoma e-commerce team walked out as a group while
the site was still under development to join a startup bankrolled by a
European luxury goods firm. (The startup failed, and the group was again
on the move, with multiple offers.)

Mixing internal and external people poses other dilemmas. In Honeywell's e-hubs, and even in the e-business units within the mainstream
divisions, newly hired employees demanded higher wages, greater flexibility in the workplace, and stock options if and when the e-hubs went
public. Whether and how to change the internal compensation structure
was an organization-wide challenge. For Tom Galanty, head of Honeywell's first e-hub, MyPlant.com, it was a daily concern. Galanty wanted the
best talent, and he did not want to settle for Honeywell veterans just
because he couldn't bend the rules enough to attract external people. He
reported that he was criticized by some Human Resources staff for not
posting all open job positions, "But I felt we must act like executive
recruiters, and selectively pick individuals with the talent and drive
needed for us to succeed. Certain positions make sense to post, but others don't." How could Galanty as head of a small startup convince an
industrial giant that Internet employees were different and should be paid
more and differently than the scales in the traditional business?

High turnover is often the result of a failure to resolve this New Econ-
omy/Old Economy clash. This was apparent at barnesandnoble.com,
whose high turnover was widely reported in the press. Many Internet-side
employees who left still expressed to my e-culture team great respect for
the parent company's leaders and for the dotcom itself. "It was a really
cool place to work, and it was a lot of fun," one former staffer said, "but
they've had a lot of turnover lately, a lot of turnover, because the stock is
nowhere, and there are other fish in the sea."

Compensation and responsibility at barnesandnoble.com mirrored
that of the parent company rather than reflecting the needs of an Internet company, an ex-executive explained: "Len Riggio built the retail chain
with five guys close to him and 25,000 hourly employees. Turnover at the
hourly employee level, that's just a fact of life. Those people are easily
replaced." There was not enough understanding of the different demands
of an Internet company and how much harder it was to find and hold
talent: "You have to manage 400 dotcom employees differently than you

manage 25,000 retail store employees. We're just a different animal. We are in higher demand and can get jobs anywhere. They just never really got that, never really internalized that." Another former employee concurred: "The coolest book job in New York—the center of the publishing industry—was at barnesandnoble.com. So if you were a book person, that was the place to be. I think the company knew that and didn't have to pay a lot to those book people. But for people with Web skills, while Barnes & Noble was pretty cool there was also N2K and CDNow and Big Star and lots of other places that someone with basic HTML or other Web type skills could go. So people could demand a lot more because they had so many other opportunities."

To some employees, compensation felt disproportionate, weighted to the ten top people. What was fair on the retail side was considered highly unfair on the Internet side. "They compared the stock option plan to Walden Books and Borders, their chief competitors in the retail world. But nobody, nobody on the Internet side compared the options plan to Walden Books. They compared it to Amazon, Yahoo!, and eBay, and it didn't hold up too well."

Not only wannadots are running scared. Pure Internet companies face their own attraction and retention issues. In mid-2000, many of those who used stock options as their bait found their employees jumping ship when a stock market downturn put the options under water, below their exercise price. And the chance to get rich quick on stock options works best before a company goes public. One post-IPO company that we observed in depth had very high turnover and an overreliance on financial incentives that no longer seemed enough to attract and hold people. Their lament could be a song title: "How you gonna keep them down on the farm, after the IPO?"

Yet, despite the mobility surrounding Internet opportunities, people still work hard and show every sign of deep commitment to their work, if not fierce devotion to the company. They define loyalty as contribution rather than tenure. Although length of service is no longer appropriate as the main indicator of commitment, some workplaces have greater "stickiness" than others. And some companies, including those surrounded by knowledge nomads, do a better job of attracting, motivating, and retaining people a little longer than their peers. There are clues in the experiences of companies with the best workplaces about a new kind of commitment—renewable commitment.

Mastery, Membership, and Meaning:
Three Dimensions of Commitment

Old-fashioned bureaucracies were characterized by universal rules and uniform treatment of people; those features were considered virtues at the beginning of the modern industrial age. Machine Age corporations made a high art out of mass production of everything, including workplaces as well as products. Managers used a narrow motivational toolkit, treating people as though they were all the same and wanted the same things—and if they didn't, too bad. Those were the rules.

E-culture begins with a different set of premises. The Internet pushes segment-of-one customization to the individual level and allows individuals to change their minds frequently. Inside organizations, customization of work environments is not always so clear, but some of the best companies have started to offer more choices and more flexibility at work to fit people's varying lives outside work, while also building organizational community.

Today we see people as more variable than psychology once did. Howard Gardner observed geniuses in many fields and identified a range of forms of intelligence. Others have identified a range of learning styles and a range of work motivations. Motivations change over a person's whole life cycle. They can also change over the phases of a project. For example, Teresa Amabile found that both intrinsic and extrinsic motivation support creativity; intrinsic motivation is more important for generating new ideas, whereas extrinsic motivators can play a role in completing the effort to get them off the ground.[6]

Variability extends to the things that influence people's choices. There is no one single magic ingredient that accounts for commitment; it is a mix of factors. Survey data indicate that people are willing to work hard, and even make long-term commitments, if employers provide challenging work and compatible colleagues—two clear but different variables. WetFeet.com, a career information site, polled 889 undergraduate, business, and graduate school students from top universities in the spring of 2000. WetFeet found that good-quality job training was the most important factor in graduates' job selection that year, far outranking dotcom incentives such as stock options and also rated as much more important than the ability to dress casually, have a personal office, and take weekends off. Consistent with 1999 findings, training for future work ranked first, followed by challenging assignments, good colleagues, and salary. Financial benefits such as stock options and bonuses were far less important than attributes of the job and the workplace. Results clearly showed that money is not always the key factor in job commitment, for young graduates as well as seasoned employees.[7]

For those already at work, similar factors are important. A December 1999 study of 6,357 workers by Randstad North America found that 73 percent of employees would rather work harder and receive performance bonuses than work with minimal deadlines and low stress. The study also showed a high proportion indicating loyalty to their current company. The top reasons employees gave for staying put included affection for coworkers (71 percent), a pleasant work environment (68 percent), an easy commute (68 percent), challenging work (65 percent), and flexible work hours (54 percent).[8] Among Europeans, the nonmonetary side of employment is even more striking. An aggregation of data from nineteen countries showed that job satisfaction, working relationships, and company identification topped the list of fifteen possible aspects of employment as being the most important to people, while pay ranked at the bottom.[9]

With all the fuss over money in discussions about Internet recruitment, it is a little surprising that its importance is underplayed on surveys. People clearly expect compensation to be fair and equitable, with fairness defined by the right peer comparisons: One of the complaints on the Internet side of wannadots is that the parent corporation uses the wrong peer group (other old companies, not dotcoms) in determining financial incentives. Money is important, and as long as there's a bidding war for talent, it will always be salient—although some people value it for its own sake more than others do. But logic suggests that money cannot be an important factor in commitment. As a universal medium of exchange, one employer's money is as good as another's (once all the calculations are made about the value of various cash and noncash compensations). Money is fungible. Other aspects of the work environment are not. They are company specific. And even if companies can copy aspects of each other's practices, as they do, the multidimensional nature of commitment makes the whole package important, not just single features. Social psychologists have long distinguished between "hygiene factors"—the basic must-haves-because-everyone-else-does—and true motivators—the things that make a difference in level of effort and length of service.

Commitment, as my earlier research showed, involves a set of linkages between people and organizations that build on human capabilities.[10] People have cognitive, emotional, and moral skills. We rationally calculate instrumental advantages and seek mastery of the elements that will provide advantage in the future, using our cognitive skills. We develop relationships and feel connections with other people along an affective dimension, through our emotions. And we search for meaning and purpose, an almost spiritual dimension, based on a moral impulse. These three kinds of human information processing correspond to three broad qualities that organizations offer, which serve as the basis for commitment: the three Ms of mastery, membership, and meaning. (And, of course, we shouldn't forget that the fourth M, money, is always lurking somewhere in the scene in the talent-hungry e-world.)

Mastery: Caring about Today, Thinking about Tomorrow.

The first dimension of commitment involves an assessment of whether it is worth it to stay or leave, to put in a great deal of effort or slack off. That involves a variety of rational calculations about the job today and where it will lead in the future. Underlying these calculations is a generic desire for mastery: for satisfaction and success coupled with increasing opportunity to achieve success in the future. Challenging work, training and the chance to learn, paths to greater success, and a stake in the future are all components of mastery. Ideally, these would all be found together; in reality, there are personal preferences and trade-offs. With more of one thing, people might settle for less of another, depending on their own situation.

Still, it is striking that the e-culture project's comparison of higher- and lower-commitment organizations (a rough approximation, since some companies are still young) yielded an almost-universal agreement about the centrality of mastery goals for knowledge workers with Internet-relevant skills. These workers are attracted by the chance to take on big responsibility and stretch their skills even further. The "stickiest" work settings (the ones people leave less frequently and more reluctantly) involve opportunity and empowerment. Cutting-edge work with the best tools for the best customers is important in the present because it promises even greater responsibility and rewards in the future. Knowledge workers want to build their human capital—their individual package of skills and accomplishments—as much as their financial capital. (Anyway the former is also seen as a route to the latter.) This was true across the range of Internet types and company sizes.

Stretch and Empowerment: The Chance to Learn, Speak Up, and Be Heard. David Palmieri, vice president of product development for Mondera.com, gave the e-culture team deep insights into the importance of mastery. Mondera, a rapidly growing online retailer of fine jewelry and luxury items in New York City, was engaged in fierce competition to attract the best and the brightest, especially on the technology side. "In my area, the website and technology, it is particularly difficult. I think the key is to look for smart young people with a can-do attitude and then give them more responsibility than they are likely to get elsewhere. Technology people are highly motivated by technical challenges and take a lot of pride in their abilities. I've found that if you create an environment in which everybody is slightly over their head, it's infectious. The word gets out that it's a good place to learn and that attracts other good technical people."

At Honeywell, one of Tom Galanty's strategies for attracting creative new talent to MyPlant.com was to ask people to write their own job descriptions and include a business proposition to explain how they would grow a particular part of the business. "This scares away 80% of the people, but the ones that come back and are aggressive are the ones I want to hire," Galanty explained. He tried to create an agile organizational culture that "empowered people to do what they can do to the point where they're out of their comfort zone. A lot of people think they're constrained by organization. But I've removed virtually every constraint you can think of." At Reuters Greenhouse in London, "The incentive is to give smart people absolutely outrageous responsibilities," senior associate Norman Fiore said. "One of our new associates, a just turned 25-year-old, closed three deals in one week. He's talking to CEOs. He's doing absolutely obscene stuff, stuff that he shouldn't be doing for 10 years."

Abuzz attributes its unusually high retention rate to the opportunity to stretch. That began as an almost accidental byproduct of a cash-strapped startup, but then became a company value. "It's funny, the retention stuff," Jess Brooks mused. "When I first started at the company, we couldn't afford to hire people who really knew what they were doing, and so everybody got to do a little bit of everything. I think that's a value that is still really important here. If someone has a really good idea, we're not going to let job title or job description get in the way of that. And so it's really easy for a person to come in with a great idea and end up going in a totally different direction from the direction that they were hired in, both in terms of their official job and then also in terms of the other things that they do that are part of who they are. The company allows people to branch out and do different things. We don't ask people to narrowly define themselves."

Examples abound at Abuzz:

- When Jay Brewer came as a casual drop-in to work on a specific project, he was immediately assigned to what he called "amazing work," so he wanted to find a more permanent job at Abuzz. Brewer (eventually chief of product design) recalled the freedom he was given to take on any responsibilities he could: "Andres said in his accent, 'Mr. Brewer, I know what you'll do tomorrow; you'll get this thing working. I don't know what you'll be doing in three months, but it will be the right thing to do.'"

- A graphic designer pitched in to work with the engineers when they were short staffed and up against a big deadline. "It was a stretch for her; she had to learn Java in like two days," a colleague reported. "But then when she came back to the marketing group, it was really good that she had that tie with them."

- Vivian Wong interviewed for the job of community coordinator, but was told she would be good at user research, so she plunged in to a bigger job than she had imagined. Compared with her previous employer, she said, Abuzz put a lot of confidence in the staff. That, in turn, motivated her to learn: "They placed their confidence in me, so I'd better learn this stuff to catch up."

People uncomfortable about stretching to do unfamiliar things reminded themselves that the whole domain was unfamiliar, so they did not have to be intimidated by the assumption that there were experts out there or afraid of a hierarchy when speaking up.

In contrast, an Internet star I'll call "Joshua Jones" abandoned a prominent, growing online venture for a smaller company where he would be more influential. He found it easy to poach former coworkers because "they were all looking to operate at the next level. They really couldn't before, because the organization was too big and moved too slowly. Producers and developers that I've hired wanted more responsibility." His previous company was "an incredible training ground, an incredibly high volume site, very competitive, high profile, so you really learn your craft well across all the disciplines. But [at] some point, you just want to call the shots." A company will successfully retain people, he said, to the extent that it empowers people.

Focus, Clarity, and Discipline: Aids to Mastery. Empowerment should not be confused with open-ended responsibilities with no boundaries. Higher-commitment settings are also characterized by a great deal of focus, clarity, and discipline. People like projects that are challenging but in which priorities are clear. In contrast, many people told us that they left dotcoms because of poorly articulated goals, shifting priorities that made it impossible to complete anything, time that was wasted in endless rambling meetings, and a lack of focus in the business model. To become attractive work environments, dotcoms have to overcome the natural chaos of a startup.

In big as well as small companies, rigorous goals and deadlines are considered an asset—and seen as a stimulus to creativity, not a stifler of it. At CNBC.com, Pamela Thomas-Graham said she appreciated the discipline imposed on her Internet venture by corporate parent General Electric because it made CNBC.com a "real business, with deliverables" and a disciplined plan as well as accountabilities for results. Similarly, PlanetRx.com, an independent dotcom, brought the discipline of the founders' MBA training and consulting experience to create temporary order out of chaos, which allowed people to focus on completing projects successfully. Regular companywide communication of major themes guided the overall purpose of the work. Employees used the themes to determine which tasks were necessary, which could wait, and which should be eliminated.

The most satisfying projects for engineers and other knowledge workers involve complex technological feats that no one believes can be done. Focus and clarity help them accomplish the impossible. For example, over a nearly two-year-period at Sun Microsystems, in the largest project Sun had ever undertaken, Helen Yang's and Mark Walden's SunPeak team moved the company from a mainframe-based ERP system to a network-centric Sun-driven ERP system, minimizing the impact on customers and business partners even during a three-week shutdown for conversion to the new system. There were monthly, weekly, and daily milestones. Action items were constantly revised and communicated to account for surprises or new developments. There was a firm deadline—go live in August 1998—and Yang and her team constantly revisited the schedule to make sure they could hit the date. The priorities were schedule, then quality, then cost. "That helped the team tremendously because there was a clear goal and a clear priority. There was no confusion about what we had to accomplish." This underscores the importance of one of my favorite management lessons about dealing with change: Certainty of process can enable effective action even when there is uncertainty of outcomes.

Organizational clarity is equally important to people: who is working on what, who can make decisions, where to go for fast approvals, and what tasks the person himself or herself will be held accountable for. In rapidly changing e-culture environments, this clarity comes not from dissemination of organization charts but from frequent, abundant communication. Clarity is especially important after major organizational changes, such as mergers and acquisitions. This is why Cisco Systems, the reputed master at acquisition integration in the Internet technology space, strives to ensure that jobs and reporting lines are clearly defined from day one of an acquiree's association with Cisco.

Opportunity, Options, and Ownership. Mastery also involves a feeling of opportunity—that today's success will lead to greater satisfactions in the future. That is where future-oriented financial incentives can play a role. If stock options make people act more like owners of their companies with a longer-term stake, that can only benefit performance. James Toledano, founder of brandnewmusic.com in London, feels that it is important to give options to his employees because the startup's pay is low; a piece of the pie would breed enthusiasm for long hours. Shaun Cutts, co-founder of Abuzz, made it clear that Abuzz "was not stingy" with stock options. Options are part of a larger ownership ethic, even in traditional offline companies; Motorola CEO Christopher Galvin uses options to build commitment to "one Motorola."

Money alone is not the issue. It is money coupled with responsibility that generates commitment. An Abuzz employee who had worked as a trader reported: "On Wall Street people were in it for the money you made yourself. Abuzz employees have an amazing sense of ownership, even as we get larger. They say, 'This is mine, I built it,' even though they don't do any coding.... There's this incredible degree of employee ownership of the product and the goals. Like it's not just the engineers who actually built the web page."

One opportunity that companies can hold out to people is the chance to run something and benefit directly from an ownership stake. Lucent Technologies' New Ventures Group uses internal startups as a retention tool; its ventures kept talented engineers from leaving for Silicon Valley, as I reported in chapter 4. At the other end of the size spectrum, iXL, a young, high-growth Internet strategy consulting firm with high turnover even by industry standards, decided to use venture opportunities to reward people who successfully completed a few years of service—they could earn a chance for leadership of one of the company's portfolio of Internet-related startups.

When an Internet company that had used stock options to attract talent before the IPO asked me what they could do after their IPO, I included the elements of mastery in my advice about motivating professionals:

- Signal to new hires that the company has a future, that it is built to last, or they won't join (or will keep their names out there in the market).

- Recognize that e-culture incentives are not the IPO but career capital —not just getting rich but getting ahead, playing at the top of the game. So make sure people get to work on the biggest, most important new problems. Company innovation builds motivation.

- Give the most talented, the "rock stars" of the field, reputation enhancers such as external visibility, the chance to build knowledge that gets embedded in the company's practices with credit to them, and inclusion in the senior leadership of the company, making its decisions and charting its course.

- Motivate younger, less experienced hires through cutting-edge tasks, the chance to work with the rock stars, the best training, and clear expectations for future responsibilities.

MEMBERSHIP: CEMENTING THE WE, CARING ABOUT ME

Membership, the second dimension of commitment, has both collective and individual dimensions. It involves cohesion among members as a group, warm and strong relationships. It also derives from respect for individuals and their differences, so that people feel included for who they are. A feeling of community emanates from many people's feelings of belonging. Numerous organizational practices can encourage this.

Welcome to the Community. Membership begins with how people enter. Abuzz made this a high art. New hires receive a range of gifts in the office and at home, and then, at the end of the first day, a surprise party. "There are all the people you're going to be working with, celebrating you," Jay Brewer recalled. Vivian Wong said, "When I walked in after my first day and saw the party, I was ready to cry."

"Someone to Watch over Me." Buddies and mentors connect individuals to the community, helping them with numerous personal questions as well as job issues. Another sign of caring comes from managers with responsibility for nurturing the person's career. The SunPeak project at Sun Microsystems made a special point of assigning a home-base career manager as well as a changing task manager to people on the team, because the tasks—and hence the specific project leadership—kept changing as the project evolved. Helen Yang said that this special management structure meant that people could move around freely without worrying about "Who is my manager and who's responsible for my review? Who's looking after me?"

Honoring Personal Interests. Abuzz's Cool Talks over a free lunch every few weeks allow people to present other aspects of themselves not generally visible at work: ballroom dancing, video games, musical performances, Sue Ellen's art, Dala's Nigerian wedding. "It really cements the relationships here when you realize that Dala has this whole other life in Nigeria, and Sue Ellen has a studio where she goes in the evenings and creates all these gorgeous prints, and Jed is writing a musical," a leader said. Another one indicated, "For me, the cool thing about this company is: I can do my work stuff, and I can carve it out so that it's stuff that is really interesting to me. But in addition to that, the company allows me to come up with other things that are important to me and lets me do them here. . . . We all work crazy hours, but there aren't any real set hours here. And as long as you're getting your work done, if you want to spend another ten hours this week working on the personal stuff, that's not an issue at all."

Recognition. Recognition is abundant in high-commitment settings. In the best instances, it is not only ceremonial. It is used to reinforce community values as well as honor individuals. Abuzz created RAVEs (Respect and Value Everyone) as a way for employees to recognize each other for above-and-beyond contributions, such as pitching in to help someone else. RAVEs can be filled out on the corporate website; at the weekly company meetings, someone reads the RAVEs and which core values they demonstrate. SunPeak's recognition was more formal. At completion, sizable bonuses were awarded to team members. Helen Yang also nominated three key project leaders from her team for the coveted President's Award (twenty-five people in all of Sun recognized by Scott McNealy for their outstanding achievement), all three of whom were chosen. Then she held a weekend celebration in Monterey, California, for all team members and their families.

Supporting Life outside of Work. Speaking of families, American employers can no longer act as though they do not exist. Finally—after more than twenty years of exhortation by women's advocates—U.S. companies are starting to recognize that people have lives and families outside of work. Discovering unacceptable rates of turnover among women professionals, Deloitte & Touche, the accounting and consulting firm, took steps to add flexible schedules, control travel, and help employees balance work and family responsibilities. Those changes, useful for men as well, landed Deloitte in the top ten list of best companies to work for in America—helping the firm attract still more talent. Flexibility is not hard to provide, as a survey of 769 HR professionals by an outplacement firm showed; 68 percent agreed that telecommuters at their companies are no more difficult to manage than on-site employees.[11] As of 2000, an estimated 11 million to 22 million Americans telecommuted at least one day a week.

In addition to flexible work, e-culture involves attention to personal needs. At Abuzz, an employment contract might specify not only job responsibilities but also individual regimens. An employee reported that her contract said: "You must listen to music or go jogging or whatever it is that helps you relieve stress. You must do something that gets you out of the office and helps you be sane." The workplaces of pacesetter companies such as Gap Inc. and others include conveniences that help people balance work and the rest of life: dry cleaning services, bank branches, fitness centers, and cafés with takeout food to carry home.

Trust and Respect. In high-commitment settings, we heard people say that they not only like each other, they respect each other. Numerous knowledge nomads now happily at work in a company with open communication mentioned previous companies where people operated with hidden agendas or were guarded and full of fear.

Contrast the inclusiveness of high-commitment companies with a prominent dotcom afflicted with high turnover, firings, and lawsuits. Respect for employees was so low that if a junior person wasn't working out, the CEO brought in someone over him, which made the company top-heavy and created seemingly unnecessary layers. "It felt very hierarchical," reported a former executive. "It was a cliquey and personality driven culture—the people who are close to the founder or not. The founder has a strong personality and places a lot of value on personal relationships. That's good if you have a good personal relationship and death if you don't. . . . It was a very small company, but it was a more political place than other dotcoms, and it felt more bureaucratic than the phone company—so many channels to go through."

MEANING: BELIEVING IN A LARGER PURPOSE

The third commitment mechanism is a sense of meaning: the belief that the work itself has meaning, that the company's output creates social value, and that belonging to the organization provides a chance to help change the world for the better. When time with a company comes to mean something that resonates with the human quest for a higher purpose to life, people are more likely to solidify their commitment.

Missionary idealism is not typical of traditional businesses, but it does characterize many dotcoms. Their revolutionary rhetoric of Total World Domination and their search for "believers" is a big part of their workplace culture. An executive at Women.com reported on the founding period, "We were all overqualified for our jobs; we had all taken a calculated risk. We had a tremendous challenge—to push this new media onto the world. . . . We were missionaries [and] needed to hire people who would buy into our vision."[12]

Some companies earn employee affection by making people proud to work there; others give employees the chance to do more than just their job. One way to extend the company's purpose into a broader realm of meaning is involvement in community service. This can make concrete statements of values that are otherwise abstract, long term, and not particularly credible. Allaire, a rapidly growing producer of e-commerce software that was number 22 on *Business Week*'s Information Technology 100 list in 1999, proclaims on every occasion its founding mission ("Empower people with technology") and accompanying statement of values. But that mission became more meaningful to Allaire's 400 people when the company committed to sponsoring City Skills, a nonprofit organization training inner-city youth for Internet jobs. Now Allaire people could see their capabilities put to direct use in their community, and they could volunteer their own services.

Community service can solidify a shared identity. When the Swiss pharmaceutical giant Novartis was formed from the merger of Sandoz and Ciba-Geigy, new CEO Daniel Vasella worked with his top team to craft a new statement of mission, aspirations, and values that included acknowledging the company's social purpose. As a consultant on merger integration, I recommended that this could become real to all employees through a global day of community service involving teams of volunteers making a difference in their local communities in every Novartis country. At the one-year anniversary of the decision to merge, Novartis held its first annual Global Community Day. This was not a Swiss tradition nor much of a European tradition either, but the reports from countries such as France were glowing. It was the most inclusive and meaningful thing Novartis could have done to announce its new identity to employees and the world.

Community service activities performed jointly allow people to "feel together" in a literal sense—that is, to share a direct emotional experience. That explains an apparent paradox: that virtual, place-transcending e-culture should include hands-on, local community service. The chance to serve the community through one's employer is among the hottest new employee benefits in the United States. Timberland offers its employees five days of paid company time to work on community service projects, often through City Year, a national youth corps that Timberland sponsors along with other global companies such as Adobe, Compaq, and Cisco.

Community service is most meaningful when there is a match with the business mission. Service creates commitment not just because of the company's charitable impulses but because the company's core skills can make a contribution to solving major social problems. Akamai, a high-flying Internet technology startup, was looking for a way to get involved in the community when it hosted a fundraiser for a new charter school focused on media and technology. IBM is an award-winning role model. IBM gets high marks from employees because of its big commitment to public education innovations through its Reinventing Education projects in twenty-one local and state school systems in the United States and seven large projects in countries such as Brazil, Italy, the United Kingdom, Vietnam, South Africa, and Singapore.

Community service can be a recruitment tool, as Timberland finds. Bain, an international consulting firm, uses community service to attract MBAs; new recruits can volunteer anywhere in the world with Habitat for Humanity before starting their full-time jobs, receiving up to $3,000 per person for travel expenses. Abuzz mentions its involvement in the Dante Alighieri Elementary School on its corporate website; it comes up frequently in recruiting. "When candidates come in to interview, it's definitely something they ask about," Jess Brooks reported. "We absolutely consider it an advantage."

In some companies, a service ethic emerges by example. EarthWeb does not mandate community contributions, believing that would not fit the individualistic nature of people working in an Internet company. But people are given opportunities to contribute to organizations in which founder-CEO Jack Hidary is a leader, such as MOUSE, Trickle Up, and policy groups concerned with the digital divide. EarthWeb has provided technical expertise, designing Trickle Up's website. Hidary also sends some of his people to represent him at community events, and there they catch the spirit (as well as catching facetime with celebrities) and get involved. They find such community activities "a very satisfying part of their job experience," Hidary reported. This gives EarthWeb a higher profile in New York than other companies of its size, and the visibility helps it attract talent ("I have had people come to me and apply for jobs because they know about our community activities," Hidary said) and also retain people. "I think it does help your retention. It helps with the job experience and makes it more than just a job," noted Hidary.

Hidary was quick to say that the core work environment is the most important thing, but he sees that making a difference in the world outside the business is a strong secondary factor. "It may not be the primary determinant that someone chooses this company or another company, but I think it is a factor for more and more people. If people are choosing between two of the same kind of companies, [their choice] is probably due to a working environment that is empowered, it is based on training, and then on some of these secondary issues, such as does the company get involved in public policy and charity."

Business is still business, and the work comes first. But infusing it with meaning adds to the mix that produces commitment.

Instant Culture: Seeking Commitment at a Click

Corporate culture used to just happen to companies. Today, building community is an explicit topic on Internet entrepreneurs' To Do list. PlanetRx.com was eager to establish guiding values from the beginning. PlanetFeedback documents its startup experience on its website as a way to reinforce a shared cultural history for everyone who joins. John Clare, chairman of FreeServe, the United Kingdom's first free Internet portal, as well as its parent company Dixon's, told us that FreeServe managed its rapid growth through special efforts to create a culture around social events as well as business meetings. New York Times Digital set up a culture committee across its portfolio of dotcoms, with Abuzz as a leader, almost as soon as it had the portfolio assembled. Sapient, a Web services firm, appointed Courtney Dickinson as its Culture Architect. Of course, culture of the traditional kind takes years to build and generations to solidify. In typical Internet fashion, new companies want instant culture.

Fun and games vie with attempts to create near-religious experiences as the cornerstones of explicit culture. Razorfish, a successful e-strategy and Web design firm in New York's Silicon Alley with a hip corporate ambience, uses large events to jump-start a common culture. The biggest and boldest was a company-wide Las Vegas trip in December 1999.

RAZORFISH FISHFRY 1.0

Hilary Glazer, then a producer at Razorfish, kept a diary for me about "Razorfish FishFry 1.0," "the first ever world-wide gathering of Razorfish employees to meet, share ideas and foster a sense of community within a worldwide growing company."

Prior to take off for Las Vegas, Fish from around the world were pointed toward the FishFry 1.0 intranet where we could check out the city, the hotel, the weather and get a general sense of what the 3-day weekend would be all about. It didn't give too much away. The element of surprise was an important factor in making the weekend a success. Any of us with prior "conference" experience probably expected a sleepy, conference-room style experience. Wrong. Over 1300 fellow Fish and I found a super-organized, super-fun and incredibly eye opening experience. Everything was in Razorfish style, unique and unexpected.

On the first day of the conference, we gathered in an enormous room in the hotel with stadium style seating, flashing lights, huge video screens, loud music, and a spinning stage in the center from where we would observe our sequined MCs throughout the weekend. [Co-founders] Craig and Jeff rolled in on scooters to much applause from a crowd of employees, many of whom they had not yet met. For the rest of the weekend, we met in this central room for announcements and a chance to hear first hand from our founders and representatives from newly acquired offices such as Lee Hunt Associates and I-Cube. All employees sat together, blending in, getting acquainted and in general, just learning about what we all do. The breakout sessions consisted of creative exercises such as drawing out your most embarrassing moment in crayon and explaining it to a crowd of strangers or constructing skits about our vision of Razorfish's future. Fun and games, but also a chance to showcase our creativity and get to know each other.

FishFry 1.0 was also an opportunity to spend time with our fellow New Yorkers and friends who had moved to other offices such as London, San Francisco, Stockholm and Los Angeles. A Razorfish value is to foster growth and learning through sharing projects with other offices. Many projects have tapped talent from other offices, most recently from the newly acquired and technically strong Cambridge office (formerly I-Cube). There really aren't 'typical' Fish. Only personal style and colorful expression. Fish ages range from right out of college to people on their third career. Most were in their 20s and early 30s. FishFry 1.0 fell on the first night of Chanukah, so Jeff and Craig led those of us who celebrate in candle lighting, latke eating and song. Jeff's parents were visiting that night and got a chance to see for themselves just how much Razorfish had grown.

What will I remember most about this experience? The never ending clink of quarters, the amazing view from my hotel window and the feeling of belonging to a smart set of people spread across the globe. I've seen exponential growth and am continuously awed by our collective knowledge, creativity and teamwork.

Such events can stir emotions and deepen relationships while establishing rituals that produce a company identity and a feeling of a special bond among those who know the rituals. They create memories of feelings that transcend the more mundane business information that is transmitted. As Novartis planned a gathering of its top 400 executives worldwide in Bermuda to begin the postmerger integration process, I talked with CEO Daniel Vasella and others about the need for emotional experiences to supplement the strategic sessions. I used the casual example of a company song. "Just an example," I said, "too American for a Swiss company." To my surprise, an older Swiss gentleman in corporate communications decided to write one. The charming song featured the company's mission as its refrain ("the science of life"). Everyone sang it after dinner at the conference.

For large global companies, the common culture formed by such events is a business asset because it enables people to recognize each other as fellow members. They now have artifacts and experiences in common that help them see beyond their differences. Sun's Helen Yang commented about the SunPeak project, "Running my team was like running a third world country. Or a United Nations. Not only do I have the normal ethnic cultural difference and the company cultural differences. I also have a large population of independent contractors and Andersen and Oracle consultants. So for everyone to work very well together and stay aligned for one goal—to go live in August '98—that was a challenge." Emotional experiences reinforce the power of a shared goal.

What is endearing to insiders about corporate culture, however, can seem cloying or corny to outsiders. Companies with strong cultures invite jokes about brainwashing. (When I told friends I had spoken at Cisco's top management conference, they asked if I had been "assimilated," a reference to the Borg colony on *Star Trek* that absorbs individuals into a single collective mind.) As more and more outrageous activities are performed in the name of "team-building," cynicism can easily grow. E-strategy firm Mainspring's week-long training program for new hires, mostly in their twenties, included a scavenger hunt involving a series of bizarre tasks, such as proposing marriage to a stranger, getting permission to don scrubs in a hospital operating room, and obtaining a store mannequin legally.

Not even insiders always find fun and games or value-shaping events appealing. Abuzz is self-conscious about its abundant rituals, knowing they can seem corny, and is careful to point out that they emanated from the people themselves. The company meetings were an Andy Sack decision. The beer hour became margarita socials at Andres Rodriguez's instigation when the office moved to the Brickyard. The buddy system for newbies (new hires) was started by Jess Brooks herself in April 1998. Maribeth, no longer with Abuzz, started RAVEs in September 1998, but she left her legacy, if not her last name. Brooks observed, "It's kind of corny, but there's this whole competition that's developed around writing a really good rave. Some people write it in verse, some people do a drawing or graph. Then someone will throw a piece of candy at your head. . . . People go away, but the culture endures. . . . This creates an incredible sense of accomplishment. Something exists that is greater than the people." A designer said, "It's not cult-like. These little things keep us team-oriented." Co-founder Shaun Cutts reflected, "I think having a clear sense of culture is self-reinforcing. People who don't fit in, don't come in. . . . That is sort of the start of it, that you set expectations right from the beginning." An Abuzz executive who returned after taking another job commented: "When I left, I thought this was touchy-feely. When I got back, I thought it's really cool."

Another Abuzz co-founder, Andres Rodriguez, was initially skeptical about the Abuzz style: "There were some people who felt that all the gushy, corporate stuff was fake, and there were people who felt that all my harsh stuff was vulgar, and in between, we cover the entire territory. We [the co-founders] gave people a lot of room for whatever they wanted as 'us.' A lot of the most fun people are not us, were never us. One sales guy decided that he was going to bring this dome hockey thing. All the developers are playing Quake. The big thing is you just trust them. In the beginning, one of the mistakes we made was being afraid of those things. We would say, 'no playing Quake until it's 5 o'clock,' or 'let's monitor Quake.' I remember Andy and I having this serious conversation about what we are going to do now that someone had brought in Quake."

For their part, Abuzz employees seem to value the trust and autonomy even more than the specific activity they create under the culture banner. At one point, several employees mocked up videotapes and elaborate news reports with photos depicting a cat and a monkey. A participant said, "Being creative promotes friendship and something to share." He added that he was grateful that "we have the freedom to do that."

Forced fun has its discontents. The *New York Times* reported on a modest exodus from dotcoms even before the stock market downturn because of the self-conscious culture: "Carla De Luca, a former CNN producer, moved from Atlanta to California and took a job at Beyond.com. . . . Top executives, she said, spent a lot of time spinning their wheels in endless meetings. But what really bothered her was the atmosphere of mandatory fun. Employees were told that if they wanted to have a meeting over a game of Ping-Pong, they should. And a 'dogs welcome' policy turned the office into a near-kennel. Ms. De Luca lasted four months, leaving behind a pile of stock options when she quit."[13]

The culture is also irrelevant if the work is not right. An Internet veteran reported that the prominent dotcom company he left "was a fun place in a lot of ways. It was relaxed and casual and everybody goes and has coffee together at one of the hot spots. But the company didn't know what to focus on in the time that I was there, and it's one of the reasons why I left." There were plenty of rituals and bonding mechanisms and discussions of values, but there was no clear business model. "If you asked the founders who were their competition, they would say we didn't have any competition, because no one was doing what we were doing—which I felt was a bad sign. If you have no competition, then you don't know what you're doing."

Return of the Nomads:
The Virtuous Circle of Attract and Retain

In a community, people leave, but they also come back. Knowledge workers operate less like feudal serfs dedicated to the land for life than like members of medieval craft guilds who take their craft from place to place and bring their friends with them. Companies attuned to e-culture have stopped shunning those who leave and have begun to consider them alumni who meet for reunions and continue to support the institution even after leaving. Bain invites former consultants to return to the consulting firm. Autodesk sends postcards to former employees a few months after they leave. (Of course, companies don't want to make it too easy for people to leave by holding the door open for their return.)

Abuzz, whose strong culture appears to build strong commitment, often has nomads return to the fold. Liesel Pollvogt, who came back to Abuzz as marketing vice president in 2000, had worked there for nine months in 1998 after leaving Firefly. She resigned from Abuzz, she said, because she was more interested in the Internet than the enterprise model Abuzz was then developing. But she left feeling good about the people and the company and continued to refer recruits to Abuzz while she was gone. "It felt very natural to return," she said.

Knowledge nomads also bring others with them. Mondera.com's David Palmieri deliberately leverages the network of people who had worked together before, trying to attract them as a group. Online Retail Partners recruited over twenty-five former barnesandnoble.com employees, including CTO John Kristie. For Abuzz's first few years, staff gathered mostly through friendships. "It starts with one person psyched about their job," a leader said. "I want to stay up late talking about this, so I want to talk to my friends." A computer expert reported, "A friend of the head of engineering had passed my work to Jay Brewer. It was word of mouth. Friends of friends is the best means of hiring. Then you know what you're getting, that the people will fit in." Andres Rodriguez concurred: "The best consequence of having a good place to work is that people bring their friends.

It's like tribes. There are groups of five or six that go around in groups. You get one, if he is great, you get the whole team."

Note the multiplier effects. Committed employees are not only more likely to stay longer, but they will also bring their friends. An increasing number of companies find referrals from current staff an excellent source of recruits. Even with online job search sites, word of mouth remains important, especially in the upper ranks. A 1999 survey of 7,400 U.S. executives who changed jobs within the previous year showed that 64 percent found their new jobs by networking, and only 4 percent found them through the Internet.[14] Some companies offer incentives to refer; one e-strategy firm offers stock options for referrals that result in hiring. But the best impetus for referrals is the way employees feel about the company. Retention of people reinforces attraction. It is a virtuous circle: *The stronger the commitment, the higher the enthusiasm, the easier to retain, and the easier to attract new people.*

High-commitment organizations are more likely to do more things across all three dimensions of commitment. The bond between people and organizations is multifaceted. The three clusters of commitment mechanisms overlap, and they work better in concert than they do alone. The same organizational practice can play many roles. When we asked an Abuzz technologist who had worked elsewhere and had numerous offers while at Abuzz what had attracted him to the company, he rattled off a long list that included the culture: *the opportunity to be designing at an early stage; coworkers who are intelligent and motivated and enjoy teamwork, being fun and serious, getting things done, and being on top of things; respect for the individual that promoted respect for the company and hard work; and the security of ownership by the New York Times.* "Everyone is really happy to be here," he concluded; "they're not dying to get to the door at 5 P.M."

Multiple commitment mechanisms can also save the company money. Many potent commitment mechanisms, such as trust and respect, are free. Others don't cost much, and can even bring immediate returns—such as extra treats for people who volunteer to meet tough deadlines that win key contracts.

The hard part for many companies is not giving financial incentives, it is giving people opportunity, power, and meaning. Some employers don't trust or respect people enough. For many years the U.S. auto manufacturers bought labor peace with high wages rather than ceding control over the workplace—that's why Saturn, with its high-involvement and high-performance culture, was so different. Other companies find it easier to offer financial incentives (a bold stroke, possible with a single decision) than to change the behavior of managers who are not adept at being leaders of people. And some otherwise successful companies have neglected cultivating people skills. Their lack of emphasis on people will be a limit to growth. At Sun, for example, we found skilled innovators and change leaders, some of whom are role models throughout this book. But we also found concerns that the company had grown to $12 billion without being explicit about creating talent nurturers. And Sun has no record of community service, unlike IBM and Cisco. One Sun executive said: "If you ask people managers in Sun what they do, they don't mention the people. They say, 'I make these decisions. I provide this technology input. I solve these problems,' and they might as an afterthought say that they get their teams to do them. But it's more a command-and-control type mentality—an individual contributor-technocrat type mentality—than a people manager mentality."

Are We All Volunteers?

Recounting some of the commitment mechanisms can make it sound like Internet companies and their offline counterparts are producing a workers' paradise. This is far from the case. Telephone call centers are the faceless factories of the Internet Age, complete with oversupervision and limited autonomy. In many dotcoms there are two or more cultures. Highly paid knowledge workers in e-commerce companies find food and fun in nurturing offices, while people in the warehouses who might not speak English toil to fulfill online orders with low wages and minimal appreciation—not to mention the workers making the products in Third World plants for whom the words *sweatshops* and *exploitation* might still apply. But in tight labor markets, some of the positive practices spill over to traditional offline companies. Jordan's Furniture, a multistore chain in the Boston area, is just as fun filled as any dotcom: It takes the entire company on trips to Bermuda, and runs festivals and celebrations in its warehouses.

Paying attention to people's needs and acknowledging their freedom of action means treating them not like subordinates who can be ordered around but like volunteers who are there of their own free will and can leave anytime. Charles Schwab, the pioneering online financial services company, has especially high volumes in the first quarter of each year, peaking at tax season. The company serves call center workers complimentary breakfast, lunch, and dinner during this period. "People who work extraordinarily long hours are treated like volunteers," reported Schwab San Francisco IT executive Parkash Ahuja.

In a certain sense, all employees are volunteers for some portion of what they do. People are paid for showing up at work, and they are given incentives for producing certain kinds of results. But many activities that affect longer-term company performance require voluntary effort unrelated to financial compensation in any direct way. The SunPeak team that converted all of Sun's IT systems had a punishing work schedule; for months, Saturday was a mandated work day. But despite the term "mandatory," vice president Helen Yang treated her people like volunteers who were thanked for being there. Meals were brought in. A "stress-free zone" was created. Yang established valet parking in response to the team's frustration at accumulating piles of parking tickets when they couldn't find legal spaces. She scheduled motivational speakers—stress specialists, an Olympic skier, an Apollo astronaut, and CEO Scott McNealy. "You are on a mission from God," McNealy would tell the team, Yang said. "The company's counting on you to get this done." (McNealy's rhetoric was perhaps not just hyperbole. Religious missionaries are the world's best sales forces. They make cold calls, face rejection, and persist for the long term.)

Classic research in psychology has shown that people are more committed to efforts that they perceive are voluntary rather than coerced or demanded. One set of studies found that paying people for certain kinds of tasks actually diminished their commitment. People attributed more importance to unpaid efforts that they believed were justified by strong personal beliefs. Just ask software industry executives about this motivation. Leading software companies enlist unpaid volunteers from outside their companies to commit significant blocks of time to answering customer questions and educating customers about product use. One leading producer of client-server programming tools enlisted thirty-two skilled outside professionals as unpaid volunteers to spend several hours a day participating in online forums. They signed on to be available for ten to twelve hours a week on the Internet in exchange for advance copies of products and travel expenses to three user conferences a year. That arrangement cost the company 15 percent of what it would take to deliver similar customer advice through an in-house paid staff.

The concept of volunteerism does not apply perfectly to profit-making companies, of course. Most of us who work for a living care about the money. But treating employees as volunteers and tapping into their self-propelled desires provides a valuable edge above and beyond incentive programs. Acknowledging that employees have freedom of choice is a thought exercise that enlarges the motivational toolkit from which managers draw.

From Blind Loyalty to Renewable Commitment

The emergence of knowledge nomads who are temporary volunteers instead of permanent fixtures makes some leaders wonder whatever happened to loyalty as a virtue. But I think the problem of loss of loyalty is overstated. Loyalty does have a nice ring to it: a long-term bond that transcends the caprices and greed of the moment. But loyalty can also sound like servitude. Unquestioning obedience. Blind conformity. Sticking with something that's not working. "My company, right or wrong." All things that are decidedly not part of e-culture.

Hewlett-Packard's great corporate culture that valued long service kept some people in place who were unable to innovate fast enough to compete with Sun Microsystems, whose culture valued constant change. For companies like Sun, length of service is not a value in itself but only an outcome of giving people such exciting project opportunities that they are constantly recommitting themselves, secure in the knowledge that they could leave anytime. Companies need people who are committed to doing the best possible job, and they need people who will stick around long enough to offer a return on the investment in training them. But that's not the same as loyalty to the company no matter what. High performance is not necessarily equated with long-term employment.

In the early 1990s, at the height of the reengineering craze, American and British commentators decried the other end of the employment equation: downsizing companies shedding long-term employees. Companies at that time expected loyalty without being loyal to their people. In the tight labor market for knowledge workers at the turn of the 2000s, is it any surprise that employees have reciprocated, deciding that loyalty is not a virtue? The past always looks better in retrospect, so suddenly there arose nostalgia for an earlier Golden Age of company loyalty in which people were reluctant to change employers. But in too many organizations people were "loyal" not because they really cared but because they had little choice. Seniority reigned. People could not afford to get off the career ladder; they had to climb it. Status, influence, and big pay increases were tied to promotion. People didn't have stock options; they had pension plans that handcuffed them to the company. For workers without career opportunity who were stuck in the same job for many years, the "loyalty" they seemed to demonstrate by sticking around was really just a lack of choices. Many of them secretly dreamed of escape and retired on the job.

Old-fashioned corporate loyalty in which all status and rewards accrued to seniority stopped being good for the economy when global competition heated up. Productivity and wages stagnated under the old corporate bureaucracy. In a U.S. economy characterized by entrepreneurial churn and high workforce mobility, productivity is up and wages are rising. Other countries want the same thing.

The money has to be right, but you can't buy loyalty just with money. Building long-term commitment depends on the nature of the work itself, the opportunity to grow and stretch, the chance to speak up and be listened to, and the feeling of making a difference. Members of the new generation in the workforce don't want to be subordinates; they want to control their own fate. They are more interested in building wealth than climbing a career ladder. They seek meaningful work with redeeming social value without sacrificing the chance to have a life.

E-culture has no room for blind loyalty. With so many choices and so much information readily accessible with a few mouse clicks, neither employees nor customers need to close their eyes to new offers and opportunities. E-culture does not discourage loyalty, but it does make it depend on constantly updated value. E-culture is based on eyes-wide-open renewable commitment. It is based on commitment that also recognizes the importance of change.

PART THREE

❖

Morphing

*Leading Fundamental Change at
Internet Speed*

8

◆

ON TRACK TO TOMORROW
Getting Change Rolling

You've got to be prepared to change the genetic code of the organization.
—David Weymouth, CIO, Barclays Bank, London

THIS IS A roll-up-your-sleeves-and-get-to-work chapter, so be prepared. If all you want to do is become an instant dotcom billionaire by starting MakeMeRichQuickOnTheWeb.com, then this won't be the place to find advice. This chapter digs into the leader's toolkit and introduces tools for systemic change to ensure that the system is in gear to create and sustain the business culture of tomorrow. I consider this chapter more like HowToGetThereAndKeepItGoing.com.

For wannadots, the big question is how to transform themselves into Internet-enabled organizations. CEOs of large manufacturing companies are jumping on the bandwagon, convening large meetings almost overnight to make it happen—whatever "it" turns out to be. For dotcoms and new dotcom-enablers, in contrast, the question is how to scale up while building and maintaining the right culture, how to grow without spinning out of control. Despite the difference in starting points, the interests of wannadots and dotcoms converge on the need to understand and guide their underlying organizational systems.

These are the kinds of questions that CEOs ponder. They are high on the worries list that top leaders generated in response to my inquiry about "what keeps you up at night?" But even if you are not the CEO, if you are charged with any responsibility for organizational change—as a leader of a new venture, as an entrepreneur-founder trying to take a company to the next level, as a department head or project team leader—then this is the time to take a systemic perspective. This chapter provides the view from the control tower about how to build a dynamic vehicle that can keep moving forward.

E-culture is not lipstick on a bulldog; it is a fundamentally different way of life. It is not just a new wardrobe (casual tops, jeans, ponytails, earrings) or a little redecoration (wild colors, game rooms, kitchens, music). It presents a demanding set of requirements for change, as we have just seen:

- The need for rapid innovation turns strategy into improvisational theater.

- The principle of *big everywhere fast* increases reliance on a network of partners.

- Customer power fuels the need to operate seamlessly, to become more like a community pulling together for the common good, showing one face to the customer and responding quickly before protestors grab mind-share.

- Competition for talent means emphasizing empowerment and renewable commitment through mastery, membership, and meaning as well as money.

These are broad requirements that reach down into day-to-day tasks. E-culture comes complete with new jobs and new titles, appearing throughout the cases in this book: *content managers, webmasters, alliance executives, directors of communities and affiliates, partner advocates, business information executives, product evangelists, managers of e-business enablement, culture architects.* And it includes roles such as *blue sky watchers, idea scouts, integrators, change agents, thought leaders, network facilitators, rock stars, ambassadors and diplomats, wandering minstrels,* and *collabronauts.*

This list of novel titles is a change in itself—a signal that new kinds of work are being done, in old organizations as well as startups.

Constant change is built into the very nature of the e-world. The Web and associated network technologies are both stimuli for e-culture (making it necessary) and facilitators of e-culture (making it possible). It is like a spiral of increasing force: *The more the Web is used, the more uses are identified, and the more it must be used to do more things. Change produces the need for more and deeper change.* Mastering deep change—being first with the best service, anticipating and then meeting new customer requirements, and applying new technology—requires organizations to do more than adapt to changes already in progress. It requires them to be fast, agile, intuitive, and innovative. In change-adept organizations, people continuously learn and adapt, spread knowledge, and share ideas. By making change a way of life, people are, in the best sense, "just doing their jobs."

Thus, it is not surprising that attitude toward change distinguishes pacesetters compared with laggards among the 785 companies in my global e-culture survey. Those indicating that they are better than competitors, compared with those that said they were worse than competitors, also report having these characteristics:

- Internal changes are considered a way of life, and people seem to take them in stride (instead of viewing them as disruptive, inconvenient, or a source of discomfort).

- Conflict is seen as creative and something to be encouraged (instead of disruptive and something to be avoided).

- Ideas that are unusual, controversial, or "different" are strongly encouraged and well received (instead of being viewed with skepticism and resistance).

- When the organization is considering a major strategic change, most people generally hear about it in advance, so they have a chance to comment (instead of learning about change at the same time as outsiders, or even later).

A positive approach to change, as reported on the survey, is also strongly associated with empowerment (decisions are made by people who know most about the issue regardless of rank) and collaboration (departments and functions work actively with other groups on a regular basis). And there is some association with fast decisions—approval for unforeseen or nonroutine activities by one or two people (instead of many sign-offs through many levels)—and with the ability to do anything that's not prohibited.

It is possible to learn something about change-embracing cultures from the more highly evolved. At Cisco Systems, for example, waves of rapid innovation and investments in startups, leverage of a large partner network, "one company" principles, managing crowds, reverse mentoring, and the care and feeding of talent were built in from the start. We expect this of high technology companies—though it is instructive that Sun Microsystems's e-commerce initiative, e-Sun, had to struggle to get acceptance despite Sun's culture of improvisation.

A system for change is not considered as common in much older bricks-and-mortar companies, such as retailers. But in the United Kingdom, supermarket chain Tesco was first mover to the Internet not only ahead of retail competitors but also ahead of most other companies of any kind, and its leaders attribute this to its culture. Tesco has built an organizational structure that supports constant change. Its leaders are young, fast, and dynamic. A flattened hierarchy allows their energy to permeate all the way down to the front lines in the form of "hungry 25-year-old store managers," as a leader described them. Store managers are given freedom to take risks (and are expected to perform), which results in Tesco's ability to change on a dime. It has put its money where its mouth is, with a big investment in Web technology compared with competitors: a large IT team of hundreds of internal staff and contractors, plus planned year 2000 Internet investments that were extensive by British—or American—standards. Complacency is avoided by continually setting new targets. Tesco leaders discovered their early mistakes in online grocery sales—poor customer service, incomplete understanding of skill and staffing requirements, lack of incentives for cooperation across channels—corrected them, and moved on.

A culture for change does not mean doing everything perfectly; it means doing everything quickly, learning from it, and then doing it differently.

Now for the hard question. How can companies not born to change manage to transform, and do it at Internet speed? Many people give up on existing organizations altogether, believing that large-scale change is possible only by starting independent ventures—whether e-commerce spin-offs, "greenfield" sites where everything is new, or charter schools. They think that big established organizations move too slowly, change too reluctantly. But it would be premature and foolish to relegate such organizations to the recycle bin. Too much value is created in those organizations, and too much of the economy depends on them.

So it is important to find the gears that can get change rolling, and get it done quickly. And that is not simply a matter of making one big change. A culture for change, the platform for e-culture, needs to be programmed into the organization's method of operating. Without fundamental systemic change, organizations will always revert to their basic pattern, like the default position on a computer program. Leaders must thus reset the organization's default position. They must change the template and get to the underlying code. To become an e-business, David Weymouth, CIO of Barclays Bank in the United Kingdom, said, "You've got to be prepared to change the genetic code of the organization."

I have developed a simple model that enables leaders to implant the important elements of e-culture in their organization's genetic code. I call it the Change Wheel, because each spoke contains an element that, when combined with the others, gets systemic change rolling.[1] (See the illustration of the wheel.) A wheel is the right image, especially when seeking radical change. After all, the turn of a wheel is a *revolution*. And the circular shape means that no one element automatically comes first; there can be many starting points. But all elements must reinforce the change, or the wheel will stop turning.

The Change Wheel

- *Common theme, shared vision:* The change message must be well and widely understood. Initially, this is a matter of articulating it well and broadcasting it to many audiences. It can be crafted by a small group, but it becomes truly shared—internalized—as it is used by large numbers of people.

- *Symbols and signals:* People are always reading the organizational tea leaves, looking for signs of whether the change is serious and how it will feel. Small symbols can have big consequences. The right early signals can show people what the change will mean for them. (Eliminating reserved parking is how some companies signal a reduction of hierarchy.)

- *Guidance structure and process:* Change needs someone at the controls, even if ultimately everyone has to get involved in change. And there needs to be a process for steering it in the right direction. This involves the nuts and bolts of project management, on a large scale. Assigning accountability for the big picture—the overview of all the elements of change—is an important step.

- *Education, training, action tools:* How do people know what to do to make the change operational, to make it real in their activities? The same words can be understood differently by each part of the organization, interpreted from their own perspectives. Therefore education is necessary to communicate the why and what of change. Training is necessary for people to become adept at the new behavior implied by the change. And action tools help people relate the change to their own day-to-day work.

- *Champions and sponsors:* Changes need people who become passionate about seeing that they take place. Champions are the activists and cheerleaders for change, often carrying out mini change projects themselves. Sponsors make sure that the change has the backing of those with the power to fight for it.

- *Quick wins and local innovations:* Early successes show that change is possible and indicate what the change means in practice. It is important to get the grass roots involved in shaping the change by picking projects that particular units can tackle. This is improvisational theater at its best—a clear overall direction, but details created as units take hold of the change and make it their own. That's why "shared vision" is directly opposite this element on the Change Wheel; pilot projects, demonstrations, and local modifications make the vision concrete and ensure its acceptance.

• *Communications, best practice exchange:* Change requires even more communication than routine activities. Top leaders need to know what's happening in the field so they can make adjustments to support it or steer it in a different direction. Local units need role models to learn from the experience of their peers, to see what's possible, and to be spurred on to new heights. Change can be chaotic without a way to communicate what's happening everywhere.

• *Policy, procedures, system alignment:* Every organizational rule, routine, requirement, or procedure can either reinforce or undermine the desired change: human resource systems (hiring criteria, promotion criteria, compensation policy), information systems (what data are shared, with whom, when), policies about who gets to talk to customers or to the press. Rules and processes need to be reassessed and adjusted to support the new direction.

• *Measures, milestones, and feedback:* It is important to know whether the change is on track. Establishing measures of progress is important, especially for softer changes (such as a shift of culture) or ones that will not show up in conventional financial results. Dividing big changes into small increments with clear milestones is helpful for measurement and morale; each milestone successfully passed is a cause for celebration, or each one missed a cause for readjustment. There needs to be a feedback loop based on agreed-upon measures of progress.

• *Rewards and recognition:* Who gets rewarded and for what reasons is an essential component of change. The organization's carrots and sticks combine with its publicity engine to create heroes of the revolution or enemies of the change.

Companies that struggle with change are often unwilling to engage all the gears. Change starts, and then stalls because a few spokes were activated but nothing happened in the others. For example, after a slow start Williams-Sonoma eventually embraced the e-commerce theme with active sponsors and champions and quick wins, but was not yet ready to change a compensation system that rewarded divisions primarily for their own results. In contrast, IBM consistently reinforced e-business transformation around the whole wheel, through elements described in chapter 6: a common theme for the entire company ("One IBM" and e-business leadership), signals of change (e.g., eliminating divisional CIO titles), a governance structure for Web activities, abundant training and tools, e-business plans within each business unit, internal and external publicity, new information systems, specific metrics, and a new appraisal and incentive system.

To change the code and reset the default position requires action on every element of the Change Wheel. This lesson applies to any organization, not just to business. Thomas Highton, school superintendent in Union City, New Jersey, led a transformation of his ailing inner-city district into perhaps the world's first demonstration of e-culture in a K–12 public school system, with striking improvements in student achievement, as discussed in chapter 1. It wasn't the computers that made the difference—it was a commitment to fundamental systemic change that pervaded the entire school system.

Check off the spokes of the Change Wheel as used in the Union City schools. Highton's theme was to use technology to transform teaching and raise student performance. He sent the signal that teachers are important by assessing their needs first and using the results to set the agenda; an early symbol was investment in improving run-down school buildings. The head of instructional programs, Fred Carrigg, became the designated e-change champion, and extensive training was undertaken early and often to shift teaching to a team-oriented collaborative approach. With Bell Atlantic as a partner and major sponsor, Union City developed a major local innovation—a demonstration project in a new middle school that became an e-school. Computers were put in the homes of entering seventh graders as well in their teachers' homes, and soon parents joined students and teachers in computer classes before and after school and on weekends. The school curriculum was changed to support the use of the Internet in teaching. Students and teachers in the demonstration project began sharing their new ways of working through numerous events and a student-designed website. The efforts were measured extensively, and a two-year project turned into a long-term commitment to fundamental educational change. Among the many forms of recognition were appearances on national television (principal Bob Fazio on CBS-TV's *60 Minutes*); visits from President Clinton, Vice President Gore, and Congressional leaders; and widespread publicity that attracted additional partners, such as Microsoft, to further the e-agenda.

Organizations cannot always do everything at the same time, and what happens within one element of change influences the others. So there is logic to the order in which I've presented the spokes of the wheel. Theme/vision, symbols/signals, and guidance structure/process make sense at the very beginning. Next, educational events can help identify and groom champions and sponsors, and quick wins/local innovations can then more easily follow. The activities at the grass roots then trigger the next three elements: lessons to communicate; clarity about what needs to change in rules and procedures to support the kinds of innovations and activities that are emerging as the change idea becomes actualized; and measures of progress. Rewards help lock the whole thing into place. The elements overlap, because the same action can have multiple ramifications—for example, identifying change champions to lead local innovations and communicate with other groups to exchange best practices puts many of the spokes into gear.

The challenge in the Internet Age is to get the wheel revolving faster, toward a more highly evolved organization that can keep the momentum going. Let's watch it in motion in an industrial giant that tried for an accelerated push toward the culture of tomorrow.

A Year around the Change Wheel: How Honeywell International's AlliedSignal Got to E

This case is about an organization that changed in several ways over one year, 1999. The corporation began 1999 as AlliedSignal (aerospace and chemicals) and ended it as Honeywell International, having folded in Minneapolis-based Honeywell (aerospace and controls). But an even bigger change was starting the long march to e-culture. It began 1999 as a typical bricks-and-mortar, product-centered manufacturer and entered 2000 as a budding e-business, reexamining AlliedSignal's operations while building on Honeywell's Web experience. (See chapter 3.) And more change was ahead—General Electric planned to acquire the whole company in late 2000.

A year is not a lot of time in the life of an old, complex industrial firm. Pre-Web conventional wisdom always held that transforming the culture of a large company is a five- to seven-year process. But then, this is Internet time. AS/HI convened meetings on a short time frame, worked with large crowds, expected fast action, and set stretch goals for breakthrough ideas.

Keep in mind that this story is about positive change in a successful company. The change was not a response to crisis. It was not accomplished by massive layoffs or across-the-board cost-cutting. It was carried out while many other things were going on (such as a major merger) that could easily have derailed the focus on e-business. But also keep in mind that reality is messy—much messier than corporate public relations departments ever want us to report. Companies like to paint pretty pictures—or rather, pretty diagrams on PowerPoint slides—that make it seem as if their change popped into life full-blown, with the curtain rising on a perfect ending. In reality, even successful change contains mistakes, setbacks, and unresolved issues.

At AS/HI there were early traps, such as management by committee rather than leadership by champions. There were low-risk baby steps instead of breakthrough ideas. Many people were following orders instead of embracing change. Resources were often inadequate, and policies and procedures got in the way. This drama, like all transformation tales, unfolded unevenly, without a prepared script, and with audience reactions that were unexpected. It is also ongoing. The first year revealed numerous additional challenges as it was discovered that e-business required even more fundamental systemic changes to support the new direction.

The stage for the AS/HI story was set in 1991, when Larry Bossidy joined the aerospace and chemical company AlliedSignal as CEO after serving in top executive posts at General Electric. Bossidy took pride in making the numbers. An oft-told company legend concerned the one quarter when the earnings forecast was missed by a penny, and the stock price plummeted. He dramatically increased the then-troubled company's performance on every dimension: 500 percent growth in stock price in seven years, with double-digit earnings growth every year. By 1998, AlliedSignal had 70,000 employees and sales of $15 billion. Teams forming and reforming to make business improvements were an ingrained element of AlliedSignal's culture. Still, e-business transformation involved changes beyond anything the company had known.

In January 1999, Bossidy had less than sixteen months before his planned retirement in April 2000. He turned his attention to ensuring the company's future. One goal was to seek an acquisition. In the summer of 1999 AlliedSignal and Honeywell announced their attention to merge, and their marriage was completed in December to form Honeywell International, with Honeywell's CEO, Mike Bonsignore, as head of the combined company. Bossidy's second New Year's resolution for 1999 was that the company must compete in cyberspace. Bossidy told me he had been watching e-commerce sales accelerate during the Christmas season in 1998, and soon after saw the potential for a business like his: "I went to the Bill Gates conference, the one held at Microsoft every year. It had Jeff Bezos from Amazon, Jack Welch, a host of others. Much of the conversation was about how best to exploit the opportunity provided by the Internet. It was the first time that I recognized that this was not about technology—it was about market opening. It needed the same kinds of disciplines it takes to open new market. I believed that we had to get moving and get moving quickly."

COMMON THEME, SHARED VISION

Change is just random motion without a direction, a theme just a grand idea in the leader's head without widespread understanding of its meaning and a dramatic presentation that makes it memorable. Soon after Bossidy returned from the Microsoft meeting, roughly 100 company leaders from around the world heard the "first shot of the revolution" (as it later became known).

Michael Dell, founder and CEO of Dell Computers, and John Chambers, CEO of Cisco Systems, came to company headquarters in Morristown, New Jersey, in February 1999 to describe their experience with e-business. Dell challenged the group's assumptions about nearly every business issue, from net receivables (AlliedSignal's was a typical industrial standard of thirty to sixty days; Dell's was negative seven days) to inventory (Dell had none), to quality management. But it was Chambers who really opened executive eyes to new possibilities, a participant reported. Like AlliedSignal, Cisco was a business-to-business supplier with tangible products. Yet Cisco had only about 500 manufacturing employees, Chambers said; AlliedSignal had over 50,000. Don Redlinger, AS Senior Vice President of Human Resources, recalled: "The idea that you could have a company in our industry, in the manufacturing business, and yet have only 500 people in manufacturing, was just a bizarre proposition. Cisco has a radically different structure, facilitated by technology. It was mind-boggling." A follow-up meeting with Cisco CIO Pete Solvik for a smaller group of leaders "blew away everything people had ever learned."

The theme took shape at the next top management meeting. To provide a common vocabulary and common direction, Bossidy introduced the "four pillars" model to frame the change. The model—which he developed with five of the functional leaders on his team—defined the areas of the value chain in which technology-enabled processes would transform current business. *E-business* described the entire chain: pulling Internet technology into all aspects of the business—not just the customer channels—to create new capacity, efficiency, cost advantage, and customer connections. *Global sourcing* focused on creating new vendor relationships—particularly from low-cost regions of the world—that could deliver lower costs, better quality, and expanded capacity. *Manufacturing* focused on the value-driven "make or buy" decision, or "deverticalization" (outsourcing portions of the product value chain instead of owning all the capacity to make everything themselves, end to end). *Reengineering* focused on using the Web for greater speed, efficiency, and cost advantage in administrative functions. The first three pillars were expected to fund the fourth, *e-commerce*, which focused on business-to-business and business-to-customer revenue-generating projects.

This one-page model provided a common framework, the theme that would kick off business unit improvisation. It was easy to communicate and could be widely shared. Better yet, it showed that e-business change was truly comprehensive and systemic, with change implications for every single part of the business. It was not just applying a little lipstick to the bulldog.

Symbols and Signals

For AS the early signal that change was serious was the personal time Bossidy devoted to conveying the new theme himself. Because of his disinterest in computers in the past, his conversion to chief e-business cheerleader was a potent symbol. An Aerospace vice president commented about the impact of his message: "He made it clear to everyone that e-commerce is important and that it will change how we do business. We would not have anticipated this coming from him. He never struck me as an extensive user of technology. It made the importance that much more believable." Over nearly a year, the top team dedicated a portion of all regular meetings and many additional meetings to e-business, setting goals and reviewing accomplishments. Bossidy became so convinced about the Internet future that he made it known that he wanted to dedicate his postretirement time to working with small B2B startups.

People knew he was serious about e-business, but was he also serious about risk-taking to get there? After all, improvisation includes the risk of mistakes. Bossidy preached revolution. He told me: "You're not going to change a company by making incremental change. We're going to have some colossal failures here. We'll just have a party that night and talk about all the things we screwed up and then go back the next day and fix them. No way are we going to bat 100% on this, but we are going to execute it in a way that we're going to stop things we do wrong and we're going to accelerate things we do well. That's how, at the end of the day, we're going to create value."

The turning point was when Bossidy publicly praised an e-commerce initiative that stumbled badly—moreover, one that was in "Handy Gadgets," my pseudonym for a unit that was so troubled that any mistake could be used as an excuse for punishment. The news quickly circulated that it was okay to experiment, to try things without full certainty about the ending.

GUIDANCE STRUCTURE AND PROCESS

Someone has to steer change, guiding it, monitoring the actions it entails. It is not good enough to say that change is everyone's responsibility; then it becomes no one's responsibility. (That's one of the clear lessons from companies that tried to run e-commerce by committee with a weak part-time staff.) And there has to be a process, a set of steps that put change in motion. Using an existing, familiar process to do something unfamiliar can help ground people and keep them focused on the task, rather than fumbling to figure out how to use a new procedure before they can even think about getting to the goal.

Bossidy was a devotee of process-led change, so process came first, even before the leadership structure was in place to guide his e-business transformation. Bossidy needed a way to convert awareness to action "without a burning platform," he said. Choosing the existing planning process, he required every business unit to develop an e-business strategic plan (dubbed an e-STRAP). This meant that he could hold people accountable for getting moving, even if he did not yet know what the results should be, and that motion would reinforce the message. He explained, "Skeptics said, 'Why us, why me? We're not Amazon.com.' But the more that they worked on the strategic plan and evolved the strategy, the more they saw it." Bossidy required that e-STRAP projects be self-funded and be executable in three months, to create quick wins. (We'll get to the pro's and con's of those requirements later.)

Because strategic planning was the initial process for change, the senior management formed the early guidance structure at the top, with equivalent committees within the business units. Meanwhile, there was a period of some confusion as the units got bogged down in committee processes without anyone clearly accountable for e-business activities, and there was a scramble to find e-business heads. Finally, in the fall of 1999, when the Honeywell merger was close to approval, a corporate e-business council was formed, consisting of eighty heads of e-business for each AlliedSignal and Honeywell unit, to take over the role of steering change. (Most of the AS e-business heads were new hires.) Russel McMeekin, an experienced Honeywell e-business leader, became corporate e-business director after the merger was approved in December 1999.

Bossidy did not wait until all the players were in place. He set the process in motion and kept control at the top until there were accountable leaders of change. The positive result was that action could get underway fast. The problem was confusion and false starts in the business units, because responsibility for e-business was unclear and shifting. Because of the complexity of a large corporation, with its layers of sectors, divisions, and business units, it was sometimes not even clear where e-business accountability should fall. Specialty Films, for example, a business unit with the Polymers Group, put its marketing head in charge of e-business and was off and running with innovative proposals, but then an e-business vice president was appointed at the group level, and responsibilities had to be sorted out. The new leader added capability and depth to the implementation process, but also another layer of governance and an additional step in any decision process.

Aerospace, the largest sector at $8 billion in sales and 37,000 employees in thirty-two major locations in ten countries, had just undergone a reorganization into a seven-unit matrix. Answering Bossidy's call for e-business initiatives while the structure was in flux was challenging, although Aerospace already had e-business experience with FlightSite, an Internet portal for general aviation. Because resources were limited, the heads of the segments' marketing groups were named the e-business leaders. A ten-person Aerospace e-business council was formed. Most of the representatives had operations experience and many had marketing experience, but no one had e-business experience. What ensued was an attempt at innovation by committee—something that rarely works. The council held frequent meetings and teleconferences but did not work as a team, because each represented a separate cell. They worked individually, each developing a different set of ideas. The result was a list too long to execute: over fifty project proposals, deriving from seven different e-STRAPs, and little or no ownership of individual initiatives.

EDUCATION, TRAINING, AND ACTION TOOLS

Picture the scene: A major event with inspirational celebrity speakers (AS's February conference with Michael Dell and John Chambers) excites and inspires people about new possibilities, and everyone leaves all charged up. The morning after, people remember the warm glow but have no idea what to do next. In-depth education must follow quickly to turn inspiration into practice. To do this at Internet speed means getting working with large numbers, assembling crowds, and reaching the masses all at once.

To provide training and tools for the e-STRAPs, Bossidy invited Cisco's managing director of interactive business solutions, Amir Hartman, to lead a training session for his leadership team, including functional heads, presidents of the twelve strategic business units, and Bossidy himself. A few weeks later, in April 1999, over 700 AlliedSignal leaders from around the world attended a one-day version of the same session in Morristown, in person or via satellite. They were then expected to carry the message deeper into their organizations.

Hartman introduced a Cisco-trademarked Internet strategy portfolio matrix to assess Internet initiatives. The first part of the model could characterize initiatives in terms of their business impact (magnitude of opportunity or threat and alignment with company business objectives) and likelihood (the feasibility of the model and its necessity in light of competitive threats). A second step helped prioritize individual Internet commercial projects using a matrix defined by *business criticality* and *newness or innovation.* According to Hartman, the trend of Internet-based projects is from "radical experimentation" (new but not business critical) to "break-through strategies" (both new and critical), then to "operational excellence" (critical but not new) and ultimately to "new fundamentals" (neither critical nor new, but necessary to stay competitive). Projects could be assessed in terms of *business impact* and *ease of implementation*—another Cisco tool—to ensure that a portfolio contained primarily break-through and operational excellence projects. Among the new learning for AS managers was a vocabulary for e-business activities: for example, *storefront, infomediary, trust intermediary, infrastructure provider,* and *marketspace enabler.*

Participants saw that Web technologies could reinvent every point in the value chain, from customer care to internal knowledge management. One manager called the session "an adrenaline shot. It got all of us going, 90 miles an hour, in one day." AS leaders left the training sessions with the directive to apply new thinking to their e-STRAPs: how to embed e-business into daily operations and drive radical change in their organizations.

To support the development process, an e-business website on the company intranet offered information about resources, such as contacts for e-business partners or preferred suppliers, and corporate software and hardware standards. Updates included corporate contracts, new projects, and best practices. Senior leaders also sponsored several corporatewide teleconferences in late spring on topics such as the strategic intent behind new business models, and the creation of a new market-driven value proposition for AlliedSignal. Like IBM and Cisco, AS was using e-business mode to push e-business transformation—the process of change demonstrating the direction of change.

This was a great starting point, but education and training became an ongoing challenge, and this was an area in which this company, like many, was tempted to underinvest. Tools to develop new business models were one thing, but notably lacking were tools for changing the organization that would have to execute the plans. ("You have to spend a lot of time and attention on training in change management," Ed Huston, vice chairman of Ryder Systems, concluded from his own experience. "I don't think people totally understand how their role is supposed to change.")

CHAMPIONS AND SPONSORS

Members of the corporate executive committee served as the major sponsors of e-business change, with an expectation that business unit heads would play a similar role throughout their businesses. In contrast, the champions who would be the day-to-day agents of change were often outsiders. Bossidy encouraged the units to hire e-business leaders, sending a memo to the leadership group outlining the skills needed: strong business leaders with a good combination of marketing and information system skills who would think differently from traditional AlliedSignal management, visualize more radical opportunities, and challenge the organization to move more quickly.

In the troubled "Handy Gadgets" division introduced in chapter 1, president "Michelle Hellman" appointed "Craig Lebolt" as e-commerce vice president. Lebolt's previous roles in manufacturing and supply base management gave him no experience with e-business. Hellman was willing to be an active sponsor of Lebolt's activities. He recalled: "She said to me, 'You're a change agent, and that's why we want you in this role.' I probably was the first appointed to this role, because I remember calling Morristown to ask who the others were to do some benchmarking, and they said they were still structuring the role."

Given limited resources, he became the "Craig Lebolt one-man show." Lacking a network of e-business colleagues, he immersed himself in learning about e-business, the Cisco training, and Handy Gadget's North American and European customer base. He gave himself six weeks to assess Handy Gadget's readiness to deliver on an e-business strategy. He received some help from marketing on creative ideas, and customer service helped him evaluate his options. But his e-business efforts, as he said later, "just flew in the face of our traditional organization. I kept hearing people say, 'that's not how it's done here.' I drove these projects with the force of my personality." He felt that Hellman was his greatest asset. "She is a great advocate and sounding board. She always has time. It was so important, like when I thought I was crazy because thirty people were against my idea." Furthermore, Bossidy was a powerful sponsor. Lebolt enthused that "Larry supported us—even when we were challenged. He has significant capacity for change and risk. He makes our efforts easy because of his level of support."

But the support of the boss and the boss's boss is not enough without a wider set of sponsors and champions. Lebolt's efforts were perhaps doomed from the start because the rest of his own organization was not behind him, and there was not yet a peer network to lend their ideas and support. Lebolt's launch of GadgetPlus.com, a website for do-it-yourselfers (30 percent of the whole gadget market), received negative reviews (more like death threats) from an important part of the external audience, Handy Gadget's traditional distributors, causing a flurry of apologies and backpedaling. This was a problem that could have been avoided had the sales force felt more involved and had Lebolt not felt the pressure to rush—alone—to the Web.

QUICK WINS AND LOCAL INNOVATIONS

In the spirit of improvisational theater, a vision or a strategy does not become real until the actors create the story through the actions they undertake. One AS leader said, "Execution is our strategy."

On a fast track between April and June 1999, teams in each of the businesses and functions assessed their markets, customers, and business priorities and developed the first-ever e-STRAPs. Time was limited, so businesses worked primarily with existing market information. Teams formed for intense periods of work, went back to the normal content of their jobs, and regrouped to pick up on the next step in planning. Few businesses could devote anyone on a full-time, dedicated basis to strategic planning. In most units, people took on the e-STRAP work as an addition to an already-demanding workload. But volunteerism was high; there was energy, excitement, and a sense of challenge.

In late June and July 1999, about ninety days after the top 700 managers had attended the company's first training session on e-business, leaders representing fifty-two lines of business and major corporate functions appeared at headquarters over several days to present their plans to Bossidy and other senior leaders. The quantity of ideas was impressive—over 600 project ideas—even if the quality was uneven. The ventures covered a range. Some were basic process quick wins such as online travel reservation systems or product information websites (brochureware). Others were larger efforts, such as business-to-business order management or developing an online store locator and parts finder. Many company intranets were proposed for internal communication, project management, and other uses.

This was a good start, because minds were opened to a wide range of new possibilities. But that was also the problem. The rush to have plans—any plans—inevitably meant that units would pick the low-hanging fruit, the obvious ideas already within reach. They would make lists without thinking through the feasibility of implementation. (Craig Lebolt spent only six weeks developing the idea for GadgetPlus.com.) And they would minimize the amount of change implied by their projects, so projects would emerge cell by cell, silo by silo, even though the best ideas inevitably cut across silos and require their cooperation. I have already mentioned the fifty project ideas from the Aerospace sector. Although grouped under six broad headings, they were still isolated projects without prioritization, and there were too many to provide a big win on the Web.

It was not until much later in 1999 that Aerospace, now merged with its Honeywell counterpart, defined a "killer app" in MyAircraft.com, one of the e-hubs described at the end of chapter 3. This idea involved a new way of segmenting the marketplace (by whether customers handled their own maintenance) that cut across the divisions within the sector. The

Aerospace organization chart suddenly looked very different from the perspective of cyberspace. The e-hub had to be carved out as a separate venture. Turning to existing units to create revolutionary plans will almost guarantee that plans will stick within the walls of established, known parameters, unless new, cross-cutting units are formed.

By the fall, the mind-set at AS had changed to include e-business concepts in business plans, but true innovation to create e-business breakthroughs remained a challenge. In November 1999, when the merger was close to consummation, CEO heir-apparent Mike Bonsignore called the hundreds of projects currently underway in AlliedSignal "bunnies"—they were small, cute, and didn't eat a lot. (I can add another rabbit-like feature: They were reproducing wildly and becoming a nuisance.) What the new company needed were "tiger" projects that could transform the business and create new markets. Some business unit managers thought Bossidy was disappointed that his drive to e-business had not generated any truly revolutionary initiatives. In December Bossidy responded to my question about progress to date by recognizing the big changes still ahead: "I'm going to say something that sounds contradictory. I am enthusiastic about progress, and yet I still think we're at the beginning."

The Specialty Films (SF) experience was an example of how to stifle innovation prematurely. Its team developed three new business models that were considered among the more innovative, but changes at the levels above it kept derailing forward motion. Reorganizations, budget cuts, new bosses, and new corporate IT requirements undercut choices SF had already made. Fastest out of the box with creative new ideas, SF was unable to implement any of them.

By the end of 1999, business units were executing some of their e-STRAP projects. Despite setbacks—inevitable with something so new, underway so fast—there was growing confidence that Honeywell International could succeed as an e-business. Three e-hubs were in the works as stand-alone ventures: MyPlant.com, brought in from the Honeywell side; myFacilities.com; and MyAircraft.com. They emerged as cross-business applications from the experimentation within the units. The lesson is clear: Innovation requires local units to breach boundaries and let go of territory.

COMMUNICATIONS AND BEST PRACTICE EXCHANGE

Multidirectional communication is a big part of e-culture. After all, messages can have big audiences whether the sender intends them to or not.

AS used numerous communications media to kick off its year of change: events for large numbers of managers, satellite broadcasts, teleconferences, websites with a growing array of information and best practice models. The review sessions dedicated to e-STRAPs were a form of communication from the periphery to center; after fifty-two different presentations, issues and challenges would become rather clear.

Like many companies, AS tended to emphasize what management wanted to tell the troops, rather than using multimedia channels to learn from the experiences of local innovators. The risk was that innovations would remain isolated endeavors. Though horizontal communication was not a particular formal emphasis, the needs of those active in leading the march led to informal exchanges. Jeffrey Ritz, Specialty Films's e-business head, described "informal alliances forming among those of us who were doing things to share information and learn faster." The gradual addition of dedicated e-business heads within business units and then the formation of the e-business council helped greatly with best practice exchange, and by the end of the year, the council was the vehicle for conveying information about e-business opportunities and progress.

Policy, Procedures, System Alignment

Many pieces have to be adjusted to ensure that the change is supported by the underlying system and that the default position is set at a new level: how performance is measured, resources are allocated, people are hired, supplies are purchased, information is collected and disseminated. A major new direction should be an occasion for reassessing and rewriting organizational programs.

AS corporate functions worked first on their own e-STRAPs—how to Internet-enable their own activities. The supply chain staff group was quickly on board with an e-business-driven, integrated, global supply chain that built on current activities but would require new job competencies, hiring patterns, and career paths. Marketing sought to implement a customer relationship management (CRM) system, including sales automation, a customer complaint system, data mining, and an Internet-enabled call center. The corporate human resource staff worked on new approaches for e-business talent. Then–HR Vice President Laurie Siegel reflected: "We want all these e-businesses, but we still have a traditional unionized work force that comes to work with a lunch pail. So if the work force is segmented, we must segment HR. We need a different set of programs and to give people choices. A rich pension plan isn't right for people who might leave in two years. And there is nothing more evocative of old-line HR than a policy manual. We could have other ways of solving problems online that would actually help people."

Lining up the pieces was not easy or smooth. Those who controlled policies and procedures were not always in synch with the business units. For example, the Internet standards and preferred vendor lists developed by the corporate IT group were intended to create integration on the Web and save the business units the time of screening and educating partners. But because some of them were not ready until September, business unit plans were already underway. And some e-ventures bumped up against corporate rules that had not yet been adjusted for their needs, such as posting jobs internally when the talent was coming from the outside.

There was another alignment task that could reinforce or undermine e-business transformation: the merger. Appropriately for the Internet Age and e-business goals, merger integration was managed on a fast track with crowds of players. Bonsignore and Bossidy studied other companies' merger experiences and vowed to avoid the pitfalls. Teams started working on it one week after the announcement on June 7, 1999, and were ready to roll out implementation plans as soon as the merger was approved on December 1. (Aerospace was an exception; merger planning had to wait for antitrust clearance.) Over 600 people were deployed in 130 teams. Because there was minimal overlap between AlliedSignal and Honeywell businesses, leaders felt there was less turmoil than mergers that displaced many people or created winners and losers.

Merger execution was fast and smooth because of the large numbers of people participating who were able to adjust their activities to fit the thrust of the combined company. But adjustment of other policies and procedures to support e-culture was only beginning by the end of 1999. In 2000, e-business heads were starting to push back on corporate routines that were getting in the way of their new ventures.

The biggest issue was resource allocation—the routine budgeting process. Many AS business unit leaders tied their ability to execute to three things: resources, governance, and leadership. Where resources had been allocated and e-business leaders named and given full support, e-business projects had moved forward. But where internal buy-in and resources had been lacking, where skills for understanding markets and e-business were not accessible, and where funding and local budget issues could not be resolved, projects had stalled or even died. There was much discussion of Bossidy's edict that e-business projects be self-funded by the business units, one of the three initial requirements for the e-STRAPs, and one that fit existing AS procedures. Some managers considered this a serious obstacle, both because it would starve promising ventures too big to fund within established budget lines and because it made cross-silo projects very difficult. By November, Bossidy agreed to reassess this policy and announced that promising business-to-business e-commerce plans might merit corporate funding.

Clearly, it is difficult to get to the big change—successful e-ventures—without numerous supporting changes in every function in the organization. Sometimes that's a message senior leaders don't want to hear; they want revolutionary breakthroughs without really wanting change. The emergence of e-business exposed more issues than AS leaders had imagined, and they were not only internal matters of ongoing policies and procedures. E-business raised new questions about appropriate partners for new ventures and the choice of organizational forms: outright ownership, spin-offs, joint ventures, or working through someone else's e-commerce venture. After a year of improvisation, the company found that e-business was not just a matter of new ways to reach customers with new communication tools; it seemed to suggest entirely new ways to organize the business that could be even more disruptive than a merger. As Bossidy passed the CEO baton to Bonsignore, the big challenge was to dig deeply into the organizational code to rewrite it.

MEASURES, MILESTONES, AND FEEDBACK

It is a cliché of management that you get what you measure. To jumpstart change, AS set short-term targets and milestones: e-STRAPs within ninety days that could be executed within another ninety days. Having a plan at all was the first milestone, and business units proudly displayed their large numbers of ideas at review sessions that served as occasions for feedback about progress. But the next set of milestones was more difficult: to actually do something that top management would consider a breakthrough. There were serious questions about what the measurements for e-business were—how progress would be tracked, what success meant. Some leaders, particularly those with long AlliedSignal experience who worked most directly with Bossidy, felt that their traditional business metrics should apply to e-business: revenue growth, earnings per share, productivity, and margins. Other leaders, particularly those newer to AlliedSignal, felt that the measures of value for e-businesses should be radically different from traditional ones, and that utilizing traditional measures was counterproductive to speed. There was agreement, however, that intervals for measurement (i.e., annual budgets) were a mismatch for the requirements of e-business.

E-business was challenging traditional assumptions in ways that the company was not prepared for. Among all the obstacles that Specialty Films faced as they tried to execute their creative ideas, the one that struck the final blow for Specialty Films's e-business initiatives derived from the clash between traditional business measures and the needs of new ventures. When the Polymers Group as a whole reported poor quarterly results, SF's parent group was reorganized in response. People working on various e-business initiatives were moved into new roles with a new set of priorities, and e-business projects were handed new business imperatives and sign-off rules. "The focus in our whole business shifted quickly from strategic, e-business, to short-term, make-the-numbers," e-business VP Ritz recalled. Specialty Films's e-business efforts were caught between two worlds and two set of measures. They were immobilized.

REWARDS AND RECOGNITION

It is logical to put rewards at the end of this tour around the Change Wheel because it is hard to know who to reward for what until quick wins and early successes give shape to the vision. But this doesn't imply that rewards can be an afterthought. Indeed, announcements of new incentives or forms of recognition can be the starting point, a tool for getting people to pay attention to the new theme. Still, too many companies think there should be no special incentives for change because people are just doing their jobs. And companies are reluctant to touch their compensation system for changes that have not yet produced results.

In 1999, dotcom stock options had made compensation one of the thorniest issues in the e-world for established companies, and AS was no exception in delaying efforts to grapple with this challenge. AS/HI incentives didn't change. E-business leaders received corporate attention but not much else. But as the company's need for e-business talent grew, the question of rewards loomed large; the topic was pondered by the human resource staff and discussed frequently, with grumbles from those trying to hire for new ventures.

The talent race posed other challenges, too. People had already demonstrated that they would plunge into e-business planning with great enthusiasm, behaving like volunteers dedicated to a cause, a mode I discussed in chapter 7. But without the tools to succeed, to achieve mastery, would people remain committed? A new package of rewards and recognition was needed to encourage the people who were leading the change and to publicize the projects and behaviors that were to be role models for everyone else. That would certainly be on the agenda for the next year of change.

Honeywell International entered the year 2000 as a budding e-business. It was slated to end 2000 as a pending General Electric acquisition. The former AlliedSignal had laid a foundation for e-culture. Adding e-savvy Honeywell provided a track record of innovation and promising e-ventures that Honeywell had underway. The process of e-business change reflected some aspects of e-culture: improvisational theater, abundant communication, and opportunities to empower creative people. The year of change opened eyes and minds, uncovered mistakes and obstacles still to be overcome, created some successes, and provided experience of a new way of working, on Internet time. If not all spokes of the Change Wheel were strong yet, at least systemic change was rolling.

If You Want Revolution, Keep Revolving

The important thing about the Change Wheel is that it has to keep turning. All of the spokes are necessary to build momentum and keep change rolling forward. All of them must be strengthened and adjusted as change rolls down the track. The elements of the wheel are the underpinnings of e-culture—indeed of all organizational culture. They set the terms under which people work. They create the conditions that enable people to apply their skills.

Leaders manage the vehicles that shape culture and give it expression. They set the direction, define the context, and help produce coherence for their organizations. They set the boundaries for collaboration, autonomy, and the sharing of knowledge and ideas, and give meaning to events that otherwise appear random and chaotic. And they inspire voluntary behavior—the degree of effort, innovation, and entrepreneurship with which employees serve customers and seek opportunities.

Shifting toward the fast pace, empowerment, and community spirit of e-culture helps not just with a one-time transformation but with the constant change necessary in the Internet-enabled world. A combination of the willingness to experiment and the will to always do better triggers the ability to change. Companies that stay ahead of change are ones in which their people see change as something they themselves accomplish and not as something that is merely imposed on them. They seize opportunities to take initiative. They take pride in challenging themselves to higher and higher performance.

Increasingly, the assets that are carried by people are most critical to success. People's ideas or concepts, their commitment to high standards of competence, and their connections of trust with partners are what set apart great organizations. All these requirements can be enhanced by leaders, but none can be mandated. That's where e-culture comes in. Times of rapid technological change produce upheavals that can be viewed as either threats or opportunities. To stay ahead of change, to anticipate and create the future, requires a culture with the momentum to seek constant innovation and productive change. Without this culture, and without leaders to direct it, you could just be spinning your wheels.

9

━━━━━━━━━━━━━━━ ✦ ━━━━━━━━━━━━━━━

LEADERSHIP FOR CHANGE
New Challenges and Enduring Skills

"We must find the radicals, the true revolutionaries, and support them."
—Louis V. Gerstner, Jr., Chairman and CEO, IBM

TO LIVE WITH E-CULTURE is to live with change. Not just isolated, one-time, occasional changes, but ongoing, continuous, ubiquitous, never-finished change. Change as a condition of existence . . .

Wait a minute. Haven't we heard this before? Of course we have. Calls to "embrace change or else" have been issued for decades, well before the World Wide Web was a gleam in its creators' eyes. And leaders responded to that call to action long before the advent of a New Economy. So some lessons of the past are still relevant. But what *is* different today is the pace, depth, and scope of change, and how many people must get involved in coping with it. Change moves faster, and so do the reactions to change, as viral marketing spreads the good news but e-organizers and Web protestors create bad news almost as quickly. The reach of change is broader and deeper: to bigger audiences in more places at greater distances, and into the inner workings of long-taken-for-granted institutions and daily routines. Internet-enabled change has the potential to reshape nearly every aspect of life, all at once.

Each aspect of change by itself might be manageable, but together they can seem overwhelming. So the skills to deal with change can't be casual afterthoughts, they must be well understood parts of everyone's repertoire. More people, at more levels in more organizations, must learn to master change and lead it. More of us must play leadership roles, whether we are invited to the task or appoint ourselves. Thus, the lessons to be learned from successful leaders featured in this book can be a survival guide for the Internet Age.

The first thing any one of those star performers will say is how easy it is to make a decision about change and how tough it is to bring it about. The complexity of steering the wheel of change is not the only difficulty leaders encounter. Change is also emotionally hard. We might have to live with change, but that doesn't mean we have to love it—and we usually don't. People often resist change for reasons that make good sense to them, even if they don't correspond to organizational goals. Emotions that provoke resistance interfere with the best-laid plans of the most effective innovators, as we have seen repeatedly in earlier chapters. John Taysom was fired from Reuters because his proposals were surrounded by so much uncertainty, and that was threatening. Leaders at Sun had to overcome the desire to cling to territory on the part of those who thought e-business would turn them into losers. CEOs dragged their feet on e-business investments because of anxiety over their own lack of computer skills.

My ten classic reasons people resist change can pop up in the early stages of any new endeavor, and leaders must work around them:

1. *Loss of face.* Fear that dignity will be undermined, a place of honor removed; embarrassment because the change feels like exposure for past mistakes

2. *Loss of control.* Anger at decisions being taken out of one's hands, power shifting elsewhere

3. *Excess uncertainty.* Feeling uninformed about where the change will lead, what is coming next—a sensation like walking off a cliff blindfolded

4. *Surprise, surprise!* Automatic defensiveness—no advance warning, no chance to get ready

5. *The "difference" effect.* Rejection of the change because it doesn't fit existing mental models, seems strange and unfamiliar, and challenges usually unquestioned habits and routines

6. *"Can I do it?"* Concerns about future competence, worries about whether one will still be successful after the change

7. *Ripple effects.* Annoyance at disruptions to other activities and interference with the accomplishment of unrelated tasks

8. *More work.* Resistance to additional things to do, new things to learn, and no time to do it all

9. *Past resentments.* Memories of past hostilities or problems that were never resolved

10. *Real threats.* Anger that the change will inflict real pain and create clear losers

Established organizations have no monopoly on resistance to change. These issues apply to organizations of all sorts, whether or not they have *e* before their name or *dotcom* after it. Resistance to change pops up in early-stage companies, too. With each shift of business model, there is job displacement and the potential for resistance to change. When Abuzz moved to the Internet under NYTD ownership, it had to eliminate a sales department dedicated to enterprise sales. When eBay focused on community safety, its virtual service representatives drawn from users were supplanted by a professional department in Utah. At hongkong.com, internal staff initially created all the content themselves; under a new business model, the website featured other people's content, in part because they could be charged for the postings. "So obviously the people whom we originally hired in to produce content feel uncomfortable," Rudy Chan explained, and they find ways to slow down the change. Even in deferent-to-authority Asia, change causes resentment and resistance. There are fewer complexities when an organization is small and new, but there's still a human tendency to sink into comfort and fight change.

With resistance to change possible even under benign circumstances, leaders must be even more skillful at handling the human side of change when the environment is turbulent and the impact of change revolutionary. The skills of New Economy leaders are similar to those of Old Economy leaders, but the pace and complexity is much more demanding, and the audiences for every act are much bigger. E-culture requires leaders who are especially adept at leaping over barriers and converting resistance to commitment. The new challenges of the Internet Age increase the need for leaders who are masters of change. Like webmasters who guide the images that appear on-screen, changemasters guide the activities that occur behind the screen.[1] More people, in more walks of life, must add "changemaster" to their skill set.

Seven classic skills are involved in innovation and change: tuning in to the environment, kaleidoscope thinking, an inspiring vision, coalition building, nurturing a working team, persisting through difficulties, and spreading credit and recognition. These are more than discrete skills; they reflect a perspective, a style, that is basic to e-culture.

Skill 1. Sensing Needs and Opportunities: Tuning In to the Environment

Innovation begins with someone being smart enough to sense a new need. Of course, being "smart enough" comes from focusing time and attention on things going on in the environment around you that send signals that it's time for a change. Changemasters are adept at anticipating the need for change as well as leading it. They sense new ideas or appetites emerging on the horizon—sometimes because they feel hungry themselves. The concept for eBay came from the desire of Pierre Omidyar's girlfriend to swap Pez dispensers, and the idea for Worldroom.com, a Hong Kong startup, came from journalists who needed a way to download files and get local information on the road.

Changemasters sense problems and weaknesses before they represent full-blown threats. They see the opportunities when external forces change—new technological capabilities, industry upheavals, regulatory shifts—and then they identify gaps between what is and what could be. Recall the divergent paths to e-business success taken by pacesetter companies compared with the laggards in chapter 3. Whereas laggards respond to hints of new developments on the horizon with denial and anger, pacesetters exhibit curiosity.

Changemasters find many ways to monitor external reality. They become idea scouts, attentive to early signs of discontinuity, disruption, threat, or opportunity. They can establish their own listening posts, such as a satellite office in an up-and-coming location, an alliance with an innovative partner, or investments in organizations that are creating the future. Reuters Greenhouse founder John Taysom began to see the potential of new technology when posted in Bahrain, because the peculiarities of transmitting financial information (Reuters's mainstay) suggested problems that technology could solve. Then he put himself in the middle of Silicon Valley and started tuning in. After a few strategic investments, the Reuters Greenhouse Fund opened for business with a philosophy that getting an inside look at a number of innovative companies would be the best way to learn about what was about to happen, not what had already been created. Partnerships and alliances not only help you accomplish particular tasks, but also provide knowledge about things happening in the world that you wouldn't see otherwise.

Max Jones, managing director of Kerry Logistics in Hong Kong, attributes his company's early lead as an e-commerce fulfillment house (with Internet capabilities ahead of American counterparts) to the ability to tune in: "There's a word in Cantonese with no direct translation, *jahp sahn*, that means to be forever mindful, watch the environment around you, and respond to it on the spot." Improvisational theater begins with becoming very aware of every nuance of the context. Robin McCulloch, who founded Corporate Agility in Toronto to teach improvisational techniques to business teams, comments: "Once you have placed yourself in context, you must prepare for working in the moment. You can't react to change if you can't see it. And you can't see it if you are preoccupied and not looking for it." Sensing change is a subtle skill, and it requires first-hand contact, not distilled, packaged, second-hand information.

Changemasters are more likely to emerge in companies already open to change. It's a self-reinforcing cycle: those companies already successful at change create the circumstances that make it easier for people to sense the need for the next changes, because they have opened minds and broken through walls already. Pacesetter organizations produce more need-sensors because they encourage encounters with customers, competitors, and challengers that provide opportunities to sense needs, if people are open to intelligence about new threats or opportunities.

For some, opportunity is triggered by customer encounters. CEOs Louis Gerstner at IBM and Mike Bonsignore at Honeywell both spend a great deal of their time with customers, not at headquarters but in the customers' own environments. At Sun Microsystems, telephone calls to CEO Scott McNealy and President Ed Zander from a new kind of customer—Internet service providers—triggered Doug Kaewert's effort to make changes that would turn ISPs into partners and open new markets. For others, the change sequence begins with challenges. Williams-Sonoma's CEO, Howard Lester, began his conversion to an Internet fan when students at Berkeley's business school challenged his biases. John Chambers of Cisco has a teenager in the office of the CEO for a similar challenge to orthodoxy. Tuning in to competitors—individual as well as organizational—helps, too. It was rumored that then-AlliedSignal CEO Larry Bossidy's e-business "aha!" at a Microsoft golf outing came in part because General Electric CEO Jack Welch was doing it.

Laggards, in contrast, are much more likely than pacesetters to fall into traps that prevent tuning in to new possibilities from customers, competitors, or challengers:

- *The customer avoidance trap:* Assuming you already know what customers are thinking. Asking customers questions about past experiences, rather than about future hopes. Being content with overall positive averages, instead of getting agitated about the few minor negatives.

- *The competitor avoidance trap:* Making yourself feel good by concentrating on your competitors' flaws and flops, while thinking about your own successes. Imitating their practices, seeing only their mistakes, and not considering what they could do to wipe you out. Looking only at current competitors and failing to see emerging competition that might be coming from far outside the industry.

- *The challenger avoidance trap:* Talking only to people who agree with you and think exactly the same way. Enjoying that classic perquisite of attaining a top position in a hierarchy: never again having to talk to someone who disagrees. Never meeting people who come from a different place, speak a different language, practice a different specialty, fall in a different industry, use a different set of tools, or feel differently about the value of your field.

Changemasters need to be a little neurotic—a bit paranoid about competition overtaking them and never quite satisfied, even with success. John Chambers's audacious goal of quadrupling Cisco sales in less than three years was accompanied by his warnings of complacency at Cisco's top management conference in May 2000. Chambers requires occasional belt-tightening and expense reduction even in the face of soaring profits to "put the brakes on," he says, so people will "remember where the brakes are"—but I suspect it is also to shake people out of their routines and cause them to question their habits. Steve Kaufman set up Arrow.com to ensure that Arrow Electronics could cannibalize its own business before somebody else did it to them. A change leader at Sun Microsystems opened meetings with a chart headlined "old-line vs. on-line": "Because Barnes and Noble screwed up, there's an Amazon.com. Because Merrill Lynch screwed up, there's an e-Trade. Because Kroger screwed up, there's a Peapod. Then I'd say, 'Sun.' You guys tell me. Who's going to put us out of business? And some people still didn't get it. They'd say, 'But we're doing great, our stock's high, everything's cool.' And we'd say, 'It was at Compaq, too.'"

When people are encouraged to tune in all the time, to be conscious of the context, and to become restlessly dissatisfied, they are less likely to be jarred by change. Mindless habitual behavior is the enemy of innovation. Changemasters begin by being mindful.[2]

Skill 2. Kaleidoscope Thinking: Stimulating Breakthrough Ideas

Sensing an opportunity on the horizon is only part of the picture; an additional mental act of imagination is needed to find a creative new response to it. Changemasters take all the input about needs and opportunities and use it to shake up reality a little, to get an exciting new idea of what's possible, to break through the old pattern and invent a new one.

Creativity is a lot like looking at the world through a kaleidoscope. You look at a set of elements, the same ones everyone else sees, but then reassemble those floating bits and pieces into an enticing new possibility. Innovators shake up their thinking as though their brains are kaleidoscopes, permitting an array of different patterns out of the same bits of reality.[3] Changemasters challenge prevailing wisdom. They start from the premise that there are many solutions to a problem and that by changing the angle on the kaleidoscope, new possibilities will emerge. Where other people would say, "That's impossible. We've always done it this way," they see another approach. Where others see only problems, they see possibilities.

Kaleidoscope thinking is a way of constructing new patterns from the fragments of data available—patterns that no one else has yet imagined because they challenge conventional assumptions about how pieces of the organization, the marketplace, or the community fit together. A yard sale down the street? So why not a giant yard sale on the Internet? (We call that eBay.) Often it is not reality that is fixed, it is assumptions about reality—such as Williams-Sonoma executives telling e-commerce champion Patrick Connolly that their customers would never buy upscale kitchenware on the Internet. Connolly said customers would buy, and he was right.

The first-mover advantage in cyberspace stems from more than just market lock-in by reaching large numbers of users fast. Innovators reframe the situation, resetting the kaleidoscope on a new pattern that then becomes the convention for everyone else. Consider how many dot-com propositions are now copy-ware, just "me-too" variations on a theme set by the early innovator. New value is created only by an imaginative leap into another pattern altogether. For many wannadots, e-business transformation is now considered a cost of doing business rather than an investment in innovation to create new opportunities, because they are simply imitating a model developed elsewhere—whether they are imitating Federal Express's way of allowing customers to track their own shipments, or Amazon.com's one-click ordering. Even in "me-too" changes, a leader has to be willing to shake up assumptions about existing routines. On my e-culture survey, laggard companies often claimed limited capital for investment in new projects as a primary barrier. But their problem is not lack of money, it is lack of imagination.

The casual, free-expression atmosphere of dotcoms (wild colors, personal art on the walls, music on all the time) is often an attempt to stimulate creativity, and it probably succeeded the first few hundred times it appeared. Now it is almost a workplace norm, not an expression of challenging anything. We visited the e-commerce unit of an industrial company in which the venture manager had decorated the facility in what he considered dotcom style; he spoke repeatedly about open communication and dialogue to build community and encourage creativity. But then we watched a meeting that could have taken place in any stifling bureaucracy. The venture head made announcements; the staff sat around looking bored and not saying anything. Colorful walls and pets in the office do not by themselves induce people to challenge assumptions or seek new approaches. It's not the office layout that induces changemasters to step forward, it is the mental layout—whether the person's mind is engaged in a constant search for fresh ideas.

The revolutionary potential of e-business encourages some companies to rethink assumptions. Honeywell International's commercial airline unit had traditionally segmented its customers by size and type of aircraft: large airlines or regional/commuter airlines. But when managers used an e-business kaleidoscope, they asked a different set of questions. A fresh look at the marketplace, focusing on the aircraft maintenance activity, caused a different cut through their customer base: those who wanted to do their own maintenance as a core competency, such as Lufthansa; those who did not want to do their own maintenance, such as Southwest Airlines; and those who were forced to do their own maintenance because of asset or union constraints, such as American Airlines. This fresh perspective led to the idea for MyAircraft.com, a website for managing aircraft maintenance. Sometimes it takes outsiders to ask the new questions. At Tesco.com, a logistics manager was assigned to head what others had viewed as a marketing initiative; in turn, he built his team from general managers without preconceived perspectives of how it should be done.

Organizational practices can encourage kaleidoscopic thinking. For example:

- *Monday morning quarterbacking* (named after the dissection of each Sunday's game common in American professional football). Change-masters second-guess their own successes as well as their own mistakes. Looking for root causes but also for unexpected juxtapositions of events can challenge assumptions and suggest new approaches.

- *Expeditions to Labrador* (in honor of frozen food innovator Clarence Birdseye, who got his idea while fur-trapping in Labrador). Sending people outside the company and the industry—not just on field trips, but "far afield trips"—can shake kaleidoscopes. When John Taysom took Reuters's CEO and top executives to California in 1997 for two days of meetings with Silicon Valley entrepreneurs, complete with fast electric car rides in one company's parking lot to jar minds (as well as bodies), that was probably as strange as Labrador to many of them. But it opened minds to how the Greenhouse could trigger innovation.

- *Blue sky events* (designed to look up, beyond the horizon). Large brainstorming sessions consisting of people from a wide variety of areas allow interested outsiders to ask questions, make suggestions, and trigger new ideas.

- *Talent shows* (everyone has a hidden talent). Humor, play, artistic expression, and poking fun at tradition signal that it is okay to question the status quo. Abuzz's Cool Talks are twice-monthly lunchtime talent shows that allow people to get to know each other's out-of-work pursuits, but they also reinforce a spirit of creativity throughout the company.

Skill 3. Setting the Theme: Communicating Inspiring Visions

A raw idea that emerges from the kaleidoscope must be shaped into a theme that makes the idea come alive. Ideas don't launch productive changes until they become a theme around which others begin to improvise, a vision that raises aspirations.

"If you can dream it, you can do it," the saying goes. Not exactly. There is a gap between dreaming and doing that is filled by the support of others. A vision remains just a dream unless it can inspire others to follow. The third skill for mastering change is to shape ideas into a theme that makes a compelling case for the value and direction of change—especially when you are pursuing a new idea that has not yet taken shape.

Successful organizations are often the hardest to sell on the need for change. You would think they would be easy because they have the time, money, and desire to remain on top. But they are often complacent, and their people are too comfortable to want to rise from inertia for the hard work of change. Sukyana Lahiri's analysis of a subset of respondents to my global e-culture survey showed that financial service and retail companies with the highest revenues per employee (one measure of success) are more often laggards than pacesetters on e-business change.[4] (Perhaps those rich laggards think they are already perfect, so they don't want to rock the boat by adopting strange new technology. Or perhaps they are running so tightly that there is no time to dream about change.)

Leaders must wake people out of inertia. They must get people excited about something they've never seen before, something that does not yet exist. The theme provides the setting for a story that has to come to life in order to raise aspirations and inspire action. A vision is not just a picture of what could be; it is an appeal to our better selves, a call to become something more. It reminds us that the future does not just descend like a stage set; rather, we construct the future from our own history, desires, and decisions. And we have to stretch our imaginations just as we take on stretch goals—Cisco CEO John Chambers's favorite kind of goal. The aspiration must be so compelling that it is worth the extra time and effort to achieve. That means an appeal also to our pragmatic selves, addressing the classic first question of "What's in it for me?" One answer might be that the hard work of change now will make life easier later (a message conveyed by many of the e-business change agents at IBM and Sun). Changemasters have to focus people's eyes on the prize—to get them to see the value beyond the hardship of change to the prize waiting at the end. When hongkong.com changed its business model and set a new theme, director Rudy Chan reported: "We needed to go through quite a bit of explaining. We had to tell them why. And what's in it for them in terms of career opportunities. And we needed to do that several times. It was a lot of communication."

Setting the theme involves more than a lot of communication; it's a special kind of communication, with dramatic flourishes. Recall the *Total World Domination* film commissioned by Abuzz. PlanetFeedback memorialized its own startup experience on its website. "Nigel Brown's" Internet team turned Hong Kong offices into an art gallery to help "Empire International Bank's" bankers visualize what they could do on the Web. Inspiring visions provide a picture of the future combining poetry and prose, imagination and pragmatism, drawing on six elements:

- *Destination:* Where are we headed?

- *Dream:* What will be different because of this goal? What will our world look like then?

- *Prize:* What positive outcomes will be obtained? Who will benefit? How?

- *Target:* What deadlines or metrics make the outcomes concrete?

- *Message:* What memorable image, slogan, or headline conveys the essence of the goal?

- *First step:* What tangible step can be taken that will give reality to the goal?

These pieces of the picture are important because sometimes people just don't understand what the change leader is talking about. They nod at the words, but do not hear the music or get the meaning. Sometimes they prefer to misunderstand. The one kind of power that is universal, held by every person in every role in every organization, is silent veto power, such as the pocket veto, in which a person simply puts a request in his or her pocket and forgets about it. People exercise this power by doing nothing to support or advance the change. People can ignore change by denying that it requires anything they are not already doing. Or they can disclaim any responsibility for it. Time is the most valuable commodity, and people can only do so many things. Things that not part of their immediate goals can fall by the wayside. So unless they have a compelling reason to cooperate, they can slow down even changes ordered by the top. When Albert Ormiston, vice president for direct sales at Sun Microsystems, began to communicate the vision for e-Sun, he reported that: "We found people that said, 'Hey, it's not my job' or 'I'm doing the best I can.' This really meant 'Take a hike, I'm not interested.'"

Words matter. The rhetoric of change can open wounds or heal them. How the vision is conveyed makes a difference because symbols matter to people. Sun Microsystems's e-Sun project was considered both mysterious and threatening to some in the direct sales force; the way my Sun informants talked about the macho character of the sales force made me think they felt that the coming of Web sales was a loss of manhood. The elimination of business unit CIO titles at IBM in 1997 was a loss of status and of face that got in the way of some of the former CIOs (newly named business information executives) understanding the bigger "One IBM" goal. They saw "reengineering," not a journey to e-business leadership. Healing visions avoid blame and maintain respect for traditions, but still keep the dream and destination in clear focus. John Browitt, CEO of Tesco Direct, said that Tesco never talked about cannibalization internally during the move to Internet sales, instead stressing a broader vision that this was a way to follow customers where they wanted to go.

The big-picture element of a new aspiration is critical for the message even being heard by people bogged down in daily routines. The skeptics Philip Nenon encountered at Sun Microsystems for his team's new network product were "people who were more focused on the tactical, day-to-day, status quo type of product growth," he said. Albert Ormiston and his colleagues not only had to compete for time and attention to get the e-Sun vision understood, but as leaders based near Boston, they also had to overcome a bias against things that did not emanate from California. Only a big-picture aspiration can lift people out of their own immediate tasks and make a change effort appear central to the community rather than just more work piled on by peripheral people.

A vision isn't a written goal distributed to people, like a business plan or mission statement; nor is it communicated once as an announcement of a new venture. It is embodied by the changemaster's personal enthusiasm, reflected in his or her passion for the cause, communicated over and over again in every encounter. If the project is viewed as just another assignment, then either it's so routine that it doesn't produce much change, or skeptics and resisters (who are already too busy) have good reasons to slow it down. So it is important for potential change leaders to make sure that their passion matches their aspiration, asking themselves questions such as the following:

- Do I feel strongly about the need for this?

- Am I convinced that this can be accomplished?

- Can I convey excitement when I talk about it?

- Am I willing to put my credibility on the line to promise action on it?

- Am I committed to seeing this through, over the long haul?

- Am I willing to make sacrifices to see that this gets done?

Personal passion helps the changemaster do whatever it takes to get started, to demonstrate the value of the vision even when others cannot yet see it. An e-commerce head of a large bank reported that "Those of us who are believers are dedicated to what we want to do, but the others are not sure or convinced of the right path to follow, especially given the big expenses involved. . . . So I rather sneakily chunk out big projects into smaller pieces that I can approve myself." The small projects then produce tangible results that help others picture the goal.

Skill 4. Enlisting Backers and Supporters: Getting Buy-in and Building Coalitions

As every entrepreneur knows, a great idea is not enough. Even a great mandate from a powerful sponsor to "just do it" isn't enough. Potential changemasters must sell the idea more widely: attract the right backers and supporters, entice investors and defenders, get buy-in from stakeholders in a position to help or harm the venture at later stages. The newer the idea, the more critical this coalition building. Recall that list of barriers to e-business change in chapter 3. Most of them concern reluctance or outright resistance to change from employees, managers, and even the CEO, as well as customers and suppliers. A great deal of the work of innovation and change is to reach deeply into, across, and outside the organization to identify key influencers and get them interested and supportive. Does the idea have financial implications? Better get buy-in from Arthur in Accounting. Will it affect company image? Involve Peggy from PR. Does it change sales channels? Speak to Don from the Distributors.

Coalition building requires an understanding of the politics of change and the skills of a community organizer. Instead of trying to recruit everyone at once, changemasters seek the minimum number of investors necessary to launch the new venture and then to champion it when they need help later. Each successive round of buy-in brings more people and groups on board—a process that is similar for both stand-alone startups and internal change.

"To make anything successful, you must work a personal network," many successful innovators repeated to me like a mantra. Without that network of contacts, identifying the people to ask for support can be challenging. When a newcomer took on responsibility for a centralized Web initiative at one large manufacturing company in our e-culture research, she couldn't get information on websites and URLs owned by the company, and she found it hard even to get the names of the right contacts in the divisions. That's why changemasters are often more effective when they are insiders bringing a revolutionary new perspective. A foundation of community and a base of strong relationships inside large organizations can speed the change process; people already trust each other. An independent entrepreneur's file of phone numbers is one of his or her most important early assets. For intrapraneurs and internal change agents, potential coalition members are not limited by the walls of the company; they can extend to suppliers, customers, and partners. At Sun Microsystems, innovators routinely drew on key customers as backers of ventures that had not yet secured the full approval of senior management. An enterprising innovator at a dotcom made an external strategic partner her ally in convincing peers to back her vision for change. The spirit of community and a network of partners are key elements of e-culture.

Early in the change process, leaders need the support of power holders—those who possess resources, information, and credibility that can be invested in the venture to get it moving. Resources can include people or technology as well as funds. Information includes political intelligence and savvy as well as data or expertise. Both are important, and they are often widely available. Equally important is the intangible asset of legitimacy. Powerful, well-connected sponsors make the idea credible, open doors, speak on behalf of the changemaster at meetings he or she does not attend, and quell opposition. Early coalition members help sell others. Just as dotcom entrepreneurs seek strategic investors, so Union City school superintendent Thomas Highton used Bell Atlantic for credibility with New Jersey officials when he wanted to buy an old parochial school and turn it into a technology showcase connecting home and school via the Internet.

Effective coalition building proceeds through three kinds of actions. First is *preselling*. The change leader speaks to many people, to gather intelligence (such as where people stand, who is likely to support or resist the idea) and to plant seeds, leaving behind a germ of an idea that can blossom and gradually become familiar. Changemasters must be willing to reveal an idea or proposal before it's fully developed, following the Rule of No Surprises. Secrecy denies you the opportunity to get feedback, and when things are sprung on people with no warning, the easiest answer is always no. Smart leaders pave the way for a good reception to new ideas by one-on-one preparation before convening people, and they avoid initiating discussions or holding meetings where people hear something they are not prepared for.

A second action is *making deals*. Having identified those likely to provide strategic support, the leader gets them to chip in ("tin-cupping," one company calls the process of "begging" for resources). This can involve some creative exchange of benefits ("horse trading"), so that supporters get something of value right away. Some changemasters seek contributions beyond the amount they actually need because investment builds the commitment of other people to helping them. It lets other people in on the action, even if what they are investing is minor—a little time, a little data, a staff member to serve as a liaison. This is a good preemptive move, because otherwise "every one who is left out secretly wants to see you fail," an e-commerce head said.

A third piece of coalition building is *getting a sanity check*—confirming or adjusting the idea in light of reactions from backers and potential backers. Changemasters want to secure the blessings of those with experience, but they also need their wisdom to ensure that "I'm not out of my mind," as one said. A coalition is generally a loose network, with people chipping in various things at various levels of commitment. Sometimes, when the project is significant and controversial, the coalition can become an official advisory board. Internal boards for e-commerce initiatives build a set of spokespeople and cheerleaders for the venture while reassuring others in the mainstream that their views are represented, as we saw in chapter 6.

Throughout, changemasters do not just communicate, they overcommunicate—communicating more than seems necessary through more media more times. One leader who successfully bridged silos to establish e-commerce for a large manufacturer attested to the truth of this principle: "You've got to go back over it over and over and over again. You have to present it orally, present it visually. You have to get consensus and buy in from their peers and the people above them."

Having a mandate from top management to make radical change does not guarantee that other supporters will fall in line. (Remember the veto power I mentioned earlier—the ability to slow down anything by just doing nothing.) At a large manufacturer, the CEO and other officers underscored their support for the unified website and the e-commerce group at a senior management conference, and then business unit heads seemed to conveniently forget some of the messages when they got home.

Under some circumstances, being too close to the bosses can provoke backlash, and efforts to persuade colleagues can be seen as spying on them and reporting their resistance. This is a risk particularly in cases in which e-business change forces managers to give up territory; e-business looks so revolutionary that it seems likelier to leave the losers out completely. At IBM, some former business-unit CIOs who lost power in the centralization of Web initiatives had little desire to cooperate with the people leading the changes, and instead raised objections or engaged in passive resistance. Albert Ormiston commented about his e-Sun team: "I would say that this is not a real popular group at Sun. People that work for me say it is like being in the internal affairs department of the police."

Coalitions are fragile, especially when they contain people who look to see which way the political wind is blowing. Top management might withdraw their support if organizational opposition swells instead of declining. Thus, changemasters try to widen their coalition—to move people up a continuum toward more active support, if they are neutral, and to the neutral zone if they are opponents. So to develop e-Sun, Ormiston focused on constant selling: "You have to really work hard on communicating that message. And then you must have a whole bunch of hooks in that message, where you can come back and sneak up behind people to see if they really got it. The fact that I know what I want to do doesn't really cut much if I can't clearly get you to understand what I'm going to do. [A]nd the fact that I want to get to the end game doesn't mean much to people either. So you show them benefits, how it fits what they need."

Support from power holders gets the venture underway; other stakeholders help it move forward. Bringing key stakeholders into the coalition (which means active communication) avoids problems later. And stakeholder representatives can be co-opted to help sell their peers. That's how Vauxhall was able to win support from car dealers for its growing e-commerce initiatives. In 1995, Vauxhall (a General Motors subsidiary) was the first U.K. manufacturer to have a website of any sort. In September 1999, Vauxhall moved from brochureware to electronic sales completed by a dealer, and by 2000 Vauxhall had launched an exclusive range of "dot-com cars" available only over the Web, with the entire transaction online. Paul Confrey, Vauxhall's changemaster in his position as manager of relationship marketing and new media, faced the same channel conflict as other manufacturers: Online sales threatened offline dealers. Confrey used the franchise board of 20 dealers with whom he met frequently to provide the sanity check and then to sell the idea to the rest of the 400 dealers. (The early supporters were undoubtedly flattered to get so much attention from the company and a chance to shape the initiative, despite its potential to displace them.) He did some horse trading, offering the dealers a partial commission on Internet sales in their region. He also displayed his other support, bringing in heavy hitters, such as the company chairman, to meet with the dealers. Although about half the dealers were wary at first, eventually all of them accepted the dotcom cars and began to feature computers on the showroom floors to differentiate themselves from other dealers.

Backers and supporters help avoid the risk that e-business pioneers will be viewed as mavericks to be undercut. "Nigel Brown," leader of an Internet skunk works at "Empire International Bank," had several sources of funds from managers for which his group provided services, so he was not undermined when the IT group in London froze his official budget. At "Handy Gadgets," as discussed in the previous chapter, "Craig Lebolt" described himself as the "Craig Lebolt one-man show." He got some help from marketing on creative ideas, and customer service helped him refine his options. But his e-business efforts "just flew in the face of our traditional organization. I kept hearing people say, 'That's not how it's done here.' I drove the e-commerce projects with the force of my personality."

His boss, "Michelle Hellman," was very helpful as a sounding board and advocate to other groups, especially "when I thought I was crazy because thirty people were against my idea," Lebolt said. Like the wise old hands that invest in new ventures, Hellman helped her associate pass the sanity check. Now he could pull the team together to get Gadgets.com online.

Skill 5. Developing the Dream: Nurturing the Working Team

Once a coalition of backers is in place, changemasters enlist others in turning the dream into reality. Too often executives announce a plan, launch a task force, and then simply hope that people find the answers—instead of offering a dream, stretching their horizons, and encouraging people to do the same. In contrast, the areas where people feel that they are in charge of creating the future always seem to hum with communication. People cluster to help each other over rough spots. There's a team identity, maybe a team name. The team has deadlines that are considered milestones whose accomplishment can be celebrated.

Leaders now shift their role in the drama of change from lead actor to producer-director. They bring on stage the rest of the improvisational actors who take on the task of translating an idea into implementation, a promise into a prototype. There are two parts of this job: team-building and team-nurturing. The first consists of encouraging the actors to feel like a team, with ownership of the goals and a team identity that motivates performance, like a sports team that wants to win. A working team that feels deep commitment and responsibility for delivering on deadlines and promises is the best way to ensure high performance at Internet speed. The second involves care and feeding of the team as it does its work—supporting the team, providing coaching and resources, and patrolling the boundaries within which the team can freely operate.

Team is one of those overused words, like *partner*, that is part of corporate-speak even when it doesn't fit the reality of the situation. Even though a group of people has a common assignment, they are not a team unless more stringent criteria are met: a common identity, strong respect for each other as individuals, and a desire to do whatever it takes to support each other in succeeding. In short, they need to reflect the spirit of community at a micro level, with both structure (deadlines, routines, tools, disciplines) and soul (bonds among people). There is a big difference between the e-commerce committees that have trouble getting anything done at lagging wannadots and the high-performance product development teams that meet impossible deadlines to get Web applications up and running at Abuzz. Both involve groups, but beyond that, there are no similarities. Committees are often convened to ensure that many voices are heard and no unpopular decisions are made, and that by definition slows down the action. Working teams, in contrast, should be designed to make sure things happen quickly. Honeywell captures this speed goal when it establishes "tiger teams."

Team-building begins with allowing a set of people to embrace the goals rather than just being told what to do by their manager. This encourages a more voluntary commitment through face-to-face relationship-building. At Abuzz, product development teams meet as a large group over several days to create the plan together, with individuals making commitments to pieces of the schedule, and lots of back and forth among all team members until everyone knows what they can expect from everyone else. The result is full ownership for stringent deadlines, such as turning enterprise software into an Internet offering in record time. In e-culture, teams need to be considered offshoots of crowds; they take shape out of a larger, amorphous group of people as some step forward to take more responsibility than others. Getting everyone together from any function that might have anything to do with the solution to hear the same message at the same time has long been associated with faster product development or process implementation.[5] Rapid prototyping and parallel development are a big part of the improvisation that produces innovation and shapes a strategy, as I showed in chapter 4.

Team names, slogans, T-shirts, and mascots symbolize identity, but these can be empty of meaning unless the team has first taken ownership of its tasks. The theme set by the leader provides a starting point, and the vision offers inspiration, but details are best left to the team to create through their own interactions among themselves and with their audiences. That approach not only confers team ownership, but also allows for creative approaches. Unleashing team creativity involves intensity and focus, with brains fully engaged—a contrast with the mindlessness possible when people are just following a script.[6] Leaders must give team members the time and the space to focus, protected from distractions. Creative effort, whether development of new knowledge or the solving of challenging problems, takes full attention to the task and excellent communication among team members so that elusive bits of not yet fully understood knowledge can be pinned down and shared quickly.

Communication over the Web through e-mail and team chat rooms, with everyone looking at the same documents or drawings, can facilitate speed and seamlessness. But face-to-face communication at the beginning and at critical moments throughout the team's work is more commonly associated with success than is pure virtuality. People looking each other in the eyes and talking directly to one another live and in person builds the foundation that permits virtual communication to be effective in between face-to-face meetings.

The second big job is to see to the care and feeding of the team—to be their advocate to the world around them, to get them whatever they need to get the job done. Successful teamwork is determined not just by the person-alities of the people on the team or the particular process they use, but by whether or not the team is linked appropriately to the resources they need from the wider world around them. In e-business environments, the *feeding* part of care and feeding is often literal. E-business team leaders as diverse as Parkash Ahuja at Charles Schwab or Helen Yang at Sun Microsystems described meal delivery as an important act. Yang, who led the SunPeak project that converted Sun to run on its own systems, also secured valet parking, stress management, and pep talks for her team. But even more important than amenities are the best tools to do the job. Among the biggest differences between pacesetter and laggard wannadots is whether people creating their e-ventures have leaders who helped them get the resources they needed.

Skill 6. Mastering the Difficult Middles: Persisting and Persevering

My personal law of management, if not of life, is that everything can look like a failure in the middle. Every new idea runs into trouble before it reaches fruition, and the possibilities for trouble increase with the number of ways the venture differs from current approaches. The more innova-tion, the more problems. The more problems, the greater the importance of skills in getting over the difficult middles.

One of the mistakes leaders make in change processes is to launch them and leave them. There are many ways a new venture or change initiative can get derailed. These tempt people to give up, forget it, and chase the next enticing rainbow. Stop the effort too soon, and by definition it will be a failure. Stay with it through its initial hurdles, make appropriate adjustments and midcourse corrections, and you are on the way to success. Of course, if the process takes too long, you have to return to the beginning—monitor the environment again, recheck assumptions, look at the way the theme is being played out, and reset the vision. In the e-business environment, outcomes are often emergent, not planned. Constant monitoring is important to keep ideas on track or to redirect them if circumstances change—and they change constantly in the e-world.

Four common problems arise in the middle of developing new products, implementing new processes, or getting new ventures off the ground.

1. Forecasts fall short. You have to have a plan—but if you are doing something new and different, the plan often does not hold. Plans are based on experience and assumptions. When attempting to innovate, to do something that has never been done before, it is difficult to predict how long it will take or how much it will cost. Change leaders must be prepared to accept serious departures from plans. They must also understand that if they hope to encourage innovation it is foolish to measure people's performance according to the script. That's why improvisational theater is so important; the team is expected to take the project in a direction that could not have been envisioned in advance. That's positive, part of the process of innovation. But projects designed to be completed on Internet time often involve a scramble. An aggressive fourteen-week launch time for Vauxhall's e-commerce site featuring Internet-exclusive cars meant that not all the back-end systems were ready when the front end went live. In situations like this, leaders must secure additional resources, beg for additional time, or be even more innovative in figuring out how to work around limitations.

2. Unexpected obstacles pop up. Everyone knows that a new path is unlikely to run straight and true, but when we actually encounter those twists and turns we often panic. Especially when attempting to make changes in a complex system, diversions are likely—and sometimes unwelcome. It's a mistake to simply stop in your tracks. Every change brings unanticipated consequences, and teams must be prepared to respond, to troubleshoot, to make adjustments, and to make their case. Although scenario planning can help identify the possible problems that can pop up, the real message is to expect the unexpected. Not only do projects hit potholes, but external events can disrupt the best-laid plans as well—for example, AlliedSignal's Specialty Films business was reorganized in the middle of multiple new e-business projects, and IBM's Reinventing Education projects experienced turnovers of several school superintendents, stopping the action. External events can also create new opportunities, such as the New York Times's offer to buy Abuzz and divert its software to the Internet just as Abuzz was in the middle of launching an enterprise software product.

Leaders must ensure that there is sufficient flexibility to redirect the venture around obstacles, or to mount a second project to deal with the new challenge. This kind of flexibility is apparent in pacesetter companies but is not characteristic of the laggards. The e-commerce head of a Canadian bank ran into a roadblock when a study was issued reporting that Canadian consumers did not want to give credit card information on the Internet; his CEO, already wavering about the Web, was ready to cancel the project. (It was still hanging in limbo as of this writing.) If success or failure of a new venture rests on one factor only, without flexibility to explore other approaches, then the venture is doomed from the start.

3. Momentum slows. Most people get excited about things in the beginning, and everybody loves endings, especially happy endings. It's the hard work in between that demands the attention and effort of savvy leaders.

After the excitement and anticipation of a project launch, reality sinks in. You do not have solutions to the problems you face; the multiple demands of your job are piling up; the people you have asked for information or assistance are not returning your calls. After longer-than-normal work days (and nights, in dotcoms), the team is tired. And within the team, after the initial warm glow of membership, differences among team members—in work styles or points of view—start to surface, and conflict starts to slow things down.

At Sun Microsystems, the SunPeak project to convert all of Sun's systems to its own networks almost got hurt by sagging morale. The team had a punishing work schedule (mandated Saturdays) and a firm deadline (go live in August 1998). Then two months from completion, Vice President Helen Yang told the team that the date would slip by six weeks. "No one was thrilled to work 80 hours a week for six additional weeks," one of her sponsors recalled. To her existing morale boosters (free meals and more) she added days off on July 4 and 5 ("That got the loudest cheer in our meeting," she reported), and she brought in the project's chief backers to pick up team spirit by reminding them how much more successful they would be because of the extra effort.

It is important for change leaders to revisit the team's mission, to recognize what's been accomplished and what remains, and to remember that the differences in outlook, background, and perspective that now may divide the group can ultimately provide solutions. When teams are stuck in the middle, shuffling assignments, breaking into subgroups, and trying a different tack can often break the logjam. The best morale booster and team unifier is a successful solution.

4. Critics get louder. The final problem of middles is often the most frustrating. Even if you have built a coalition and involved key stakeholders, the critics, skeptics, and cynics will challenge you. They will be strongest and loudest not at the beginning but in the middle of your efforts, just when the project itself is not quite ready and thus is most vulnerable. It is only then that the possible impact of the change becomes clear. And those who don't like it have had time to formulate their objections and harden their positions. In the beginning, the theme is just a distant possibility, and the vision is just rhetoric. Perhaps people don't even understand what the words mean, or what the venture implies for their own activities, until the unfolding project makes the consequences concrete. And now that it looks like the venture might succeed, the threat to those who oppose it increases.

At a number of companies, enthusiastic public commitment at the executive committee level to support e-business is followed by dissension once those same business unit heads find out what it means for their territorial sovereignty. The e-commerce team at a manufacturing company thought the opponents of a unified corporate website were converted by top management speeches and a beautiful demonstration at a leadership meeting in February 1999. "You might think it would be easy to get acceptance for the website from rank and file management after that demo, but that's not how it worked in reality," recalled the head of Web initiatives. "We never did really sell it. Even right before we went live no one really believed it would happen. People would tell me, 'You are never going to get it done.' But we had to keep pushing." As Albert Ormiston of e-Sun observed, "The very generality of the theme leaves room for low level folks to speculate, are we really doing to do this? Even now people are saying we're really not going to do this. That goes on forever." And so the same venture that was authorized and backed by power holders and has a working team well underway remains open for discussion. An e-business change leader reported: "One of the things that's been discouraging for me is you think you're past a certain point, and then you find, no you're not, you're revisiting that point again. Why is it? It's not just the resisters, it's sometimes even people in your own organization. You think you've got an agreement, you think you've communicated something. And then you come back later, and the whole thing is stuck again in arguments. Maybe there was just one little detail that you assumed that everybody understood that they didn't."

Critics and skeptics can be internal and external. At Sun, internal skeptics dismissed the (ultimately successful) network computer being designed by Robert Gianni's team as an old-fashioned model, a dumb design that would never work and would never be bought. Even customers doubted it would work, or grumbled about having to change networks they had just installed. Gianni is an engineer, but he had to become a salesperson, explaining the product to key customers even before they could see it in full operation.

In the middle, then, the persistence and perseverance of a changemaster makes the difference between success and failure. While the working team soldiers on, the changemaster needs to be there to fight for additional resources, remove obstacles, boost team morale, and deal with the critics. And now the real value is derived from having taken the time to create a clear and compelling vision, a strong and committed coalition of backers, and a team that feels ownership. Each of these—the vision, the supporters, and the team—helps weather the middles. With the help of coalition members and their own team, changemasters can make adjustments, veer around obstacles, and push forward.

Leaders can remind people of the vision. Powerful sponsors can neutralize or remove the critics. Team members can be enlisted for the political campaign. Sun changemaster Robert Gianni, responsible for a new network computer, turned his engineers into educators, teaching people at Sun about the product at big events in each major geography—how to sell it, how to understand it. Sun's Philip Nenon drew on internal and external coalition members. His unit's venture into telecom products involved a tough, evolving marketplace and customers such as Cisco with very stringent standards. When unexpected technical problems appeared, upper management supporters were brought in to help. "It's a tribute to [the] management team that when implementation issues came up, they did not freak out," Nenon recalled. "They got closer to it. They got directly involved and gave both the attention and support that were needed for us to execute." Having key customers in the coalition of backers also proved useful; they served as unofficial consultants. The venture found additional engineering resources, worked around obstacles, and eventually proved the value of Sun's "billion dollar bet" on this market.

Sometimes power holders use their clout to silence the critics. The finance vice president of a manufacturing company opposed the coming of e-commerce because he would have to merge a portion of his operation with the sales group. He frustrated the e-commerce team leader by appearing to agree (after a seemingly endless set of meetings and slide presentations) and then throwing up objections or letting schedules slip. At a major meeting, the finance head was confronted by the sales vice president and embarrassed in front of his peers. With the CEO watching closely, the finance executive committed to an aggressive implementation schedule.

One venture head compared leading change to pushing a boulder up a hill: It takes muscle power and the determination to never let go, or the boulder will roll down and you'll be crushed. To another agent of e-business transformation, a changemaster is like a pest, never taking no for an answer, never letting go, following up relentlessly, staying on top of people to make sure they do what they promised. "You have to constantly come back. Someone said, 'You guys are like a bug around my head. You're bothering me, go away.' Well, I'm not going away," he said. That kind of persistence helps turn difficult middles into successful achievements.

Skill 7. Celebrating Accomplishments: Making Everyone a Hero

Remembering to recognize, reward, and celebrate accomplishments is the final critical leadership skill, just as it was the final stop on our tour around the Change Wheel in chapter 8. E-culture thrives on celebration. Dotcoms, with their spirit of fun, are likely to celebrate everything in sight, including the fact that it's Friday afternoon. But some are better than others at publicizing the accomplishments that give change leaders and their team members that warm glow that comes from being recognized by other members of their community.

Recognition is important not only for its motivational pat on the back but also for its publicity value; the whole organization and maybe the whole world now knows what is possible, who has done it, and what talents reside in the community gene pool. Steve Socolof, vice president of Lucent Technologies' New Venture Group, uses the press to publicize achievements internally and externally. Formal recognition—awards, merit badges, or medals of honor—is also a way to boost the reputation of knowledge nomads, who can list awards on their resumes. Of course, the company doesn't want to lose talent, but promising to make someone a star is a good way to attract and hold talent. That's the value of the RAVEs for employee achievements that Abuzz posts on its website and communicates at companywide meetings.

In traditional organizations, recognition is probably the most underutilized motivational tool. There is no limit to how much recognition you can provide, and it is often free. Recognition brings the change cycle to its logical conclusion, but it also motivates people to attempt change again. So many people get involved in and contribute to changing the way an organization does things that it's important to share the credit. Change is an ongoing issue, and you can't afford to lose the talents, skills, or energies of those who can help make it happen.

The Rhythm of Change

The seven skills of changemasters—tuning in to the environment, kaleidoscope thinking, conveying the theme through an inspiring vision, building coalitions, nurturing the working team, persisting through the difficult middles, and making heroes—correspond roughly to the phases of change projects. But this is not to suggest that there is an orderly sequence, one careful step at a time. In the everything-faster e-world, where innovation is improvisational theater, opportunities become themes before the need is fully documented, the actors start the play while the producer is still finding backers, and the team celebrates milestones while the ending is still undetermined.

Sometimes a set of people share responsibility, sometimes people enter after the idea has already been formulated, and sometimes they hand it off to another leader to pick up. At Williams-Sonoma, Patrick Connolly shook the Internet kaleidoscope and set the e-commerce theme, but then stood back to become a sponsor while other change agents picked up the challenge of building coalitions, nurturing teams, and managing implementation.

Depending on the nature of the effort, projects move through these phases at different rates of speed. Even Internet time has different rhythms—faster at some points, slower at others. Some ventures gestate in the minds of innovators and then spring into being seemingly all at once, because the gestation period got everything lined up for incredible speed once the action began. (Even "instant" success takes time.) Others get organized quickly and then bump up against those murky middles, so time slows down again—for example, as the go-live date is postponed, features are delayed, the front end promises something the back end can't yet deliver, or audience members intervene and must be dealt with. The successive iterations, rapid prototypes, and unexpected creative bursts that characterize e-culture mean that there are many simultaneous innovation projects, and they are likely to overlap. One is hardly finished before another is underway. Changemasters are often protecting still-embryonic projects from the ripples of neighboring ventures.

Certain kinds of change appear simple and fast. If you're a senior executive, you can order budget reductions, buy or sell a division, form a strategic alliance, or arrange a merger. Such bold strokes do produce fast change, but they do not necessarily build support for the work that follows, the work that creates the value the leader hoped to gain from the bold stroke.[7] Bold strokes are decisions. Decisiveness is important for moving at Internet speed (one of the lessons Pamela Thomas-Graham learned when she moved from being a McKinsey consultant to CNBC.com CEO). But change is not just a decision, it is a campaign. IBM announced a centralized Web group, a change of CIO titles, and "One IBM" on the Internet—a *big everywhere fast* bold stroke—except that it took a year or two to align all the pieces, convert all the systems, and commit all the stakeholders. That's a long march.

It takes long marches to turn decisions into new sources of value, to produce and ultimately sustain change. Long marches can proceed at a run, but they still involve voluntary, discretionary, ongoing efforts of people throughout the community. Real change requires people to adjust their behavior, and their behavior is often beyond the control of top management. A senior executive can allocate resources for new product development or reorganize a unit, but he or she cannot order people to use their imaginations or to work collaboratively. Shaking things up with a bold stroke makes good external press (that's why some leaders like dramatic moves), but that doesn't necessarily change anyone's behavior.

Some revolutionaries make a big splash, attacking the castle head-on. Such moves create drama and heroics, but the fortifications harden, and even if the battle is won, there is blood everywhere. Other change leaders operate by stealth, tunneling underneath the castle. They take actions that are hardly visible until suddenly the castle collapses. Consider this contrast within the same company. One change agent talked about the fast immediate painful changes that he "muscled" through ("April 12, 1999, a day that will live in infamy")—cutting people and changing their jobs—and then the longer period of persuasion that followed (perhaps longer because the pain caused backlash). Another, however, reported a slow seven months—identifying supporters and resisters, letting people get familiar with the change, getting the team to develop the idea a little further—and then an accelerated four months as he started to use clout to force faster progress ("The 'golly, gee, I hope we can all work this out and still be friends' day is gone").

Leaders must sense what the context will handle and then pick the rhythm of change that appears right for their organization. But as a general tendency, starting more slowly and then accelerating for a really fast finish reduces the risk of being blindsided by obstacles or resistance. Dot-com leaders who manage by press release, making big public announcements before they know they can deliver, often have to backpedal furiously. Better to take a little time to build the coalitions, get the buy-in, nurture the team, and then make a huge splash everywhere at once.

Individuals in the audience for change dance to different rhythms, too. Some like their music fast (get it over with), others like it slow (time to get ready and get it right), and some would prefer to sit it out, hoping it goes away. Some jump on every bandwagon; others hold back no matter what. After leading a major new Internet initiative, a Silicon Valley executive concluded: "When you move to a new business model, there are those precious few who say 'I get it, let's go.' Folks who can see the bigger picture. Then there are folks that say they get it, but they don't really mean it; they're pretending. And then there are folks that just screw themselves to the floor, don't communicate, and are thinking 'I ain't doing that.' The hardest to deal with are the people who consider what you're doing totally insignificant to what they're doing, so they ignore you." For some kinds of changes, he said, "Folks just don't want to go there. The eyes glaze over. Don't want to talk about it, don't want to think about it, don't want to know about it." If we take his informal categorization of people in reverse order, we have the phases through which wannadot laggards pass, as I identified them in chapter 3: denial, anger, cosmetic change, and (we hope) full acceptance.

Like community organizing, organizational change is a numbers game: a few early enthusiasts to carry the message, then a building of critical mass until even avoiders can no longer remain in denial. There are always holdouts, there is always pushback (Is she serious? Will he fold?), so maintaining the momentum for the long march makes a difference. When changemasters are successful, what started as a rogue initiative—an opportunity that one person seized—becomes a real option, then the norm, and ultimately embedded everywhere. Sometimes people who think they have the assignment to create a bold-stroke change discover that they must instead be organizers and shapers of initiatives already underway elsewhere. A corporate team given the goal of creating a globalization strategy for a large retailer found that several groups within the business units were already working on the same thing. The team used kaleidoscope thinking. They shifted from seeking decisions to working with the other globalization groups to make sure that they all moved in roughly the same direction.

The most important personal traits a leader can bring to any kind of change effort are imagination, conviction, passion, and confidence in others. To turn these qualities into successful ventures, just add a few political lessons:

- Position power is not enough. Personal passion and force of personality aren't enough. Other people must become believers, too. Their behavior shapes what the change turns out to be.

- Marshal data in support of change. Make the theme memorable and the vision concrete. Prototypes and test programs can be effective in demonstrating the power of change and in building momentum.

- Endorsers and investors lend credibility and wisdom. Tap into the experience of others inside and outside the organization. Utilize relationships to get resources.

- Winning supporters can take time. Try iterative waves of coalition building, in which many get the message and some become champions who reach out to many more.

- Seek to minimize loss and uncertainty for those who will be affected by change. Listen to the resisters; sometimes they are telling you things you need to hear. Walk in the shoes of resisters; show them you understand them and are on their side. Co-optation of your opponents through a role in the venture can be effective. If they can't be converted, get them out of the way.

• Choose the rhythm that fits the situation. Know the audience. Know what people and the organization can handle, and push—but not too much too fast. Stretch people, but not to the breaking point.

• Persistence pays off. Stick with it. Follow up and follow through.

• Respect and recognition win friends. Throughout the process, make all those who are part of the change look good.

In the Internet Age, *morphing* has become a common synonym for changing. To morph is to undergo transformation. In cyberspace, on-screen, morphing is instantaneous. One image dissolves into another through the magic of programming. Offline, behind the screen, change is not so simple. Skillful leaders in receptive environments can speed it up, but they cannot altogether avoid the hard work of convincing others to join them in mastering change.

10

◆

CHANGING OURSELVES
Human Skills and Social Evolution

The computer is a chameleon. It can be seen as a theater, a town hall, an unraveling book, an animated wonderland, a sports arena, and even a potential life form. But it is first and foremost a representational medium, a means for modeling the world that adds its own potent properties to the traditional media it has assimilated so quickly. As the most powerful representational medium yet invented, it should be put to the highest tasks of society.

—Janet Murray, *Hamlet on the Holodeck:*
The Future of Narrative in Cyberspace

On the Internet, nobody knows you're a dog.

—Oft-quoted 1993 *New Yorker* cartoon

WHAT'S WRONG with this picture?

• Renren.com, serving Greater China with electronic communication, invokes a "no e-mail" rule for its own staff for some kinds of discussions.

• A new dotcom, drugstore.com, can start from any location but chooses to settle close to investor and partner Amazon.com in Seattle.

- Hewlett-Packard and German software giant SAP open a joint facility in Germany to develop a new product and later another one in the United States.

- John Taysom takes the Reuters Greenhouse companies skiing after the large InfoWorld conference in Geneva, Switzerland, to encourage the companies to work together.

- Staffs for IBM CEO Louis Gerstner and Cisco CEO John Chambers compare their travel schedules so they can meet when they're in the same city.

- Razorfish, which puts businesses on the Web, builds its own culture by flying the whole company to Las Vegas.

- The most creative act by Williams-Sonoma's e-commerce executive is winning friends and influencing colleagues, not designing websites.

- Innovators at Sun Microsystems and Hewlett-Packard travel extensively to build support for their ventures, reporting that resistance increases with physical distance. Even projects endorsed by top management get more resistance from people whose offices are furthest from a venture's home base.

Actually, nothing is wrong with this picture. These examples, and others throughout this book, show that New Economy success rests on the same face-to-face human relationships as Old Economy success. And the best companies solidify relationships in old-fashioned ways: golf outings, ski trips, meetings and conferences, informal encounters around the coffee machine, or walking into someone's office to nail down his or her commitment.

The Web is a great facilitator, enhancer, and multiplier, but it is not a substitute for personal relationships. Hermits with Internet access will not take over the world. Being virtual is like having a battery that runs down after a while if it isn't recharged by being plugged in to real people. Cisco and IBM, for example, get enormous leverage (and cost savings) from Web-enabling nearly every business process and routine communication, but they still convene large meetings face to face—and then get even more leverage from webcasting those events or setting up team rooms on their intranets to continue the discussion (which sometimes provoke more face-to-face meetings). The Internet enables distance communication among faceless crowds and anonymous audiences who can post messages, get the information or product they want, and disappear without any human intervention or interaction. But—and here's the irony—the companies behind the explosion of the Internet work best through face-to-face relationships at vital moments.

Let machines handle the routine, the mundane, the mindless. The best improvisations, innovations, alliances, collaborations, silo bridging, culture building, and organizational transformations—all the elements of e-culture I have discussed throughout this book—all require strong interpersonal skills and the mental acuity to juggle complex relationships.

Think of that! A technology that apparently makes place and face irrelevant is best built and deployed in a context rich with human relationships. Effectiveness online is backed by strong relationships offline. I opened chapter 1 with this I-paradox—that for all the personalization, customization, and empowerment of the Internet, rampant individualism (isolation and separatism) destroys the potential to develop economic and social benefits from the technology. Social philosopher Anthony Giddens, director of the London School of Economics, distinguishes between me-first egoism and a "new individualism" of self-improvement and self-realization coupled with acceptance of mutual responsibility.[1] The best businesses involve this new individualism, operating more like communities—with fluid boundaries, voluntary action, stakeholders who feel like members, a shared identity and culture, collective strength, and community responsibility. We have seen that pacesetter companies that were the early adopters of e-business models are more collaborative than laggards, more team oriented. Operating as a community permits speed, releases human energy and brainpower, engenders loyalty, and reaches across walls and beyond borders to include volunteers, entice partners, and turn unknown audiences into fans. But if the Internet isolates people, it then undermines the very skills needed for the organizations that form around the Internet.

Competition for talent is the number one issue for companies and other organizations in the New Economy. A scarcity of people with the right skills is the number one barrier to e-business change—and a major barrier for nearly 40 percent of the 785 companies in my global e-culture survey. To have the talent to build communities in cyberspace, we must build supportive communities for learning and development on the ground. Our next step in human evolution is not to become cyborgs attached to our machines. It is to become more fully human, attached to each other, with our machines on our toolbelts for use when we need them. The challenge is social evolution: to develop shared consciousness of the human community.

The case studies throughout this book illuminate the skills and sensibilities people require to succeed in a fast-paced work world, and all of them involve the best of human intelligence—or, following Howard Gardner, multiple human intelligences. Success stories such as Williams-Sonoma, Sun Microsystems, IBM, Abuzz, or Reuters Greenhouse came about because people used their heads—or to put it more technically, their intellectual/analytic skills (cognitive intelligence) plus intuitive/empathic skills (emotional intelligence).

The star performers of this book are characterized by seven qualities of mind, drawing on both analytic and emotional abilities:

- They display curiosity and imagination that allow them to envision and grasp new possibilities as they emerge, to find new patterns in the kaleidoscope.

- They are adept at communication with others, near and far. They work to make themselves understood and to understand people who have not shared their life experiences.

- They are cosmopolitans who are not confined to a single world view but are able to understand and create bridges of thought.

- They can grasp complexity—connecting the dots that make sense out of complicated multipartner alliances. They can tune into the reactions of multiple audiences with conflicting points of view and chart a course that takes the complexity into account.

- They are sensitive to the range of human needs as well as to the messages conveyed by actions that create organizational cultures. They care about feeding their teams' bodies and spirits.

- They work with other people as resources rather than as subordinates, respecting what others bring to the table and listening to their ideas.

- They lead through the power of their ideas and the strength of their voices more than through the authority of formal positions.

This could be a definition of what it means to "evolve."

In addition, the stars of the digital culture of tomorrow have one other characteristic especially helpful for 24/7 settings where the work is never done: stamina. Their high energy depends on being healthy, well-nourished, and psychologically supported by family and friends. Behind every successful person is a supportive environment that fuels and refuels his or her brainpower.

There has been a great deal of attention in the United States and other developed countries to the Digital Divide—the fact that people in poor neighborhoods and less-developed countries lack access to computers and related Internet-relevant technology and, thus, could fall further behind. But it's not the Digital Divide we should be worrying about, it's the Social Divide—the fact that some people live in an environment that does not develop the intellectual and social skills I just outlined, nor ensure physical health and psychological support.

It's not very complicated to figure out how to put computers and network connections everywhere. Between public subsidies and private donations, facilitated by falling prices, I have no doubt that we'll get devices into every nook and cranny. That's easy compared with the challenge of building enriching social environments. In Singapore and Taiwan, two countries with lots of computers and programmers, executives and government officials told me repeatedly that their biggest concern was whether their people will be creative enough for the Internet age. A Singaporean economic minister asked me how America encourages the arts and reinforces community volunteerism; these dimensions of human experience form part of Singapore's strategic plans for technology competitiveness in the twenty-first century. In the United States, at the same time, there are concerns about a loss of "social capital" (local bonds of service and support) that is considered critical to child development. And in an ironic reversal, American technology advocates want to make sure that children in lower-income households and poorer schools have Internet access, while affluent parents worry that Internet access is not good for their children.

Does the Internet itself help or hinder the development of the skills that Internet-enabled organizations need to operate? Concerned citizens and outright critics express three kinds of worries about the impact of the Internet. These worries involve social ties and skills, intellectual development, and community responsibility. Reviewing a few of the prominent arguments and evidence regarding each worry brings us back to the social challenge: The issue is not the computer or electronic communications but the social environment itself. The Internet and its close cousins can have a positive effect when the right social context is in place, but a negative effect when it is not. Getting the best of what the online world can offer requires a well-connected offline community.

Worry 1: Social Graces

Is Internet use good or bad for relationships? Let's begin with the argument of the critics. Some people worry that time spent on the computer is not time spent with other people. Some admit that computer use is less passive than television watching, and the Web is less isolating than individual computer use. The Web includes communication as well as interactivity. Still, critics argue, people could end up more isolated, relationships could become more fleeting and superficial, and both social skills and social support could decline, tearing the social fabric and damaging mental health. Critics are concerned that Internet use further erodes people's face-to-face connections to one another. Even e-commerce gets attacked for making it easier for people to shop in private rather than venturing into public places where they can encounter one another.

There is ample evidence about the positive impact of electronic communication for specific tasks in the workplace when it is used in addition to other communication. For example, survey data from a large U.S. multinational corporation showed that employees who used e-mail extensively were better informed about the company and more committed to management's goals, in part because of information spillover as people forwarded messages.[2] An experiment in another company compared the work of two large task forces over the course of a year, one with and one without electronic communication. Electronic communication increased people's involvement—the computer network users served on more than one subgroup, developed more complex relationships among the working groups, created new groups, and kept meeting after the official year was over.[3] Under those circumstances, relationships were strengthened, and performance was better.

The Internet also seems a good way for busy people to find others who can help them with their work, anywhere in the world—tapping so-called weak ties to get advice they can't get from colleagues close at hand. Nearly 150 employees at Tandem Computers broadcast internal requests for technical information over a six-week period, and eighty-two replies were posted in a public file for study by researchers. The investigators found that the most useful information over the Web came from people with whom there was no relationship, no similarity (even in country base), and no expectation of reciprocity—and it came from peers, not from those higher in the hierarchy. The number of replies did not increase usefulness—it was the ability to find just that one person somewhere else who had just the right piece of the puzzle. The givers of the most useful information did it, they said, for organizational benefit, not for an expectation of rewards— in my terms, because they were part of the community.[4]

But these are adults at work on tasks. Even in the workplace, some consultants find backlash against e-systems that appear to reduce face-to-face relationships, such as employee assistance on the Web rather than through meetings and counseling. Cheryl Shearer, a director at IBM Global Services in London responsible for e-business consulting throughout Europe, saw a backlash against e-systems there: "There are challenges particularly in cultures like, for example, the Italians, who like to work person to person, to go and see someone to discuss a problem. Elements which look to systematize, mechanize, even robotize our lives are culturally not acceptable in Europe."

Worse than resistance, some critics hold, is acceptance of virtual work that then spills over to personal life, undermining social graces. A business psychotherapist in New York, who had worked in corporate employee assistance programs for fifteen years, expressed common concerns about the impact of work styles in which people do not have to face each other directly: People working in the same location must know how to get along with each other or they are not likely to get much done. But if relationships are conducted via e-mail or on the Web, how are people going to learn to negotiate, learn to read subtle signals about others' true views, or learn to work out differences and recover from missteps?[5] The worry is that social skills will decline, with dire consequences for people and organizations.

To test the social and psychological impact of Internet use, ninety-three Pittsburgh families were given computers, phone lines, free Internet access, and a battery of psychological tests. Some of the families started their Internet use in 1995, and others in 1996. A year later, the researchers found, the seventy-three families remaining in the study had experienced a modest reduction in social involvement, family communication, and psychological well-being. People who had large social circles tended to use the Internet less, but holding constant the initial size of social circles, there was a decline over the year in contact with people nearby with whom the subjects had previously socialized at least once a month. Being initially depressed or lonely didn't predict Internet use, but over the year, those who were heavier Internet users reported larger increases in loneliness and depression and marginally more daily life stressors.[6]

A flurry of rebuttals greeted publication of this study. Objections were raised to the study's methodology, findings, and claims. One psychologist pointed out that all the effects were small: People in the study used the Internet infrequently (contrast their three hours a week to the three hours a day the average American watches television) and showed only a small increase in distress. A group of female mental health practitioners cited their own experience with an ongoing e-mail discussion forum that gave them "permission to be authentic" and "expand our very real feelings." Far from becoming lonely or depressed, they said, the Internet helped them feel "freer—we bring our voices onto the screen."[7]

Which is it, isolating or enriching? Answer: It depends. Anything can be taken to pathological extremes; the really Net addicted—who spend over thirty nonworking hours a week online—are likely to lose sleep, ignore family responsibilities, and let job performance slip. But what about average people? A pair of reports of large surveys in 2000 present contradictory evidence. A study by Norman Nie at Stanford University made headlines with its claims that "the more hours people use the Internet, the less time they spend with real human beings." Nie called the Internet "the ultimate isolating technology that further reduces our participation in communities even more than television did before it."[8] But a daily tracking poll of 3,533 Americans, 1,690 of whom were Internet users, in March 2000 found the opposite. The Pew Internet and American Life Project reported that its survey provides clear evidence that e-mail and the Web enhance users' relationships with family and friends. About 60 percent of the Internet users have more contact with family and friends thanks to e-mail. Internet users are more likely than nonusers to have a robust social world with deeper social connectedness to a significant network of helpful relatives and friends—although differences are small, and those in touch with family don't seek advice from them or discuss things that worry them.[9]

The latter result is a clue to resolving the contradictions—the fact that people who stay close to their families and friends may still prefer to discuss their worries with strangers over the Internet. Research at Harvard Medical School showed that parents of special needs children who use electronic support groups have experienced more stress and stigma in real life. They feel that family and friends are less supportive, so they turn to the Web to find people with whom they could exchange experiences and advice.[10] The impersonality and anonymity of the screen makes it possible for people to confess things they wouldn't reveal face to face, for young people to ask questions of adults they would be embarrassed to ask in person, and to find people far outside their usual circles who might have a useful new perspective. This is the "weak ties" point made by the research at Tandem Computers.

Worry 2: Intellectual Development

Some people worry that not only is the computer isolating, but that its use also shapes a world view, a particular way of using one's mind and seeing the world. So it is not only the time online that is a problem, it is what happens in on-screen interactions.

The argument by critics begins with the social isolation assumption—that even when the Internet is used for communication, it is used alone. This perspective holds that on-screen dialogue lacks the richness and unpredictability of face-to-face communication, thus inhibiting the development of children's (and adults') intellectual as well as social skills. One extrapolation from poll data estimated that children aged ten to seventeen in 1999 will experience 31 percent fewer face-to-face interactions than the previous generation and will thus be more reserved, with fewer social skills (though, the authors added, five times as worldly because of exposure to other cultures).[11]

In a widely reprinted article, Todd Oppenheimer said that it is a "computer delusion" to imagine that the computer improves education when its use might hurt real education. It encourages, he wrote, a "fundamental shift in personal priorities—a minimizing of the real, physical world in favor of an unreal virtual world." It teaches that "exploring what's on a two-dimensional screen is more important than playing with real objects, or sitting down to an attentive conversation with a friend, a parent, or a teacher." It downplays the "importance of conversation, of careful listening, and of expressing oneself in person with acuity and individuality. In the process, it may also limit the development of children's imagination." He lumped it with television for giving the illusion of acquiring information without work and without discipline, despite the extra interactivity. And as the final blow, he cited Hewlett-Packard—a computer company that rarely hires people who are predominantly computer experts, favoring people who are flexible, innovative, and have a talent for teamwork. Moreover, he said, HP's contributions to public schools involve math and science lessons involving hands-on work with real materials such as seeds and magnets.[12]

MIT sociologist Sherry Turkle is one of the few experts who has studied the ways children interact with computers and what they learn. The computer, she argued in an influential book, "evokes both physical isolation and intense interaction with other people" through MUDs (multiuser domains). Kids raised with computers and video games know that "to learn to play, you play to learn. You do not first read a rulebook or get your terms straight." One popular game, Myst, included a blank journal for collecting information, instead of an instruction book; a nine-year-old user was able to differentiate between "rules" for the game (there are none) and "information" (the codes and secrets players collect). Although simulation games can teach players to think in an active way about complex phenomena as dynamic, evolving systems, she argued, they also accustom people to manipulating a system whose core assumptions they do not see and that may or may not be "true." A culture of simulation threatens to devalue direct experience, in Turkle's view. "Direct experience is often messy; its meaning is never exactly clear. Interactive multimedia comes already interpreted. It is someone else's version of reality."[13] Simulations could even replace real actors on webcasts, further obscuring the distinction between the virtual and the real. In the spring of 2000, Britain's Press Association introduced Ananova, heralded as the "world's first virtual newscaster"—a real-time computer with a female face in front of it, programmed to exude a range of human emotions. On-screen simulations using emotion databases could eventually confer a weird kind of immortality, as dead actors could spring back to life in new films.

Of course, some of the same arguments can be used against any idealized or sanitized representations of life, whether in literature or in films. So perhaps the objection is that computer simulations are more powerful because of greater audience participation in shaping the outcome. Another MIT scholar, Janet Murray, offered a more optimistic view of the potential for computer-based complex role-playing games to build skills. Role-plays require players to get inside characters, understand the implication of their attributes, and negotiate the rules or the story line with others. (In short, these are exactly the features associated with children's play in general, but now augmented by the ability to communicate at a distance with so many more variables involved.) Murray identifies properties of "cyberdramas"—the narratives that can be created in digital environments—that are particularly intriguing in terms of the skills needed for e-culture:

• *Procedural.* Characters follow a set of rules.

• *Participatory.* A virtual world can respond to every possible combination of commands it has been programmed to accept. Users can construct alternatives, cast characters, perform voices. Objects can react as users explore them.

• *Spatial.* The screen can represent space, not just display it, and users can move through it.

• *Encyclopedic.* The virtual world can hold a wealth of detail—background, spaces to explore and discover.

Consider Murray's sweeping conclusion in terms of my argument in chapter 4: "The computer is providing us with a new stage for the creation of participatory theater. . . . We are all gradually becoming part of a worldwide repertory company, available to assume roles in ever more complex participatory stories. Little by little we are discovering the conventions of participation that will constitute the fourth wall of this virtual theater, the expressive gestures that will deepen and preserve the enchantment of immersion."[14] Indeed, I feel that simulations involving complex role-playing games can enhance the awareness of complex interactions that helps people master the alliance-rich world described in chapter 5, in which competitors must collaborate, and multilateral relationships must be negotiated and managed.

Whether the ability to live another life in cyberspace is an enhancement (opening new horizons) or an escape (preventing coping with reality) could depend on how appealing reality is. Young people are particularly prone to posturing and experimentation, trying on a variety of selves, and the Web provides a handy medium. The most frequent users of anonymous chat rooms, Nie's study at Stanford showed, are teenagers and people barely out of their teens, with use declining after age twenty-five. Those flocking to chat rooms and adopting new personae tend to have problems in real life; other psychologists have found that most people are themselves online.[15] The escapist qualities of the Web for children can be a healthy outlet. In Hong Kong, a Web consultant helped an upstart local telecom company called Sunday develop a creative website to help kids design their personal fantasies online. They could customize their own cyberrooms and cyberself, choosing furniture and different hairstyles and clothing for their Web personae. David Mok, a founder of the Web consultancy, saw this as a positive way to enhance the quality of life for children growing up in small, cramped quarters.[16] Critics may call this the technological form of an "opiate of the masses," but I feel that anything that stretches imagination and raises aspirations can have positive benefits.

Does the Web make fantasy more attractive than reality, or does it provide a place to test and develop responses to a wide range of real situations? The value of cyberspace for learning new skills depends on how supportive the social context is on the ground.

In the normal middle, not the pathological extremes, there is evidence that children can be sensible Internet users, letting the Web takes its place as another tool for managing various aspects of their lives. A Toronto-based research firm studied Canadian teenagers, 85 percent of whom were wired, with boys online more than ten hours per week, and girls more than eight hours. The researchers reported that the teenagers are "normal"— playing sports, valuing friendships, and even going (physically) to the library to do research, despite the fact that homework was the single most common reason they used the Web.[17] The Canadian study, like others, found that the Internet expands kids' social connections. Advertising agency Saatchi & Saatchi's Kid Connections group reported that preteen girls often have up to 100 people on their instant message lists, whereas older teens (who did not grow up with this capability) have about 10. "Lifelong interaction with multimedia technologies has created a generation which communicates in an interdisciplinary language: the marriage of words and images," their report said. The children studied felt empowered by their expertise, because their parents came to them to learn about computers and the Web—like the reverse mentoring I described in chapter 2.

The most heartening Kid Connections finding is that the preteenagers placed a tremendous emphasis on learning. "Being smart has become cool."[18] And evidence is mounting for the benefits of a range of Web-related technologies for helping kids get smart. As I indicated in chapter 1, computers in classrooms are the least important manifestation of technology in education—and often the counterproductive one attacked by Todd Oppenheimer and other critics. The value of technology in education comes from the positive impact on teachers and parents—the on-the-ground real relationships that help children develop and education take hold.

In 1997, consultants at strategy firm McKinsey conducted an exhaustive review of hundreds of studies of the use of computers and electronic communication in K–12 education and visited dozens of classrooms. They cited increases in student reading and writing skills through e-mail use. Distance learning courses led to higher achievement because of the availability of highly skilled teachers. Connecting teachers to administrators and parents also showed up in enhanced student performance.[19] In 1998 and 1999, even more positive evidence was presented about the positive impact on children's achievement when computer networks were part of systemic reforms in teaching and school operations. Evaluations by the well-regarded Center for Children and Technology (CCT) in New York of the highest-profile and most comprehensive use of intranets and the Web—Project Explore at the Christopher Columbus Middle School in Union City, New Jersey (which I described in chapters 1 and 8) and the U.S. sites for IBM's global Reinventing Education initiative—concluded that network-enabled schools can raise academic performance. (I saw this first-hand in my visits and interviews at Reinventing Education sites.) But with respect to Union City, Margaret Honey and other CCT researchers are careful to distinguish the impact of the technology itself, which was modest, from the impact of school reform, which was significant. In Union City, students' test scores started to rise before they had computers for Internet use because of longer class periods, new books, after-school programs, and team projects. IBM itself is interested in how the networks are used to empower teachers and parents, not in replacing face-to-face instruction with computers.[20]

The big experiments are yet to come, as e-learning becomes the "next big E," and new dotcoms spring up in partnership with education. Scholastic Inc. and Harcourt General are partnering with tutor.com and thinkbox.com on online tutoring networks for children. IBM's Learning Village software offers a suite of online services to school systems. The New York City Board of Education's Teaching and Learning in Cyberspace Task Force was dreaming big dreams in 2000: to give all students and teachers an Internet-ready laptop computer—perhaps even funded by a public-private partnership with an ISP to create a revenue-generating K-12 Internet portal. Although the fate of the New York City proposal is unclear, plans to offer universal Internet access to school children (for example, through their own e-mail address and a dedicated network) are underway in many American states as well as countries as diverse as the United Kingdom and Costa Rica.

Such actions could take care of one aspect of the Digital Divide: access. But simple access alone will not address the larger question of educational quality: excellence, not just equity. Nor will it address the Social Divide. The evidence to date shows that those who already have rich social connections and supportive interpersonal relationships in a healthy environment will find electronic networks a huge enhancer. But those who don't—children without adult mentors, students in crowded classrooms with no change in teacher effectiveness, young people isolated in neighborhoods with few safe places to gather, families without access to health care or clean water—could continue to fall behind, with or without computers. It's the quality of the community, not the availability of the technology, that matters most.

Worry 3: Social Responsibility

A third worry is about that very issue: the quality of the community. If the Internet has any isolating effects, could that combine with loss of connection to particular places to erode mutual help, civic participation, and social responsibility? What happens if virtual communities take over from real ones? In chapter 1, I described a plea for help by a desperate single mother on eBay's Giving Board. There is always the risk that charitable eBay users could decide to help her instead of an equally desperate single mother down the block—whom they've never met because they spend their time on the screen, not on the street. Even eBay's CEO Meg Whitman wonders how far the boundaries of caring and concern can be stretched, questioning what would happen to community values as eBay grows rapidly from cybertown to big Net-city.

A clearly positive potential of the Internet lies in increased global consciousness. The mental boundaries of community can be stretched to encompass more people in more places. That builds the cosmopolitan sensibilities and awareness of multiple audiences needed for the innovators and collabronauts discussed in chapters 4 and 5—or, for that matter, for the e-organizers described in chapter 1. Through the Web, significant contributions can be made to improving life anywhere, such as IBM's assistance in reuniting refugee families in Kosovo, described at the end of chapter 6. Dot-orgs are springing up to match philanthropic donors and non-profit causes without geographic restrictions. But the critics weigh in here, too, with worries that local causes will suffer and that people will be generous and supportive only at a distance.[21]

It's not just the virtual world that could threaten the real one. The workplace supporting cyberspace also threatens to overwhelm other aspects of community. Consider the 24/7 world of dotcoms. When people wander in and out of the office all night, the kitchen is right there with meals available around the clock, and sleeping facilities are available (as in Cambridge Incubator's "start-up hotel"), is there any time for community life outside the workplace? Abuzz, whose workplace activities are described in chapters 2 and 7, proves that dotcoms can value personal life (letting people bring their avocations into the workplace) and engage in on-the-ground community service (adopting a local school). But even Abuzz has to be very self-conscious about this. Its leaders work hard to achieve balance.

Consider another kind of example. Nortel Networks, a leading dotcom-enabler, made a "city" out of its new headquarters in the Toronto suburb of Brampton, co-locating 3,000 people who had previously been scattered. There are indoor parks, a Zen garden, a full-service bank branch, fitness centers, basketball and volleyball courts, a physiotherapy area, a dry cleaning service, a spirituality room, a café, and public areas for television viewing. Insiders report greater job satisfaction and more productive relationships with colleagues.[22]

Yes, and does anyone need to go home? In chapter 6 I argued that organizations need to become more like communities. But they should not do that at the expense of the rest of community life. We need to nurture the places where families bond, children go to school, amateur sports teams practice, artists create, religious rituals and personal milestones are celebrated, and people meet outside of their work roles and help each other.

LET ME SUMMARIZE THE WORRIES and try to resolve them. The worries all involve either/or trade-offs, which is the wrong way to think about things in a multichannel world. The Internet is said to strengthen weak ties (mere acquaintances and even strangers who are far away) but at a price: the potential to weaken strong ties (family, friends, and coworkers in the next office). It is said to increase social identification (bigger numbers of people from more places are in the contact circle) but also at a price: a potential decline in face-to-face social interaction. These are set up as competitions, like a sports scoreboard: *weak ties 1, strong ties 0; social identification 1, social interaction 0.*

Why must this be either/or? An IBM virtual team provided assistance in Kosovo (distant), but some of those same team members are active in local schools in IBM Reinventing Education projects (close). To me, the worries stem from false assumptions—that the Internet simply takes us over and we have nothing to say about it, or that it is so powerful that it overwhelms everything else. These assumptions have interesting echoes of the dotcom frenzy that dominated the capital markets in 1998 and 1999, when some fervent e-believers said that e-commerce would replace bricks-and-mortar stores—not just augment them or enhance them, but eliminate them.

A more likely outcome, one that we are starting to see in every field, is that the real and virtual will live side by side. The Internet means that even local businesses and local organizations, rooted in one place, must be aware of the rest of the world and must create connections to all those places. Acting as a good global citizen, everywhere a company operates, is an excellent way to create a culture that employees care about. Yet, without the services and supports and strategic discussions that take place locally, even global giants of cyberspace cannot operate. This is not an idealistic statement, but a pragmatic one. Amazon.com cannot function without warehouses and package handlers and delivery trucks.

The Grande Finale or the Grand Beginning?: Evolve!

If Internet technology erodes the skills and sensibilities that technology companies (and other organizations) need to run, that would be a tragedy for them. But it would be an even bigger disaster for humanity.

Part One of this book opened with the observation that we are in the midst of a technological revolution and searching for guidance. Many people in many companies want "the" answer—the simple thing to do. But the Internet doesn't give you one answer, it gives you many. It is open ended, and it will grow through imagination and creativity. We have to be open to the discovery of new possibilities, in the spirit of IKIWISI (I'll Know It When I See It), but we can still set clear guidelines for the direction in which we want to head.

In every best-practice case in this book, from businesses to public schools, the real and the virtual interact. They reinforce each other. They push each other for change. Already, dotcoms and wannadots are starting to meet in the middle. E-business will simply become business, e-commerce will become just another one of many ways to buy and sell, e-learning will enhance but not replace classrooms, and e-culture will be simply the culture of tomorrow. Electronic communication will connect people on the other side of the world, or it will facilitate the work of people a few steps away. (My research associate Michelle Heskett's desk is only fifteen feet from mine, yet nearly every day one of us yells across the hall that we have just e-mailed a message to the other.)

I am both conscious of the dangers and optimistic about our ability to avoid them. The Internet is powerful but neutral. It reinforces relationship building, intellectual development, productivity, and collective responsibility where there is already an appealing social environment and face-to-face relationships. It can diminish those positives where the social context is impoverished. The Internet can feed into the worst human tendencies or the best. It can be an excuse for turning our backs on each other as we fly off into cyberspace, or it can be a tool for helping us create online and offline communities, at work and at home. After all, we can only become grounded on the ground.

Am I predicting the future, or indulging in wishful thinking? Perhaps the latter. But we don't know enough yet to let science be our guide— there is still too little experience, too few reliable studies. It's up to us to take a stand, and I hope we decide in favor of community. We need shared consciousness to solve social problems. To feel responsible to wider communities, even to posterity. To appreciate our interdependence.

We're on the verge. Will we evolve? That's a question about us—about people, about our humanity and values—and not about technology. So, which will it be: the lonely crowd or the connected community?

It is our choice.

◆

Appendix A
Cast of Characters
Company Descriptions

Nearly eighty companies were included in the interview portion of my e-culture research project, along with a dozen assorted other kinds of organizations, such as public school systems, law firms, and nonprofit organizations. This appendix lists only those companies in which multiple interviews were conducted or that play a significant role in this book. Interviews were conducted between November 1999 and July 2000 for almost all companies. Harvard Business School cases are available for a portion of the companies, as shown at the end of each listing.

Abuzz Technologies, founded in 1996 and headquartered in Boston, Massachusetts, is an online knowledge-sharing community website with twenty employees. Acquired by The New York Times Company in July 1999, Abuzz launched www.abuzz.com with New York Times Digital to bring its business to the Web in January 2000. See Rosabeth Moss Kanter with Katherine Chen, "Abuzz," Case 301-024 (Boston: Harvard Business School, 2000).

Acer, incorporated in 1981 and headquartered in Taiwan, manufactures high-end computer and multimedia products and operates a range of e-commerce websites.

AlliedSignal, see *Honeywell International.*

Amazon.com, founded in 1995, is an online retailer based in Seattle, Washington, with 7,600 employees. It is best known for its flagship Internet bookstore, but now offers a range of other items and services, including tools, gifts, and auctions.

Arcadia, a leading fashion retailer in the United Kingdom, is home to fifteen diverse fashion brands with thousands of outlets in the United Kingdom and hundreds more worldwide and has a growing Internet presence. In 1999, the London-based company, which was known as the Burton Group from 1969 to 1997, hit $2.4 billion in revenues. (A Harvard Business School case was in progress as this book went to press.)

Arrow Electronics, headquartered in Melville, New York, is the world's largest distributor of electronic components and computer products, with sales of $9.3 billion in 1999.

Audible, Inc., founded in 1995 in Wayne, New Jersey, enables its customers to listen to spoken audio programming, such as radio shows and audio books. It has a strategic partnership with Amazon.com.

barnesandnoble.com, founded in 1997, is the second-largest online book distributor, and consistently one of the most popular websites on the Internet. Headquartered in New York, barnesandnoble.com had over 1,200 employees by mid-2000.

Blackboard.com, founded in 1997, offers an enterprise software product for course management for educational institutions, and a public website on which instructors can create their own course websites. See Todd Pittinsky and Rosabeth Moss Kanter, "Blackboard: Growing Up @ Internet Speed," Case 301-014 (Boston: Harvard Business School, 2000).

brandnewmusic.com, founded in 1999, is a dotcom in London, England, promoting new and unsigned musical talent over the Internet in several countries.

Cisco Systems, headquartered in San Jose, California, with over 21,000 employees and 1999 sales of nearly $13 billion, offers end-to-end networking products and services, including routers and other communication devices.

CNBC.com, located in Fort Lee, New Jersey, is a subsidiary of NBC (whose parent company is General Electric). It was founded in 1997 out of CNBC, a leading cable broadcaster of business and financial news; it was relaunched on the Web in 1999. See Rosabeth Moss Kanter, "CNBC.com (A): NBC Incubates E-Business," Case 300-090 (Boston: Harvard Business School, 2000).

Deloitte & Touche, headquartered in Wilton, Connecticut, has over 80,000 employees and is primarily involved in accounting, auditing, tax, and management consulting services. See Rosabeth Moss Kanter and Jane Roessner, "Deloitte & Touche (B): Changing the Workplace," Case 300-013 (Boston: Harvard Business School, 1999).

Digitas, located in Boston, Massachusetts, with over 1,200 employees, is an Internet professional services firm. See Rosabeth Moss Kanter, David Lane, and Courtenay Sprague, "Digitas: Managing Growth," Case 300-130 (Boston: Harvard Business School, 2000) and "Digitas: Working with Bausch & Lomb," Case 301-014 (Boston: Harvard Business School, 2000).

EarthWeb, founded in 1994 and headquartered in New York City, provides information technology knowledge and career solutions. EarthWeb has over 350 employees and year 2000 revenues of about $60 million.

eBay, founded in 1995 and headquartered in San Jose, California, is the world's largest online auction website and trading community. Material on eBay in this book stems from original research performed as a part of the e-culture project, augmented by two cases by other Harvard faculty members: Jeffrey Bradach and Nicole Tempest, "Meg Whitman at eBay Inc. (A)," Case 400-035 (Boston: Harvard Business School, 2000); and Stephen Bradley and Kelley Porter, "eBay, Inc.," Case 700-007 (Boston: Harvard Business School, 1999).

"Empire International Bank" is a pseudonym for a large global bank headquartered in the United Kingdom and operating in over fifty countries, with an important base in Asia.

"FashionCo" is a pseudonym for a chain of luxury apparel stores in the United States.

"Handy Gadgets," see *Honeywell International.*

Hewlett-Packard, a leading provider of computing and imaging solutions and services, is located in Palo Alto, California, with over 80,000 employees. See Rosabeth Moss Kanter and Alida Zweidler-McKay, "Hewlett-Packard Global Alliance Program (A): Alliance Strategy," Case 300-014 (Boston: Harvard Business School, 2000); "Hewlett-Packard Global Alliance Program (B): Managing Alliances," Case 300-015 (Boston: Harvard Business School, 2000); and "Hewlett-Packard Global Alliance Program (C): Implementing Change," Case 300-016 (Boston: Harvard Business School, 2000).

Honeywell International, headquartered in Morristown, New Jersey, has over 120,000 employees and 1999 annual sales of $23 billion; in October 2000, General Electric announced its intention to acquire it. HI produces aerospace products and services; control technologies for buildings, homes, and industry; automotive products; power generation systems; specialty chemicals; fibers; plastics; and electronic materials. It was formed when AlliedSignal bought Minneapolis-based Honeywell in December 1999. "Handy Gadgets" is a pseudonym, used by request, for Honeywell International business. See Rosabeth Moss Kanter, "E-Business at Honeywell International (A): AlliedSignal," Case 300-088 (Boston: Harvard Business School, 2000); and Rosabeth Moss Kanter and Daniel Galvin, "E-Business at Honeywell International (B): E-Hubs," Case 300-125 (Boston: Harvard Business School, 2000).

hongkong.com, launched in 1998, is a source for news, travel, life, technology, and business information pertaining to Hong Kong, and also provides e-mail and shopping. It has over 200 employees.

IBM, located in Armonk, New York, is the world's largest information technology company, with over 300,000 employees and 1999 annual sales of over $87 billion. IBM provides information technology solutions, manufactures computer hardware and peripherals, and develops software; it popularized the term *e-business*. IBM's Reinventing Education sites include Broward County, FL; Charlotte-Mecklenburg, NC; Chicago, IL; Cincinnati, OH; Philadelphia, PA; San Francisco, CA; San Jose, CA; the state of Vermont; and the state of West Virginia. IBM's Reinventing Education 2 sites include Atlanta Public Schools, GA; Boston Public Schools, MA; Detroit Public Schools, MI; Durham Public Schools, NC; Houston Independent School District, TX; Maryland State Department of Education; Memphis City Schools, TN; New York City Public Schools, NY; New York State Education Department; Rochester Public Schools, MN; South Carolina State Department of Education; and Texas State Education Agency. International sites include the state of Rio, Brazil; Ireland; Italy; Singapore; South Africa; United Kingdom; and Vietnam. See Rosabeth Moss Kanter, "IBM's Reinventing Education," Case 9-399-008 (Boston: Harvard Business School, 1999), and Rosabeth Moss Kanter and John Scannell, "IBM Ireland: Reinventing Education Crosses the Atlantic," Case 300-034 (Boston: Harvard Business School, 1999).

iSteel Asia, founded in 1999 and headquartered in Hong Kong, is the first publicly listed vertical industry-specific Asian portal offering a neutral marketplace for the steel trade. See Pamela Yatsko and Rosabeth Moss Kanter, "iSteel Asia," Case 301-025 (Boston: Harvard Business School, 2000).

iXL, Inc., an Internet consulting company founded in 1996 and headquartered in Atlanta, Georgia, had over 2,000 employees in twenty-one cities around the world at the start of 2000. See Rosabeth Moss Kanter and Michelle Heskett, "iXL, Inc. (A): Growth and Change," Case 300-058 (Boston: Harvard Business School, 2000); "iXL, Inc. (B): Tessera Enterprise Systems," Case 300-115 (Boston: Harvard Business School, 2000); and "iXL, Inc. (C): Acquiring and Integrating Tessera," Case 300-116 (Boston: Harvard Business School, 2000).

Kerry Logistics is a Hong Kong–based company operating warehouses and fulfillment and distribution centers for e-commerce companies. It is owned by the Kerry Group, an Asian property company and diversified conglomerate.

Lucent Technologies, the New Jersey–based telecommunications equipment and software giant that was spun out of AT&T in 1996, had $38 billion in revenue and 153,000 employees in 1999. Its New Ventures Group was established to help capture value from research in Bell Laboratories. See Rosabeth Moss Kanter and Michelle Heskett, "Lucent Technologies New Ventures Group," Case 300-085 (Boston: Harvard Business School, 2000).

Lycos, headquartered in Waltham, Massachusetts, with 785 employees in 2000, is a leading Internet portal that provides navigation, browsing, searching, and advertising services.

Mainspring, Inc., founded in 1996 and headquartered in Cambridge, Massachusetts, is a growing e-strategy consulting firm.

Mary Kay, Inc., is a leading direct seller of beauty products in the United States. The Dallas-based company was founded in 1963 and has grown to include 620,000 independent beauty consultants selling $1 billion in products worldwide.

Motorola, headquartered in Schaumburg, Illinois, with over 150,000 employees, provides integrated communications solutions and electronic components.

NBC (National Broadcasting Corporation), see *CNBC.com.*

Online Retail Partners, founded in 1999 and headquartered in New York City, develops and runs e-commerce sites for brand-name manufacturers.

PlanetFeedback, headquartered in Cincinnati, Ohio, specializes in using the Internet to channel consumer feedback to businesses. Launched in February 2000, the company received $25 million in second-round funding in May 2000.

Razorfish, founded in 1995 and headquartered in New York City, with over 1,300 employees worldwide, provides digital change management services. Razorfish conceives, plans, and executes strategic technology solutions to integrate its clients' business functions for the Web.

renren.com, founded in 1998 in Hong Kong, is an Internet portal for the global Chinese community. It went live in 1999 and by May 2000 had grown to over 300 employees.

Reuters, headquartered in London, England, supplies financial information and news, as well as other services such as transaction and information management systems, and owns Instinet and a sizable portion of TIBCO Software. Reuters Greenhouse Fund, the venture capital division of the company, invests in companies that affect Reuters's business in the areas of e-commerce and e-markets, technology infrastructure, and digital content. Portfolio companies include Adero, Equinix, Harmony Software, and Persistence. See Rosabeth Moss Kanter and Daniel Galvin, "Reuters Greenhouse Fund," Case 301-012 (Boston: Harvard Business School, 2000).

Sun Microsystems, headquartered in Palo Alto, California, with over 27,000 employees, is a global provider of products, services, and support solutions for building and maintaining network computing environments. See Rosabeth Moss Kanter and Jane Roessner, "Sun Microsystems, Inc. (A): An Enterprise of Change," Case 300-074 (Boston: Harvard Business School, 1999); "Sun Microsystems, Inc. (A1): 'Dot-comming' the World: Philip Nenon on a Billion Dollar Bet," Case 300-075 (Boston: Harvard Business School, 1999); "Sun Microsystems, Inc. (A2): Network Visions, Mike Clary on the Product that Hid in HR," Case 300-076 (Boston: Harvard Business School, 1999); "Sun Microsystems, Inc. (A3): Network Computer: Robert Gianni on Answering the Skeptics," Case 300-076 (Boston: Harvard Business School, 1999); "Sun Microsystems, Inc. (A4): Sun Peak: Helen Yang and Mark Walden on 'Running Sun on Sun,'" Case 300-078 (Boston: Harvard Business School, 1999); "Sun Microsystems, Inc. (A5): Solaris 7: Rich Green on Product Strategy and Culture Change," Case 300-079 (Boston: Harvard Business School, 1999); "Sun Microsystems, Inc. (A6): Enterprise 250: Mark Canepa on the Newcomer as Change Agent," Case 300-080 (Boston: Harvard Business School, 1999); and "Sun Microsystems, Inc. (B): Nurturing Entrepreneurs and Change Agents," Case 300-081 (Boston: Harvard Business School, 1999).

Tesco, based in Cheshunt, England, is a leading food retailer in the United Kingdom with almost $30 billion in revenues for fiscal year 2000. Wholly owned subsidiary Tesco.com was launched in mid-2000 with 250,000 regular Internet customers purchasing not only groceries but also books, CDs, and a variety of nongrocery items.

theglobe.com, founded in 1995 and taken public in 1998, is a global online community that helps its members find and communicate with other people with similar interests.

Vauxhall, founded in 1903 and headquartered in Luton, United Kingdom, is a subsidiary of General Motors. Vauxhall employs 10,000 people and produced over 315,000 vehicles in 1999. Also in 1999, Vauxhall introduced "dotcom cars" for purchase on the Internet.

Williams-Sonoma, headquartered in San Francisco, California, with over 4,800 employees, is a specialty retailer of products for the home. Williams-Sonoma, Inc., owns Williams-Sonoma, Pottery Barn, Pottery Barn Kids, Hold Everything, and Chambers. See Rosabeth Moss Kanter and Daniel Galvin, "E-Commerce at Williams-Sonoma," Case 300-086 (Boston: Harvard Business School, 2000).

APPENDIX B
SELECTED SURVEY FINDINGS
The Global E-Culture Survey

My GLOBAL E-CULTURE SURVEY was an enjoyable online and offline endeavor in its own right. It had all the challenges and pleasures of connecting my research team at Harvard Business School with important collaborators on several continents. It also featured some fingernail biting as we waited for responses to come in, the excitement of discovery as we viewed the statistical data and open-ended responses, and the fun of meeting new people and companies.

The survey debuted at the January 2000 meeting of the World Economic Forum in Davos, Switzerland, where it was publicized in *Worldlink*, the Forum's magazine, and distributed to participants, who could return hard copy or respond through an online poll on the Harvard Business School website (http://www.hbs.edu/e-culture). The February 2000 issue of *Inc.* magazine, the other major survey collaborator, publicized it through editor-in-chief George Gendron's regular column, a column I wrote on managing change, and online versions of both articles on the *Inc.* website (http://www.inc.com), all directing readers to the online poll on the HBS website. Electronic responses began to flow in immediately.

Hard-copy questionnaires were subsequently mailed by *Worldlink*, based in London, to its global list of top-level executives belonging to the World Economic Forum, and by *Inc.* to present and past *Inc.* 500 companies, members of the Young Entrepreneurs Organization, and related groups. These brought airmail and fax responses to my Harvard Business School office from all over the world. Links on EarthWeb's Datamation site and an e-culture club at theglobe.com (run by my research team member Daniel Galvin) generated additional electronic responses. Another cluster of survey responses was facilitated by Mainspring, a growing e-strategy consulting firm, who gave research team member Sukyana Lahiri access to members of its e-council (generally e-commerce vice presidents or directors), initially through an e-mail poll with a subset of the survey questions. Lahiri's follow-up with thirty-nine financial services and retail companies based on survey questions (and probing of their meaning through telephone interviews with fifteen of them) resulted in her honors thesis at Harvard College and became part of the data set used in this project.

By our cutoff date of May 15, 2000, we had received 785 completed questionnaires, nearly 300 of them online through the Harvard Business School website. The survey was designed to identify general trends and tendencies, as discussed later in this appendix, but it also helped us find people willing to discuss their specific experiences through in-depth interviews. In addition to the ambitious interview roster we prepared ahead of time, the survey generated several dozen interviews around the world with individuals and companies we would not have otherwise known to contact; research team member Michelle Heskett took leadership of the survey and identification of follow-up interviews. Our scope and perspective were widened by the enthusiastic response of survey respondents who wanted to tell their stories—positive and negative. Further, those interviews allowed us to explore the actual events behind the check marks on forced-choice survey items.

The findings discussed here cover only the written survey, but by the time my e-culture project team was ready for vacation in August 2000, we had conducted over 300 in-depth interviews with informants representing nearly eighty companies, primarily in the United States, United Kingdom, and Hong Kong.

WHAT WE ASKED: THE QUESTIONNAIRE

The survey consisted of 116 items grouped in six sections:

- *Background:* Identification of the unit for which respondents would answer survey questions (e.g., independent organization or subsidiary of a larger organization); country of head office; corporate form (e.g., publicly traded, closely held, professional partnership, government entity, nonprofit, joint venture); primary industry; country scope; respondent's own position.

- *Opinions about the Internet:* Agreement/disagreement with five broad statements about the Internet (detailed in "Views of the Internet and Its Future," later in this appendix). Results from this section allowed us to draw general conclusions about how different cross sections of respondents perceive the magnitude of change the Internet will cause.

- *Website experience:* How involved respondents' units are with the Internet, how closely their own responsibilities intersect with the Internet, and how they perceive their unit's progress in using the Internet. In this section of the survey, we gathered valuable data about how companies are currently using the Internet and how they plan to use it two to three years in the future. These data could then be correlated with other characteristics to identify, for example, what uses self-proclaimed leaders are putting the Internet to, or which industries use the Internet for which purposes.

- *What helps or hinders:* How various stakeholders may have helped or hindered them from taking advantage of the Internet or profiting from e-commerce; barriers they have faced (from a list of seventeen possibilities); and whether eight core characteristics and business metrics have increased, decreased, or stayed the same over the past few years, identifying any of those items in which the Internet played a significant role.

- *Organizational style:* Sixteen items, drawn from my previous research on aspects of culture and structure, representing two alternate responses to an organizational scenario. For example, the statement "The steps and actions needed to do most jobs tend to be:" was followed by two responses at either end of a 1–5 scale: "Spelled out in great detail; procedures count" or "Left to the person's judgment; results count." Respondents chose where on the scale their organizational culture fit. Alternative statements were framed in a neutral manner and randomly assigned to one side or the other on the scale to reduce bias.

- *Organization and respondent demographics:* The size and age of the respondent's whole organization (instead of just unit), as well as personal work experience and age.

Throughout the survey, respondents were given the opportunity to add their own responses and comments to augment the numbers they circled or responses they checked. To conclude the survey, they were asked for open-ended comments, including general views on the Internet, and for contact information if they were willing to be interviewed about their responses. (Survey respondents were promised complete anonymity but could provide their e-mail addresses or contact information separately to receive early reports of survey findings.) Approximately 520 of the 785 respondents provided addresses. Nearly half of the survey respondents indicated a willingness to spend additional time in follow-up conversation—and those volunteers ranged from top-level executives in Global Fortune 500 companies to young new recruits in Internet startups. We were able to follow up with only a fraction of those willing to go on the record, but all respondents who provided contact information received a "first findings" report in June 2000.

Survey Respondents

Respondents were almost entirely top management (CEOs or other high-ranking executives or board members), so we are confident that they can speak authoritatively about their organizations. They represented 247 publicly traded corporations; 479 closely held corporations (including pre-public Internet companies), professional partnerships, and joint ventures—a cluster reflecting limited exposure to capital markets; and fifty-one government or nonprofit organizations. Almost half of the respondents were from pre–Information Age companies (founded twenty or more years ago); slightly more than half can be called Information Age companies (founded less than twenty years ago).

In line with our sampling strategy, there were 519 responses from organizations headquartered in North America, where the e-business wave began. From Europe, which is quickly following North America into e-business, there were 160 responses. We received 22 responses from Asia, 16 from Latin America, and 68 from the "other" category, which includes missing information (we suspect some of those are from the United States and did not feel that they needed to include location because they were sending the survey to a U.S. address). There were 308 responses from purely domestic companies (defined as producing in one country for use in that country); 185 from exporters (producing in one country for international use); 19 from off-shore producers (producing internationally for use in one country); and 252 from fully international companies in both production and markets. Over 100 respondents identified themselves as part of pure Internet units—including the dotcom unit within established offline companies—and 657 said they were not pure Internet companies.

Respondents do not constitute a random or representative sample, since survey participation was voluntary and responses were anonymous. We oversampled people who are interested in the Internet. This is simply an opportunistic, suggestive sample that can be used to generate hypotheses and glean insights, and that is how I have used it.

Selected Findings

Views of the Internet and Its Future

We asked respondents for their opinions with respect to five common statements about the Internet and e-business.

1. Revolution? "The Internet will completely transform every aspect of business in the foreseeable future."

Overall, 75 percent strongly agree or agree with this statement; only 9 percent disagree. The rest are in the middle, expressing neither agreement nor disagreement, but there are fewer fence-sitters on this issue than on any other.

Our small set of government and nonprofit organization representatives are much more likely to strongly agree, perhaps a sign that government officials and leaders of nongovernmental organizations see the importance of the Internet to their country's future and, one hopes, that they will support infrastructure investments. They are followed in their enthusiasm for revolution by publicly traded corporations, which tend, on the average, to be larger than the "closely held" cluster, and which, by definition, must respond to the pressures of global markets. The "closely held" cluster (closely held corporations, professional partnerships, and joint ventures) are the least likely to agree, perhaps because they have few investors and all of them operate privately, thus relieving the pressure that publicly traded companies feel to jump on technology bandwagons.

Domestic or international scope makes no difference in responses, nor does headquarters region. People from every country are equally certain of revolution— if they are interested in this topic enough to respond to my survey. Not surprisingly, pure Internet units are much more likely to strongly agree, and much less likely to strongly disagree. When we grouped Internet-dedicated and primarily Internet units, a full 88 percent agree; this difference between online and offline organizations is statistically significant. However, respondents' own age makes no difference; the revolutionaries are found among the oldest as well as the youngest respondents.

2. Competitive necessity at any cost? "It is important for every company in my industry to have a web presence and be actively engaged in e-commerce even if they do not make any money doing it."

Overall, 63 percent strongly agree or agree; 18 percent disagree. We know that we oversampled advocates and zealots, but it is striking that so many leaders endorse expenditures without requiring a return. Less than 20 percent are fence-sitters.

Agreement is even stronger among the publicly traded corporations, at statistically significant levels. Similarly, the more international the company, the more likely is strong agreement (also statistically significant). This can reflect the cosmopolitanism of international companies but also their larger size and greater likelihood of exposure to global supply chains and global capital markets. Clearly, larger public companies feel pressure to invest in the Internet regardless of ability to show immediate earnings, but our interviews indicate that this issue of long-term investment versus short-term earnings creates constant tension within the company. (One respondent e-mailed us after the "first findings" report that he is not surprised at this, because the Web is now just another factor of business and thus a cost to be borne, like advertising expenditures.)

It is interesting that respondents from companies headquartered in Europe are much more likely to agree and agree strongly (a statistically significant difference). (Latin American responses are similar to Europeans' in this respect.) Although pure Internet units are more likely to agree, the difference is not strong or statistically significant—of course, those units may also be under pressure to bring in revenue and head toward making a profit. However, they should be heartened by the fact that units and executives engaged in tasks other than Internet-related activities see the necessity for investment.

3. Just another tool? "The Internet is not really that different from any other business tool; it should not change enduring wisdom about how companies should operate and how leaders should behave."

Overall, 30 percent strongly agree or agree; 56 percent disagree. This question starts to get at who sees the necessity for deep, systemic change, in contrast to narrow, ad hoc approaches to using the Web.

The closely held corporations, professional partnerships, and joint ventures are most likely to agree with the "no change" point of view. Publicly held corporations are most likely to disagree with the "no change" statement, at statistically significant levels. Larger, publicly traded companies exposed to global competition and capital markets are the most likely to understand that the Internet calls for significant departures from their traditional methods of operation. This is confirmed by a glance at other cuts through the data.

Companies domestic in scope are much more likely to see this as just another tool that doesn't require much change on the part of the company; companies international in scope are more likely to strongly disagree, thus indicating that major change is necessary (a statistically significant difference). Asians are much more likely to agree with the "no change" point of view, which some interviewees explain in terms of low labor costs, which makes it less necessary to replace human-mediated processes with e-business processes. Europeans (with high labor costs) are more likely to disagree and see the need for major changes in thinking (a statistically significant finding). The Internet craze has already hit Europe, but it is only starting to penetrate Asia, despite centers of technology excellence in India, Singapore, Taiwan, and the Philippines.

There is a slight tendency for respondents whose units are not dedicated solely to the Internet to be more likely to agree that the Internet is just another tool, but the difference is not statistically significant. Based on our in-depth interviews, we hypothesize that responses to this question reflect degree of experience with the Internet. Those who think it doesn't really change much organizational behavior are unlikely to have done much with it yet. Those who are trying to do more with e-commerce and e-business find that they must rethink many organizational assumptions.

4. Bricks versus clicks? "Established 'bricks and mortar' companies with strong brands still have the advantage and will ultimately win in competition against pure Internet companies."

Overall, 38 percent strongly agree or agree, 32 percent disagree, and almost the same percentage are smack in the middle. Clearly, this is an area of mixed views and a great deal of uncertainty. This is where the battles of the future will be fought.

Closely held corporations, partnerships, and joint ventures are slightly more likely to agree and slightly less likely to disagree (a statistically significant difference). These are also the organizations, as we see from the other opinion questions, that are least likely to see a revolution in the making or a necessity for much change—so naturally they would think that whoever is winning today will continue to win tomorrow. There is also a slight tendency for the importers—companies with international production for domestic use—to agree (statistically significant). There are no real differences among regions in responses to this issue. And there are no discernable differences between pure Internet units and others; the former are just as uncertain as the rest of the respondents and just as likely to spread their bets among bricks-and-mortar companies, Internet pure plays, and hybrids somewhere in the middle.

5. *Must a generation die off?* "The Internet and e-commerce will not really take hold until the old generation of corporate leaders gives way to a new generation of young entrepreneurs."

Only 18 percent strongly agree or agree; 65 percent disagree. This could reflect confidence that established companies and mature leaders can change, or it could reflect a view that the advent of e-business is so far along regardless that it does not require that much future change. We heard both points of view reflected in interviews.

There are no real differences among types of companies, their international scope, or their headquarters region. Age of respondents also makes no difference. There is a tendency for respondents from pure Internet units to be more likely to agree that the old generation needs to go—a quarter of them agree with generational replacement.

Uses of the Internet

The 657 respondents who are *not* in pure Internet businesses answered questions about the characteristics of their most important website. Overall, 92 percent say their most important website is run as part of the preexisting organization rather than set up as an independent unit; 61 percent report that it is designed to be used by both individual consumers and other businesses/organizations; only 16 percent have consumers-only sites. This finding, coupled with the data described in this section on uses of the Internet, indicates that many of the respondents are in the early stages of tapping the full potential of e-business and so do not yet see the necessity for establishing a separate venture or unit to handle it. As shown below, many of those that are lagging behind use their website only for publishing general information.

Because this activity is so new, and hard data on effectiveness are hard to come by, we used a crude proxy for effectiveness in order to get a rough picture, namely, self-reports of whether the unit's uses of the Internet are better or worse than what competitors are doing. Because the sample is split almost equally between self-reported "better" and "worse," we feel that this rough cut can be illuminating.

Just under 100 respondents (94 of them) claim that their unit's activities are much better than that of their competition, 256 say they are somewhat better, 286 say they are somewhat worse, and 21 say they are much worse (a brave admission, even anonymously). Our probing of these responses through selected interviews indicate that there is reason to take the claims at face value.

The only use in which the competitively "worse" match the competitively "better" is the most basic and simplest: to publish information, or what is called *brochureware*. Nearly 60 percent of both the best and the worst report that they use the Internet to provide news and information about the unit or its products or services. Slightly over half of both the best and the worst report that they advertise the unit's products and services on the Internet.

However, the "better" are much more likely than the "worse" to use the Internet today to do more things. The following list presents uses of the Internet in order of the percentage that consider this an important current use; the asterisks indicate that this difference between "better" and "worse" is statistically significant.

- Attract new kinds of customers not previously reached (67 percent of the best consider this an important current use)*

- Sell products and services over the Internet to traditional customers (61 percent of the best consider this an important current use)*

- Work with customers online (exchange data, track deliveries, modify designs, solve problems) (57 percent of the best have this as an important current use)*

- Work with suppliers online (exchange data, track orders, modify designs, solve problems) (55 percent of the best cite this as an important current use)*

- Purchase online (51 percent of the best consider this an important current use)

- Conduct meetings or get work done over the Internet across locations (47 percent of the best have this as an important current use)

- Get employee reactions and feedback online (45 percent of the best cite this as an important current use)

- Deliver education and training online (44 percent of the best have this as an important current use)

- Allow telecommuting (43 percent of the best consider this an important current use)

Those reporting that they are "better" today are also much more likely than those who are "worse" today to envision more uses for the Internet in the future. In short, those who lag behind see the Internet in narrower terms, as just a way to post information. Some are force-fitting the Internet paradigm onto existing businesses; some in this category are not sure that they should be doing much with the Internet but feel forced to do something. Those who are pacesetters integrate the Internet into every aspect of their operations, becoming fuller e-businesses.

Frequency of Barriers to Change

Percentage of Respondents	Barrier
38	The unit does not have staff with adequate technical or Web-specific skills.
37	Customers and key markets do not want to change their behavior.
35	There are more important projects that require existing resources and time.
34	Technology and tools are inadequate, unavailable, or unreliable.
31	It is hard to find the right partners to work with.
28	Suppliers are not cooperative or are not ready for electronic business.
25	Employees are not comfortable with change.
21	Leaders are not sure where to begin; they don't understand how to make the right choices.
16	Top executives do not personally use computers and are not personally familiar with the Internet.
15	"Friendly rivalries" or conflicts between internal divisions get in the way.
13	It is hard to find capital for new investments.
12	Managers fear loss of status or privileged positions.
10	Employees fear loss of jobs, or unions and employee groups fear loss of membership.
10	Government rules and regulations get in the way.
10	The company is successful as it is; leaders see no need for change.
9	The company had a bad previous experience with new technology.
4	It is a waste of time or money; it is not relevant to the business.

Barriers to Change

We asked respondents to check any specific barriers they had encountered, from a long list of possible barriers. This table lists the barriers in the order of frequency with which each was checked and provides the percentage of the total set of respondents that identified that barrier, regardless of sector, region, company size, or Web experience. (Chapter 3 also includes a comparison of older and younger companies on this question.)

Note that staffing problems are identified most frequently, and these center around obtaining new skills. Current employees' fears of change are much more prevalent as a barrier than their fear of losing jobs. Lack of market readiness and technology readiness also poses major barriers largely external to the company, along with finding partners, but those barriers are more likely to be encountered by newer and younger companies, not by the corporate giants. Government rules and regulations are a barrier for just a small number of companies concerned about censorship. And a mere 4 percent feel that the Internet is irrelevant.

Within the company, the barriers involve conflict and internal competition for resources. Relatively few companies check barriers such as top executives' computer phobias or lack of interest in change (in part because the survey includes many pure Internet companies who start out dedicated to e-business and also many smaller, closely held companies that don't want to change much anyway). However, our interviews and case studies in established companies make clear that those barriers often play a major role in slowing down the pace of change. For the larger companies, internal barriers to change are the most prevalent problems. Top management reluctance to invest is a barrier overcome only by extraordinary advocacy by credible internal entrepreneurs. E-believers in established companies tend to be younger and to be outsiders, coming from other companies; they can have a hard time getting resources and support from the mainstream organization. Those who are successful tend to separate out the e-business group and pamper it, but that takes strong support at the top of the mainstream company. Thus success can depend on the top leadership's view of the Net's importance. If top leadership's support is equivocal or lukewarm, then e-business is not given attention and even an advocate cannot do much. And if there is a legacy of internal rivalries, as well as resentment of e-commerce and e-business units in the mainstream company, then the barriers can seem insurmountable.

E-Culture in Leadership and Management

Those claiming that they are better or much better than the competition also are much more likely to report that they have flexible, empowering, team-oriented organizations supportive of innovation. The pacesetters—those claiming to be ahead of the competition in the move to e-business—are more likely, at statistically significant levels, to identify the following as characteristics of their organizational culture:

- People can do anything not explicitly prohibited (as opposed to doing only what is explicitly permitted).

- Conflict is seen as creative (as opposed to disruptive).

- Ideas that are unusual, controversial, or "different" are strongly encouraged and well received (as opposed to viewed with skepticism and resistance).

- To get approval for an unforeseen or nonroutine activity, an OK from just one or two people is usually enough (as opposed to needing to get many sign-offs or go through many levels).

- Decisions about significant activities are made almost immediately (as opposed to taking a long time).

- Decisions are made by the person with the most knowledge (as opposed to the person with the highest rank).

- Departments collaborate (as opposed to stick to themselves).

- People shift their job responsibilities in the course of a year (as opposed to sticking with preplanned tasks).

- When the unit is considering a major strategic change, most people generally hear about it in advance, so they have a chance to comment (as opposed to hearing at the same time as outsiders).

- Changes are considered a fact of life, and people take them in stride (as opposed to finding them disruptive and uncomfortable).

Differences between pacesetters and laggards in work hours (whether work spills over into personal time), alliance approach (whether highly formalized in advance or based on trust), and community service (whether encouraged by the company on its time or left to employees on their own time) are small, mixed, and not statistically significant. Interviews, rather than the survey, guided our interpretation of these factors.

These are the most important findings. According to the survey data, national differences and industry differences are minor notes. The successful transition to e-business is a matter of organizational culture and leadership, that is, whether an organization is change ready and change adept. This finding holds across countries and industries.

NOTES

Unless otherwise noted, all quotes and company information in this book come from over 300 personal interviews and other original sources, including personal observations of meetings, internal company documents, and information posted on company websites. Citations in the notes that follow cover only material beyond the e-culture project team's original database. Also see Appendix A for Harvard Business School teaching cases prepared by the e-culture project team on core companies described in this book.

Introduction

1. The *New Yorker* cartoons appeared in the 29 May 2000 issue.
2. Mark Jurkowitz, "E-Coverage Shakes Off the 'Fairy Dust'," *The Boston Globe*, 20 April 2000.
3. *Evolve! The Song* was stimulated by my desire to reach young people who might not read a book like this, by speaking to them in their idiom. I was inspired by my service on the national board of City Year, the urban youth service corps that was the model for Americorps and that now operates in thirteen American cities, to think about how to take my message from the corporation to the community. The song is simply a translation of the themes of the book into poetic

form. I have recorded the song with Michael Boston, a rap musician on the City Year staff, who helped the song itself evolve.

Chapter 1

1. This discussion draws on research and original interviews for the e-culture project and also two excellent Harvard Business School cases on eBay: Jeffrey Bradach and Nicole Tempest, "Meg Whitman at eBay Inc. (A)," Case 400-035 (Boston: Harvard Business School, 2000); and Stephen Bradley and Kelley Porter, "eBay, Inc.," Case 700-007 (Boston: Harvard Business School, 1999).
2. Bradach and Tempest, "Meg Whitman," 6.
3. Bradley and Porter, "eBay, Inc.," 10.
4. Bradach and Tempest, "Meg Whitman," 2.
5. Bradley and Porter, "eBay, Inc.," 2.
6. Ibid., 9–10.
7. Ibid., 8; Bradach and Tempest, "Meg Whitman," 14.
8. Bradley and Porter, "eBay, Inc.," 10
9. An overview of evaluations by the Center for Children and Technology in New York, as well as a detailed chronicle, can be found in Rosabeth Moss Kanter and Ellen Pruyne, "Bell Atlantic and the Union City Schools (A): The Intelligent Network," Case 399-029 (Boston: Harvard Business School, 1999); "Bell Atlantic and the Union City Schools (B): Education Reform in Union City," Case 399-043 (Boston: Harvard Business School, 1999); "Bell Atlantic and the Union City Schools (C1): Project Explore," Case 399-065 (Boston: Harvard Business School, 1999); "Bell Atlantic and the Union City Schools (C2): Project Explore," Case 399-066 (Boston: Harvard Business School, 1999); "Bell Atlantic and the Union City Schools (D): Results and Replications," Case 399-084 (Boston: Harvard Business School, 1999); and "Bell Atlantic in Union City, Video" 399-501 (Boston: Harvard Business School, 1998).
10. Citations to evaluations as well as further details of the projects are found in Rosabeth Moss Kanter, "IBM's Reinventing Education," Case 399-008 (Boston: Harvard Business School, 1999); Rosabeth Moss Kanter and John Scannell, "IBM Ireland: Reinventing Education Crosses the Atlantic," Case 300-034" (Boston: Harvard Business School, 1999); and Rosabeth Moss Kanter, "IBM: Reinventing Education, Video," 399-502 (Boston: Harvard Business School, 1998). See also Rosabeth Moss Kanter, "From Spare Change to Real Change: The Social Sector as Beta Site for Business Innovation," *Harvard Business Review* 77, no. 3 (May–June 1999): 122–132.
11. Philip Willan, "Italians Urge Telecom Site Attack," *ComputerWorld*, 26 October 1998.
12. "BT Internet Goes Toll-Free," *Network Briefing*, 3 June 1999.
13. Suh Hae-sung, "Disgruntled Korean Consumers Take Their Complaints to the Net," *Asia Pulse*, 10 January 2000.

14. William Finnegan, "After Seattle: Anarchists Get Organized," *New Yorker*, 17 April 2000, 40–51.

15. At Joseph Sweeney's urging, we supplemented our interview with him (and his memory) with a search for contemporaneous press accounts. See Peter Stein, "Hong Kong Internet Raids Strand Users," *Asian Wall Street Journal*, 7 March 1995; Maggie Farley, "Next Step Hong Kong's Remedy for Subversive Use of Cyberspace," *The Los Angeles Times*, 25 April 1995; and Arman Danesh, "Police Call Halt to Net Investigation," *South China Morning Post*, 23 May 1995.

16. "Technology Playing to the Cowed: A Japanese Consumer Incites a Web Revolt," *AsiaWeek*, 6 August 1999.

17. Pam Dixon, "Cyber Artists' War Is Not Child's Play," *San Diego Union-Leader*, 5 March 2000; James Surowiecki, "Eminent Domain," *Artforum*, 1 March 2000.

18. "Chat Attack: (Message) Board Games," *PR News*, Phillips Business Information, 8 May 2000.

19. The haiku was forwarded throughout the Web and made it into *Business Week* on 10 April 2000.

20. Peter Haapaniemi, "What's in a Reputation?" *Chief Executive*, 1 March 2000, 48–51.

21. Kevin Maney, "Cybercurtains Could Partition Off Wide-Open Internet," *USA Today*, 23 February 2000.

Chapter 2

1. I am a fan of Disneyland and Disney World, and my use of the Tomorrowland image bears no relationship, real or imagined, to Disney theme parks.

2. Michael Diamond, "Teen Success Story," *Netrepreneurs*, 14 March 2000.

3. Albert Baime, "The Way We Live Now: 4-2-00: Questions for Ryan Zacharia," *New York Times*, 2 April 2000.

4. Spencer Stuart, "Internet Board Index '99, A Report on 200 Publicly Traded Companies" (Chicago: Spencer Stuart, 2000).

5. Myra Hart, "Women.com," Case 800-216 (Boston: Harvard Business School, 2000).

6. Kimberley A. Strassel, "Top Deal Makers: The Entrepreneur: Schambach Pushed Intershop into Gear," *The Wall Street Journal Europe*, 21 June 1999.

7. "The Messiah of Cyberasia: Asia's Mr. Internet," *The Economist*, 8 January 2000.

Chapter 3

1. This phrase comes from a Fortune 100–level CIO via Abigail Kramer of Empact Inc., who indicated that the CIO prefers to remain anonymous.

2. In addition to the general analysis of survey findings, e-culture research team member Sukyana Lahiri compared a subset of pacesetters and laggards in financial services and retail industries using both the survey and a personal interview.

She created regression models and performed analyses that confirmed the differences between the groups. See Sukyana Lahiri, "The Organizational Determinants of Success in E-Business: A Socio-Economic Approach" (Cambridge, MA: Harvard College Honors Essay, March 2000). Full details of the complete survey and selected findings from all 785 companies can be found in Appendix B.

3. Zeynep Ton and Ananth Raman, "Borders Group, Inc.," Case 600-067 (Boston: Harvard Business School, 1999).
4. Warren St. John, "Barnes & Noble's Epiphany," *Wired* 7.06, June 1999.
5. Doreen Carvajal, "Superstore's Online Unit Seeks Stability," *The New York Times*, 17 April 2000.

Chapter 4

1. Stephen Bradley and Richard Nolan, *Sense and Respond: Capturing Value in the Network Era* (Boston: Harvard Business School Press, 1998).
2. Eric von Hippel, *The Sources of Innovation* (New York: Oxford University Press, 1988); Rita Gunther McGrath and Ian C. MacMillan, "Discovery-Driven Planning," *Harvard Business Review* 73, no. 4 (1995): 44–53.
3. John Kao, *Jamming* (New York: HarperBusiness, 1996); Shona L. Brown and Kathleen M. Eisenhardt, *Competing on the Edge: Strategy as Structured Chaos* (Boston: Harvard Business School Press, 1998), 25–56. Others include E. Eisenberg, "Jamming: Transcendence through Organizing," *Communication Research* 17 (April 1990): 139–164; Karl Weick, "Managing as Improvisation: Lessons from the World of Jazz" (Aubrey Fisher Memorial Lecture, University of Utah, 19 October 1990); Karl Weick, "Organizational Redesign as Improvisation," in *Mastering Organizational Change*, eds. G. Huber and W. Block (New York: Oxford University Press, 1993), 436–379; and Frank Barrett, "Creativity and Improvisation in Jazz and Organizations: Implications for Organizational Learning," *Organization Science* 9 (September/October 1998): 605–622.
4. Inspiration for IKIWISI comes from WYSIWYG, computer lingo for "What You See Is What You Get," referring to graphic user interfaces.
5. Myra Hart, "Women.com," Case 800-216 (Boston: Harvard Business School, 2000).
6. Teresa Amabile, "How to Kill Creativity," *Harvard Business Review* 76 (September/October 1998): 77–87.
7. Stephen Bradley and Kelley Porter, "eBay, Inc.," Case 700-007 (Boston: Harvard Business School, 1999).
8. Michael Picken, "Reuters: Initiating Coverage with a Buy Recommendation" (London: Credit Suisse First Boston Ltd., 2000).
9. Anirudh Dhebar, "Reuters Holdings PLC—1850–1987: A (Selective) History," Case 595-113 (Boston: Harvard Business School, 1995).

Chapter 5

1. Donald Tapscott, "Digital Economy: Rewriting the Rules of Engagement: Business Webs are Destroying the Old Competitive Models," *National Post*, 26 May 2000; Donald Tapscott, *The Digital Economy: Promise and Peril in the Age of Networked Intelligence* (New York: McGraw-Hill, 1996); James F. Moore, *The Death of Competition* (New York: HarperBusiness, 1996). See also Benjamin Gomes-Casseres, *The Alliance Revolution: The New Shape of Business Rivalry* (Cambridge, MA: Harvard University Press, 1996).
2. Robert D. Hof, with Heather Green and Diane Brady, "Suddenly, Amazon's Books Look Better," *Business Week*, 21 February 2000.
3. Ibid.
4. Richard L. Nolan, "drugstore.com," Case 300-036 (Boston: Harvard Business School, 1999).
5. Ken Bensinger and Daniel Costello, "Sotheby's Push onto the Internet Faces Problems," *The Wall Street Journal Europe*, 9 March 2000.
6. Rosabeth Moss Kanter, *World Class: Thriving Locally in the Global Economy* (New York: Simon & Schuster, 1995), chapter 11.
7. "CIBC World Markets Starts Netglomerates," *News Traders*, 8 June 2000.
8. Adam Brandenburger and Barry J. Nalebuff, *Co-opetition* (New York: Doubleday, 1996).

Chapter 6

1. Charles Handy, "Balancing Corporate Power: A New Federalist Paper," *Harvard Business Review* 70, no. 6 (November–December 1992): 59–73.
2. I first identified and labeled this tension in Rosabeth Moss Kanter, *When Giants Learn to Dance: Mastering the Challenges of Strategy, Management, and Careers in the 1990s* (New York: Simon & Schuster, 1989).
3. Bold strokes versus long marches are explored in the final chapter of Rosabeth Moss Kanter, Barry A. Stein, and Todd D. Jick, eds., *The Challenge of Organizational Change* (New York: Free Press, 1992).
4. Jody Hofer Gittell, "Programmed and Interactive Coordination Mechanisms: Toward a Theory of Complementarity," working paper, Harvard Business School, Boston, 2000.

Chapter 7

1. Jerry Useem and Wilton Woods, "For Sale Online: You," *Fortune*, 5 July 1999; Dylan Loeb McClain, "For Job Hunters, Networking Beats the Net," *The New York Times*, 17 May 2000.
2. Todd L. Pittinsky, "Knowledge Nomads: Commitment in a Transient Workforce" (forthcoming Ph.D. diss., Harvard University, 2001).

3. See Rosabeth Moss Kanter, *When Giants Learn to Dance,* and Rosabeth Moss Kanter, "From Climbing to Hopping," *Management Review,* 1 April 1989, for an early and fuller discussion of the Hollywood model of careers.

4. Interim Services, Inc., in conjunction with Louis Harris & Associates, "1999 Emerging Workforce Study" (Fort Lauderdale, FL: Spherion, February 1999).

5. Kerry A. Dolan, "GE's Brain Drain," *Forbes Global,* 1 November 1999, 21.

6. Howard Gardner, *Intelligence Reframed: Multiple Intelligences for the 21st Century* (New York: Basic Books, 1999); Teresa M. Amabile, "Motivational Synergy: Toward New Conceptualization of Intrinsic and Extrinsic Motivation in the Workplace," *Human Resource Management Review* 3 (November 1992): 185–201; Tereas M. Amabile, "The Motivation for Creativity in Organizations," Note 396-240 (Boston: Harvard Business School, 1996).

7. "Top Grads Foregoing Lure of Dot Coms, According to WetFeet.com Research," *WetFeet.com,* 8 May 2000, <http://www.wetfeet.com>.

8. The Randstad North America study was reported in *The Wall Street Journal,* 11 April 2000.

9. International Survey Research, "Tracking Trends: Employee Satisfaction in the '90's" (Chicago: International Survey Research, 2000).

10. Rosabeth Moss Kanter, *Commitment and Community* (Cambridge, MA: Harvard University Press, 1972).

11. Lee Hecht Harrison poll, reported in *The Boston Globe,* 23 April 2000.

12. Myra Hart, "Women.com," Case 800-216 (Boston: Harvard Business School, 2000).

13. Laura M. Holson and Katie Hafner, "Some Enticed by Dot-Coms Now Have Second Thoughts," *The New York Times,* 14 April 2000.

14. Dylan Loeb McClain, "For Job Hunters, Networking Beats the Net," *The New York Times,* 17 May 2000.

Chapter 8

1. I first introduced the Change Wheel in the concluding chapter of Rosabeth Moss Kanter, Barry A. Stein, and Todd D. Jick, eds., *The Challenge of Organizational Change* (New York: Free Press, 1992). I have since expanded and refined the wheel, and it is now found in the Rosabeth Moss Kanter Change Toolkit, an electronic, Web-based leadership kit. (Reprinted here by permission; not to be copied or reproduced without explicit written permission.)

Chapter 9

1. I coined the term changemaster in a slightly different form in an earlier book: Rosabeth Moss Kanter, *The Change Masters: Innovation and Entrepreneurship in the American Corporation* (New York: Simon & Schuster, 1983).

2. For an excellent discussion of mindfulness and its benefits, see Ellen J. Langer, *Mindfulness* (Reading, MA: Addison-Wesley, 1989).

3. Steven Pinker, *How the Mind Works* (New York: W.W. Norton, 1999).

4. Sukyana Lahiri, "The Organizational Determinants of Success in E-Business: A Socio-Economic Approach" (Cambridge, MA: Harvard College Honors Essay, March 2000).

5. Kim B. Clark and Takahiro Fujimoto, *Product Development Performance* (Boston: Harvard Business School Press, 1991); Stephen C. Wheelwright and Kim B. Clark, *Revolutionizing Product Development: Quantum Leaps in Speed, Efficiency and Quality* (New York: Free Press, 1992).

6. Dorothy Leonard and Walter Swap, *When Sparks Fly* (Boston: Harvard Business School Press, 1999).

7. The distinction between bold strokes and long marches is elaborated in Rosabeth Moss Kanter, Barry A. Stein, and Todd D. Jick, eds. *The Challenge of Organizational Change* (New York: Free Press, 1992).

Chapter 10

1. Anthony Giddens, *The Third Way* (Cambridge, England: Polity Press, 1998).

2. Robert E. Kraut and Paul Attewell, "Media Use in a Global Corporation," in *Culture of the Internet*, ed. Sara Kiesler (Mahwah, NJ: Lawrence Ehrlbaum, 1997), 323–342.

3. J. D. Eveland and Tora Bikson, "Work Group Structures and Computer Support," *Transactions on Office Information Systems* 6 (1988): 354–369.

4. David Constant, Lee Sproull, and Sara Kiesler, "The Kindness of Strangers: The Usefulness of Electronic Weak Ties for Technical Advice," in *Culture of the Internet*, ed. Sara Kiesler, 303–322. See also Morton T. Hansen, "The Search-Transfer Problem: The Role of Weak Ties in Sharing Knowledge across Organization Subunits," *Administrative Science Quarterly* 44 (1999): 82–111. The original analysis of weak ties is in Mark S. Granovetter, "The Strength of Weak Ties," *American Journal of Sociology* 6 (1972/3): 1360–1380.

5. Ellen Oler, Brooklyn, Letter to the Editor, *The New York Times Magazine*, 16 April 2000.

6. Robert Kraut, Michael Patterson, Vicki Lundmark, Sara Kiesler, et al, "Internet Paradox: A Social Technology That Reduces Social Involvement and Psychological Well-Being?" *The American Psychologist* 53, no. 9 (1998): 1017–1031.

7. Jill Rierdan, "Internet-Depression Link?" *The American Psychologist* 54, no. 9 (1999): 781–782; Toby Silverman, "The Internet and Relational Theory," *The American Psychologist* 54, no. 9 (1999): 780–781.

8. Norman Nie and Lutz Erbring, "Internet and Society: A Preliminary Report" (Stanford Institute for the Quantitative Study of Society, Stanford University; interSurvey, Inc.; and McKinsey & Company, 17 February 2000).

9. Pew Internet and American Life Project, "Tracking Online Life: How Women Use the Internet to Cultivate Relationships with Family and Friends," 10 May 2000. <http://www.pewinternet.org/reports/toc.asp?Report=11>.

10. Kristin D. Mickelson, "Seeking Social Support: Parents in Electronic Support Groups," in *Culture of the Internet*, ed. Sara Kiesler, 157–178.

11. "Study Finds American Families on the Verge of an Internet 'E-Mergency,'" *Business Wire*, 17 November 1999; Sara Hammel, "Living Their Lives Online," *US News & World Report*, 29 November 1999.

12. Todd Oppenheimer, "The Computer Delusion," *Atlantic Monthly* 280, no. 1 (1997): 45–62.

13. Sherry Turkle, *Life on the Screen: Identity in the Age of the Internet* (New York: Simon & Schuster, 1995), 60, 69–70, 238.

14. Janet H. Murray, *Hamlet on the Holodeck: The Future of Narrative in Cyberspace* (New York: Free Press, 1997), 125.

15. Peter Doskoch, "Personality Crisis? Not on the Net," *Psychology Today* 31, no. 2 (March–April 1998): 70.

16. Maholon Meyer, "Hong Kong Gets Its Groove Back," *Newsweek Asia*, 13 March 2000.

17. Sue Ferguson, "The Wired Teen," *Maclean's* 113, no. 22 (2000): 38–40.

18. "New Study Examines the Effects of Digital Media on Kids/Teens," *Youth Marketing Alert*, 1 March 1999.

19. McKinsey & Company, "Connecting K–12 Schools to the Information Superhighway," Report to the National Information Infrastructure Advisory Council, 1997.

20. Rosabeth Moss Kanter, "Bell Atlantic and the Union City Schools (D)," Case 399-084 (Boston: Harvard Business School, 1999); Rosabeth Moss Kanter, "IBM's Reinventing Education," Case 399-008 (Boston: Harvard Business School, 1999). See also Rosabeth Moss Kanter, "From Spare Change to Real Change: The Social Sector as Beta Site for Business Innovation," *Harvard Business Review* 77, no. 3 (May–June 1999): 122–132.

21. In an earlier study. I found that globalization affects local community service when it causes companies to move their headquarters, since companies headquartered in a particular place contribute more time and money to that place—and even their employees contribute more. See Rosabeth Moss Kanter, *World Class: Thriving Locally in the Global Economy* (New York: Simon & Schuster, 1995), chapter 7. Andrew Shapiro makes a similar point about the need to ensure local involvement in the wake of the Internet. See Shapiro, "The Net that Binds," *The Nation*, 21 June 1999, 11–15.

22. Branda Paik Sunoo, "Redesign for a Better Work Environment," *Workforce*, 1 February 2000, 38ff.

CREDITS

"Acknowledgments" sounds so bland, in light of all the people who deserve to have their names in lights for their contributions to this book. This is my way to give credit where credit is due. (But any blame is mine alone.)

I am asked all the time, by audiences to which I speak, to identify my favorite website. I always answer www.hbs.edu. I mean that only partly tongue-in-cheek. I realize that there is no dot-edu bandwagon, and a few of my interviewees even assumed that the Harvard Business School website would be hbs.com—but there we are, still solidly hbs.edu, dedicated to education. Without the generous support of the Division of Research at Harvard Business School, the enthusiasm of Teresa Amabile, Michael Yoshino, and the other directors of research for this project, and the ability to use hbs.edu for so many things—the e-culture survey, virtual meetings, a flow of documents—this book would never have been written.

I conceived of this project on the island of Martha's Vineyard, and there I returned to write. I benefited from conversations at key moments with the remarkable people a Vineyard summer attracts: for example, President Bill Clinton and First Lady Hillary Rodham Clinton about the Digital Divide; General Electric Senior Vice President Ben Heineman about e-business; and others in diverse fields, such as Dominique Borde, head of a pan-European law firm in Paris, about e-culture and their professions. After writing all day, I tested the resonance of various themes at gatherings at night, learning from the reactions of people such as Alan Dershowitz and Carolyn Cohen, Eli and Phyllis Segal, Carol and Frank Biondi, Glenn Hutchins, Zoe Baird, Bob Vila and Diana Barrett, Mary Steenburgen and Ted Danson, Max and Cheryl Batzer, Bill Rollnick and Nancy Ellison, Wolfgang Puck and Barbara Lazerow, Bill Hambrecht, and Alan and Ruth Stein, among many others. Writers such as Richard North Patterson, Clyde Phillips, Gerri Sweder, Connie Borde, Larry Mollin, Nancy Aronie, Laura Roosevelt, and Roseline Glazer had insights into the process. Tom and Chris Murphy and Joanne and Tom Ashe also helped.

I shared a platform at the White House Conference on Philanthropy in October 1999 with Steve Case, CEO of AOL, and started to think about the potential of e-culture to reshape the nonprofit world. (And perhaps my desire to write a song was stimulated by sharing that same occasion with Justin Timberlake of 'NSync.) At the millennium meeting of the World Economic Forum in Davos in January 2000, I had to clarify my then-embryonic analysis in order to serve on a panel with John Chambers, CEO of Cisco Systems; Ed Zander, president of Sun Microsystems; Steven Shepard, editor of *Business Week*; and others. (It was both encouraging and challenging to see Mayoshi Son of Softbank in the front row.)

The e-culture research project team had a flow of talented people—paid staff as well as unpaid volunteers—working on particular ventures. But, as I indicate in chapter 7, in many ways everyone is a volunteer, and so I want to thank an extraordinary group for above-and-beyond efforts, based on commitment to the quest.

Daniel Galvin and Michelle Heskett were the continuing threads, e-culture champions, and team leaders, as my chief research associates at Harvard Business School. Dan (my designated culture scene observer) is energetic, talented, persuasive, insightful, and willing to jump in with enthusiasm to do nearly anything. Micki (outstanding writer and calming influence) is equally talented, insightful, and willing to tackle complicated tasks, from survey logistics to pinning down the U.K. side of the project. They worked on, and coauthored with me, a range of the in-depth company cases, and were on the ground in New York and London. Their good cheer as well as numerous intelligent observations made this effort a pleasure.

I was lucky to entice Pamela Yatsko, an accomplished journalist and author of the exciting book, *The New Shanghai*, to join us temporarily to conduct over twenty interviews in Hong Kong. Pam is one of those "alumni" I mention in chapter 7; she worked for me at Harvard Business School from 1992 to 1994, then moved to China and soared as an analyst and writer. Pam and her investment banker–husband, Brewer Stone, became my friends. I am grateful that she returned briefly to lend her formidable interview skills to this project.

Katherine Chen, Jane Roessner, Lisa Rubin-Johnson, and Alida Zweidler-McKay (in alphabetical order) also did heroic things as my research associates for waves of interviews and writing of particular cases. Their contributions were especially helpful toward the beginning of the project, before hypotheses were fully formed or conclusions fully reached. Sukyana Lahiri devoted her Harvard

College honors thesis to research on this project, lending her intelligent perspective and ability to manipulate quantitative and qualitative data with grace. Rachel Lindell joined the team with good cheer for a range of insightful interviews, as did Karen Weigert and Russell Grieff. I am very grateful to Russell Braterman for collaboration on Tesco, to Hal Hogan for pitching in on interviews, and to Courtenay Sprague and David Lane for an excellent handoff on an important case series. Doctoral candidate Todd L. Pittinsky contributed a great deal of knowledge of the dotcom world as well as company research and a social science perspective; his own work on knowledge nomads will be timely and important.

I am also very grateful to Robert Gandossy, friend and global organizational effectiveness leader for Hewitt Associates, for lending the skillful Erin Owen and Karen Barnes to work on the AlliedSignal portion of the Honeywell International cases, and for paving the way. David Lehrer worked on that venture, as well as others, with his usual speed and intelligence. Through an earlier project, Thomas Dretler (now CEO of Eduventures.com) helped me with the work on technology in education, as did Ellen Pruyne and Robin Root. Willa Reiser was her usual cheerful presence, a responsible communicator always there to support us in the office.

The global e-culture survey benefited from strong collaborators and distribution partners. Thanks are due to Lance Knobel, orchestrator of the Annual Meeting of the World Economic Forum and chief editor of *Worldlink* magazine, and Kamal Mehta and Sami Aknine of *Worldlink*, for seeing the significance of this project and for the World Economic Forum membership mailing. Thanks are also due to George Gendron, editor-in-chief of *Inc.* magazine, for similar friendship and support and, along with managing editor Evelyn Roth and David Young, for survey distribution through *Inc.*'s own website and list and also for the involvement of the Young Entrepreneurs Association, a distinguished group in its own right. Datamation and theglobe.com helped with some electronic links, for which we are grateful. Michael Sorrel at Harvard Business School and his great team provided incredible help with the online poll, data entry, and data analysis. John Buehler was the guru of quantitative analysis, playing a very important role in translating data to wisdom.

Several people deserve credit for knowledgeable door-opening—knowing who to contact and why is sometimes as important as the introduction itself. Carl Syman, chairman of IBM U.K., and Sir Martin Sorrell, chairman of WPP Group (whose WPP Interactive is a leader among Web-centric agencies) were very helpful in lending staff members to assist with seeing the right people in London, as was Laurence Borde, imaginative and accomplished founder/CEO of MediaTree in London. Henry Nasella of Online Retail Partners in New York City opened a vital door and contributed ideas from his new model. Kathy Biro, vice chair of Digitas and a founder of Strategic Interactive Group, stimulated my thinking in the early stages. Daniel Isenberg and Israel Drori offered insights into Internet companies in Israel. In Hong Kong and Taiwan, the Harvard Business School

Asia-Pacific Research Center was helpful, as was William Reinfeld. My faculty colleague Richard Nolan's invitation to speak at a symposium in Silicon Valley for Harvard Business School alumni leading dotcom companies opened other doors. Serving on the Oxygen/Markle Pulse advisory board with Geraldine Laybourne, Zoe Baird, Sherry Turkle, Meryl Streep, and other smart people provided additional leads and opportunities.

Thanks are due to Peter Simon for another demonstration of photographic genius. My "virtual title team" brainstormed creative possibilities by e-mail: Dr. Michael Wertheimer, Alex MacDonald, Michael Brown and Charlie Rose of City Year, and John Scannell in Ireland. Michael Boston, a talented musical performer and a City Year Fellow, helped with the song. I am grateful for important guidance from readers of early drafts: Nancy Aronie, Lisa Foster, Leslie Jacobs, Stanley Litow, Richard Nolan, William Reinfeld, John Scannell, and Kenneth Sweder. Bestselling novelists Richard North Patterson and Clyde Phillips were especially generous with their comments. (But they bear no responsibility for the final result.)

I am also very grateful for the experiences and insights shared by the 300-plus people to whom we spoke at eighty or so companies and other organizations. Unless you requested anonymity, I tried to thank you by quoting you by name—until my editor asked me to be reasonable and cut the number of stories and quotes. So please look yourself up in the index, but if you do not find your name, please know that it was impossible to list everyone, and that you have my appreciation.

Speaking of editors, Hollis Heimbouch is a delight—witty, creative, knowledgeable about the content as well as the presentation, willing to work at Internet speed, and herself an exemplar of the best of e-culture.

That leaves only my friends and family, whom I did not drive crazy this time because I worked on this book so fast, on such a compressed schedule, that I was done before some of them noticed. But my son, Matthew Moss Kanter Stein, noticed. Matt supported me every day with some form of encouraging communication, whether e-mail, phone calls, or in person. He also was my first teacher about computers and the Internet, way back when. Browser, our aptly named cocker spaniel, was the best animal companion, sitting at my feet while I sat in front of the screen. (Browser was my pet in the office.)

And what do I say about my husband, Barry Stein? It is hard to imagine a better life partner, intellectual partner, critic and collaborator, support system, and loving presence. Barry continues to give me so much more than I could ever have dreamed of, hoped for, or expected. And his talents—there's that word again, but it fits—are reflected on nearly every page of this book.

Rosabeth Moss Kanter
Cambridge and Edgartown,
Massachusetts

INDEX

About the Author

---◆---

ROSABETH MOSS KANTER is an internationally known business leader, award-winning author, and expert on strategy, innovation, and the power to change. She is the Ernest L. Arbuckle Professor of Business Administration at the Harvard Business School and an advisor to major corporations and government entities worldwide. *Evolve!* is her fifteenth book. She is also the author of the bestsellers *Men and Women of the Corporation, The Change Masters, When Giants Learn to Dance,* and *World Class.*

Considered one of the most prominent business speakers and strategy consultants in the world, she has delivered keynote addresses for trade associations, civic associations, and national conventions in nearly every U.S. state and in more than twenty countries, including national agenda-setting speeches following the presidents or prime ministers of Norway, Malaysia, Peru, and Venezuela. Her consulting clients have included many of the world's largest global companies as well as Internet and technology startups. She serves on advisory boards for many privately held growth companies.

At Harvard Business School, she brings her latest work to business executives and MBA students through her courses on managing change. In 1997–1998, she conceived and led the Business Leadership in the Social Sector (BLSS) project, involving more than 100 national leaders (including senators and governors, corporate CEOs, national association heads, and First Lady Hillary Rodham

Clinton) in dialogue about business-government partnerships to improve American communities.

Before joining the Harvard Business School faculty in 1986, Kanter was a tenured professor at Yale University and a Fellow in Law and Social Science at Harvard Law School. From 1989–1992, she served as Editor of the *Harvard Business Review*, which was a finalist for a National Magazine Award for General Excellence in 1991. She co-founded Goodmeasure, Inc., a consulting firm that has developed leadership and consulting tools based on her work. The *Rosabeth Moss Kanter Change Toolkit* is now being translated into electronic form for dissemination over the World Wide Web in partnership with IBM.

Named one of the 100 most important women in America by the *Ladies Home Journal* and one of the 50 most powerful women in the world by the London *Times*, she has received nineteen honorary doctoral degrees and more than a dozen leadership awards. She is a judge for the Ron Brown Award for corporate leadership in the community (established by President Bill Clinton to honor the late Secretary of Commerce), has served on the Board of Overseers for the Malcolm Baldrige National Quality Award, is a Fellow of the World Economic Forum, served on the Massachusetts Governor's Economic Council (for which she was co-chair of the International Trade Task Force), co-chaired with Timothy Shriver the Youth Service Advisory Board at the initiation of General Colin Powell's America's Promise organization, co-led the effort to establish a Year 2000 Commission for legacy projects for Boston, and served as a vice president of the NOW Legal Defense and Education Fund board in recognition of her advocacy for women. She serves on numerous other national and civic boards, including City Year, the national urban youth service corps.

She lives in Cambridge and Edgartown, Massachusetts, with her husband, son, and a very friendly cocker spaniel. She can be contacted at rkanter@hbs.edu or through websites featuring her work: www.hbs.edu/faculty, www.goodmeasure .com, and www.rosabeth.com.